WITHDRAWN
HARVARD LIBRARY
WITHDRAWN

HUSSERL AND HEIDEGGER ON BEING IN THE WORLD

PHAENOMENOLOGICA

SERIES FOUNDED BY H.L. VAN BREDA AND PUBLISHED
UNDER THE AUSPICES OF THE HUSSERL-ARCHIVES

173

SØREN OVERGAARD

HUSSERL AND HEIDEGGER ON BEING IN THE WORLD

Editorial Board:
Director: R. Bernet (Husserl-Archief, Leuven) Secretary: J. Taminiaux (Centre d'études phénoménologiques, Louvain-la-Neuve) Members: S. IJsseling (Husserl-Archief, Leuven), H. Leonardy (Centre d'études phénoménologiques, Louvain-la-Neuve), D. Lories (Centre d'études phénoménologiques, Louvain-la-Neuve), U. Melle (Husserl-Archief, Leuven)

Advisory Board:
R. Bernasconi (Memphis State University), D. Carr (Emory University, Atlanta), E.S. Casey (State University of New York at Stony Brook), R. Cobb-Stevens (Boston College), J.F. Courtine (Archives-Husserl, Paris), F. Dastur (Université de Nice), K. Düsing (Husserl-Archiv, Köln), J. Hart (Indiana University, Bloomington), K. Held (Bergische Universität Wuppertal), K.E. Kaehler (Husserl-Archiv, Köln), D. Lohmar (Husserl-Archiv, Köln), W.R. McKenna (Miami University, Oxford, USA), J.N. Mohanty (Temple University, Philadelphia), E.W. Orth (Universität Trier), P. Ricœur (Paris), C. Sini (Università degli Studi di Milano), R. Sokolowski (Catholic University of America, Washington D.C.), B. Waldenfels (Ruhr-Universität, Bochum)

SØREN OVERGAARD
*Danish National Research Foundation: Center for Subjectivity Research,
University of Copenhagen, Denmark*

HUSSERL AND HEIDEGGER ON BEING IN THE WORLD

KLUWER ACADEMIC PUBLISHERS
DORDRECHT / BOSTON / LONDON

A C.I.P. Catalogue record for this book is available from the Library of Congress.

ISBN 1-4020-2043-0 (HB)
ISBN 1-4020-2239-5 (e-book)

Published by Kluwer Academic Publishers,
P.O. Box 17, 3300 AA Dordrecht, The Netherlands.

Sold and distributed in North, Central and South America
by Kluwer Academic Publishers,
101 Philip Drive, Norwell, MA 02061, U.S.A.

In all other countries, sold and distributed
by Kluwer Academic Publishers,
P.O. Box 322, 3300 AH Dordrecht, The Netherlands.

Printed on acid-free paper

All Rights Reserved
© 2004 Kluwer Academic Publishers
No part of this work may be reproduced, stored in a retrieval system, or transmitted
in any form or by any means, electronic, mechanical, photocopying, microfilming, recording
or otherwise, without written permission from the Publisher, with the exception
of any material supplied specifically for the purpose of being entered
and executed on a computer system, for exclusive use by the purchaser of the work.

Printed in the Netherlands.

CONTENTS

Acknowledgements vii

Abbreviations viii

Introduction 1

Chapter I: Natural Attitude and Everyday Life 9
   1. Objects in the Lifeworld 10
   2. Subjects in the Lifeworld 15
   3. "Inside" or "Outside" the Natural Attitude 19
   4. The Thesis of the Natural Attitude 21
   5. Anxiety 27

Chapter II: The Question of Constitution 31
   1. The Need for the Question of Constitution 31
   2. The Epoché 36
   3. The Transcendental Reduction 45
   4. The Noematic Correlate 55
   5. Reduction and Constitution 59
   6. Constitutive Phenomenology 61

Chapter III: The Question of Being 69
   1. The Need for the Question of Being 69
   2. Phenomenology 74
   3. Husserl's Epoché 77
   4. Formal Indication 82
   5. Fundamental Ontology 90
   6. The Destruction of the Ontological Tradition 95
   7. Phenomenological Ontology 100

Chapter IV: World 104
   1. Object-Intentionality and World 104
   2. World as Horizon 109
   3. World as a Referential Whole 117
   4. The Phenomenon of World 126

Chapter V: Subjectivity 131
   1. Intersubjectivity 131

2. Transcendental vs. Mundane Subjectivity:
   Some Initial Considerations..136
3. Dasein: Some Initial Considerations 142
4. Transcendental Subjectivity and the Body 148
5. Subjectivity 161

Chapter VI: Constitution, Transcendence, and Being..................164
1. Understanding of Being and Intentionality 164
2. Constitution and Transcendence...169
3. Understanding the Being of Equipment: Some Clarifications............173
4. The Being of Equipment 180
5. The "Mundane" Subject 183
6. The Being of the Subject 190

Conclusion 202

Bibliography 207

Index of Names 224

ACKNOWLEDGEMENTS

This book is a revised version of my Ph.D. dissertation presented at the University of Aarhus, Denmark, in 2002. The revision was funded by the Carlsberg Foundation and carried out at the Danish National Research Foundation: Center for Subjectivity Research (University of Copenhagen).

Thanks are first of all due to the staff of the Husserl-Archives at the Katholieke Universiteit Leuven for their help during my short stay there in January 2000, and to the director of the archive, Rudolf Bernet, for allowing me to consult, and quote from, unpublished manuscripts.

I am indebted to Maxine Sheets-Johnstone for her kind support, and for the many conversations I have had with her, stretching back to long before I began writing this book. I also want to express my gratitude to Donn Welton for his help with arranging my stay at Stony Brook in 2001. He also read and commented on the first draft of Chapter I, and he took the time to engage in stimulating discussions with me. For that I am especially grateful.

A number of people read and commented on an earlier version of the manuscript. I am thus indebted to Hans Ruin, Anders Moe Rasmussen, and Jim Jakobsson for their valuable suggestions and constructive criticism. Special thanks are due to Dan Zahavi for his many insightful comments on the manuscript. More than anyone else, he has helped me make a publishable manuscript of my dissertation – something for which I am particularly grateful. I am also very much indebted to Thomas Schwarz Wentzer for the way he has tried, with perceptive comments and encouragement, to keep me on the right track through all stages of this work. Especially in the early stages of the work, his confidence in me (often greater than my own) was invaluable. And the fact that he not only tolerated, but even encouraged me to develop my own argument, even when it conflicted with his views – which I think it did more than once – stands for me as a model of academic virtue.

I am grateful to my colleague Deborah Licht for reading the manuscript and suggesting many stylistic and linguistic improvements, and to Maja de Keijzer of Kluwer Academic Publishers for helping me with formatting the manuscript.

Finally, I wish to express my gratitude to my wife, Deborah Vlaeymans. Without her, I doubt that I could have completed this work. I dedicate this book to her.

ABBREVIATIONS

Works by Husserl published in the *Husserliana* are cited as "*Hua*," followed by volume number (Roman numerals) and page number.

Works by Heidegger published in the *Gesamtausgabe* are cited as "*GA*," followed by volume number (Arabic numerals) and page number.

(I thus refer to volumes of the collected works of Husserl and Heidegger in the standard ways. Information about these volumes is found in the Bibliography, not in the list below.)

I list only the author and title. Full information about all works can be found in the Bibliography.

BZ	Martin Heidegger, *Der Begriff der Zeit*
EU	Edmund Husserl, *Erfahrung und Urteil*
HuDo II/1	Eugen Fink, *VI. Cartesianische Meditation. Teil 1* [Parts written by Husserl]
HuDo II/2	Eugen Fink, *VI. Cartesianische Meditation. Teil 2* [Parts written by Husserl]
HW	Martin Heidegger, *Holzwege*
KPM	Martin Heidegger, *Kant und das Problem der Metaphysik*
LV	Edmund Husserl, "Phänomenologische Methode und phänomenologische Philosophie. <Londoner Vorträge 1922>"
PIA	Martin Heidegger, "Phänomenologische Interpretationen zu Aristoteles: Anzeige der hermeneutischen Situation"
RB	Edmund Husserl, "Randbemerkungen Husserls zu Heideggers *Sein und Zeit* und *Kant und das Problem der Metaphysik*"
SZ	Martin Heidegger, *Sein und Zeit*
WDF	Martin Heidegger, "Wilhelm Diltheys Forschungsarbeit und der gegenwärtigen Kampf um eine historische Weltanschauung"

WM	Martin Heidegger, *Wegmarken*
ZSD	Martin Heidegger, *Zur Sache des Denkens*

The present work is based on my study of the original German editions of Husserl's and Heidegger's works. The majority of the quotations presented in this book are the standard English translations. However, I have sometimes modified the translations slightly, without indicating it. When English translations were not readily accessible, I translated the relevant passages myself (fully aware of all the dangers this entails, when neither language is one's mother tongue).

All page numbers refer to the German editions of Husserl's and Heidegger's works. The original page numbers are retained in the English translations for the most part. However, there are a few works from which I quote several times where this is not the case. Here I have included section numbers as well as page numbers, when this has been possible – and only when I quote directly from the texts. (Husserl's *Erfahrung und Urteil*, *Logische Untersuchungen*, and the main text of the *Krisis* are cases in point.)

Square brackets ("[…]") within quotations indicate additions or changes made by me – this usually entails the original German phrases when important, or when I am uncertain about the translation. Angle brackets ("<…>") indicate additions and changes made by the editor of the original German work, or by the English translator.

I have not insisted on using entirely consistent terminology. Instead, I have attempted to keep a certain "openness" of terminology hoping that this will help the reader understand the issues, rather than concentrate on learning a particular Husserlian or Heideggerian jargon. (*Vorhanden* is here a case in point. I generally translate it with "present-at-hand," following Macquarrie and Robinson, but I also sometimes use "on hand" and "occurrent.")

INTRODUCTION

> "Away with empty word analyses! We must question the things themselves. Back to experience, to seeing, which alone can give our words sense and rational justification." Very much to the point! But what, then, are these things? And what sort of experience is it to which we must return [...]?
>
> *Husserliana* XXV, p. 21.

> Whence and how is it determined what must be experienced as "the things themselves" in accordance with the principle of phenomenology? Is it consciousness and its objectivity or is it the being of beings [*das Sein des Seienden*] in its unconcealedness and concealment?
>
> *Zur Sache des Denkens*, p. 87.

"To the things themselves!" Thus sounded the battle cry of the movement of phenomenology, inaugurated in 1900-1901 by Edmund Husserl. Among the philosophers who would subsequently associate themselves with this movement, and eagerly reiterate Husserl's maxim, was Martin Heidegger. The final story of the personal relationship of these two major figures of twentieth century philosophy still remains to be told,[1] but it is certain that it ended in personal tragedy, at least from Husserl's point of view. As far as the relation between their philosophical doctrines is concerned, Husserl and the early Heidegger's agreement that philosophy had to be carried out as phenomenology has not led to consensus among commentators. It has been and remains unclear to what extent "phenomenology" actually means the same thing to Husserl and Heidegger. Opinions range from the view that "Husserlian and Heideggerian phenomenology are radically different, and have virtually nothing to do with each other,"[2] to the contention that "the whole of *Sein und Zeit* springs from an indication given by Husserl," and amounts to nothing more than a detailed elaboration of a particular Husserlian theme.[3]

What is the "truth" of the matter? At least it is clear that Husserl and Heidegger agreed on one or two negative points concerning phenomenology. Neither suggests that agreement on the phenomenological slogan ensures any common theme. What *are* the "things themselves" that we should go back to? The answer to this in no way follows from the maxim itself. Secondly, Husserl and Heidegger are equally worried about the *method* of phenomenology. They are both unhappy with the way other phenomenologists construe all kinds of theories and ideas and easily pass them off

---

[1] Though a good deal is written on the subject, it remains a difficult as well as delicate issue. For various accounts of the relationship, see Hugo Ott, *Martin Heidegger: Unterwegs zu seiner Biographie*, esp. pp. 167-179; Theodore Kisiel, "Husserl and Heidegger"; and Thomas Sheehan, "Husserl and Heidegger: The Making and Unmaking of a Relationship."
[2] Richard Schacht, "Husserlian and Heideggerian Phenomenology," p. 294.
[3] Maurice Merleau-Ponty, *Phenomenology of Perception*, p. vii.

as "essential insights" (*WM*, p. 5; *Hua* XXVII, p. 180).[4] For both Husserl and Heidegger, phenomenology is hard work. Despite their negative and formal agreements, however, there is good reason to think that "phenomenological work" has very different meanings for Husserl and Heidegger. Husserl, after all, conceives of his phenomenology as a "transcendental," even an "epistemological" project, whereas Heidegger's phenomenology is to be "ontology." On the one hand, the "things themselves" are thus "consciousness" and the question of how it "reaches" transcendent things, and on the other hand, the being of entities is the phenomenon *par excellence*. In the last analysis, so it seems, there is no single phenomenolog*y*, but rather a number of different phenomenolog*ies*.

But is Husserlian constitutive phenomenology really without further ado to be identified with epistemology? And is it so obvious that Heidegger's "ontological" phenomenology is opposed to transcendental philosophy? In the present study, I shall attempt to answer these questions. My guiding hypothesis is that "being" somehow sums up what phenomenology is all about, although under the heading of "being" we find two different, but still essentially connected, types of inquiries. Though both types of questions are not given equal weight by Husserl and Heidegger, and although each question is not equally consistently pursued by the two phenomenologists, both types of questions are nevertheless present in Husserlian as well as Heideggerian phenomenology. In other words, perhaps there is after all some unitary notion of phenomenology underlying the many differences between these two major figures of twentieth century philosophy. Moreover, in addition to arguing that the study of Husserl and Heidegger allows us to formulate some unitary phenomenological project, I shall also claim that there are some points of convergence in the actual phenomenological analyses provided by Husserl and Heidegger, and in the methods with which they obtain those analyses. Specifically, I shall argue that there are important similarities between the two accounts when it comes to the characterizations of world and subjectivity. However, as we will also see, there are significant differences concerning the interpretation of intra-mundane entities.

It is usual in an introduction such as this to specify whether the aim of a study is "systematic" or "historical." As the early Heidegger repeatedly stresses, however, these two things cannot be separated. We really only philosophize in dialogue with the history of philosophy, and yet as philosophers we engage in this dialogue for reasons that are "systematic." We want to understand the world, ourselves, history, society, and for this reason we turn to other thinkers, past and present. The present study is "historical" in the sense that I attempt to present a reading of Husserl and Heidegger that in important ways differs from the main currents in the literature.[5] I

---

[4] Cf. *GA* 19, p. 587: "They come to the point where they think phenomenology is an easy science, in which one intuits essences, sort of lying on the couch with one's pipe."

[5] A note on the previous literature. Ernst Tugendhat's landmark study *Der Wahrheitsbegriff bei Husserl und Heidegger* is still an important work, not least because of the critical distance the author displays in relation to both Husserl and Heidegger. Tugendhat also offers an interpretation of their relation that, in

shall develop my account of Husserlian and Heideggerian phenomenology through a discussion with the various other interpretations of the relationship, and it will at times perhaps look as if the "historical" business of providing the "right" interpretation of the Husserl-Heidegger relation is my sole objective. Along the way, however, I hope to throw considerable light on the phenomena of subjectivity, world, and intra-mundane entities. If the task of philosophy, as Merleau-Ponty once put it, is to understand "the system 'Self-others-things,'"[6] then, through the dialogue with Husserl and Heidegger, I attempt to do philosophy in the study that follows. I am not satisfied simply with pointing out difference and similarities; I also make it my business to evaluate phenomenologically how convincing the Husserlian and

---

some respects, is close to the one presented here. However, Tugendhat's focus is on the concept of truth, not on the phenomenological projects of Husserl and Heidegger as such. Though it mainly deals with Heidegger, Carl F. Gethmann's *Verstehen und Auslegung* is also an important work in this context. It offers a lucid interpretation of Heidegger as an exponent of transcendental phenomenology that in important ways agrees with the present study. However, I do not agree with Gethmann's presentation of Husserl, and I shall discuss some of the points of disagreement in the footnotes to the chapters that follow. Timothy J. Stapleton, in *Husserl and Heidegger*, provides a very interesting interpretation of Husserl and Heidegger, according to which Husserl's project is an ontological one. Despite my general agreement with this, it becomes clear that there are significant differences between Stapleton's interpretation and my interpretation. Barbara Merker's *Selbsttäuschung und Selbsterkenntnis* presents a very weak Husserl. Heidegger's critique is mainly accepted, and new points of criticism of the Husserlian position are even added by the author herself – all based on an uncharitable reading of Husserl. Burt C. Hopkins' *Intentionality in Husserl and Heidegger* is basically a defense of Husserl's position. Though in some points illuminating, the study, I believe, does not give Heidegger his due. Herrmann Schmitz's mammoth study *Husserl und Heidegger* offers a very idiosyncratic reading of the two phenomenologists, portraying Husserl as "the most malignant opponent of phenomenology in the Twentieth Century" (p. 561). In my view, this book is more informative concerning the philosophy of its author than it is regarding those of Husserl and Heidegger. Jean-Luc Marion's *Reduction and Givenness* is a very interesting work that contains a multitude of ideas; the book is much more than, and perhaps not mainly, a commentary on Husserl and Heidegger, but it contains abundant material suited for a discussion of the two. Pierre Keller's *Husserl and Heidegger on Human Experience* contains interesting material as well, e.g., on the (American) discussion of the role of *das Man*, but both Husserl's and Heidegger's positions are presented idiosyncratically. I shall discuss some of Keller's theses, with which I disagree very much, in Chapter IV. Friedrich-Wilhelm von Herrmann's *Hermeneutik und Reflexion* (a much expanded edition of a work previously published under the title *Der Begriff der Phänomenologie bei Heidegger und Husserl*) follows Heidegger's critique of Husserl on all points, and although the book contains important readings (e.g., of the recently published *GA 17*), again I think Husserl is portrayed rather uncharitably. *The World Unclaimed*, written by Lilian Alweiss, presents a reevaluation of Heidegger's critique of Husserl. Alweiss' unorthodox thesis is that Heidegger's phenomenology of *Dasein* ultimately issues in an "immanentism" that is more severe than that of Husserl's transcendental subjectivity. There are many problematic claims in Alweiss' study, and I shall point out some of them in Chapters V and VI. Among the authors that present both Husserl and Heidegger as transcendental phenomenologists, *and* manage to keep an equally critical (and equally sympathetic) stance towards transcendental phenomenology in both its Husserlian and Heideggerian versions, are Steven Crowell (*Husserl, Heidegger, and the Space of Meaning*), and Daniel Dahlstrom (*Heidegger's Concept of Truth*). Although the contents of their books are not similar to the argument that I present in the following six chapters (for one thing, because neither Crowell nor Dahlstrom, as far as I can tell, offers an exposition of Husserl as detailed as the one I shall present below), I think the general drift of my interpretation is similar to what characterizes these two important works.

[6] Maurice Merleau-Ponty, *Phenomenology of Perception*, p. 57.

Heideggerian accounts of world, subjectivity, and intra-mundane entities are. More importantly, one of the ultimate aims of the study is to elucidate the nature of phenomenology, perhaps even philosophy, as such. What is it that phenomenology can provide us with? Can one, through an examination of two so seemingly different versions of phenomenology as those of Husserl and Heidegger, conclude something in general about the tasks of phenomenology?

I thus hope to accomplish no less than four things in this book. *First*, I want to provide a fair, original, and well-argued interpretation of the relation between the phenomenologies of Husserl and Heidegger – an interpretation that takes into account the debate in the literature. *Second*, I want to describe in detail the phenomenological methods of Husserl and Heidegger. *Third*, I want to discuss and evaluate some of the central phenomenological analyses provided by Husserl and Heidegger, notably those of world, intra-mundane entities, and (especially) subjectivity. *Fourth*, I hope to substantiate the claim that phenomenology as such has two tasks, both concerning "being," albeit in different ways. In other words, my interests are "historical," as well as "phenomenological" and "meta-phenomenological." These issues could perhaps have been described more independently of each other than they are in this study. In the chapters that follow, the four strands are deeply interwoven rather than separated from each other. However, I think this to some extent reflects the "matters themselves"; by pursuing one of the four issues, one is led quite naturally to considering the others as well.

My study of the Husserl-Heidegger relation consists of six chapters and a conclusion. In Chapter I, I discuss Husserl's and Heidegger's accounts of pre-philosophical or non-philosophical life. Both Husserl and Heidegger believe that the real philosophical problems are found precisely where the "naturally attuned" subject or "everyday Dasein" sees *no* problem whatsoever. But if this is so, then how does one become a philosopher? What is it that allows one to see problems where one did not see any problems previously? I argue that, contrary to what Husserl proposes, there can be no theoretical motivation to "give up" the natural attitude; but the unproblematic way one goes about in everyday life can be disrupted, for instance, with *anxiety*, as it is described by Heidegger.

Chapters II and III are dedicated to unfolding the kinds of problems Husserl and Heidegger believe are hidden in everyday life. In Chapter II, I turn to Husserl's constitutive phenomenology. The chapter is an attempt to develop in some detail the nature of the "question of constitution" that Husserl poses, as well as the method by which he proposes to answer the question. Is the problem of constitution just another version of the problem of "the external world," or is it in fact better described as a question concerning being? But if it is the latter, how does that square with the method of epoché – often described as the method by which we precisely *ignore* the "being" of things? I argue that the epoché has in fact nothing to do with ignoring anything; it is rather intended to allow us to keep a certain (viz. transcendental) problematic in view. I also argue that Husserl's constitutive phenomenology, in a way, is precisely about "being."

The theme of Chapter III is Heidegger's question of being. Again, I not only try to sort out what that question is really about, but I also develop in detail the method by which Heidegger proposes to answer it. I argue that Heidegger in fact poses two questions, rather than one; both questions *concern* "being," but one is better labeled the question of "transcendence," so that we may reserve the title "question of being" for the other issue Heidegger addresses. I also argue that Heidegger's method to a large extent is that of Husserl, although as concerns terminology, Heidegger is more careful and methodical than his mentor. This chapter raises important questions about Husserl and Heidegger: What relation is there between Heidegger's problem of "transcendence" and Husserl's constitutive problematic? In Husserl's phenomenology, is there anything like Heidegger's specific question concerning *being*? These issues, which are at the systematic heart of the study, are postponed until Chapter VI.

In the subsequent chapters, I leave the abstract project-oriented and methodological considerations and turn instead to concrete phenomenological analyses. These chapters are dedicated to a treatment of some of the frequently debated issues in the literature on Husserl and Heidegger, and in addition, they provide phenomenological analyses of world and subjectivity. Taking up two charges that are often brought against Husserl – viz. the charge that he has no conception of world except that of a totality of entities, and the charge that Husserlian transcendental subjectivity is "worldless" – I discuss Husserl's and Heidegger's phenomenological characterizations of the world (Chapter IV). I argue that Husserl's notion of world-horizon is in many ways similar to Heidegger's conception of the world as a referential web, and that the former indeed seems to have the advantage of being less tied to a specific intra-mundane mode of being.

In Chapter V, I turn to subjectivity. One of the "guiding clues" is still the charge of worldlessness, but Husserl's accusation that Heidegger's phenomenology is a type of "anthropology" is also considered. I argue, among other things, that Husserl's phenomenology of the embodied transcendental subject exhibits traits very similar to those exhibited by Dasein: both are "in" the world, rather than simply "related" to it, yet they are "in" the world precisely *as* subjects, not as objects. Thus, just as one cannot say that the transcendental subject is worldless, then it is equally wrong to claim that Heidegger's phenomenology of Dasein is a type of anthropology. Both Husserl and Heidegger are analyzing the structures of the *transcendental* subject, and both are providing a radically new interpretation of it.

In the sixth and final chapter, I attempt to tie up some of the loose ends the first five chapters left hanging. Going back to pick up a question postponed in Chapter III, I discuss what the relation is between Husserl's question of constitution and the question of "transcendence" posed by Heidegger. Are they mutually exclusive, or could it be that they are equally indispensable to a transcendental clarification of how things can "be there" for us? I present the latter view as the more attractive one. Another question, posed but not answered in Chapter III, is taken up in this chapter as well. To what extent does Husserl's phenomenology try to determine phenomenologically the modes of *being* of different entities? Bearing in mind the analyses of especially Chapter V, I discuss this question using the examples of intramundane entities (equipment, as well as what Husserl calls the "mundane" subject) and subjectivity. I argue that Husserl's interpretation of the mode of being of intramundane entities is phenomenologically inaccurate, whereas Heidegger's account is more persuasive. Husserl, however, poses and answers in an unprejudiced way the question concerning the mode of being of the transcendental subject, I claim. In his phenomenology of the embodied subject, Husserl is essentially giving the correct interpretation of the mode of being of subjectivity. Yet, I also argue that Heidegger's reflections on the being of Dasein are, in an important way – viz. *terminologically* – even more adequate. Because of his more serious concern with problems of terminology – leading him to develop a method of "formal indication" – Heidegger is able to capture the being of subjectivity in terms that entirely escape the traditional "dualistic" terms, which Husserl, despite his revolutionary insights, appears to remain entangled in.

In the conclusion, I leave the concrete analyses, in order to provide a general characterization of the problems that phenomenology, in both its Husserlian and its Heideggerian guises, tries to deal with. I here claim that, in a certain sense, Husserl's as well as Heidegger's phenomenology is essentially ontological, transcendental, and "hermeneutic." Phenomenology is in both cases about "understanding" or "interpreting," in both cases interested in accounting for the conditions for the possibility of entities "appearing," and in both cases the phenomenon *par excellence* may indeed (albeit equivocally so) be called *being*.

My way of presenting Husserl and Heidegger bears witness to my mainly, though not exclusively, "systematic" interests. The present study says nothing about Husserl and Heidegger's personal relationship. In a similar manner, although I sometimes refer to and discuss criticisms brought forth by one of the two phenomenologists concerning the other, I make no attempt to provide a systematic account of their interpretation of each other. Finally, matters concerning philosophical development are largely ignored; instead Husserl and Heidegger are presented as each having a more or less coherent and stable position. One may with some justification present Husserl thus: although his thought, as Heidegger once remarked, is "fully in flux" (*GA* 20, p. 167), real ruptures seem rare if not completely absent. Heidegger, on the other hand, in the words of one commentator, "at every instant of his career […] made more twists and turns than we can readily navigate."[7] So how can one possibly justify presenting Heidegger as if he has one stable position? The "systematic" aims supposedly help to justify my procedure. In addition, in contrast to Husserl, whose whole phenomenological production is taken into account, I only consider Heidegger's writings from the years 1919-1929, indeed with special emphasis on the Marburg period. With a few exceptions, later material is only introduced insofar as it contains retrospective remarks on Husserl, or on phenomenology in general. Despite

---

[7] David Farrell Krell, *Intimations of Mortality*, p. 99.

Heidegger's twists and turns, presumably some *approximation* to a stable position may be extracted from Heidegger's Marburg production.

But why choose this period? Apart from the desire to be able to present some coherent Heideggerian phenomenology, is there any reason why one should focus especially on the years 1919-29? Why not consider instead Heidegger's work from the thirties or forties? It seems evident that one cannot simply claim that only the earlier Heidegger associated himself with phenomenology, since there are a number of texts in which the later Heidegger unequivocally declares his sympathy for and commitment to at least some type of phenomenology.[8] Nevertheless, researchers keep returning to the notion that some kind of break with phenomenology takes place around 1929.[9] Apparently there is something that makes the twenties especially interesting in the context of phenomenology. In *Zur Sache des Denkens* Heidegger remarks that he has attempted since 1930 to conceive the problematic of *Sein und Zeit* more "primordially" (*anfänglicher*) than it is done in that work itself (*ZSD*, p. 61). If one examines the lecture course Heidegger gave in Freiburg in 1929/30, one can no longer doubt that, in important ways, the years of 1929 and 1930 mark a turning point in Heidegger's philosophical career. Here Heidegger digs deeper than or goes beyond the project of *Sein und Zeit* in announcing that the ontological difference – a crucial "operative concept"[10] in his thinking in the mid-twenties – should *itself* be questioned, and indeed that the project of *ontology*, the very heart and soul of *Sein und Zeit*, should be dismissed as "metaphysically inadequate" (*GA* 29/30, pp. 522-523). Although Heidegger perhaps agreed with Husserl up to then that some type of phenomenological "science" was the true philosophy – whether under the thematic title of "constitution" or under the title of "ontology" – as of 1929/30, he no longer appears to be in agreement. The period up to 1929, in other words, seems to be the period where Heidegger explicitly associates himself with the idea of phenomenological *research* in the "scientific" style of Edmund Husserl, and thus the period most suited for a comparative study such as the present one.

But still, even granted the legitimacy of these decisions, I do not present the whole picture of either Husserl or Heidegger. Husserl is portrayed as being very far indeed from Descartes, and yet Husserl probably never abandoned Cartesianism entirely.[11] Heidegger, on the other hand, is presented in a "scientific" and transcendental version that bears almost no trace of the "plethora of different

---

[8] See *GA* 12, p. 114; *GA* 29/30, p. 534 (a speech given on the occasion of Eugen Fink's birthday in 1965); *ZSD*, pp. 48, 90; and "Preface/Vorwort," pp. xv-xvii.
[9] Cf., e.g., Otto Pöggeler, "Die Krise des phänomenologischen Philosophiebegriffs (1929)," and *Der Denkweg Martin Heideggers*, p. 358. Theodore Kisiel has dubbed the period 1919-1929 as Heidegger's "phenomenological decade" (*The Genesis of Heidegger's Being and Time*, p. 59).
[10] Although the technical term "ontological difference" does not appear in *Sein und Zeit*, the distinction between being and entities is used throughout the work. I borrow the notion of "operative concepts" from Eugen Fink, *Nähe und Distanz*, esp. pp. 184-190.
[11] As Donn Welton subtly puts it, "while he [Husserl] did 'depart' from Cartesianism, to echo Landgrebe's well-chosen term, he never abandoned it" (*The Other Husserl*, p. 97).

thoughtpaths" that characterizes especially his early Freiburg lecture courses.[12] Furthermore, a number of important issues are not dealt with in any detail in this study, including the problems of *temporality* and *historicity*. In both Husserl and Heidegger, temporality is absolutely central to an understanding of subjectivity and of being. The most fundamental structure of the mode of being of what Heidegger calls Dasein and Husserl calls transcendental subjectivity is – in a particular sense that should be carefully distinguished from that of appearing *in* time – *temporality*. And, as we know from *Sein und Zeit*, Heidegger believes time can be shown to be the "horizon for any understanding whatsoever of being" (*SZ*, pp. 1, 17, 437). But against this background one might argue that temporality is such an important and vast issue that it deserves a study of its own. As for historicity, this could be seen as one of the topics concerning which Husserlian and Heideggerian phenomenology must part ways (cf. *GA 63*, p. 75; *GA 17*, pp. 213-214; WDF, p. 176), and thus something not to be ignored in a study aiming to compare these two philosophies. However, it is not entirely clear that Husserl remains oblivious of historicity, even if he initially excludes it from his phenomenological focus. Husserl scholars have thus spoken of a "turn," a *Kehre* in Husserl's thinking, in that, in contrast to the early Husserl, the later Husserl begins to take historicity very seriously indeed (cf. *Hua VI*, pp. 378-382, 495).[13] In other words, the problem of historicity in Husserl and Heidegger perhaps is not such a simple affair after all; and its crucial importance might thus again constitute a reason for setting it apart for discrete study, rather than giving it what is bound to be inadequate treatment. Fully recognizing the importance of the problems of temporality and historicity for any exhaustive account of the Husserl-Heidegger relation, the present study leaves these issues for other studies to address. The present book focuses on the (bodily) situatedness or embeddedness of subjectivity in the world, or "in the midst of what there is," as Heidegger puts it (WM, p. 166; *GA 27*, p. 328). It aims to describe subjectivity as thus situated, as well as the world "in" which it is situated, and the kinds of entities it finds itself already occupied with. Temporality and historicity, crucially important as these topics are, thus fall outside its scope.

So all in all, the present study paints a quite incomplete picture of Husserl and Heidegger. It is tempting, here, to paraphrase Heidegger: *Den 'Heidegger (bzw. Husserl) an sich' zu entdecken bleibe der Heideggerphilologie (bzw. Husserlphilologie) überlassen* (cf. *KPM*, p. 249). However, as Husserl emphasizes in his analyses of perceptual intentionality, the fact that we see a thing from a certain perspective and thus do not see all of its sides or aspects does not mean that we do not see the thing *in itself*. The present study, in other words, intends to portray Husserl and Heidegger *an sich*, but in both cases, it does so only from a certain perspective, dictated by certain, mainly "systematic" interests.

---

[12] Cf. John van Buren, *The Young Heidegger*, p. 365.
[13] See Bernet, Kern, and Marbach, *Edmund Husserl: Darstellung seines Denkens*, pp. 10, 213.

CHAPTER I

NATURAL ATTITUDE AND EVERYDAY LIFE

As we know from his lecture course of the summer of 1925, Heidegger is very critical towards Husserl's description of the "natural attitude" (*GA* 20, pp. 155-156). Furthermore, Heidegger apparently views the task of describing the world in the way we naturally experience it in our everyday life as a crucial one, a task on which the success of the whole of phenomenology could depend (cf. *GA* 20, p. 156; *SZ*, p. 52).[1] Thus, if Husserl's analyses of the natural attitude are flawed, as Heidegger claims, in the eyes of the latter this would not be a minor detail in Husserlian phenomenology. Heidegger must be granted this point. We phenomenologists have not always been phenomenologists, and some of us are not even constant phenomenologists, at least not constantly doing phenomenology. We all start in, and often return to, perhaps even mostly remain in a "natural attitude," busy with pursuing "natural" goals, going about our "everyday" business. On this Husserl and Heidegger agree. They also agree that somehow this "natural" or everyday life is what feeds phenomenology. Phenomenologists are not people who turn their eyes to a different world, but women and men for whom *this world*, indeed especially in its most "obvious" and "trivial" aspects, has become a problem, or even an "enigma."

From the beginning the phenomenologist lives in the paradox of having to look upon the obvious as questionable, as enigmatic, and of henceforth being unable to have any other scientific theme than that of transforming the universal obviousness [*Selbstverständlichkeit*] of the being of the world – for him the greatest of all enigmas – into something intelligible [*eine Verständlichkeit*]. (*Hua* VI, § 53, pp. 183-184; cf. p. 115; *Hua* VII, p. 247; *Hua* XXVII, p. 167)

But to philosophize precisely means to be fundamentally and constantly moved by, and directly sensitive to, the completely enigmatic nature [*Rätselhaftigkeit*] of that which common sense [*dem gesunden Verstande*] finds obvious and self-evident. (*GA* 21, pp. 23-24; cf. p. 198; *GA* 24, p. 80; *GA* 26, p. 6)

In other words, the world of natural, everyday life holds within itself the proper theme of phenomenology. If correctly approached, this life, or this attitude must be made to reveal its "blind spots" in need of phenomenological elucidation.

Therefore, a lot does indeed depend on our description of the world of the natural attitude. Different descriptions of it could lead to different phenomenologies, some of these perhaps dealing with pseudo-problems that could have been excluded from the beginning, had the analysis of the natural world been carried out properly. In this chapter I present Husserl's and Heidegger's descriptions of some of the things we encounter in the world of the "natural attitude," or everyday life. I argue that significant differences are few, but (as we see in the course of the first three

---

[1] This is emphasized by Daniel O. Dahlstrom in "Heidegger's Critique of Husserl," p. 238, and in *Heidegger's Concept of Truth*, p. 123.

chapters) enough differences exist to account for the different tasks the two thinkers envision for phenomenology – although I also argue that these tasks should be regarded as much more similar than often assumed. An initial discussion of the entities we encounter when in the natural attitude, or everyday life, must lay bare the roots of the Husserlian question of constitution and Heidegger's question of being.

1. OBJECTS IN THE LIFEWORLD[2]

Husserl is very clear that the world in which we find ourselves is not a world of "pure" objects, pure material things bereft of significance. I am sitting here in front of a computer screen, with books and sheets of paper lying around on my desk, and sometimes I look out the window at the building opposite, noticing that there is light in some of the windows there, etc. I do not encounter, according to Husserl, any neutral, meaningless objects, or pure things of nature. As he aptly puts it in *Ideen II*: "In ordinary life, we have nothing whatever to do with nature-objects. What we take as things are pictures, statues, gardens, houses, tables, clothes, tools, etc." (*Hua* IV, p. 27; cf. *Hua* VIII, p. 151). Thus, the founder of phenomenology would have no reason to argue with Heidegger when the latter describes the immediately given object in Dasein's everyday life as a "tool" (*Zeug*; often translated as "equipment") (*SZ*, p. 68). Both thinkers readily agree that the kinds of "things" we humans mostly encounter are things for some kind of *use*, be it practical, esthetic, or whatever. Husserl even admits that it is an abstraction to talk of "value free" things that are simply "there," since everything means something to us; everything has its role to play, even if it is just the negative role of "uselessness" (*Hua* XV, p. 56).

To all appearances, Heidegger not only agrees with this description, but also recognizes it as Husserl's. In other words, Heidegger does not believe that Husserl would claim that the world of the natural attitude is one of "pure" matter with no significance. What he does accuse Husserl of, however, is the failure to offer any adequate account of the mode of *access* a subject could have to the equipment encountered in the lifeworld. How do I encounter a piece of equipment *as* just that: a

---

[2] "Lifeworld" (*Lebenswelt*) is supposed to refer simply to the world of everyday, natural life. It is of course a famous term of Husserl's from the thirties, but is even found in manuscripts dating back to Husserl's *Ideen* project (cf. *Hua* IV, pp. 288n, 374-376). What makes the concept of "lifeworld" so apt for my purpose of describing both Husserl's "natural attitude" and Heidegger's "everydayness" is, of course, that the term is also evident in the early Heidegger. It appears in most of Heidegger's early Freiburg lecture courses (e.g., *GA* 56/57, pp. 210, 214; *GA* 59, pp. 58, 151; *GA* 60, pp. 11-12, 328, 336; *GA* 61, pp. 6, 94, 96-97, *et passim*), but nowhere as frequently as in the winter course of 1919/20 (cf. *GA* 58, pp. 59, 62-63, 66-71, 75-77, 79-80, 174-176, 207-208, *et passim*). A natural question, of course, is who coined the term in the first place. Apart from the fact that establishing "rights of ownership" is not a purpose of this study, perhaps we should agree with Gadamer that Husserl and Heidegger's relationship in 1919 must have been such that it would have excluded as irrelevant and improper any questions of ownership (cf. Gadamer, "Die phänomenologische Bewegung," p. 127n). In any case, Ernst W. Orth has documented that the term *Lebenswelt* was coined neither by Husserl, nor by Heidegger (cf. Orth, *Edmund Husserls "Krisis der europäischen Wissenschaften und die transzendentale Phänomenologie,"* pp. 132-136).

piece of equipment? Not by watching it, not by "gaping" or "staring" at it, as Heidegger polemically puts it.[3] No matter how hard you stare at a piece of equipment, determining its appearance and properties, you will not be able to discover it as what it is as a piece of equipment (*SZ*, p. 69), viz. *something that can be used for...*("*etwas, um zu...*") (cf. *SZ*, p. 68). You encounter the equipment *as* equipment, when you *use* it: "the less we just stare at the hammer-thing, and the more we seize hold of it and use it, the more primordial does our relationship to it become, and the more unveiledly is it encountered as that which it is – as equipment" (*SZ*, p. 69). Knowing Husserl's preoccupation with perceptual experience (noted, indeed, by Heidegger himself; cf. *GA* 20, p. 125), we would expect this to be a criticism of Husserl. Whereas Husserl does recognize that the usual objects we find ourselves surrounded by are by no means "pure things," and whereas he even describes them as very much like the Heideggerian *Zeug*, he does not realize that *being equipment*, these "things" are not properly "experienced" in a perception. Although one is tempted to conclude this, such a criticism is not entirely justified. Let us divide the issue into two questions. First, does Husserl think, acknowledging that something not unlike a Heideggerian *Zeug* is what we mostly encounter in our daily life, that our principal mode of approaching these things must be a kind of "beholding"? And secondly, if he agrees that this is not the case, would he then also agree that our *original access* to these things, i.e., the way we are presented with these "objects" *as just that kind of object*, could hardly be through an inquisitive gaze?

As to the first question, Husserl does think that various forms of perception must be a part of what goes on in our going about our daily business. But this, he stresses, does not mean that perceptual experiences are what we *live* in:

We can live in willful self-resolve or else in the activity of actually carrying out that resolve. Then, what is presupposed are certain representing acts, perhaps thinking acts of various levels, and valuing acts. But these acts, all of them, are not ones performed [*vollzogen*] in the eminent sense of the word. The true and proper performance [*Der eigentliche Vollzug*] lies in the willing and the doing. (*Hua* IV, p. 10)

The ego, living in its concrete environing world, given over to its practical ends, is in no way a subject which is contemplative above all. (*EU*, § 14, p. 67)

Perception is a necessary component in the complex act of using a hammer, but when busy using the hammer, one would not be "watching" the hammer as such, actively, but rather be preoccupied with getting this board to fit next to the other, etc. But certainly, in order to do just that, being engulfed by the constructing of whatever it is one is constructing, one must *see* the nail and the boards, *feel* the hammer in one's hand, and so forth, according to Husserl (cf. *EU*, p. 67). It is, in other words,

---

[3] Husserl notes in the margin on p. 74 in his copy of *Sein und Zeit* (here Heidegger again polemically speaks of "staring" at pure objects): "mere things – staring" (RB, p. 22). Husserl frequently writes "*Einwand*" (objection) in his marginal notes to *SZ*, when he senses a hidden attack on his own philosophy, and even if he doesn't write "objection" here, he would hardly have noted Heidegger's use of "staring," if he did not feel that it had a critical edge to it. After all, this word is not one of the important technical terms in *Sein und Zeit*.

essential to distinguish between the kind of acts we live in, and the "underlying" acts in "serving function" that enable us to live in those "higher order" acts (*Hua* VIII, pp. 100-101). Whereas Husserl admits that we do not necessarily, or even mostly, *live* in acts of perception, such perceptions are, nevertheless, necessarily involved – functioning as a "principal aid," as Husserl says.[4] He is clear that practical interests *govern* our perceiving activities. Husserl would contend that if I am entering into a dark room, for instance, looking for a piece of equipment, then I do not usually try to achieve an "optimal" view of the wanted tool. Or rather, the *optimal* view is simply the one that allows me to *find* what I need. And of course, once I spot the tool I need, I waste no time looking at it but immediately commence using it for my purposes (cf. *Hua* XI, pp. 23-24; *Hua* XVI, pp. 127-128).

One might be tempted to launch a counter attack against Heidegger at this point, arguing that if he would deny that perception is involved in our activities, he would face serious difficulties in explaining why it is much more difficult to go about one's business of hammering with one's eyes closed, than when they are open and focused on the head of the nail that one intends to hit. But of course, Heidegger by no means wants to deny that perception has a part to play in our everyday life. He is emphasizing only – more strongly, perhaps, than Husserl, but in basic accordance with him – that perception hardly ever appears as an *independent* act:

Natural perception as I live in it in moving about my world is for the most part not a detached observation and scrutiny of things, but is rather absorbed in dealing with the matters at hand concretely and practically. It is not self-contained; I do not perceive in order to perceive but in order to orient myself, to pave the way in dealing with something. (*GA* 20, pp. 37-38)

As Heidegger expresses this point in *Sein und Zeit*, there is a certain kind of "vision" (*Sichtart*) involved in our everyday activities playing a significant part in everything we do (*SZ*, p. 69). "Vision," one should hasten to add, must here be understood to include not only visual perception, but tactile and acoustic perception as well – indeed any possible type of access to entities (cf. *SZ*, p. 147).[5] The kind of "vision" Heidegger wants to attribute to everyday life must be seen as an *integral moment* in, and wholly obedient to, our everyday activities. As these activities are given the general label *Umgang* (interaction, involvement; literally "intercourse") by Heidegger, he consequently names their integral "vision" *Umsicht* (circumspection) (*SZ*, p. 69). Although Husserl and Heidegger might seem to be in perfect consensus here, we see later in this chapter that there is a slight difference between the two thinkers on this point; one that will prove crucial.

But what about the second question? The founder of phenomenology agrees that in our natural life, or natural attitude, we rarely (if ever) encounter "pure objects" bereft of any significance, and he would also agree that we do not spend most of our

---

[4] "And experiencing and knowing can indeed be a major help for other <kinds of> concern" (RB, p. 20).
[5] Likewise, if visual perception seems to occupy the principal part in my discussions of Husserl's analyses of perception, this must not be taken to mean that Husserl is simply a "philosopher of the visual sense." Husserl analyzes tactile perception extensively in his lectures and manuscripts, and in general, neither Heidegger nor Husserl should be accused of "visualism."

time "gaping" at things, but rather plunge ourselves into various activities, in which our perceptual "acts" only serve "assisting" functions.[6] But does not Husserl subscribe to the view that *perception*, after all, is what presents us with things *as they are*? Even if Husserl emphasizes that there is another "presenting" act for mathematical equations, and yet another for other humans, and so forth – doesn't he still maintain that when it comes to *things*, objects, then perception is the original type of access? Much would seem to support this assumption.[7] But Husserl, in certain reflections, does acknowledge the fact that this might not be the right way to approach equipmental objects. In a compact working manuscript from around 1920, dealing among other things with cultural objects such as tools, Husserl describes a tool as "an 'I or someone can do this or that with it'" (*Hua* XIII, p. 358). Following up on that definition, he concludes that "*the accomplishing and confirming perception* would in this case be the *using of the tool*" (*das ausführende, bewährende Wahrnehmen wäre hier das Verwenden des Werkzeuges*) (*Hua* XIII, p. 359, my emphasis). Husserl is thus no stranger to the notion that the objects we mostly encounter could be objects that are truly given to us, not in an act of beholding, but in our activity of *using* them (cf. *Hua* IX, pp. 115, 118).[8] Whether or not Husserl decided to properly develop such insights, at least his thinking has the means to realize that perception in the narrow sense might not be the original access to the objects around us. In other words, also on this point a Husserlian phenomenological description of the objects of the "natural attitude" can agree with its Heideggerian counterpart.[9]

There is, however, yet another rung on Heidegger's ladder. But first, let us recapitulate what has been agreed on thus far. (1) We are not surrounded by pure objects, but rather by equipment of various sorts; (2) we do not normally just behold the objects around us; and (3) the original access to the equipmental things *as such* is not an act of beholding, but rather the using *Umgang* with them. What Heidegger wants to claim in addition to this is that what things are *as equipment* – in Heidegger's terminology, the "being" of a piece of equipment *as* a piece of

---

[6] Therefore, accusing Husserl of having "theoretician's narcissism" (cf. Barbara Merker, *Selbsttäuschung und Selbsterkenntnis*, pp. 79, 194) is wrong. Because it is such a superficial criticism it might lead one to miss any true critical potential that Heidegger's account might have vis-à-vis Husserl.

[7] See, e.g., Husserl's marginal note to *SZ*, p. 69, line 20. Heidegger writes: "If we look at things just 'theoretically' we are without an understanding of readiness-to-hand." And Husserl replies: "But naturally a theoretical look at the implement [*Zeug*] is required if we are to grasp and have it as such objectively and to explain it descriptively" (RB, pp. 21-22).

[8] Thus, Hubert Dreyfus is hardly justified in claiming that Heidegger has to "force" Husserl to acknowledge that there could be other types of access to objects than just that of perception (cf. Dreyfus, "Introduction," pp. 20-21).

[9] One cannot disagree with Rudolf Bernet's declaration that "[w]hat Heidegger says about daily life corresponds fairly well to Husserl's notion of 'the natural attitude'" (Bernet, "Phenomenological Reduction and the Double Life of the Subject," p. 257). Nevertheless, "fairly well" still leaves room for differences that can later prove significant.

equipment should be labeled "readiness-to-hand"[10] (*Zuhandenheit*) – is what they are *an sich*: "*readiness-to-hand is the way in which entities as they are 'in themselves' are defined ontologico-categorially*" (*SZ*, p. 71). When we are trying to give nothing more (and nothing less) than a faithful description of the objects in our natural, everyday world, we must stick to describing and not smuggle into our description unwarranted assumptions. The objects, so we have concluded, are by no means pure things, but rather equipment. Thus, according to Heidegger, there is every reason to say that equipment is what they truly are, what they are *an sich*.[11]

But Husserl wants to say something slightly different. For Husserl, the question of what the objects are *an sich* is ultimately a question that can only be answered by constitutional phenomenology. However, speaking "from within" the natural attitude, we can, according to Husserl, say that a piece of equipment consists of different *layers*. As explained above, Husserl agrees with Heidegger that perception in the narrow sense is not normally the kind of act we *live* in, but Husserl insists that acts of perceiving are nevertheless present on a fundamental level, supporting the acts we do live in. In a corresponding manner – turning to the thing – there is a founding "layer" of "pure objectivity" and materiality in every tool, on which other layers, such as the "can be used for…," value predicates, etc., are built, Husserl thinks (*Hua* IV, p. 214). This does not mean that Husserl imagines that we somehow only have *immediate* perceptual access to the "layer" of material objectivity, on which then *subsequent* acts of thinking or evaluating must build (*EU*, p. 57); indeed we have noted that Husserl considers such perception of value-free objectivity an abstraction, i.e., something we practically never experience. And even when Husserl seems less certain of this last point, he at least emphasizes that we not only experience "things" as pure *Sachen*, but "with the same immediacy" (*Hua* III/1, p. 58) as goods and practical objects: "*Immediately*, physical things stand there as objects of use, the 'table' with its 'books,' the 'drinking glass,' the 'vase,' the 'piano,' etc." (*Hua* III/1, p. 58, my emphasis; cf. *Hua* IV, p. 188; *Hua* IX, p. 111). In the end, however, every such piece of equipment has, at its core, a layer of

---

[10] As to the notoriously difficult question of translating Heidegger's terms, I shall try to stay within the suggestions given by Dreyfus (cf. his *Being-in-the-World*, pp. x-xii), and Kisiel (who does not strictly hold to *one* translation of each word – cf. *The Genesis of Heidegger's Being and Time*, "Appendix D," pp. 490-511), when not simply using the German phrases, or more readily understandable "traditional" terms. I believe that those who prohibit any paraphrasing of Heidegger with "traditional" concepts, in fact, are not acting in accordance with Heidegger's intentions. Heidegger's early lectures testify to a very pedagogical thinker (try comparing with Husserl's lecture courses) who strives to achieve clarity. Although he does see the need to coin somewhat "strange" (even "ugly," according to himself; *SZ*, p. 38; *GA* 20, p. 203) terms, he is very clear about his reasons for doing so.

[11] Heidegger's notions of *Zeug* and readiness-to-hand have recently been criticized by Gail Soffer ("Phenomenologizing with a Hammer: Theory or Practice"). She tries to show that readiness-to-hand can neither be shown to be "genetically," nor "statically" prior to some sort of presence-at-hand. As I see it, however, Soffer basically fails to notice that which is Heidegger's concern, viz. to demonstrate that the *being* of our everyday objects is missed if we adopt any kind of "layer ontology." Much more on this in Chapter VI.

materiality, indeed must have such a layer, according to Husserl (*EU*, p. 54; *Hua XIV*, p. 390).

In Heidegger's view, this assumption is a fateful mistake (*GA* 63, p. 88). His "critique of Husserl's construction of the 'ontologies'"[12] is unrelenting: time and again, Heidegger cautions his students not to accept this seemingly accurate description of the objects of our natural world, apparently very well aware that the path to his own phenomenological project will be closed for anyone who fails to see the inappropriateness of the description (cf., e.g., *GA* 61, p. 91; *GA* 63, pp. 88-89; *GA* 20, p. 247). Heidegger insists that "readiness-to-hand" must not in our account of the natural attitude be described as a "layer" "on top" of other layers. Viewing a tool as the "result" of several such layers is unwarranted; it is not the way we experience it to be in our going about our everyday business, according to Heidegger. And what is more, he believes that by adhering to the Husserlian description we have passed by the "blind spot" of the natural attitude, without even noticing it. If a hammer, for instance, is described as such a multi-layered "object," there is one thing philosophy can *never* ask about it, and that is *what mode of being it has* (*GA* 20, p. 247). Or rather, there is only one mode that we can attribute to it, and *will* attribute to it as a matter of course (which already indicates that the decisive point is being missed, because philosophy precisely has to make a problem out of the obvious), and that is the mode of being of a *material thing* (*GA* 63, p. 89), or what Heidegger calls "presence-at-hand" (*Vorhandenheit*) (*SZ*, p. 99). Thus, for Heidegger, it is of the utmost importance that we acknowledge that "ready-to-hand" is what the thing *in itself* is.

2. SUBJECTS IN THE LIFEWORLD

Turning to our natural, everyday experience of others and ourselves, the gap between the views of Husserl and Heidegger seems only to widen. After all, this is precisely where Heidegger, in the lecture course of the summer of 1925, explicitly objects to Husserl's description of the natural attitude. According to Heidegger, Husserl would say of the subject in the natural attitude that it is a "real object" in the world, just like houses, trees, and mountains are (*GA* 20, pp. 131-132). Heidegger then asks the rhetorical question whether conceiving the subject thus doesn't imply a *naturalistic* attitude rather than a *natural* one (*GA* 20, p. 155). We return to this question later in the study. For now, let us ask whether Heidegger is justified in presenting Husserl's position the way he does.

Heidegger very likely had a copy of Husserl's *Ideen II* in his hands just prior to giving the lecture course in question;[13] therefore it is probable that Heidegger's criticism is mainly directed at that manuscript. But if so, his criticism at first glance

---

[12] *SZ*, p. 442 (Heidegger's marginal note to p. 98).
[13] Cf. Kisiel, *The Genesis of Heidegger's Being and Time*, p. 375. Elsewhere, Kisiel relates that Heidegger studied the manuscript of *Ideen II* "intensively" while preparing for the lecture course of the summer of 1925 ("On the Way to *Being and Time*," p. 195).

looks completely misguided. For Husserl, the natural attitude, strictly speaking, is not a *single* attitude; it encompasses at least two sub-attitudes (cf. *Hua* VIII, p. 415).[14] While Heidegger thoroughly criticizes one of them, viz. the naturalistic attitude, how can he possibly defend the claim that such a criticism also holds for the *personalistic* attitude so crucial to *Ideen II*? When in this latter attitude – which Husserl contends is the attitude we almost constantly live in (*Hua* IV, p. 183) – we precisely *do not*, Husserl emphasizes, view each other as multi-layered objects: "In this attitude, it never occurs to him [the subject] to 'insert' the spirit into the body, i.e., to consider the spirit as something in the body, as something founded in it, as something belonging, with the body, to a reality" (*Hua* IV, p. 190). Rather, my fellow *persons* are the ones with whom I communicate, and with (or against) whom I act, the ones I love or hate, trust or distrust (cf. *Hua* IV, p. 194). But even given this description, it does not take much reflection to see why Heidegger might be dissatisfied with Husserl's account. However insistent that I do not *live* in acts of perception of material objects when confronting others in the personalistic attitude, Husserl maintains that such a perception is after all there (*Hua* IV, p. 244). When seeing another person, my perceptual act does not *terminate* in the material layer, but moves through it to the "higher" layers that constitute the person:

> If I turn toward a man, this act of turning-toward [*das Sichrichten*], the thematic ray of activity, goes first of all simply and straightforwardly to the body, as a matter of sensuous perception. But this ray does not *terminate* in the body; in the understanding of the expression, it goes beyond, to the ego-subject, therefore to his being in the doing of this or that: in turning-toward, in being-preoccupied-with, having-a-world, being mundanely affected by the latter, and so on – to the extent that all this attains expression. (*EU*, § 12, p. 56; cf. the identical text in *Hua* XV, p. 506)

This passage does not entirely clarify Husserl's actual view. Preventing a possible misunderstanding, we must emphasize that Husserl does not suggest that I only have intuitive or perceptual access to the material layer (*Hua* XV, pp. 83-84). Rather, in a special "perceptual" experience labeled *Fremderfahrung* (experiencing the other, the alien), I immediately experience the presence of other persons (*Hua* VIII, p. 63). Therefore, when I encounter others in my "natural" *personalistic* attitude, it is not the case that I first direct my gaze at a material thing, and then, in a series of subsequent acts of thinking, build subjective layers on top of it (*Hua* XIV, pp. 331-332). In fact, actively perceiving a material body is exactly what I *cannot be doing* when I experience other persons (*Hua* VI, p. 479).[15] Husserl does grant the Sartrean *possibility* of confronting others with an objectifying look (cf. *Hua* VI, pp. 112, 307), but like Merleau-Ponty he sees this as a distorted approach to others, and one

---

[14] John Scanlon emphasizes this in his study of the natural attitude ("Husserl's *Ideas* and the Natural Concept of the World," pp. 229-232).

[15] I think that it is, therefore, fundamentally wrong to claim that the other "at first" is a *thing*, according to Husserl. For example, Bernhard Waldenfels makes such a claim in *Das Zwischenreich des Dialogs* (pp. 45-46, 201), and strangely, so does Kathleen M. Haney, who wants to defend Husserl's theory of *Fremderfahrung*. Cf. her *Intersubjectivity Revisited*, pp. 45, 47, 50, 105, *et passim*.

that cannot do away with the personalistic *understanding* directed at the other *as* an other, but only repress it.[16]

Heidegger himself distinguishes two extreme modes of interaction with others. Although at first glance it looks as if these are totally unrelated to Husserl's naturalistic and personalistic attitudes, ultimately there is an important similarity. The negative extreme that Heidegger labels "intervening-dominating" (*einspringend-beherrschende*) solicitude (*Fürsorge*) (cf. *SZ*, p. 122) in fact entails a kind of objectification of the other person. This is evident from the lecture course where Heidegger introduces the distinction. When directed at another in the intervening-dominating mode, I approach her from the tasks she has to perform, Heidegger says (*GA* 21, p. 223). I view her as a *function*, as it were, instead of a unique individual. As a simple piece in a larger machinery, the other is degraded to a *Zeug*, or even a mere present-at-hand object:

In this kind of solicitude the other is, as it were, treated as a nothing, i.e., as a nothing of Dasein [*als ein Nichts von Dasein*]. He is not present in the solicitude as his own Dasein, but rather as an inauthentic [Dasein], and that means as something present-at-hand in the world [...]. (*GA* 21, p. 224)

The other extreme, the *vorspringend-befreiende* (*SZ*, p. 122) solicitude, respects the other as someone who cannot be defined in terms of the tasks she performs, and thus someone who *cannot be replaced* by another. As a person she is irreplaceable.[17]

Structurally, Husserl's and Heidegger's descriptions are close to identical. Just as in the case of the "objects" of the lifeworld, we must conclude that their disagreement does not lie on the level of description at all, but on the level of *interpretation*. Heidegger acknowledges that Husserl does not fail to notice the "personalistic" attitude (*GA* 20, p. 171), but he objects to the latter's interpretation of the person: "The *fundamental stratum* is still the *naturally real*, upon which the psychic is built, and upon the psychic the spiritual" (*GA* 20, p. 172). Should we, having developed something like the agreed upon description, add that what is thus described as a "person" *is after all the result of certain higher layers being founded upon more basic layers*, or is that just the kind of interpretation we *must avoid*? Both Husserl's and Heidegger's answer to this question should be obvious, given the discussion in the previous and the present section. Once again, it must be emphasized that Heidegger's position is not the clearly false one of claiming that a human being has *no* materiality or spatiality. Dasein is spatial, and it does have a certain materiality, but we will be able to understand none of these aspects properly

---

[16] *EU*, p. 56; *Hua* XV, p. 506. Cf. Maurice Merleau-Ponty, *Phenomenology of Perception*, pp. 360-361. Sartre defends the strange view that either the other is an object for me (in which case she cannot be a subject), or she is the subject for whom *I* am an object (in which case I am "degraded," "enslaved," and objectified). Cf. *Being and Nothingness*, pp. 252, 256, 267, 270, 273. For a brief survey of Merleau-Ponty's and Sartre's phenomenological attempts to come to grips with the problem of intersubjectivity, see Dan Zahavi, *Husserl und die transzendentale Intersubjektivität*, pp. 112-127.

[17] That this is at least part of what concerns Heidegger can be seen from the fact that when introducing the negative extreme of solicitude, he even calls it *substituting* (*stellvertretend-abnehmende*) solicitude (*GA* 21, p. 223).

18 CHAPTER I

if we adopt the layer theory. If we attribute the spatiality of Dasein to an "underlying" material layer, we shut ourselves off from the possibility of understanding the *genuine* spatiality of Dasein, i.e., the peculiar *way* in which Dasein, as the peculiar being it is, inhabits space, Heidegger claims (*SZ*, pp. 55-56; *GA* 20, pp. 307-308).[18]

In many ways, then, Heidegger's own descriptions of the subjects of everyday life seem in perfect accordance with what we find in *Ideen II*. For instance, it is reasonably well known that Husserl – in sentences very akin to what will later appear in *Sein und Zeit* – points out the far-reaching power of convention.[19] The analysis of the dictatorship of the "one" (*das Man*) belongs to the most famous of Heidegger's analyses of everyday life. Briefly put, *das Man* is the *subject* of everyday life (*SZ*, pp. 114, 129). In everyday life, we are essentially under the rule of convention to such a degree that we *are* "one," we *are* conventional – whether we choose to do what "one" prescribes, or rebel against it (cf. *SZ*, p. 371). Convention has always already understood and interpreted everything for us in its own "mediocre" way; it has buried possible genuine understanding under a thick layer of "idle talk" (*Gerede*), restless "inquisitiveness" (*Neugier*), and "ambiguity" (*Zweideutigkeit*) (cf. *SZ*, pp. 166-175). In a continuous, empty "hearsay" (*Hörensagen*) (*GA* 20, p. 371), a restless search for the very newest (which, once found, is already outdated) (*GA* 20, p. 386), and an ambiguity that allows no difference between genuine and fake insights to surface (*SZ*, p. 173), we spend most of our days. Although no criticism of "modern life" and likewise no moralizing are intended by Heidegger (*SZ*, p. 167), it is crucial to understand that everyday life in *das Man* is a life that, so to speak, covers itself up (*GA* 20, p. 377).[20] More precisely, it is a life whose understanding is a form of *distortion* (*Verstellung*) (*GA* 20, p. 377; *SZ*, p. 222). This, according to Heidegger, is a much more severe problem than if everyday life had simply failed to realize what goes on in it, or if it had once realized it, only to "hide" this insight from itself (*SZ*, p. 36; *GA* 20, p. 119). That is so, because having distortedly interpreted everything (rather than failed to unveil something, or hidden something), everyday life already "knows" everything there is

---

[18] Although Heidegger takes some steps towards an analysis of Dasein's peculiar spatiality, he avoids the problematic of the *body* in *Sein und Zeit* (cf. p. 108), which Husserl does not fail to notice (RB, p. 25). See Chapters V and VI of the present study.

[19] "Besides the tendencies which proceed from other individual persons, there are demands which arise in the intentional form of indeterminate generality, the demands of morality, of custom, of tradition, of the spiritual milieu: 'one' ['*man'*] judges in this way, 'one' has to hold his fork like this, and so on" (*Hua* IV, p. 269; cf. *Hua* XIV, p. 225, and *Hua* XXIX, p. 42).

[20] Dreyfus, I believe, is therefore not right in claiming that the source of the intelligibility of the world is *das Man* (cf. *Being-in-the-World*, pp. 155, 161). Frederick A. Olafson rightly criticizes this aspect of Dreyfus's Heidegger-interpretation in his paper "Heidegger *à la* Wittgenstein or 'Coping' with Professor Dreyfus" (pp. 54-63). See also the debate between Taylor Carman ("On Being Social: A Reply to Olafson") and Olafson ("Individualism, Subjectivity, and Presence: A Response to Taylor Carman"), and Pierre Keller's argument for a middle position (*Husserl and Heidegger on Human Experience*, pp. 161-167).

to know. Nothing is hidden from the distorted vision of the "one"; it cannot be taught anything because it already "knows" everything (cf. *SZ*, pp. 169, 173).

I will not dwell on the particular features of Heidegger's description of social life. What is of interest here is that Heidegger in fact attributes something not unlike Husserl's natural attitude, indeed not unlike the criticized *naturalistic* attitude, to everyday Dasein. Human beings, he tells us, have the tendency to understand themselves from the things that are not human beings, in the end from the present-at-hand material objects (*SZ*, p. 130). Even the *Zeug* with which humans are busy "coping," is generally understood this way, Heidegger admits (*SZ*, p. 201). Human beings living their everyday lives tend to *leap over* (*überspringen*) (*SZ*, pp. 43, 66, 201) their own being and the being of the ready-to-hand, and view them all as "objects." These are objects with very different "properties," to be sure, but objects nonetheless. Heidegger even calls this "objectivistic" interpretation a "natural conception" (*GA* 24, p. 92), thus clearly embracing Husserl's terminology. And yet, Heidegger views the decisive problem with Husserl's description as residing precisely in the latter's acceptance of such an understanding. Must not Heidegger be forced to take back his criticism of Husserl? And if he does not, must we not accuse him of inconsistency? It seems that Heidegger, on pains of inconsistency, must accept the criticized Husserlian description, i.e., that even the difference in *interpretation* of the agreed upon description is beginning to disappear. But this is an illusion created by a crucial difference in the standpoint from which Husserl's description of that which is experienced in the "natural attitude" is obtained and the standpoint of Heidegger's description of the "everyday Dasein."

3. "INSIDE" OR "OUTSIDE" THE NATURAL ATTITUDE

Heidegger agrees with Husserl's description of what we encounter in daily life. He even offers essentially the same *interpretation* of it. However, he insists that this interpretation is in fact a distortion. This by no means implies an inconsistency on Heidegger's part, but it does make obvious that when Heidegger describes what goes on in natural life, he does so from a *different* attitude (cf. *GA* 63, p. 109), an attitude in some sense external to (and as it were above) the life described – like Hegel describing the *sinnliche Gewißheit*. Following a hint from Eugen Fink,[21] we might be inclined to say that this is naturally so since the very notions of "natural attitude" and "everyday life" are *philosophical*, phenomenological notions, thus something that we can talk about only when we are *no longer in* the attitude thus described.[22] A thematic treatment of the "natural attitude" can only be given by

---

[21] Fink says that the natural attitude is a "transcendental" concept. Cf. *Studien zur Phänomenologie 1930-1939*, p. 113.
[22] So Sebastian Luft recently argues. See his thorough account of Husserl's notion of the natural attitude, "Husserl's Phenomenological Discovery of the Natural Attitude." Ricœur similarly argues that it is an illusion to think the natural attitude can be described from within it (*Husserl*, p. 18).

someone who no longer lives *in* it. I find this a convincing point, but it must not mislead us.

We must note that the description given so far is not, strictly speaking, a description *of* everyday life, or the natural attitude. It is rather a description of some of the entities that we experience *in* that life (things and persons), and such a description should precisely pave the way for a thematic treatment *of* (some essential aspect of) natural, everyday life. It seems plausible that someone *in* the natural attitude could and would have given something very close to the description offered in the two previous sections, only she would probably view such a description as a strange undertaking, pointless and trivial. Now, since we are not ourselves truly *in* the natural attitude, but already philosophers trying to find the way to Husserlian and Heideggerian phenomenological philosophy, there are basically two ways in which we could carry out a description of the things encountered in everyday life. We can either try to be "faithful" to the attitude in question, i.e., try to stick to describing what it experiences in the way it would itself describe/interpret it. Or we can describe it all from a different level, letting the natural interpretation appear as flawed, if we – from our present viewpoint, with our present insights – believe that that is what it is.[23]

That Heidegger takes the latter course has already been mentioned (although we have to wait until Chapter III to see how he could develop the insights allowing him to point out the distorted nature of the natural interpretation). Husserl, on the other hand, is generally *faithful* to the interpretation of the natural attitude when describing what goes on in it. Although, strictly speaking, he cannot be describing from *within* the natural attitude, at least he speaks *quasi* from within it when he describes what goes on in it. Of course, once he moves on to point out the naivety of that attitude he can no longer even be seen as *quasi* in it, but he almost always begins in solidarity with the interpretation of the natural attitude. This is evident from Husserl's description of the lifeworldly "objects": we immediately experience things as objects for use, but at the same time *we know* that they are also, at their core, material realities, Husserl claims. According to the interpretation of the natural attitude, a table just *is* something that is made of a certain material (wood), only it is made in such a way as to serve certain functions (whereby it acquires *Zeug*-properties). From *within* daily life, there is no other way of looking at it. It must be emphasized that this is so, not only according to Husserl, but also according to Heidegger's own description of everyday Dasein, with its "distorting" tendency to interpret every entity as some kind of present-at-hand object.

But then we are in a position to see what separates the two accounts. Husserl indeed – at least initially – cannot ask the question about the mode of *being* of the objects of our natural attitude. This is so because, speaking *quasi* from within the

---

[23] What is at stake here is whether we should accept the *interpretation* of the natural attitude. Concerning the *experience* of the natural attitude (which might turn out to be quite different from the interpretation the natural attitude itself gives of it), there is agreement: phenomenology must stay faithful to immediate, everyday experience.

natural attitude in his initial presentation of what we experience in the natural attitude – the presentation that must also somehow indicate the theme of phenomenology – the theme of an investigation into modes of being cannot surface. When I am in the natural attitude, a table just *is* a material thing with certain "cultural" layers, as we saw. If Heidegger is right that there are different modes of being, these *can only surface as a possible theme for phenomenology when everyday life has already been interrupted.*

The crucial difference between Heidegger's and Husserl's descriptions of that which is experienced in the natural attitude, or everyday life, is thus that *unlike his mentor, Heidegger describes everyday Dasein from a standpoint "outside" everydayness.* Of course, this is not in the sense that he is no longer in contact with, and "sympathetic" toward the experiences of everyday Dasein. Rather, insofar as he has distanced himself from the *interpretation* of everyday Dasein, Heidegger may be said to describe everyday life from an "external" standpoint. Noticing this difference between the two phenomenologists is of the utmost importance. Only then will it emerge why and when Heidegger must depart from the Husserlian project.

If the "blind spot" of everyday life calling for phenomenological elucidation can only be seen strictly speaking when we are no longer *in* that life, then the discovery of that blind spot can of course not be what *motivates* us to begin investigating our everydayness. But that does not mean that Heidegger can point out motivation for a departure from, or a radical modification of, our everyday life in *das Man*. Husserl, on the other hand, describing natural life *quasi* from within it, has not presented us with a blind spot at all. Staying faithful to the natural attitude, he has described the objects and subjects of the lifeworld as they appear, and at the same time he has interpreted them just the way the natural attitude would. No conflict or puzzle has yet emerged. In the next two sections of this chapter, we must examine what possible "fractures" in natural life could motivate one to begin to question it.

4. THE THESIS OF THE NATURAL ATTITUDE

Husserl describes the natural attitude as it would describe itself. But as the natural attitude describes itself, there is no blind spot for phenomenology to elucidate, we might presume. Husserl thinks there is, however, and he even has a name for it: *the general thesis, or general positing of the natural attitude.*

In *Ideen I*, Husserl offers only a brief sketch of the natural attitude, as he quickly moves on to emphasize the basic feature of the natural attitude, which for transcendental phenomenology will prove decisive:

I find the "actuality," [*"Wirklichkeit"*] the word already says it, as a *factually existent actuality and also accept it as it presents itself to me as factually existing*. No doubt about or rejection of data belonging to the natural world alters in any respect the *general positing which characterizes the natural attitude*. "The" world is always there as an actuality; here and there it is at most "otherwise" than I supposed; this or that is, so to speak, to be struck *out of it* and given such titles as "illusion" and "hallucination," and the like; <it is to be struck out of "the" world> which – according to the general positing – is always factually existent. (*Hua* III/1, p. 61)

Life in the natural attitude is a life in world-belief. Everything I encounter – be it equipment, persons, or the elusive "pure objects" – I experience as real, as existing. And when I am occasionally wrong, when something I "thought" I saw (as I will subsequently say) turns out not to be there after all, something else is *really* there instead. Or if I am hallucinating, and it turns out that the creatures I (thought I) saw in the closet are not there, and that indeed nothing is there "instead," what it means is that the closet is *empty*, i.e., after all the closet is really there. Illusions and hallucinations cannot shake our belief that reality is there – indeed the word "reality" itself says as much, as Husserl notes – but only lead to revisions of our belief in individual objects and their properties.

In Husserl's view, this "general thesis" is what the natural attitude cannot itself account for. That seems a reasonable claim given the fact that the "general thesis" is the *foundation* for natural life (cf. *Hua* I, p. 57; *Hua* VIII, p. 459), and that *upon* which all accounts offered in the natural attitude must build. If all accounts I can ever offer in natural life are founded on my "belief"[24] that reality exists, then surely that belief itself must be left unaccounted for in the natural attitude (*HuDo* II/1, p. 38n). The issue, however, is whether it is actually possible from *within* the natural attitude to see this "belief in reality" *as* a "belief," *as* a "general thesis." We must be able to see in the natural attitude a kind of "presumption" (cf., e.g., *Hua* VIII, p. 67), more precisely we must be able to see that there is something left unaccounted for that *should be* accounted for, if we are to begin questioning this attitude. And furthermore, *we* must be able to see this blind spot, we as people living (*quasi*) in the natural attitude. We are still only looking for a motivation for the radical transformation of, or departure from, the natural attitude, and therefore we cannot presuppose such a transformation.

But is it really possible to see that a "presumption" is present here? Husserl is very clear that the existence of reality is not something that we can have doubts about. First of all, doubting is not – according to Husserl – a matter of decision, or will. I need a motivation to doubt something (*Hua* VIII, pp. 50, 484), and such motivation seems entirely lacking in the case of the existence of reality. Even more fundamentally, I simply cannot doubt the existence of the world (*Hua* VI, p. 407; *Hua* VIII, pp. 54, 459), since the "general thesis" is that foundation of absolute certainty that makes any doubt possible in the first place, thus it is itself essentially *beyond* doubt:

---

[24] Husserl, of course, uses the unfamiliar expression "the general thesis of the natural attitude," because he knows very well that what he is trying to describe is on a level different from, and more basic than that which we would normally call "beliefs." There is, in other words, no reason to assume that Husserl would disagree with Wittgenstein's statement: "The existence of the earth is rather part of the whole *picture* which forms the starting point of belief for me" (*On Certainty*, § 209). Compare what Husserl says in *Krisis*: "The world is not a hypothesis that sole sense in which hypotheses have meaning for positive science [...]; all hypotheses in the positive sphere are hypotheses upon the ground of the 'hypothesis' of the world" (*Hua* VI, § 72, p. 265). Similarly, *Hua* XXIX, p. 268. Heidegger states in *Prolegomena zur Geschichte des Zeitbegriffs* "that the world is 'there' *before* all belief" (*GA* 20, p. 295).

When experience proceeds harmoniously [*einstimmig*], I can do nothing but receive, with certainty [*in Gewißheit*], nature as given, and remain in that certainty [...]. But what if I experience a rupture of this harmony? Then it [the rupture] appears on the basis of an experience, and a continuity of past experience, which remain certain. Without this, there can be no "certainty" of doubt, and no transition into nullity. (*Hua* VIII, p. 393)[25]

And yet somehow this absolute certainty is what must be seen as "presumptive," as a "thesis"? In the natural attitude, the existence of the world is something that is confirmed in every single perception I have (*Hua* VIII, p. 54), it is something so obvious that no one would even consider saying it in a sentence (*Hua* I, p. 57; *Hua* VII, p. 245). The world, Husserl admits, stands before our eyes as existing *without question* (*fraglos seiende*) (*Hua* I, p. 57). But if it is experienced thus, where lies its presumptive nature?

As Husserl himself emphasizes, the "presumption" cannot consist in the possibility of hallucination, or illusion. Individual experiences might be illusions or hallucinations, but they can appear as such only on the basis of other experiences that reveal the way things *really* are:

The *possibility of deception* [*Täuschung*] is inherent in the evidence of experience and does not annul either its fundamental character or its effect; though becoming evidentially aware of <actual> deception "annuls" the deceptive experience or evidence itself. The evidence of a new experience is what makes the previously uncontested experience undergo that modification of believing called "annulment" or "cancellation"; and it alone can do so. Evidence of experience is therefore always presupposed by the process. (*Hua* XVII, § 58, p. 164; cf. *Hua* XVII, p. 287)

Two hallucinations as such cannot correct each other; what is needed for a hallucination to appear as a hallucination is an experience that establishes the true state of affairs. *The whole "game" of illusion and hallucination presupposes the existence of reality* (as well as our ability to experience that reality).[26] Husserl undoubtedly agrees with that much. He does suggest, however, that something like the Cartesian "dream argument" could show that our "knowledge" of the existence of the world is not of "apodictic" certainty:

Not only can a particular experienced thing suffer devaluation as an illusion of the senses; the whole unitarily surveyable nexus, experienced throughout a period of time, can prove to be an illusion, a coherent dream. (*Hua* I, p. 57)

Suppose this is so; suppose I am convinced that I am sitting in front of my computer, writing, whereas in fact I am dreaming. Can this (implausible) possibility convince me of the "uncertainty" of the evidence I have of the existence of reality? Of course, "dreams" are that which we realize we have had only when we are awake, or at least

---

[25] The similarity with some of Wittgenstein's points in *On Certainty* is striking. Cf. the latter work, § 115: "If you tried to doubt everything you would not get as far as doubting anything. The game of doubting itself presupposes certainty" (Similarly, §§ 341, 354).

[26] The transition from the possibility of illusory particular experiences to the non-apodictic character of the evidence of world-existence as such cannot be justified. John J. Drummond seems to underestimate this important point in his attempt to demonstrate that the "Cartesian" and the "ontological" ways to the reduction are equally necessary. Cf. Drummond, "Husserl on the Ways to the Performance of the Reduction," p. 57.

in the process of awakening (cf. *Hua* XI, p. 178). For a dreamt "reality" to appear as such, it must be corrected by a truly perceived reality. So what the dream argument must be trying to convince us of is the possibility that this "world" I have constantly been experiencing is not the *real* world, but only a "dream world." This argument fails to demonstrate that a "belief" in a reality *as such* is unwarranted, instead only showing that the real world could be "different" from what I experience it to be. More importantly, Husserl is quite clear that "reality" and "world" can for me only refer to *this* world, the one in which I live and act (*Hua* VI, p. 258; *Hua* VII, p. 277). What could "reality" possibly be *for me*, if not simply this experienced world, with all its familiar places and persons? Whereas in this world I sometimes discover that I have been dreaming, these dreams only appear as such because they are embedded in a coherent system of perceptions that by and large present reality as it is. In this system of experiences, I certainly do *not* experience myself as constantly dreaming.[27]

Not only does it therefore make no sense to doubt the existence of the world; it even seems impossible to view this as any kind of "thesis." Indeed the so-called "general thesis" seems anything but a "presumption" (cf. *Hua* VII, p. 246n). Rather, it is the most immediately evident "truth." *The existence of reality is not left unaccounted for by the natural attitude in any sense meaningful to someone* in *that attitude*.

The above discussion of the alleged "presumptive" nature of world-experience, may be viewed as part of a critique of Husserl's so-called "Cartesian way" to phenomenology. The Cartesian path is the one that Husserl treads when he argues that we should look for an indubitable and completely lucid starting point for philosophy.[28] The argument usually proceeds by way of demonstrating that world-experience cannot serve as such a starting point, since doubt in principle remains a possibility for this kind of experience. We have already demonstrated in this section that – at least as long as we are speaking from within the natural attitude – world-experience in principle cannot be doubted. Does this mean, then, that Husserl's Cartesian way is impossible? We should hesitate to go that far, but it may certainly be said that there is no way "out" of the natural attitude that goes through the attempt to demonstrate – "in" that attitude – that world-experience is dubitable, or even "presumptive" in any way. But Husserl's Cartesian way has features we have not yet explored. In an attempt to show how the existence of the world is contingent,

---

[27] We could also formulate a Wittgensteinian version of this argument. As Husserl shows, a "presentifying" (*vergegenwärtigende*) act such as remembering involves "two" subjects: the one that remembers and the remembered subject (*Hua* XI, p. 309). Presumably the same must hold for dreaming. Now suppose that my sitting here wide awake in front of my computer is in fact just a dream. If I (i.e., the dreamt subject) were now to say to myself, "perhaps I am dreaming" – this *would not be true*. The *dreamt* subject is exactly "wide awake"; only it *is* just a dreamt subject. Cf. to this Wittgenstein, *On Certainty*, §§ 383, 676.

[28] A clear exposition of Husserl's different ways to phenomenology is found in Iso Kern, "Die drei Wege zur transzendental-phänomenologischen Reduktion in der Philosophie Edmund Husserls." Most of the contents of that article are also found in Kern's book *Husserl und Kant*, pp. 196-237.

while that of consciousness is not, Husserl introduces the notion of a hypothetical "annihilation" of the world. Briefly put, the idea is that if we imagine the world being annihilated, we would still have to acknowledge something as "remaining," as the "residue" of such a world-annihilation (*Hua* III/1, p. 104). That something, of course, would be the pure "ego" – not unchanged, but nevertheless unshaken in its existence (*Hua* III/1, p. 104).

Now precisely what scenario is Husserl referring to here? What does it mean to imagine the world being "annihilated," when the "ego" must somehow remain as still existing? If I imagine, say, our solar system exploding, surely I would imagine myself ceasing to exist. But of course, this is not the scenario that Husserl has in mind. Under the heading of "world-annihilation," Husserl is actually drawing attention to the possibility that my experiences could be confused to such a degree that *I would no longer be able to perceive a world* (*Hua* III/1, p. 103). The world, then, would be "annihilated" (for me), but I would remain as a changed, but still existing, experiencing subjectivity.

In the present section, we are interested in the problem of the motivation to direct our gaze at the natural attitude. Can the idea of "world-annihilation" help us? As long as we are "in" the natural attitude, living on the basis of the "general thesis," it seems that what Husserl refers to is a case of insanity (or perhaps a physical disorder affecting our cognitive capabilities *in toto*) rather than world-annihilation. Whereas insanity certainly leaves me changed but still existing the way prescribed, it does not affect the existence of the world in the least. In his lectures on *Erste Philosophie*, Husserl anticipates this objection (*Hua* VIII, p. 55), only to reject it emphatically. As his argument runs in those lectures, however, it must be dismissed in the present context. Husserl accuses the "insanity" objection of begging the question, presupposing as it does the existence of the world – something yet to be established (*Hua* VIII, p. 65). But since our question in this section is precisely whether there can be any motivation to *view* world-existence as in need of being "established" at all, it is obviously Husserl himself who is begging the question. In fact, he has little choice but to beg the question at this point. What the insanity objection has brought to our attention is the fact that when we are "in" the natural attitude we can never view Husserl's so-called annihilation of the world *as* having anything to do with the existence of the world. This, of course, is due to the characteristics of that attitude as Husserl describes them himself, above all the unshakable "belief" in world-existence. As long as we have not "abandoned" the natural attitude, we will never stop believing in a world "behind" the confused experiences in Husserl's thought experiment, and hence that thought experiment cannot in any way shake our "belief" in world-existence, nor make us realize that the world could cease existing and yet leave the ego existing as a "residue." In other words, the scenario that Husserl is describing under the heading of "world-annihilation" can only be understood the way he wants it to be understood, when we are no longer in the natural attitude.

Thus, it cannot possibly function as a motivation to begin to distance ourselves from that attitude in the first place.[29]

In sum, none of the allegedly questionable aspects of the so-called "general thesis" can be our motivation to inquire into the natural attitude, since none of them can be viewed *as* questionable. When Husserl nevertheless proposes to let the "general thesis" function as motivating, he must have left his initial position *quasi* within the natural attitude, and we are entitled to ask what prompted him to make that move. If Husserl wants to make the performance of the epoché seem a reasonable undertaking, he must, as he himself admits, present us with some kind of motivation (*Hua* VIII, p. 98). The epoché – anticipating something to be dealt with in the following chapter – is sometimes described by Husserl as an operation that attaches an "index" or a "label" to the natural attitude, to its "general thesis," viz. the label "questionable" (cf. *Hua* II, p. 29; *Hua* XXIV, p. 214). Before it makes any sense to actively perform this epoché, then, we must *already* have *experienced* this attitude as questionable – otherwise we are completely at a loss to see why we should actively perform something as *unnatural* as an "epoché," or begin to do phenomenology in the first place.[30] But to experience the "general thesis" as questionable seems impossible. More generally, it seems that *in the natural attitude no theoretical problem or difficulty could possibly arise that could motivate the first turn towards making something like the "general thesis" of that attitude itself into a problem.*[31] Indeed, this is obviously so, since the natural attitude is defined as the attitude that is thoroughly situated in, or on, the "general thesis," i.e., all of its problems and solutions appear on the *basis* of the firm "belief" in the existence of reality. What *can* happen, however, is that we experience natural life as losing its unquestionable appearance. Natural or everyday life can, so to speak, *spontaneously* become "questionable," not thereby, to be sure, revealing an unambiguous research

---

[29] Perhaps Eugen Fink is hinting at this problem when he describes the hypothetical world-annihilation as "a hypothesis that remains unilluminated with regard to its methodological presuppositions" (*Studien zur Phänomenologie 1930-1939*, p. 129). See, too, Antonio Aguirre, *Genetische Phänomenologie und Reduktion*, pp. 34, 44, 54-55, and Søren Overgaard, "Epoché and Solipsistic Reduction."

[30] Cf. Fink's similar remarks in *HuDo* II/1, pp. 39-40.

[31] I thus agree with Eugen Fink's claim that Husserl's phenomenology has no worldly problem as its motivation (*Studien zur Phänomenologie 1930-1939*, p. 110). However, that does not mean that there can be *no* motivation to set out on the path to phenomenology. It only means that this motivation cannot be a "theoretical" problem. Fink's articles on Husserl are, incidentally, very excellent commentaries, and I refer to their profound insights on more than one occasion in the course of this study. Fink seems to be guilty of only one serious mistake. Dan Zahavi convincingly criticizes Fink for falsely attributing to the very late Husserl the view that a primal life not yet divided into ego and *alter* should replace transcendental intersubjectivity as the ultimate place of constitution (cf. Zahavi, "The Self-Pluralisation of Primal Life. A Problem in Fink's Husserl-Interpretation"). Interestingly, at the time of the writing of the *VI. Cartesianische Meditation*, Fink admits that this notion of a "deeper life of absolute spirit that lies prior to all individuation" (*HuDo* II/1, p. 183) is more his own than Husserl's.

direction, but attaching to itself the "label" that will make possible a questioning of it. That is what happens, for instance, in anxiety as described by Heidegger.[32]

5. ANXIETY

Heidegger's preoccupation with the phenomenon of anxiety in the late twenties must not be seen as springing from a desire to formulate an existential philosophy.[33] Rather, anxiety serves a significant *methodological* function in Heidegger's phenomenology.[34] In what follows, I present only a rough sketch of a few features of anxiety. An adequate treatment would demand that we had already analyzed, for example, the phenomenon of world and the being of Dasein, which is to say that we would have to already be in Heideggerian phenomenology proper, whereas in fact we are searching for the path *to* that phenomenology. Another reason for the brevity of this section is that I judge anxiety less important to the project of the early Heidegger than do most commentators.[35] As the following discussion should make clear, however, I do consider the methodological role of anxiety an important one.

Heidegger claims in *Kant und das Problem der Metaphysik* that because anxiety brings Dasein face to face with *nothing,* it ultimately confronts Dasein with *being* (KPM, p. 238). Since being is just what Heidegger wants to inquire into, it seems that anxiety is what makes his investigation possible. But what kind of reasoning is this? Is this a *description* of the experience of anxiety? Quite apart from the circumstance that Heidegger's whole project is balanced on a not immediately

---

[32] Luft suggests a motivation slightly different from the one I (following Heidegger) shall suggest. Common to them both, however, is the notion that it must be something that *is not of our doing*, but rather "happens" to us whether we like it or not. Cf. "Husserl's Phenomenological Discovery of the Natural Attitude," p. 165. William Jon Lenkowski argues the same in his article "What is Husserl's Epoché?" Lenkowski even emphasizes the disruption of the familiar in the very terms that Heidegger uses to characterize anxiety: "[W]e must be able to find, at the level of passivity, an occurrence in which the world – the sphere of 'familiarity' in which one is "at home" – becomes *un*-familiar, estranged; an occurrence in which [...] *Heimlichkeit* gives way to *Un-heimlichkeit*, in its double sense of 'homelessness' and 'strangeness,' 'uncanniness'" ("What is Husserl's Epoché?", p. 309). However, Lenkowksi does not seem to notice how much this resembles anxiety as described by Heidegger.

[33] According to Theodore Kisiel, Heidegger actually avoids the existentialist vocabulary from the summer of 1923 and onwards, until the last draft of *Sein und Zeit* (cf. *The Genesis of Heidegger's Being and Time*, pp. 275, 316).

[34] Cf. Carl F. Gethmann, *Verstehen und Auslegung*, p. 130. Rudolf Bernet ("Phenomenological Reduction and the Double Life of the Subject," p. 163) and Jean-Luc Marion (*Reduction and Givenness*, p. 73) even see anxiety as performing a kind of "phenomenological reduction." Apparently, the idea is originally Jean-François Courtine's. Cf. his *Heidegger et la phénoménologie*, pp. 207-247. I am grateful to Dan Zahavi for having drawn this to my attention.

[35] Günter Figal, for instance, claims that the analysis of anxiety, the call of conscience, and being towards death, are central to the very project of fundamental ontology: "on these analyses depends the whole program of a fundamental analysis of Dasein" (*Martin Heidegger zur Einführung*, p. 75). His thesis finds support in some of Heidegger's own texts from the late twenties (see, e.g., *KPM*, pp. 237-238, 283-284). As I show in Chapter III, however, Heidegger admits in an earlier text – in the better part of which he uncompromisingly *criticizes* Husserl – that what really makes ontological research possible is something Husserl discovered.

convincing description of a possibly uncommon phenomenon, it is far from obvious that Heidegger is in fact giving a phenomenological description. Instead, he seems to be offering a sort of logical-metaphysical *argument* that runs roughly as follows: anxiety is directed at no worldly thing; therefore anxiety reveals *the nothing*; therefore anxiety makes possible the understanding of *being* (in contrast to entities) (*KPM*, pp. 283-284). The transition from "no thing" to *nothing* (cf. *WM*, p. 105) has been thoroughly criticized, and perhaps justly so.[36] But in fact – at least for the present purposes – this particular transition is not really needed. Heidegger can be presented as simply saying: anxiety reveals no thing, person, or entity as something to be anxious about (*SZ*, p. 186). Unlike fear, which has its object-to-be-feared, anxiety has *no* object-to-be-dreaded (no entity). By thus revealing *no entity*, it reveals what *is not an entity*, viz. *being*: "The nothing is the 'not' of beings, and is thus being, experienced from the perspective of beings" (*WM*, p. 123; cf. *GA* 27, pp. 190, 392).

However, this is hardly a phenomenological insight, but rather a piece of more or less convincing reasoning. Do I really "experience" *being* when I am suffering from anxiety? It is clear that I do not experience the objects and persons around me the way I usually would; perhaps we can even say that they withdraw into a kind "meaninglessness" (and thus in a certain sense are no longer there) (cf. *WM*, pp. 111-112); and we can certainly grant that there is no one particular "dreaded" entity present. But does all of this necessarily mean that I then "experience" the *being* of entities? Taking the example of stage fright as his point of departure, Günter Figal argues that anxiety makes one experience one's "potential for being," e.g., in the way that one experiences the possibility that one might not be able to give a scheduled lecture.[37] This may be a good phenomenological description, but the question at present is whether it is plausible that, as long as we remain in everydayness, we would in fact see our anxiety as disclosing a "potential for being" to us. Is Sartre's view, that anxiety – in contrast to fear – has to do with oneself rather than some external entity, not more convincing as a description of everyday Dasein's own interpretation of anxiety? When I have stage fright, do I then have an experience that I can already recognize as an *ontological* experience, or rather do I not experience simply that I "distrust myself and my own reactions"[38] once I get up to the podium? To be sure, this can very well be interpreted as an experience of "potential for being," but this is hardly the interpretation the naturally attuned person would subscribe to. For everyday Dasein, anxiety manifests itself as distrust and fear

---

[36] See Rudolf Carnap, "Überwindung der Metaphysik durch logische Analyse der Sprache," esp. pp. 230-231. Ernst Tugendhat argues along similar lines in "Das Sein und das Nichts," but emphasizes, as I do too, that this transition to the "nothing" is not important to Heidegger's argument (pp. 58-61).

[37] Cf. Figal, *Martin Heidegger: Phänomenologie der Freiheit*, p. 200: "If one wanted to articulate this experience one could say that it is questionable whether one can now give the talk – and precisely this can be interpreted as the experience of 'potential-for-being.'"

[38] Sartre, *Being and Nothingness*, p. 29.

of one's own conduct, rather than as a direct road to ontology. What anxiety obviously can do, however, is destroy the tranquility of everyday life in *das Man*.

Living under the wings of convention, Dasein is at home in the lifeworld. Everything is already understood and interpreted for us, and known to us through "hearsay." This homey familiarity with the world of everyday life is exactly what anxiety disrupts: "Everyday familiarity collapses" (*SZ*, p. 189). When one is anxious, even the most familiar of places (such as one's own home) become *unfamiliar*. With the onset of anxiety, one is no longer comfortable in the environment that was hitherto the very definition of comfort and familiarity; one feels decidedly *not-at-home* where one has always felt at home. "In anxiety one feels '*uncanny*' ['*unheimlich*']" (*SZ*, p. 188). "Being-in enters into the existential 'mode' of the *not-at-home*" (*SZ*, p. 189). It is also important that anxiety – by making the familiar unfamiliar – makes going about one's everyday business difficult, or even impossible. When I am anxious, the normal pattern of my life might be simply impossible to preserve. In other words, it is everyday life itself, as a *matter of course*, as a comfortable *Umgang* with familiar things in a familiar setting, which is disrupted by anxiety. The lifeworld has lost its natural familiarity, and everyday acting and "gossiping" is no longer a matter of course.

But as phenomenologists, our task is precisely to inquire into what, to the everyday Dasein, or the natural attitude, is simply obvious. To do phenomenology is, first of all, to make a problem of the obvious. In anxiety we have indeed found a motivation to begin to investigate everyday life, since anxiety makes the obvious and familiar problematic and uncomfortable. Anxiety, as it were, attaches the label "*questionable*" to everydayness. And this is all we need, something that can disrupt the smooth course of daily life and make it appear as something to be questioned. *Anxiety is something that makes the obvious everyday life less obvious, and thus points the way to a phenomenological inquiry into that life.*

Presumably, Husserl would have to subscribe to a motivation not unlike the one pointed out by Heidegger. There is no fracture in everyday life that demands phenomenological attention; there is no problem that can motivate us to direct our inquiries at this life itself. Phenomenology becomes possible only when the familiarity is spontaneously disrupted. Natural life does indeed hide within itself the theme of phenomenology – or the themes of phenomenolog*ies* – but that cannot be realized until something like anxiety presents natural life as questionable. But, as the Greeks knew, it is not only anxiety that can serve that function; an "irrational" – i.e., "uncalled-for," in the eyes of the natural attitude – feeling of *wonder* in the face of the world can also motivate one to become a philosopher.[39] Interestingly, Husserl's assistant in the thirties, Eugen Fink, repeatedly referred to "wonder" as the root of philosophy; so most likely Husserl, too, would have been able to accept the basic

---

[39] Cf. Plato, *Theaetatus*, 155d: "This sense of wonder is the mark of the philosopher. Philosophy indeed has no other origin." Similarly, Aristotle, *Metaphysics*, 982b: "For it is owing to their wonder that men both now begin and first began to philosophize."

argument of this section.[40] There is no problem of everyday life, or of the natural attitude, that demands phenomenology. Everyday life must already (spontaneously) render itself "questionable," before there is any motivation for phenomenology to begin inquiring into it.

To sum up the findings of the present chapter, Heidegger and Husserl are in basic agreement as to the description of the objects and persons in the natural world. They do not agree, however, on the interpretation thereof. More precisely, Husserl's descriptions and interpretations are delivered as if from "inside" the natural attitude, whereas Heidegger refuses to follow the natural line of interpretation. He can only do so because he is already viewing natural life from a standpoint external to it.

Our question then becomes what sort of motivation could lead one to begin to question natural life. The answer is some sort of uncontrolled event rather than a theoretical problem. The natural attitude or everyday life is indeed such that presumably no theoretical problem arising in it could ever lead to an investigation of it as such. At least Husserl's suggestion – "the general thesis" – proves insufficient, since it is not possible to view the "thesis" in question as a "thesis," as presumptive, while in the natural attitude.

It is of essence to note that an *alternative* to the "natural attitude" has not yet emerged. We are, as it were, on the doorstep to phenomenology, rather than in any "phenomenological attitude." Concerning the question of how to proceed to such an attitude, and what to achieve with it, Husserl has a detailed answer that I unfold in the next chapter. For Heidegger, as can be seen in Chapter III, the *ontological-phenomenological* research project will appear only as the result of initially following Husserl's phenomenological breakthrough.

---

[40] Eugen Fink, *Studien zur Phänomenologie 1930-1939*, pp. 115-116, 182. Indeed, on one occasion, Husserl himself refers to wonder as the beginning of philosophy (*Hua* VI, pp. 331-332).

CHAPTER II
THE QUESTION OF CONSTITUTION

1. THE NEED FOR THE QUESTION OF CONSTITUTION

At a crucial juncture in the first draft of the *Encyclopaedia Britannica* article, Husserl attempts to introduce the constitutive problematic in the following way:

> If it is the case that whatever is experienced, whatever is thought, and whatever is seen as the truth are given and are possible only within <the corresponding acts of> experiencing, thinking, and insight, then the concrete and complete exploration of the world that exists and has scientific and evidential validity for us requires also the universal phenomenological exploration of the multiplicities of consciousness in whose synthetic changes the world subjectively takes shape as valid for us and perhaps as given with insight. (*Hua* IX, p. 239)

Exactly this crucial transition, indicated by the words "then...requires," provokes Heidegger to ask: "Why?" (*Hua* IX, p. 239n) This question of Heidegger's sets the stage for the present section. Why is it that we need to enter into the constitutive problematic, why do we need to pose the question concerning constitution?

In an important way, our task in this section is easier than it was for Husserl to come up with a satisfactory answer to Heidegger in 1927. In the previous chapter, we have already done half the work. We have shown how natural life can be turned to some extent towards itself, how its tranquility can be disturbed in such a way as to allow it to begin questioning itself. We have, in other words, already answered the question, "Why *any* 'unnatural' questions at all?", and may proceed with Husserl to try to answer the question, "Why *this* question, why the question of constitution?"

Perhaps at this point we should return to the "general thesis of the natural attitude." We have shown already that as an attempt to point out the "blind spot" of the natural attitude, Husserl's suggestion of the "general thesis" must fail. When living wholly on the basis of "world-belief," there is no immediate possibility of seeing this "belief" *as* a "belief," as involving any kind of "presumption." It does not follow, however, that once wonder, or anxiety, has shaken the foundations of everyday life, there can be no part for the "general thesis" to play in the subsequent onset of philosophy. As I will show in this section, something like the "general thesis of the natural attitude" does indeed single out a legitimate problem, or set of problems, for phenomenology.

We live our lives in complete certainty of the existence of the world and every worldly thing within it, including ourselves as the human beings we are. The world is experienced as existing *without question* (*Hua* I, p. 57), and this experience is constantly confirmed, in every single perception (*Hua* VIII, p. 54). The world and all beings in it *are there*, and we know this because we experience it all the time. It is thus our *experiences* that reveal the existence of the world to us; it is in our experiences that the world is there for us. This, according to Husserl, constitutes a problem.

Now, it is of the utmost importance – against all temptations to immediately identify Husserl's problem with certain traditional problems – to make absolutely clear exactly what question Husserl sees as arising here. For Descartes, given the possibility of illusion, of a continuous dream, and of a vicious, deceiving demon, the problem is to establish how I may know that there is a world outside me at all, and for Descartes, as is common knowledge, the argument crucially involves establishing the existence of a benevolent God. As seen in Chapter I, Husserl has to acknowledge that, while in the natural attitude, neither illusion nor the dream argument can shake in any way the fundamental certainty of the existence of a real world. As for the vicious demon, Husserl would no doubt be quick to point out that the existence of such a creature is a completely empty possibility that has all the weight of experience against it. More fundamentally, this experienced world with all its familiar places, objects, and persons, is the only world we can ever talk about (*Hua* VI, p. 258; *Hua* XV, p. 546; *Hua* VII, p. 277; *Hua* VIII, p. 462). This world defines reality for us, thus claiming that it could be the work of an evil, deceiving genius amounts to nonsense. That is, at least while we are thoroughly situated in the natural attitude. This last point seems to be an important addition, since we are no longer thus situated in the natural attitude; we have distanced ourselves enough from it to be able to question it. Should we then say in fact that the certainty that world existence had before, it has no longer? Does Descartes' problem now become Husserl's? I think it does not.

The arguments developed in Chapter I show that the Cartesian arguments *presuppose* what they are trying to prove questionable; they presuppose precisely the validity of world-experience as such. Our newly won distance from the natural attitude does not change that, indeed it can change neither our fundamental "belief" in the world, nor the fact that any attempt to show the "presumptive" nature of that "belief" – at least any that refers to the possibility of illusion or continuous dream – must itself assume the correctness of the "belief." As pointed out, following Husserl, an illusion makes sense only against the background of experiences that establish the true state of affairs.

Of course, a different question is whether Husserl realizes that this is so; whether he realizes that his phenomenology can not set itself the task of "securing" a world that has somehow been called into question. Husserl's reflections on the degree of certainty possible for world-experience (in contrast to the experience of subjectivity) have to a great extent been carried out as an attempt to take the Cartesian path to phenomenology, the path briefly discussed above. In a number of places, Husserl does indeed argue that the experience of the world can in no way lay claim to "apodictic" evidence, whereas the experience of "consciousness" or subjectivity can. This is mostly done explicitly to show the necessity of giving up the "worldly," natural attitude, if one is genuinely committed to the ideal of scientific philosophy (cf. *Hua* I, pp. 43-58). But sometimes, as is not uncommon with Husserl, the analyses seem to have a life of their own, forcing Husserl in directions other than those he intended to pursue. The difficulty Husserl encounters in these latter reflections is of course that there *is* no convincing way of showing that the experience of the world as such (as opposed to the perception of individual objects) is less certain than the experience of subjectivity, and yet Husserl wants to insist that world-experience is less certain. These incompatible tendencies have, in places, the consequence that Husserl engages in what appears to be simple contradictions. Thus, for instance, he claims in *Erste Philosophie II* that the evidence of world experience is indeed "apodictic." However, as Husserl emphasizes, it has only an *empirical*, or a *relative* apodicticity (surely, this comes very close to a *contradictio in adjecto*), as opposed to the absolute apodicticty of the experience of consciousness (*Hua* VIII, pp. 398-400). This is clearly the result of an attempt on Husserl's part to combine his Cartesian conviction that consciousness has an absolutely indubitable existence, whereas external reality has somehow a *less* indubitable existence, with the phenomenological realization that world existence seems, nevertheless, to be something that is completely certain. In his best reflections, Husserl goes a step further in the right direction:

But perhaps universal experience, as experience of the world that in each case counts as existing, has an essential universal style that after all grants an apodicticity to the being of the world that presents itself in experience – despite the impossibility of attributing apodictic validity of being [*Seinsgeltung*] to any [...] particular experienced entity. (*HuDo* II/2, p. 285; cf. *Hua* VI, p. 407)

This "style" that Husserl is talking about is of course what we have been discussing all along: the "style" that dictates that any cancellation of the *Seinsgeltung* of an object, or range of objects (as when the series of puddles I saw further down the road turn out not to be there), must at the same time *confirm* the validity of the being of the world as such, and, in general, our experience of that world (*Hua* VI, pp. 112-113). Thus, Husserlian phenomenology cannot set itself the task of establishing the existence of the world, or providing evidence for our experience of the world, since none of this has been, or can be, called into question in the first place. We do not need to have the existence of the world established, because every single experience we have, including those in which we discover that we have been victims of illusions, is a confirmation of the existence of the world. By the same token, no evidence for our experience of the world could be provided, which is not already there. Nothing is more certain than that the world exists and that I experience it.[1]

Equally important in the present context is that Husserl sometimes clearly recognizes that, independently of whether or not we can have apodictic evidence of the existence of the world, the goal of phenomenology is fundamentally different from that of Descartes. One may safely assume that Husserl, from beginning to end, is committed to the idea of absolutely certain evidence, but – at least as far as

---

[1] Again, I do not think Husserl would be in any fundamental disagreement with Wittgenstein, when the latter tries to demonstrate how attempts to "secure" the existence of worldly objects – as if it were something we could meaningfully doubt to begin with – are in fact nonsensical. See, e.g., the witty § 467 of Wittgenstein's *On Certainty*. Where I think Husserl and Wittgenstein would fundamentally disagree, however, is on the question of whether, granted the meaninglessness of skeptical questions (as well as the attempts to "secure" what the skeptic doubts), there is, after all, a meaningful *positive* task left for philosophy, or whether only the *negative* job of dissolving all such meaningless questions remains.

Husserl's mature thinking is concerned – probably only as "an *idea*, lying in infinity" (*Hua* XVII, § 105, p. 284; cf. *Hua* VIII, p. 196; *Hua* V, p. 139). That is to say *as a regulative principle* (cf. *Hua* XVII, p. 284), as a principle that tells us how to proceed, an idea that should make us constantly vigilant and careful, an idea that ensures that we never stop improving on imperfect analyses.[2] Presumably, Husserl views such a commitment as essential to a "scientific" philosophy, and all evidence suggests that he never gives up believing in the idea of a scientific philosophy.[3] But Husserl clearly recognizes that it would be naive to expect a science to simply mass-produce apodictic, complete evidence (cf. *Hua* XVII, p. 169), and that his phenomenology, being only in the beginning stages, would harbor within its analyses "great deficiencies" (*Hua* V, p. 162; *Hua* III/1, p. 224) to be set right by coming generations. Most importantly, however, the search for certainty is hardly ever viewed by Husserl as the "constitutive" task, or *defining* task of his phenomenology. In contrast to the Cartesian enterprise, phenomenology, first and foremost, is *not* interested in achieving indubitable insights, as Husserl already points out in his 1910/1911 lecture course "Grundprobleme der Phänomenologie" (*Hua* XIII, p. 150).[4] Its main and defining tasks lie elsewhere.

In the *Krisis* – in a final attempt to fend off misinterpretations of his phenomenological project – Husserl gives an important hint as to what the defining

---

[2] For Kant's distinction between "regulative" and "constitutive" principles, cf. *Kritik der reinen Vernunft*, B 536 ff., A 508 ff.

[3] There is a famous passage from the penultimate appendix to *Krisis*, where Husserl writes: "*Philosophy as science*, as serious, rigorous, indeed apodictically rigorous, science – the dream is over" (*Hua* VI, p. 508). I used to think that Landgrebe was right in interpreting this as having become Husserl's sincere conviction in his last years (see Landgrebe's *Der Weg der Phänomenologie*, p. 187), whereas interpreters such as Herbert Spiegelberg (cf. his *The Phenomenological Movement* Vol. I, p. 77n) and Gadamer ("Die phänomenologische Bewegung," p. 129) were wrong to dismiss the passage as "bitter irony." I am now convinced that, in view of other texts from the mid-thirties (e.g., *Hua* XXVII, pp. 238-239), as well as the further development of the *Krisis-Beilage* itself (notice how Husserl describes a current of philosophy that dismisses *Wissenschaftlichkeit* as "flooding" European humanity (*Hua* VI, p. 508)), Husserl can not be expressing his own opinion. My interpretation – that although Husserl never gives up the idea of an apodictic scientific philosophy, he realizes that apodicticity is hardly realizable in practice – basically follows that of John J. Drummond in his *Husserlian Intentionality and Non-Foundational Realism*, p. 248.

[4] Elisabeth Ströker even argues that Husserl at some point realizes that final and irrefutable evidence even for phenomenology itself is "ruled out as a matter of principle" (*Husserls transzendentale Phänomenologie*, p. 67n. Cf. p. 126n). However, the references that she gives seem not quite sufficient to substantiate the claim. *Hua* VIII, p. 398, for instance, only states that no *Tatsachenerkenntnis*, whether mundane or phenomenological, could ever be apodictic. Since Husserl intended his phenomenology to be *eidetic*, i.e., not a science of facts, but of essences, it in no way follows that apodictic and final evidence is ruled out for phenomenology. The second reference Ströker gives, which is to *Hua* XVII, p. 284 (it is not p. 245, as Ströker indicates; the passage *is* found on p. 245 in the *Niemeyer* edition of *Formale und transzendentale Logik*, but not in the *Husserliana* edition), comes closer. It certainly lends support to the claim I am advancing, viz. that Husserl recognizes final and irrefutable evidence as a regulative principle, as an "idea" whose realization would be an infinite task. Insofar as it is ruled out "on principle" that one can ever *complete* an infinite task, then Ströker would appear to be right after all. Unfortunately, I know of no place where Husserl himself draws this conclusion unambiguously.

task of phenomenology might be. After complaining that many reject his phenomenology as a kind of Cartesianism, as if he wanted to "secure" objects by some kind of deduction from the "subjective" sphere, Husserl points out: "The point is not to secure [*sichern*] objectivity but to understand it" (*Hua* VI, § 55, p. 193). In other words, if the so-called "general thesis" somehow constitutes the problem of Husserlian phenomenology, it cannot be because the world or any "objects" within it are in need of being "secured." Rather, it must be because the world and the objects within it have yet to be *understood* in some fundamental way.[5]

The problem Husserl is trying to bring to our attention is that the world and all objects in it are there for us, exist for us, yet we do not understand *how* this can be so. How can a world exist for us? This is not the same problem as the Cartesian one of how to *secure* the existence of material reality, once the *ego cogito* is established. As early as 1906-1907, when Husserl introduces the problematic of constitution (as well as the epoché and the reduction) to his students, he seems to have formed the opinion that all skeptical attacks on attempts to "secure" the existence of the external world have their root in the fundamental *lack of a proper understanding* of our experiences of world-existence, and of the objects within the world (cf. *Hua* XXIV, pp. 404-405).[6] Though clearly formulated in the language of traditional epistemology – Husserl talks in the early lecture courses about the problem of how experience can "hit" (*treffen*) something transcendent – it is obvious that Husserl's description of the task of phenomenology has a different accent from that of Cartesian, as well as skeptical, epistemology: "What I want is clarity. I want to *understand* the possibility of this contact" (*Hua* II, p. 6, emphasis deleted and added). Husserlian phenomenology "wants to 'enlighten' ['*aufklären*']; it does not want deduce anything, or to re-duce [*zurückführen*] anything to its explanatory bases in laws; rather, it simply wants to *understand* what is inherent in the sense [*Sinn*] of knowledge and the objectivity of knowledge" (*Hua* XXIV, p. 190, my emphasis). Having thus laid out the task, Husserl can proceed to explain how he intends to accomplish it and what will be gained thereby. To the latter question, Husserl replies:

In this way we finally arrive at an understanding of how the transcendent real object can be encountered within the act of knowing [...]. We then *understand* how the object of experience *constitutes* itself in a continuum [...]. (*Hua* II, p. 13, my emphasis)

---

[5] Thus, Heidegger's undeniably mocking criticism, under the title of "*Sorge der Gewißheit*," of Husserl and Descartes in the first Marburg lecture course, fails to hit the mark as far as the former is concerned. It is not correct to say that *Sicherung* is what Husserl's phenomenology in the last analysis is after (cf. *GA* 17, p. 60), as Fink already demonstrates in his *VI. Cartesianische Meditation* (*HuDo* II/1, pp. 50-51).

[6] Thus, Husserl, as far as I can see, never counters skepticism directly the way Descartes does when he tries to "prove" the existence of the material realm, or by way of "retreat" the way Berkeley does, when he declares the non-existence of that which presumably could be doubted (see his *Principles of Human Knowledge*, §§ 87-88). As is well known, Husserl does try to show that skepticism contradicts itself (e.g., in the *Prolegomena*; cf. *Hua* XVIII, pp. 118-130). But his main "positive" contribution to the "struggle" against skepticism seems to me to be his constitutive explanation of the existence of what skeptics claim is doubtful, thereby not really *refuting* skepticism, but rather rendering its points uninteresting.

Husserl, in other words, wants to *understand* how the world and worldly entities come to be given in our experiences, a question that he identifies with the question concerning the *constitution* of the objects.[7] The world does exist, it is revealed to us in our experiences, but we need to understand *how* this can be so. That our experience of the world is beyond any reasonable doubt does not entail that we already understand how our experiences can "perform" this, how they can present an existing world, with existing objects, to us:

> That the world exists – that it is given as an existing universe in continuous experience, ceaselessly converging in universal harmony – is absolutely indubitable [*vollkommen zweifellos*]. But it is something altogether different to understand this indubitability, which supports life and positive science, and to clarify its validity basis [*Rechtsgrund*]. (*Hua* V, pp. 152-153; cf. *Hua* VI, p. 191)

The explanation of the "how" of this indubitable world-existence is what Husserl – under the title of "constitution" – envisions as the defining task of phenomenology. In so far as we can call the world, and the worldly entities whose "constitution" we propose to explain, *transcendent*, we can also label this constitutive phenomenology *transcendental* phenomenology (cf. *Hua* IX, p. 257; *Hua* III/1, p. 198).

2. THE EPOCHÉ

The need for a science that explains how we are able to experience an existing world seems obvious. But do not sciences dealing with this issue already exist? Surely, how we manage to experience things around us is part of what the different sciences grouped under the name of "cognitive science" are investigating; indeed, every physical science that studies how any of our sense organs function contributes to this investigation. All of these sciences supply answers to the question concerning how it comes about that our experiences present us with worldly objects. Therefore, in so far as the main problem of phenomenology is this problem of "constitution," phenomenology appears to be superfluous.

However, as Eugen Fink has tried to demonstrate on behalf of Husserl, the problem of Husserlian phenomenology is not the problem of how we experience individual things. Rather, it is the radically different question of *the constitution of*

---

[7] A number of attentive commentators notice these "hermeneutic" strands woven into the fabric of Husserlian phenomenology (cf. John D. Caputo, "Husserl, Heidegger, and the Question of a 'Hermeneutic' Phenomenology"; Jean Grondin, *Sources of Hermeneutics*, pp. 35-46; and, though he is more reserved, John Sallis, *Delimitations*, p. 78). However, none see their fundamental importance more clearly than does J. N. Mohanty. Husserl's phenomenology, Mohanty says, is a "phenomenology of respect" in that it "does not judge, but seeks to understand" (*The Possibility of Transcendental Philosophy*, p. 233). Therefore, Mohanty concludes that in Husserl's thought "[h]ermeneutic and phenomenology coexist" (ibid., p. 243). See also Husserl's illuminating comments on Kant, cited in the section on the transcendental reduction below.

the world.[8] Although Fink is basically right, a few possible misunderstandings need to be taken into consideration here.

First of all, contrary to what one might think, Husserl and Fink do not intend to say that, for example, a science that studies the functioning of the human eye is not general enough, leaving out the consideration, as it does, of sounds, and smells, etc., thereby failing to explain the "constitution" of the world as a whole. It is not as though phenomenology were simply the one, overarching science, holding together within it the sciences that study the perception of individual types of objects in the world. Put differently, Husserl's point is not that the sciences that study different types of experience need simply to be *one* science, called phenomenology, instead of a number of more or less independent sciences. Husserl may perhaps have regretted the dispersion of sciences into specialties with little or no contact with each other, and he certainly intends his phenomenology *in some way* to supply a joint "foundation" for all those sciences, thus *in some way* to tie them together again (under the title of *philosophia perennis*) (cf. *Hua* VI, p. 200). However, this is certainly not to be done by way of letting phenomenology itself be *the* natural science of cognition (as opposed to the individual sciences), nor for that matter is phenomenology intended to be *the human* science. On the contrary, from the first introduction of transcendental phenomenology and until the end, Husserl consistently maintains that phenomenology is a "science" in a *completely different dimension* (cf., e.g., *Hua* II, p. 24; *Hua* XIII, p. 112).

Second, one must not assume that phenomenology has nothing to say about individual types of objects, as though it would simply ignore them in order to focus on the world alone (if one could even make sense of such an investigation, all things, animals, and persons being excluded from the thematic field).[9] Rather, the point is that what phenomenology has to say about the different types of objects – "object" here taken in the broadest possible sense – can only be understood when one understands the completely new dimension in which phenomenology works.

The crucial thing to understand is how *universal*, how all-encompassing Husserl's question about our world-experience, or world-constitution, is. It is precisely this universality that places phenomenology in a dimension radically different from that of all natural as well as human sciences. A science that studies how the human eye functions in visual perception, for instance, studies how a specific organ of the human being works. In so far as the objective of this science is to establish how we humans are able to see the way we do, we can say that it studies the way one type of worldly entity, viz. the human organism, can achieve a certain

---

[8] See Fink's excellent article (explicitly sanctioned by Husserl himself), "Die phänomenologische Philosophie Edmund Husserls in der gegenwärtigen Kritik," in Fink's book *Studien zur Phänomenologie 1930-1939*, especially p. 145.

[9] Indeed, if that were so, we would be compelled to say that much of Husserl's work – such as the lectures on *Ding und Raum* (*Hua* XVI), the Fifth Cartesian Meditation, as well as volumes XIII-XV of *Husserliana*, dealing with, respectively, the spatial object, and other subjectivities – is not phenomenological at all.

kind of relationship to worldly entities of the same or of different types, viz. the relationship of visual perception of these other entities. But Husserl's question of constitution is not the question of how one type of worldly entity manages to enter into certain relationships (called "experience") with other entities. It is, instead, the "general thesis" *as such* that is problematic, *it is the fact that a world exists for us,* or me, *at all* that Husserl wants to make intelligible. Natural sciences do not, and cannot, answer such a question, according to Husserl. Indeed he claims they cannot supply as much as one single premise to an investigation that attempts to answer such a question, since they study entities and their properties, and thus *uncritically presuppose* that the world and worldly objects are there for us to begin with (cf. *Hua* XXV, pp. 13-15). Once again, it is not that there is any question that worldly objects indeed *are* there for us, because nothing is more certain than that. Also, it is not that there is anything *wrong* with what the natural sciences are doing, or that what they are doing has no value.[10] Quite on the contrary, Husserl sees in this "uncritical presupposition" one of the pillars that carries the success of the natural sciences (*Hua* IX, p. 191). The point is simply that when it is the "general thesis" itself, the "being-there-for-us" of the world that is in question, sciences that investigate worldly objects and relations between them can have nothing to tell us. Whatever their merits, however exact and scientifically founded (*Hua* VI, p. 193), the natural sciences are sciences in the natural attitude, i.e., the "general thesis" is their thesis, and therefore they cannot offer us any help once we embark on the voyage towards an understanding of how that "thesis" itself can come about. One does not explain anything if the *explanandum*, or anything that essentially belongs to the *explanandum*, enters into the *explanans*.

If one does try to explain the constitution of the world by reference to any natural scientific knowledge, one succeeds only in committing a *metabasis eis allo genos*, according to Husserl (*Hua* II, pp. 6, 39; *Hua* III/1, p. 130). One lets the original problem transform into a completely different problem. In so far as what results is a complete return to the questions of natural science, one simply loses the constitutive problematic in favor of a completely different, but still very much meaningful theme. There is, after all, absolutely nothing wrong with investigating how one type of worldly entity can relate to other such entities – only it is not this dimension in which Husserl wants his constitutive phenomenology to work.

However, if one still claims to be dealing with the problem of how the world can be there for us at all, the result is what Husserl calls the "transcendental" or "epistemological" *circle*. This is a special case of begging the question, the avoidance of which is viewed by Husserl as imperative: "my line of questioning requires that I avoid the transcendental circle, which consists in presupposing something as beyond question when in fact it is encompassed by the all-

---

[10] Although Husserl sometimes expresses critical opinions on the natural sciences, e.g., when he claims that all they do is "calculate" (*berechnen*) the world, without understanding it (*Hua* VIII, p. 247; cf. *Hua* VI, p. 193).

inclusiveness of that very question" (*Hua* IX, p. 273; cf. pp. 249-250). The *universality* of the present question, since it involves the entire natural attitude, is such as to exclude – on pains of a special kind of *petitio principii* – all sciences that work within that attitude. And not just the sciences, of course, also every bit of unscientific, natural "knowledge" must be excluded from this investigation (cf. *Hua* III/1, p. 66). Not, I repeat, because any of this is uncertain, or wrong, but because the universal *performance* (*Leistung*) of the being-there-for-us of the world remains to be understood.

At this point let me introduce a possible objection. We have "excluded" the existing world in order to understand how the world can exist for us, but how do we know that what in fact makes possible our experience of an existing world, and existing worldly objects isn't precisely that *the world, and the objects, exist*? In other words, it could be that the factual existence of the world and the worldly "objects" is the sought after explanation of how we can have given, in our experiences, such "objects," and such a world. Isn't the existence of this computer in front of me, the existence of light photons, the existence of retinas, etc., and all of this connected in a causal nexus, *the* correct account of my seeing a computer in front of me? Presumably, the causal explanation would run more or less as follows: the computer in front of me would absorb some of the light waves from the sun, while reflecting others, and these others would then hit my eye, and trigger off a process in my brain, which eventually would cause my experience of "seeing a computer in front of me." So the causal nexus ends with a certain mental state in me (or, for the materialist, it just ends with a brain process that is held identical with what we "call" a mental state), viz. the state of "perceiving the computer." What has been achieved? If we accept the causal account as sound, we have certainly learned how the computer can cause, or play a significant part in the process that causes, a mental state in me. Perhaps the account has even been detailed enough to make it intelligible somehow that that mental state is one of having a visual "image."

It might seem, though, that the problem of illusions and hallucinations returns with a vengeance here. It is perfectly possible, after all, to experience objects as being there, which in fact are not there at all, so how can it be the actual existence of the world and worldly things that is the explanation of my experience of them (cf. *Hua* IX, p. 32)? The reference to illusions is not sufficient to dismiss the objection under consideration, however. There is always a causal explanation for an illusion: other existing objects intervened, the eyes of the perceiver suffered from some physical malfunction, and so forth.

So is the causal account satisfactory? Have we learned how it is that the experience, the mental state caused, can be a perception of the very object that caused it (or at least played a significant part in the causation of it)? Notice that we are asking for an *explanation*; we have all along wanted to *understand how* this experience of the world, and worldly objects could come about. Can the suggested causal account, or any similar account, actually provide us with an *explanation*? I think Husserl is right in arguing that it cannot (cf. *Hua* VI, p. 193). We might understand how a mental state could result from the causal nexus, but that hardly means that we have understood *how that mental state could be such as to enter into contact with its presumed causes*. On the contrary, the problem seems only to present itself anew: how can the mental state be one of perceiving the object that causes it? The difficulty is that the causal account abandons us at the wrong end, on the side of the subjective experiences, whereas we wanted to know – to put this in a figurative, and not quite appropriate manner – how to get *from* there to the perceived entity. And that the causal explanation goes from the entity *to* the experience is not only, so to speak, a problem *for us*, with *our* present interests – it is rather a fundamental problem for that causal account itself. If the mental state is the last station in the causal nexus, being preceded by the "computer," the "eye," and so forth, and we have not established by any independent route how that mental state can bring it about (*leisten*) that it is in direct, perceptual contact with the very object(s) that caused it, we are stuck in this mental state. Being thus stuck – and this is the crucial point – there is no way of making the causal account that put us there look even plausible, because we have no understanding of how it could be possible to establish contact with the presumed *causes* in the first place (*Hua* XIV, pp. 348-349). Put differently, without an independent explanation of how to get "from" the experience "to" the object, there is no reason to suppose that there is any way that goes "from" such an object "to" the experience.[11] Therefore the causal account suffers the same fate as the infamous "picture-theory" of perception whose refutation has convincingly been unfolded by Husserl in the *Logische Untersuchungen*. The image-theory is structurally similar to the causal account, since the former, too, tries to explain our experience of worldly entities by reference to the presence of the entity. If an entity such as the computer is there, it prompts the formation in my mind of a picture or an image (*Bild*) of itself, and this is – according to the theory – what it means to perceive a computer (cf. *Hua* XIX/1, p. 436). As Husserl points out, this theory abandons us with the mental "images," with no possibility of understanding how they could ever be images *of* a transcendent entity in the first place (cf. *Hua* XIX/1, p. 437). The image-theory could only be a plausible (indeed meaningful) theory if and when there were some kind of *independent* access, i.e., an access that did not go through "images," to the entities that the images were supposedly images of (cf. *Hua* II, p. 83) – in which case it would *eo ipso* be wrong as a *universal* theory of our awareness of the world.

None of this, however, should without further ado be taken to imply that phenomenology, being in a dimension completely different from that of the positive sciences, would have absolutely no use for them. Husserl's position is more balanced than that. We are here touching upon a fundamental problem in Husserl's

---

[11] Ullrich Melle makes this case convincingly in *Das Wahrnehmungsproblem und seine Verwandlung in phänomenologischer Einstellung*. As he neatly puts it, the causal account places us in the "dilemma that, if the causal account and its implications are true, we will remain caught in the sphere of effects, i.e., perceptions and their real components; on the other hand, we could only demonstrate the truth of the account and its implications if we could succeed in breaking out of the sphere of effects and establish contact with the causes" (p. 14). See, as well, Gottlob Frege, "Der Gedanke," pp. 45-46.

thinking, viz. that of the relation between psychology and constitutive or transcendental phenomenology. There is no possibility of doing justice to the problem in the present context, and I shall therefore limit myself to making one or two simple points.

Sometimes Husserl maintains that the transcendental investigation can learn nothing from the sphere of the "positive," the constituted – indeed that something like this would be nonsensical (cf. *Hua* VI, p. 208). But, as is not unusual with Husserl, such clear-cut conviction is by no means the whole story, and we find Husserl at other times referring to psychology as "the *truly decisive field*" (*wahre Feld der Entscheidungen*) (*Hua* VI, § 58, p. 212), as if what psychology discovers would also be "decisive" (*entscheidend*), or binding, for phenomenology (cf. *Hua* VI, p. 218). Not that Husserl seems to be making thorough studies of contemporary psychology the way, for instance, Merleau-Ponty does.[12] The point is rather that he seems, at times at least, to realize that although constitutive phenomenology occupies a dimension completely different from that of the sciences of the natural attitude, it is not ruled out that what is discovered in those sciences (and especially in cognitive science) can have a function within the project of constitutive phenomenology (different from that of simply belonging to the *explanandum* of such phenomenology). As Husserl says in *Formale und transzendentale Logik*:

And yet it can be said that, if this psychology of cognition had ever gone to work with a consciousness of its aim and had consequently been successful, its results would also have been work accomplished directly for the philosophic theory of cognition. All insights into structure that had been acquired for the psychology of cognition would also have benefited transcendental philosophy. (*Hua* XVII, § 99, p. 261)

In other words, Husserl sometimes seems to acknowledge that cognitive science can provide "hints" and structural insights of use to a transcendental investigation. This interpretation is supported by the fact that Husserl clearly notices a peculiar *parallelism* between the sciences in the natural attitude (especially psychology) and the transcendental science of phenomenology (Hua IX, pp. 275, 294). I believe that Husserl's revised view on the matter is essentially correct. There is, on the one hand, absolutely no reason to rule out that discoveries in, e.g., psychology (dealing thematically as it does with the human psyche) could provide important clues, or hints, for a transcendental inquiry; one reason being that ultimately, the so-called transcendental subjectivity is none other than the human being itself, according to Husserl (*Hua* VI, p. 212). On the other hand, Husserl is right in pointing out that constitutive, or transcendental, phenomenology occupies a dimension different from that of psychology, and therefore cannot directly rely on the findings of the latter. Phenomenology occupies a different dimension, because it attempts to answer a totally different question, viz. the universal question of world-constitution. As I intend to make clear in the course of this chapter, the question of world-constitution

---

[12] See, e.g., the texts assembled in Merleau-Ponty's *The Primacy of Perception*, Part I. Merleau-Ponty was professor of psychology at the Sorbonne for a few years.

is none other than the question of *being*, or more precisely, *one* such question of being.

So the problem for Husserl is how to ensure that no natural knowledge, whether scientific, common sense, or otherwise, enters into our constitutive phenomenological investigation. In Husserl's view, what is needed is some procedure that, so to speak, will *lock up* all natural knowledge, the whole "general thesis" and all that is based upon it. All of this must be "put out of action," "bracketed" (*Hua* III/1, p. 64), or have an "index" attached to it (*Hua* II, p. 29), so that we do not *utilize it* as long as we are doing constitutive phenomenology (*Hua* XV, p. 117). The general name that Husserl gives this procedure of "bracketing" (*Einklammerung*) is *epoché* (Greek: restraint, holding back; *Zurückhaltung*).

Few philosophical notions are as controversial as Husserl's concept of "epoché." To some extent, the intensive debate about it is caused by Husserl himself. In published works such as *Ideen I* and *Cartesianische Meditationen* he associates the epoché a little too closely with the "methodical doubt" of Descartes. Although Husserl always notes that there are significant differences between his epoché and Cartesian doubt, he often fails to make sufficiently clear how radically different these procedures in fact are. Matters are only made worse by Husserl's continuous use of the notion of *Ausschaltung* to describe what the epoché does to the experienced world, since one of the meanings of the German word *Ausschaltung* is, roughly, "switching off," as when one switches off a radio (it can also mean something like "prevention," as in preventing an anticipated accident from happening). Throughout the first book of *Ideen*, we find this ill-chosen notion in play (*Hua* III/1, pp. 61-68, 107, 122-129, *et passim*). The immediate difficulty with such a characterization of the epoché is that it seems to suggest that world-belief can simply be "prevented," or "switched off," i.e., given up, at least for as long as we are doing phenomenology. It seems to suggest, in other words, that while in this peculiar professional frame of mind, we philosophers can simply let "world-belief" count as nothing to us. Husserl concedes that in fact this is hardly a possibility, and thus cannot be the correct way to understand what the epoché does: "Epoché of naïve performance [i.e., naively holding the world in *Seinsgeltung*]. *I do not really inhibit that performance*. The world continues to hold for me, it is" (*HuDo* II/1, p. 210, my emphasis).

But *Ausschaltung*, Husserl would come to realize, could lend support to an even more disastrous misunderstanding, one that would concern the very meaning and purpose of phenomenological research. Undoubtedly familiar with some of the gross misunderstandings that this notion furthers, Husserl sets things right in the twenties. In a critical reflection on earlier formulations of the procedure of the epoché he notes that

it is best to avoid talking of the phenomenological *"residue,"* and of *"switching off"* the world." This [kind of talk] easily seduces one into believing that the world would drop out of the phenomenological theme from now on, and that instead of the world, only the "subjective" acts [...] would be thematized. (*Hua* VIII, p. 432)

The interpreters who argue that Husserl's epoché is precisely intended to secure the realm of "indubitable," subjective acts, by way of excluding the real world, are far too numerous to mention.[13] The literature on Husserl abounds with proclamations to the effect that Husserl's epoché (or reduction, as these are oftentimes not separated) is a procedure of "excluding" the world, or of "ignoring" reality in favor of the sphere of subjective "immanence" (cf. *Hua* VI, pp. 179-180). Part of the reason for this is presumably that it is a good deal easier to understand what is going on in the epoché, if one sees it as shutting one type of thing out in favor of another – since after all, if it is not excluding anything, why do we need it? And, it must be admitted, a critical reading of *Ideen I* will hardly serve to refute such an interpretation. Nevertheless, I believe that the commentators who subscribe to this view miss what Husserlian phenomenology is ultimately about, viz. precisely the real world, or better, the existence of that world. Husserl's alternative descriptions of "attaching an index to" or "putting in brackets" capture much more adequately what is going on under the heading of epoché. The "general thesis" is not excluded, as though it did not belong in the theme of constitutive phenomenology, but "locked up" so that we do not utilize anything that belongs to it, or is based upon it. That is to say, the *world* as real, as existing, is not ignored, or excluded – as if we had no interest in it, and wanted to focus exclusively on something else – but rather "bracketed." And being thus "bracketed," "locked up," it is the very thematic core of our phenomenological research:

Figuratively speaking, that which is parenthesized is not erased from the phenomenological blackboard, but only parenthesized, and thereby provided with an index. *As having the latter it is, however, part of the major theme of inquiry* [*im Hauptthema der Forschung*]. (*Hua* III/1, p. 159, my emphasis)

The renunciation of the world, the "bracketing of the world," did not mean that henceforth the world was no longer our focus at all, but that the world had to become our focus in a new way, at a whole level deeper. (*Hua* XXVII, p. 173)

In fact, in view of the way Husserl's question of constitution is presented in the present chapter, this is obviously so. That question concerns precisely the world, and worldly objects. What the thematic field of transcendental phenomenology is can hardly be stated less ambiguously than it is done by Husserl in his *Nachwort* to the first book of *Ideen*: "This universal phenomenon 'world existing for me' [...] [is what] the phenomenologist turns into the field of his new theoretical interest" (*Hua* V, p. 145, emphasis deleted). How an existing world can be there for us, can show itself to us, is precisely the question we are trying to secure in its universality, against all possible lapses into questions of a different, less universal, and less fundamental character. *This* is what the epoché is supposed to do, and that is why it is necessary to "lock up" the *explanandum*, to make sure that we do not proceed by

---

[13] For just a few references, see Herbert Spiegelberg, "The 'Reality-Phenomenon' and Reality," p. 93n; Horst Gronke, *Das Denken des Anderen*, p. 96; Robert O. Schneider, "Husserl and Heidegger," p. 371. Some of these speak of the phenomenological "reduction" instead of the epoché, but in fact the "bracketing" is done by the epoché.

way of referring to anything belonging to that *explanandum*. We are by no means looking for a procedure to get the world out of view in favor of some extra-mundane subjectivity (*Hua* XXVII, p. 178).[14]

The expression "lock up" also neatly captures the second important aspect of what the epoché does, or rather, of what it *must not* do. In fact, the quotation above already presents the essence of it, but let me dwell for a moment on this important point. The epoché must not *ignore* that which it "brackets," but only "lock it up" as what we are, so to speak, aiming at. Being that towards which we are aiming, it is of the utmost importance that we *precisely do not lose sight* of the "general thesis" and all that it involves. We "lock it up" as something we may not at present utilize, but as locked up, it remains in our focus (cf. *Hua* XV, p. 117). The existence of the world for us is, after all, what constitutive phenomenology wants to explain, and it is therefore obviously not something that can be ignored or forgotten. The extent to which Husserl's constitutive phenomenology must keep the existing world and the "objects" within it in view – the extent to which phenomenology must indeed focus more or less exclusively on this – can only be appreciated once we have understood the so-called "phenomenological reduction," but for now at least we can see that ignoring the existing world is out of the question for Husserl.

As should be fairly obvious by now, the epoché implies no criticism of the natural attitude. It is neither designed to criticize the results and methods of natural science (they criticize themselves already, without the epoché), nor is it intended to scientifically scrutinize the validity claims of everyday "knowledge" and beliefs. In relation to all of this, the epoché is "neutral" (*Hua* VIII, p. 423). The natural attitude *as a whole* is transformed by the epoché, but again this implies no actual criticism, as if that attitude as a whole were in some way "wrong" – it implies only that the world of the natural attitude is "bracketed" *as that which we want to explain regarding its constitution.*[15]

Having thus introduced Husserl's epoché and established its relevance, we turn to the important issue of how to carry out the task of constitutive phenomenology within the framework of the epoché. Having "bracketed" the existence of the world for us, having "bracketed" the "general thesis of the natural attitude," how do we proceed to explain what is placed within the brackets? Husserl's answer is: by performing the phenomenological, or better, the transcendental *reduction*.

---

[14] Klaus Held expresses this point most lucidly: "Ultimately the transcendental phenomenologist is only interested in consciousness as the place where the world appears" ("Einleitung," p. 41). See the similar remark by Walter Biemel in "Husserl Encyclopaedia-Britannica Artikel und Heideggers Anmerkungen dazu" (p. 264). This phrase (*Ort des Erscheinens der Welt*) is extremely well suited to capture what both Husserl and Heidegger are after, and I use it more than once in the course of this study.

[15] In this context it is very interesting to observe Husserl's uneasiness with Fink's equation of the mundane with mere "appearance" in *VI. Cartesianische Mediation*. Husserl is, e.g., clearly unhappy with Fink when the latter calls mundane truths "appearance-truths," as if only transcendental phenomenological truths were "real" truths, and not those of the natural attitude (cf. *HuDo* II/1, pp. 133n, 143n).

3. THE TRANSCENDENTAL REDUCTION

The epoché is necessary because we need something to guard us against losing the constitutive problematic, and against corrupting that problematic by drawing directly on that which is to be explained. But in itself, the epoché explains nothing: "The empty generality of the epoché does not of itself clarify anything; it is only the gate of entry through which one must pass in order to be able to discover the new world of pure subjectivity" (*Hua* VI, § 71, p. 260).

We have now passed through that door, and are ready to proceed to making phenomenological "discoveries." But Husserl's question, we remember, is about the world, and not about any subjectivity (*Hua* V, p. 145). How, then, can "pure subjectivity" become the "new world" for us to discover?

Our problem is how to understand the being-there, for us, of the world and worldly entities. However certain, world-experience remains to be understood. In other words, our question pertains not just to the experience of individual things, but to the experience of the world and everything within it. As pointed out, Husserl's phenomenology is not interested in relations between worldly entities, but in the being-there-for-us of the *world*, including all those worldly entities. But if the world itself must accordingly be bracketed, what is left outside the brackets, what *may* we utilize as premises in the constitutive investigation? Surely, we ourselves, as well as our experiences, must be bracketed, for as human beings we are just as much worldly beings as are rocks and trees.

Indeed, as human beings we must be bracketed, according to Husserl. But "human beings" are not, Husserl points out, *all* that we are. Fundamentally, each of us is a "place" where the world, and worldly objects – including ourselves as such objects – *appear*, where everything worldly *shows itself*. For instance, I experience myself as a person among other persons, as occupying a certain position in the world, one I can change and constantly do change, and one that will nevertheless remain a position *in* the world, in space and in the "midst of that which is," to borrow an expression from Heidegger. All of this *is at the same time something that is being experienced by someone, and that could not show itself, except by being thus experienced*. No world and no objects can be manifest without appearing *to someone*; that is, there can be no manifestation without a "dative of manifestation."[16] At first, this kind of reasoning probably sounds like a platitude, as if Husserl were simply saying, "All that I experience is experienced by me" (cf. *Hua* VI, p. 168; *Hua* XV, p. 39). But in fact Husserl's apparent tautologies[17] contain within them a crucial insight, one that is essential to the kind of transcendental phenomenology carried out by Husserl – and to Heidegger's phenomenology as well, as I

---

[16] The expression "dative of manifestation" seems to have been coined by Thomas Prufer. See his article "Heidegger, Early and Late, and Aquinas," p. 200.

[17] Heidegger is clearly aware of the danger of misunderstanding phenomenology as expressing nothing but tautologies (cf. *GA* 58, p. 18). Interestingly enough, the later Heidegger himself refers to phenomenology as "tautological thinking" (*GA* 15, p. 399).

demonstrate later. As Husserl expresses the point, I am not only one of the entities within the world; at the same time I am also a subject *for* the world, I am a "place" where the world (and everything worldly) *shows itself*. Now, insofar as we can call the world and the worldly objects "transcendent," we can then say that I am a *transcendental subjectivity*. Basically, this is the sense that "transcendental subjectivity" has in Husserl's phenomenology: *the "subjectivity" to whom the world and everything worldly appears*.

Nevertheless, it becomes obvious in the later chapters of this study that Husserl's postulate of a peculiar relationship of identity and difference between the transcendental and the mundane subject is by no means without problems. However, these are not the difficulties that one would immediately be tempted to confront Husserl with. One might be tempted to assume that Husserl's notion of the transcendental subject refers to something completely different from, and separate from, the "empirical" or "mundane" subject.[18] But this would be a mistake. As Derrida proposes, there is no ontological (or rather: ontic) doubling going on here, as if there are two beings that we somehow need to establish a connection between.[19] The *same, individual* subject is at the same time a mundane being, viz. a human being, and a transcendental subjectivity, *depending on the viewpoint* we take on that subject, according to Husserl (cf. *Hua* VIII, pp. 71-72). I can view myself as one "entity" among others, as that particular being who is at the moment placed on that particular chair in that particular room, etc., or I can view myself as the one to whom all this appears so, as the one by whom I am experienced to be one entity among others, and so forth. And when I alternate between these ways of viewing myself, I clearly see, Husserl maintains, that in both instances I am indeed talking about *myself* (*Hua* VIII, pp. 71, 417). In Husserl's words:

Transcendental subjectivity, which is inquired into in the transcendental problem [...] is none other than again "I myself" and "we ourselves"; not, however, as found in the everyday natural attitude, or of positive science – *i.e.*, apperceived as components of the objectively present world before us – but rather as subjects of conscious life, *in* which this world and all that is present – for "us" – "makes" itself through certain apperceptions. (*Hua* IX, p. 292)[20]

With this definition of transcendental subjectivity, another possible misunderstanding can be dismissed straight away. In Husserl's phenomenology, the

---

[18] A position that one should not immediately associate with Kant either, as David Carr argues in his recent book *The Paradox of Subjectivity*. Cf. *Kritik der reinen Vernunft*, B 155.

[19] Jacques Derrida, *Speech and Phenomena*, pp. 11-12: "this duplication of sense must correspond to no ontological double. Husserl specifies, for example, that my transcendental ego is radically different from my natural and human ego; and yet it is distinguished by nothing, nothing that can be determined in the natural sense of distinction. The (transcendental) ego is not an other."

[20] It is significant – if one wants to contrast Husserl's notion of transcendental subjectivity to that of Kant – that Husserl speaks of "we," and "us," in this context. I touch upon this all-important Husserlian idea of a transcendental *intersubjectivity* in Chapter V of the present study. For a recent treatment of the range of problems grouped under this heading of "transcendental intersubjectivity," see Dan Zahavi, *Husserl und die transzendentale Intersubjektivität*. With its emphasis more on the ethical aspects, the account of James G. Hart in *The Person and the Common Life* is also valuable.

transcendental ego is not something that only comes into being with the performance of the epoché, as if it did not exist prior to the transcendental investigation. Of course, in the world of the *naive* natural attitude, transcendental subjectivities are nowhere to be found. The adjective "naive" is important, because Husserl does not imagine that having once discovered the "unnatural" attitude of phenomenology, the phenomenologist would constantly remain in that attitude, never to return to the natural attitude. Obviously, we must live most of our lives in an "un-bracketed" world, so to speak – in complete and active "belief" in the existence of that world. The natural attitude makes it possible for us to go about our business in the world, whether that business is theoretical or practical (*Hua* IX, p. 191). One, therefore, should make a distinction between the "*pre*-transcendental" natural attitude, the naive attitude in which one always begins (and quasi "in" which we began our journey with Husserl and Heidegger in the previous chapter), and the "*post*-transcendental" attitude to which we inevitably return (*Hua* IX, p. 472n; *Hua* XIII, p. 205). This latter, perhaps, we could call the "transcendentally enlightened" natural attitude.[21] So in the naive natural attitude, at any rate, there is presumably no trace of a transcendental subjectivity. But since an existing world and worldly entities certainly appear, and as such must manifest themselves *to* someone, this obviously cannot mean that there *is* no transcendental subject. As long as anything is manifest, there is transcendental subjectivity; transcendental subjectivity is defined as that necessary "dative" that belongs to any manifestation. However, in the naive natural attitude, transcendental subjectivity does not *know itself* as such, since it *knows* only worldly entities (*Hua* I, p. 75; *Hua* VI, p. 209), and this is why transcendental subjectivities are nowhere to be found as long as we are in the naive natural attitude. Husserl sometimes expresses this point by saying that in the naive natural attitude transcendental subjectivity is *anonymous* (*Hua* VI, p. 209; *Hua* VIII, p. 417). It is there to begin with, but only uncovered in the phenomenological investigation.

If we return to the question of what is left outside the brackets, it is very tempting to conclude that what remains is transcendental subjectivity. That is, once we bracket the existence (for us) of the world in order to explain it, the only thing that we may base our explanation upon is the study of transcendental subjectivity. In a way this is correct, yet in another way it is false. Let me admit at once that there are places where Husserl expresses the opinion that his transcendental phenomenology is, and must be, based upon the study of "unbracketed" subjectivity. And as I said, in a way that is quite correct. However, I believe that there are some important qualifications that we need to make, in order to truly understand what Husserl's so-called transcendental reduction is, and, by implication, what Husserl's project is.

First, we must be wary of expressions such as "What is left outside the brackets," since they come much too close to the Cartesian notion of the epoché. Husserl

---

[21] Concerning the problem of "*Einströmung*" – the problem of the influence that transcendental discoveries can have on subsequent life in the natural attitude – cf. *Hua* VI, pp. 213-214.

comes to see the Cartesian procedure of "hypothetical annihilation" of the world as problematic, because it seems to present us with a subjectivity cut off from the world, thus leaving us at a loss to understand what could possibly be gained by the epoché (*Hua* VI, p. 158). It is *not* – as seen in the present chapter – the case that the epoché thematically cuts off anything, as if the world were something we had to ignore in favor of something else. The epoché, rather, places the world (and the entities belonging to it) where it belongs, viz. in the *center of our research*, as that which has to be explained (cf. *Hua* XV, p. 366). And as that *explanandum*, it must never be lost sight of, it must continue to guide us as, so to speak, that upon which we must aim. Therefore, we are not left simply with whatever escapes the brackets; we will always be left with what is *in* the brackets as well. I return to a more detailed treatment of this in a moment.

Second, Husserl never intends to base his phenomenological investigations on "introspection" (cf. *Hua* V, p. 38; LV, p. 210).[22] We do not become phenomenologists by somehow shutting out the world and then turning to describe what we find in ourselves, in our experiences. In other words, the difference between the naturally attuned person and the phenomenologist is *not* that the former makes first order claims such as, "This keyboard is dirty," whereas the latter limits himself to introspective reports like, "I now see that the keyboard is dirty" – contrary, perhaps, to some of Husserl's own less fortunate formulations. This kind of introspective report cannot serve phenomenology, because phenomenology has no interest in what particular persons might be experiencing at particular points in time; its interest is devoted to the fundamental principles of *world-constitution*, as explained above.[23]

---

[22] Daniel C. Dennett's brief remarks on Husserl in *Consciousness Explained* show that there are some who hold that phenomenology is a type of philosophy or science based on introspection. On p. 44, Dennett writes: "the philosophical school or movement known as Phenomenology (with a capital P) grew up early in the twentieth century around the work of Edmund Husserl. Its aim was to find a new foundation for all philosophy (indeed, for all knowledge) based on a special technique of introspection, in which the outer world and all its implications and presuppositions were supposed to be 'bracketed' in a particular act of mind known as the *epoché*."

[23] One aspect of Husserl's phenomenology that I do not discuss in any detail in this study is his insistence that phenomenology should be an "eidetic science" rather than any "science of fact." Being an eidetic science, phenomenology can of course not be interested in the particulars of introspection. But more important in this regard, I think, is the fact that Husserlian phenomenology wants to investigate the constitution of the world, which is accordingly what I emphasize in the main text above. As to the natural objection, whether I do not rob Heidegger of one of his best arguments against Husserl by "ignoring" the eidetic dimension in Husserl's thinking, I do not believe this is so. Heidegger, after all, has no interest in the particular person *as such*, but only in the essentials of that person. Heideggerian phenomenology of being is no "science" of *facts*: even "facticity" is an *essential* component in the being of *Dasein* (cf. *GA* 26, p. 217). So when Heidegger does claim that the "eidetic variation" in Husserl's hands effects a biased (and in part faulty) understanding of the being of beings (cf. *GA* 20, p. 152), it is more a criticism of Husserl's general approach to the problematic of being – i.e., his *forgetfulness* of that problem – than of Husserl's desire to describe essentials rather than particularities. For a general argument that Heidegger's critique of Husserl's transcendental phenomenology does not concern the phenomenon or phenomena of "facticity," see Steven Crowell, "Facticity and Transcendental Philosophy."

Third, in connection to this last point it must be noted that one should not overemphasize the *reflective* character of Husserl's phenomenology. Again, some of Husserl's own remarks on this issue admittedly conflict with what I am saying. Being interested in understanding what is actually going on in Husserlian phenomenology rather than in Husserl's own interpretation of this (which is not necessarily the correct one, or the *only* correct one), I see no other option than to dismiss those kinds of remarks as self-misunderstandings.[24] My point is not, however, that Husserl's phenomenology is not "reflective" at all, but only that it is so in a less obvious way than one might be tempted to assume. If we want to call the transcendental attitude "reflective," we must take care – as does Husserl himself (*Hua* I, pp. 72-75; *Hua* XXV, pp. 162-169) – to distinguish sharply between *natural* reflection, reflection in the natural attitude, and *transcendental* reflection. Of course, it is not that reflection alone makes phenomenology; on the contrary, there is such a thing as reflecting on one's emotions, opinions, etc., as the emotions of this particular human being. When reflecting thus, I do not move on the transcendental level, but remain in the natural attitude,[25] and we should not assume that transcendental reflection has the same structure as natural reflection. Yet, keeping this distinction in mind, one should not take for granted everything Husserl says about the specifically phenomenological reflection. For instance, when Husserl claims that instead of focusing on the experienced objects we should make the experiences or the "acts" our thematic objects (cf., e.g., *Hua* XIX/1, p. 14), this is only partly correct. As it stands, it suggests that something like introspection is after all the basis for phenomenological knowledge, and as pointed out above, it is not. What is correct, however, is that we cannot allow ourselves to live naively with the "belief" in the experienced objects (and world) the way we did before – or better, for the purpose of doing phenomenology, we must simply temporarily avoid directly

---

[24] Gadamer convincingly argues that an author is generally not an authority on the interpretation of his own work. In so far as the author interprets his own work, he becomes his own reader, and as a reader he might not be better than are most others (cf. *Wahrheit und Methode*, p. 196). Many things are said about Husserl's qualities as a reader. W. R. Boyce Gibson, e.g., reports how Levinas told him that Husserl's reading was very limited because "after 2 pages the impact on his own thinking will be such that he must put the book aside" (Boyce Gibson, "From Husserl to Heidegger," p. 67). The abundance of marginal notes in Husserl's copy of *Sein und Zeit* hardly corroborates this claim, and although Husserl, to be sure, cannot be said to have understood the basics of Heidegger's thinking in that book, this is not surprising given the fact that Husserl had no precise knowledge of Heidegger's teaching throughout the Marburg years, and probably expected to find in *Sein und Zeit* an unambiguous continuation of his own thinking. With regard to the specific question of Husserl's qualities as *his own* interpreter, I do believe that there is something right in Heidegger's suggestion (with explicit reference to Husserl) that "where something is really accomplished [*gemacht*], it is mostly the case that the one who accomplishes it doesn't even know what it is all about" (*GA* 17, p. 81).

[25] Heidegger's claim that according to Husserl one never encounters "experiences" while in the natural attitude (*GA* 58, p. 251) is therefore completely false. Friedrich-Wilhelm von Herrmann also neglects the distinction between natural and transcendental reflection in his criticism of Husserl's "reflective" phenomenology. Cf. his *Hermeneutik und Reflexion*, pp. 80-85, *et passim*. This latter book clearly overemphasizes the reflective character of Husserl's phenomenology, obviously in order to contrast that phenomenology more markedly with Heidegger's "hermeneutic" phenomenology.

relying on that "belief" (it being impossible to "inhibit" it). We have "bracketed" the world and worldly entities. As "bracketed," the world remains present to us; not in the *naive* way it was before, but rather precisely in a "reflective" way (*Hua* XXVII, p. 173), as viewed from a different angle – still viewed in "belief," but no longer in *naive* "belief," no longer in a "belief" that does not know itself as a "belief." When we are doing phenomenology, we are entering (through the epoché) into a new relationship with "the world" (cf. *Hua* VI, p. 147), a relationship that may indeed be labeled "reflective." It is, one could say, the *world* that is reflected on, and *not* our experiences, since it is in relation to the world that we have been able to gain a little distance. In this sense, and – I submit – in this sense only, Husserlian phenomenology is fundamentally "reflective"; not in the sense that it bases itself on (introspective) reflections on thoughts and experiences, in spite of all appearances to the contrary. As I attempt to substantiate this claim, we can be seen to gradually unfold Husserl's notions of *reduction* and *noema*.

Husserl oftentimes speaks as though transcendental phenomenology, having "inhibited" the "positing" of the world, would itself "posit" transcendental subjectivity, or consciousness (e.g., *Hua* IX, pp. 291, 337). To be meaningful, an investigation such as the constitutive investigation needs something it can presuppose, something "posited," since without positing a thematic field, something upon which we may direct our investigating gaze, how could we possibly proceed? Could transcendental subjectivity, the way we define it, serve as the presupposed sphere of being for constitutive phenomenology? I am a transcendental subjectivity, insofar as I am not only a being in the world, but also a "locus" where the world appears. Considered only as the locus where manifestation takes place, as a "viewpoint" on the world, I am a transcendental subjectivity. But being thus considered simply as a "viewpoint" on the world, what can I then say about myself, which concerns *me* as a transcendental subjectivity, rather than the world? Is there any content that we can isolate so as to be able to say, "This is the sphere of being that we call transcendental subjectivity (in contrast to the 'transcendent' world)," or rather, will we not be thrown back upon the world, precisely due to the circumstance that what we call transcendental subjectivity is initially defined as a "point," a point that receives all the meaning it has from that with which it is contrasted? Given the way we have introduced Husserl's notion of transcendental subjectivity, it seems that it must collapse into a point with no extension, so that only the coordinated reality remains, calling to mind one of Wittgenstein's passages from the *Tractatus*.[26] Or, to be more precise, transcendental subjectivity – functionally defined as the "place" for the manifestation of the world – cannot be subjected, like an object or a region of objects, to direct scrutiny; only "the coordinated reality" can be seen in

---

[26] Wittgenstein, *Tractatus logico-philosophicus*, § 5.64: "Here it can be seen that solipsism, when its implications are followed out strictly, coincides with pure realism. The self of solipsism shrinks to a point without extension, and there remains the reality co-ordinated with it." Wittgenstein's argument is explicitly directed against "solipsism," but it applies to the present discussion as well. Indeed, in his *Notebooks 1914-1916*, p. 85, Wittgenstein makes the same point about "idealism."

this way. Initially, *transcendental subjectivity seems to have no content other than that of the manifest world; it has been functionally defined as nothing but the dative of the manifestation of that world.*[27] Therefore, to direct the phenomenological gaze against subjectivity directly will not help in the least, since we will be thrown back upon the world, rather than discover any content that might help us understand the "constitution" of the world.

What phenomenology has to "posit," therefore, can only be the *world* and the worldly objects within it. Yet, surely this is the one thing that we *cannot* do without breaking out of the confines of the epoché (and the epoché is essential to the meaningfulness of our investigation). But let us recall once again what is said about the epoché. It "brackets" what is to be *explained*, so that we can not utilize this in any direct manner (as a "premise") in the course of our explanation; but being thus "bracketed," it is important that we do not lose sight of it. So in that sense, at least, we have already granted that the world has to be "posited." When doing constitutive phenomenology we must always keep an eye on that, the constitution of which, we want to understand.[28]

The crucial point, now, is that this is all the "positing" that Husserlian phenomenology needs. Husserl posits nothing less and nothing more than the existing world and all entities belonging to it, but does so in a peculiar manner, viz. he posits the world as *that whose constitution we must understand*. That is to say, we must not "base ourselves upon" this world the way the natural attitude does, in order, e.g., to investigate mundane relations between mundane entities. Rather, all of this must be "locked up" and placed before our eyes as part of that which must be explained. Having placed it thus, we can begin to put flesh on the non-extensional "viewpoint" – i.e., to inquire into those structures that bring it about that an existing world manifests itself – using the experienced world and its entities, bracketed as they are, as *transcendental guiding clues* (*Leitfäden*). With this notion of "guiding clue" in hand, we are able finally to understand Husserl's transcendental reduction.

The reduction, to be sure, is the subject of just as much controversy as is the epoché.[29] At the basis of most of the interpretations that the present study disagrees with is the more harmless presupposition that the epoché and the reduction are identical – which means that we can dispense with a discussion of those (mis)understandings pertaining specifically to the reduction, given our brief discussion of those pertaining to the epoché in the previous section. In fact, the

---

[27] See Carr, *The Paradox of Subjectivity*, p. 94. It should be emphasized, however, that this does not mean that transcendental subjectivity has no "content" whatsoever, that it simply *is* the pure "negation of the world," as Sartre seems to think (*Being and Nothingness*, pp. 181-185). It means, rather, that the "content" of transcendental subjectivity (its manner of being) can only be caught sight of indirectly, via the manifested world.

[28] Adorno's critique that by taking the constituted thing as a guiding clue, Husserl's epistemology presupposes precisely what it had to deduce (*Zur Metakritik der Erkenntnistheorie*, p. 175) would only be valid if Husserlian phenomenology did in fact want to prove or deduce anything, which, as we have seen in detail, it does not.

[29] For references, see the note on the interpretations of the epoché above.

epoché and the reduction are not identical; they serve different functions within the framework of Husserl's phenomenological method.[30] Whereas the epoché does the "bracketing," the reduction is the *leading back* (Latin: *reducere*) of the phenomenological inquiry from the bracketed world to that which is to explain the world in terms of its constitution. The constitution of the world can only be explained by somehow focusing on the structures of that "place" *where* the world constitutes, i.e., manifests itself, and that place is transcendental subjectivity. Because transcendental subjectivity is defined as initially empty, however, that is to say, with no content except that of the experienced world, we cannot gain anything by directing our gaze directly at that subjectivity; rather, we must thematize it *indirectly*, taking our point of departure in the bracketed world and mundane entities. So we direct our thematic gaze *at the world*, and what we learn about the world must function as a *transcendental guiding clue* that will guide us in our subsequent regress into transcendental subjectivity, into the structures that explain world-constitution. *This method of regressing from bracketed world to transcendental subjectivity is what Husserl labels the "transcendental phenomenological reduction"*:

To this end we will treat the "transcendental-phenomenological reduction" a little more precisely, the method of access which leads systematically from the necessarily first given field of experience, that of external experiencing of the world, upward into all-embracing, constitutive absolute being, i.e., – into transcendental subjectivity. (*Hua* IX, p. 340; cf. *Hua* I, pp. 163-164; *Hua* V, p. 78)

It is not as though one could reach transcendental subjectivity by some other means, or as though – the epoché being performed – that subjectivity would simply be placed before our eyes as a sphere of being open to direct research. On the contrary, only with the bracketed "object" functioning as a transcendental guiding clue can we begin to say anything about transcendental subjectivity, namely, *what that subjectivity must,* so to speak, *"look like" in order to be the experiencing subjectivity of such an object* (*Hua* I, p. 86). In other words, it is the transcendental reduction that for the first time presents us with transcendental subjectivity, according to Husserl: "A pure and real presentation [*Aufweisung*] of transcendental subjectivity is first accomplished in the method of *phenomenological reduction*, known to every phenomenologist" (*Hua* VIII, p. 80; cf. *Hua* VI, p. 265).

Yet characterizing the reduction thus seems to lead to certain difficulties. At least two objections immediately come to mind.

First, how does this "indirect" method of discovering transcendental subjectivity square with Husserl's claim to be doing transcendental philosophy relying only on the *perceptually evident*,[31] in contrast to, for example, Kant, who – according to Husserl – precisely took to "regression" and "mythical construction" (*Hua* VI, pp.

---

[30] Cf. *Hua* VI, pp. 154-155, and *Hua* IX, pp. 340-341. See, too, Klaus Held, *Lebendige Gegenwart*, p. 17.
[31] It is well known that Husserl intended to widen the notions of "perception" (*Wahrnehmung*) and "intuition" (*Anschauung*) considerably, so that they would encompass much more than they do in the tradition, where they are largely equivalent with sensory perception. Cf., e.g., *Hua* XIX/2, p. 649; *Hua* VII, p. 138; *Hua* XI, p. 291.

116-118, 120)? Disregarding the question of whether such a criticism of *Kant* is justified, does the criticism then apply to *Husserl* himself? The answer is yes and no. First of all, with the crucial notion of transcendental guiding clues, there can be no question that Husserlian phenomenology must be, in some sense, "regressive." But this does not entail that it is also "constructive" (i.e., that it takes to "construing" explanations instead of heeding to the "evident"). Also, one may not assume that the *kind* of regression needed in Husserlian phenomenology corresponds to what Kant pursues under the heading of "transcendental *deduction*" – after all, Husserl's intention is not to *prove* anything, but rather to *understand*. When the later Husserl tries to bring out the difference between the two kinds of regressive endeavors, the "hermeneutic" motif of his own phenomenology is conspicuous. On the one hand, we have the regressive method of Kant, in Husserl's eyes one that is "mythically, constructively *inferring* [*schließenden*]" (*Hua* VI, § 30, p. 118, my emphasis), and, on the other hand, the regression called for by Husserl – "a thoroughly intuitively *disclosing* [*erschließenden*] method, intuitive in its point of departure and in everything it discloses" (ibid., my emphasis).

This last remark brings us to the next important point. Whereas phenomenology must "regress" (under the title of "reduction"), it can only do so starting from a *Leitfaden* described with such accuracy and in such detail as to render the regress itself "evident" – at least in some weak sense that is strong enough to rule out simple "construction." This is, I believe, where Husserl's frequent use of such words as *Anschauung* and *Evidenz* to describe the "method" of phenomenology becomes justified: *one must take care to describe the transcendental guiding clue with as much accuracy as possible, because on that depends also the "Einsichtigkeit" of the (regressive) investigation*. Stated differently, if Husserl's transcendental philosophy is not "constructive" in the bad sense attributed to Kant, this is because it describes in detail and with all possible evidence *the world* and the mundane entities, thereby allowing the "regress" to be to some extent "evident" as well. It is *not* because Husserlian phenomenology has some kind of direct *Anschauung* of the transcendental ego, considered apart from the world.[32] Phenomenological regression, so the quote goes, should be "intuitive" in its *point of departure* and in everything it "discloses" or "unveils"; my claim is that it is precisely the intuitive givenness of the point of departure that renders the phenomenological disclosing as such intuitive.

For another and more fundamental objection, let us call to mind the discussion of the "causal explanation" of world-experience from the previous section. Towards the end of that section I deny that such an account could in fact explain anything,

---

[32] In the beginning of the thirties, Husserl still holds that phenomenology has direct experiential access to subjectivity, despite the fact that we only unveil this subjectivity through the reduction. But it is important to emphasize that what Husserl has in mind when he says such things is the contrast with "speculative constructions" (*Hua* V, p. 141). Husserl clarifies his position in the *Krisis*. Here, he says that we have a "mute" evidence for the concrete ego (experiencing subject and experienced world). The muteness is only replaced by phenomenological descriptive clarity of the ego when we "inquire back" (*zurückfragen*) from the world to the subject (*Hua* VI, § 55, p. 191).

since it goes "the wrong way" – it starts from the "world" and ends in the "subject," thus abandoning us at the starting line once again. Is that not precisely what I am presenting Husserl as doing himself now? Going back from the "object" to the "subject," thus failing once again to deliver any explanation of how we get "out there" in the first place? This is definitely not the case. In fact, the causal account is "progressive"; it goes from one link in the causal nexus to the next, ending with a mental state in the subject. The phenomenological account does nothing of the sort. It, too, takes its point of departure in the "object," but not to let the object function as a link in a process that ends in the subject, but rather to "lock it up" as that which is the "result" of a yet to be understood constitutive process. In other words, one could say (using rather misleading terminology) that whereas the causal account views the state in the subject as the end result, the transcendental phenomenological explanation, by contrast, views the world as the "end result." So even if the method of phenomenology is reductive – going back from the world to subjectivity – the phenomenological explanation runs in the opposite direction of the causal account.

Since the understanding of Husserl's phenomenology *in toto* depends upon the proper understanding of the method of reduction (*Hua* IX, p. 188; *Hua* XXVII, p. 172), let me summarize for a moment our characterization of that method. The epoché, Husserl says, is the "entrance gate" to the discovery of transcendental subjectivity. It is not immediately evident that we should be interested in discovering transcendental subjectivity, since our task is to understand *the world*, more precisely its *constitution*. As pointed out, however, the world cannot constitute itself without doing so *for someone*, and this someone (the one, or one*s*, to whom the world appears) we define as the *transcendental subjectivity*. The question is whether Husserl could, or should, "posit" this subjectivity as a sphere of being to be directly investigated by phenomenology, and the answer is negative, since transcendental subjectivity as defined seems to have no content besides that of the experienced world. Instead we need to focus once again on the world inside its brackets, to see if this could function as a *guiding clue* to an *indirect* investigation of the initially empty "dative of manifestation." This *indirect* approach to transcendental subjectivity, this *going back* from the world and mundane entities to that for which it constitutes itself, we call the transcendental or phenomenological *reduction*. In what sense can Husserlian phenomenology then be characterized as based on *Anschauung* rather than non-evident "construction"? Subjectivity as we define it can not be studied directly, and thus can not yield the sought after perceptual evidence – only the world and the entities within it can yield such evidence.

For a number of increasingly weighty reasons, then, we see that the task of describing the experienced world and entities becomes all-important. First of all, we must never lose sight of that whose "constitution" we want to explain. Second, it is in fact only through a thorough description of the world that we can gain any insight into its constitution, since without the world functioning as a guiding clue, we cannot proceed. And finally, it is only an evident description of the world and of everything mundane that can render constitutive phenomenology as such "perceptual" – "perceptual" in the wide phenomenological sense of the word. Thus, before we can actually begin to unfold a constitutive investigation, we must pay serious attention to the experienced world, and the entities within it.

4. THE NOEMATIC CORRELATE

At first blush, it is far from obvious how turning to a description of the world, or the experienced "objects," could be helpful. I can describe the keyboard in front of me in great detail – the material it is made of, where the different keys are placed, etc. – without learning anything about myself as a transcendental subjectivity. Of course, I am aware that the description is one that *I* am working out, and in that sense I am obviously aware that as an experiencing subject I am "implicated" (*mit dabei*). But by describing the keyboard, how can I possibly learn anything about *how* the keyboard becomes manifest to me? More precisely put, how can I describe the keyboard in a way that *allows* it to function as a guiding clue for a meaningful investigation into its "how"?

In one of his excellent articles from the thirties, Eugen Fink points out that a transcendental analysis that moves immediately from a description of the experienced object to the supposed experiences *of* that object would soon end.[33] In order to use it as a *Leitfaden*, we need to thematize the "object" in a special way, a way that somehow "breaks open" the "object," according to Fink.[34] The keyboard – for me as I naturally begin to describe it – is a material thing that has a number of properties, some of which are known to me, and some of which are vaguely anticipated, but basically unknown to me (such as how the inside looks, how the keyboard functions, etc.). All of these properties, if one may put it thus, belong *equally* to the keyboard – not in the sense that they are all equally important to the "essence" of a keyboard, but in the sense that they are equally important to this particular thing; they are all *its* properties. It is this natural view of the object that we must tear ourselves free from.

Let us recall the task of the epoché. The epoché is the procedure intended to "bracket" the existing world and worldly entities, so that we do not utilize it – except as a guiding clue – in the constitutive investigation. This means that I cannot rely directly upon a natural description such as the one outlined above. Contrary to what one might think, Husserl insists that one should not, on account of this, view the epoché as restrictive. Indeed, according to Husserl, we instead point out a *liberating* feature of the epoché. The point is not only that we may now begin to discover a subjectivity that was "anonymous" before, but also that we may now view the *world*, and the worldly objects, in a different manner (*Hua* VI, p. 244). I anticipated this point in the previous section where I claim that the performance of the epoché brings us into a "reflective" relationship with the world. No longer living naively in world-experience, directed exclusively at the experienced entities, a different

---
[33] Fink, *Studien zur Phänomenologie 1930-1939*, p. 220.
[34] Cf. *Studien zur Phänomenologie 1930-1939*, p. 221.

perspective upon entities and world becomes possible for us: we can now view the experienced objects and world *just as they are experienced* (*Hua* VI, p. 147), in the "how" (*im Wie*) of their manifestation (cf. *Hua* III/1, pp. 217, 233, 303), without mixing up that characterization with our "natural" knowledge of the experienced objects.

Once again, something that seems to be a mere platitude in fact harbors crucial insights. As pointed out above, it is at first unclear how an object, or the world, could function as a guiding clue the way we require it. The keyboard has a wide range of properties and – for the natural description – it, so to speak, "insists" on having them *all*, at once, in such a way that I cannot begin to answer how such an object could be experienced. But by "bracketing" all knowledge of the natural attitude, it becomes possible for us to "break open" this stubborn insistence of the object, since we are now able to reflectively view it *just as it presents itself*, or just as it is given in the experience. That is to say, we are now able to describe the "object" purely as a *correlate* to any given experience, without having to take into account everything else that we (as living in the natural attitude) know about the object – and this is precisely what allows us to inquire into the "how" of its constitution. This all-important object-as-experienced Husserl also labels the *noema* or the *cogitatum* (*qua cogitatum*).

The noema is the subject of a lively debate in the literature on Husserl. For instance, it is claimed that the noema is, roughly, some kind of *meaning*-entity that stands in between the object itself and the experience of that object.[35] One cannot deny the existence of passages in Husserl's texts that favor such an interpretation (cf. *Hua* V, p. 89). But there are other texts that lend substantial support to another view, according to which the noema is the experienced object itself (rather than anything in between object and experience), precisely *as* experienced.[36] The "noema discussion" is not in itself of any interest in the present context – we are not trying to provide the final historical account of Husserl's thinking so much as we are trying to develop a viable reading of his transcendental project. For our purposes, we may simply identify the given object *as* given with the noema, or if that identification should ultimately suffer from too little textual support, we may speak instead of the experienced-object-just-as-experienced, etc. For the moment, let me suggest using the expression the *noematic correlate* when referring to the experienced just as experienced.

However marginal the noema discussion is to our present concern, we can use it as a point of departure for asking an important question, viz. the question about the relation between the noematic correlate and the "real" object. Dagfinn Føllesdal refers to a well-known passage from *Ideen I* in order to substantiate the claim that

---

[35] See Dagfinn Føllesdal, "Husserl's Notion of Noema."

[36] Varieties of such an interpretation are proposed by, e.g., Robert Sokolowski ("Intentional Analysis and the Noema"), and John J. Drummond (*Husserlian Intentionality and Non-Foundational Realism*, esp. Part II).

the noema is not to be identified with the experienced object.[37] After stating that the object (exemplified by a tree) as such is by no means identical with the noema, Husserl elaborates the point by emphasizing how the real thing, the real tree, can burn, and has chemical components, etc., whereas the *noema* that belongs to a particular perception of a tree is *not* flammable, and has *no* chemical components (*Hua* III/1, p. 205).[38] At first glance, this seems to be unambiguously in support of Føllesdal's interpretation, but one should not jump to conclusions. Notice which experience Husserl uses as an example: "Let us suppose that in a garden we regard with pleasure a blossoming apple tree" (*Hua* III/1, p. 203). Now, when I look "with pleasure" at a "blossoming" apple tree, the experienced tree is certainly one that – considered as the physical object it is – is flammable and has such and such chemical components. But considered *just in so far as it is experienced in this experience*, this joyful perception, the tree has no such components. Considered, in other words, as the *noematic correlate* of *this* experience, the tree "cannot" burn, and cannot be dissolved into chemical components. But supposing that the tree was standing in the middle of a desert, with no other tree or bush for miles around, then a person in search of firewood might very well immediately perceive the tree *as flammable*, i.e., she would probably experience a noematic object that *could burn*. However, it is by no means certain that she would immediately perceive the tree as having a certain chemical structure. This, on the other hand, would perhaps be what a chemistry professor would immediately "see" when directing his or her gaze at the tree, whereas the beauty of its bloom might totally escape this perceiver. With this notion of the noematic correlate in hand, then, we can, as it were, *break open* the object of the natural attitude and view it *just as it is experienced*.

This means, on the one hand, that the object-as-experienced, the noematic object, is not identical with the "real" object, or the experienced object (as considered in the natural attitude). The object as I would describe it in the natural attitude is beautiful *as well as* flammable *as well* as an object with a certain chemical structure, but when I happily glance at a tree in bloom, the noematic correlate to my experience has only the first mentioned property.[39] Yet, on the other hand, the noematic correlate is by no means *another* object, nor is it no *object* at all (although sometimes, as in the case of other persons, or the world, one should avoid the notion of object). It is the *same*

---

[37] Cf. Føllesdal, "Husserl's Notion of Noema," p. 684.

[38] In the thirties, Husserl still defends this passage from *Ideen I*. Cf. *Hua* VI, p. 245, and *Hua* XXIX, p. 128.

[39] A question that naturally comes to mind here, is whether it is simply the case that the "real" object is *richer* than the noematic, since the noematic object is always the correlate to a specific type of act that picks out a specific type of feature of the real object (e.g., its aesthetic qualities). As the matter is presented above, this seems to be the case. But it could be that the noematic object could tell us something about the so-called "real" object that could not possibly surface as long as we are precisely directed at "real" objects, i.e., as long as we are in the natural attitude. It could be, for instance, that the noematic object could tell us something about the *being* of objects. I argue later in this study that in fact the noematic object is indispensable for any phenomenological investigation of being.

object, but viewed *exclusively* as it presents itself in the experience – or type of experience – under consideration:

In every case the noematic correlate [...] is to be taken *precisely* as it inheres "immanently" in the mental process of perceiving, of judging, of liking; and so forth; that is, just as it is offered to us when we *inquire purely into this mental process itself*. (*Hua* III/1, p. 203)

As the perception has its noematic object, remembrance has its remembered, as such, adoration has its adored just as adored, and so forth (*Hua* III/1, p. 203). In all these cases, an object presents itself to us in a special way.

In the natural attitude, one cannot bring this "special way" into view (at least not exclusively), since natural knowledge of the object will inevitably interfere. But having performed the epoché and thus being no longer immersed in the natural attitude, we may view the object purely *as it presents itself to us* in those different types of experiences (cf. *Hua* VI, p. 151). Having thus "broken up" the object, it is possible to let it function as a transcendental guiding clue for the reduction to the transcendental subjectivity. We are now in a position to appreciate why Husserl declares that the "discovery" of the "correlational a priori" affected him deeply (*Hua* VI, p. 169n). On the surface of things, the correlation between noesis (Husserl's word for the experience as considered by phenomenology) and noema, or cogito and cogitatum seems just another version of the "correlation" between subject and object, and consequently just as empty and futile as the latter. However, the crucial difference is that the noema is the *correlate* of the act, and not the object considered in its "entirety," in view of all our natural knowledge about it. The noematic correlate is, so to speak, *the terminal of all current intentional "rays,"*[40] but also *nothing more than that*. Thus, we now have the possibility of following those intentional "rays" "backwards," to unveil the "noetic" side of the correlation. The crucial importance of the noematic correlate is precisely that it is the transcendental *Leitfaden* without which constitutional phenomenology would be impossible:

The most universal type – within which, as a form, everything particular is included – is indicated by our universal scheme: *ego-cogito-cogitatum*. The most universal descriptions, which we have attempted in a rough fashion concerning intentionality, concerning its peculiar synthesis, and so forth, relate to that type. In the particularization of that type, and of its description, the intentional object (on the side belonging to the *cogitatum*) plays, for easily understood reasons, the role of "transcendental clue" [*transzendentalen Leitfadens*] to the typical infinite multiplicities of possible *cogitations* that, in a possible synthesis, bear the intentional object within them (in the manner peculiar to consciousness) as the same meant object. (*Hua* I, p. 87; cf. pp. 122-123)

Therefore, if the epoché has until now seemed primarily "negative" – being the procedure of "bracketing" things and world – we can now see that in fact it is equally *positive*, in that it is the epoché that supplies us with a transcendental *Leitfaden*. Without the epoché, the experienced-just-as-experienced could not

---

[40] The quotation marks indicate that it hardly makes sense to speak as if one could literally discern a number of simple intentions in each act. Rather, we are faced with an intentional whole that cannot be divided up into discrete intentional "rays." The notion of "ray," however, helps to illustrate the point I am trying to make.

surface, but only the experienced objects as "real," as objects of the (natural, or life-) world. When we perform the epoché, then, obstacles are *removed* from our view (cf. *Hua* VI, p 154; *Hua* V, p. 145), rather than added.

This is the important outcome of the discussion in the present section. With the realization that only the epoché makes it possible to "see" the noematic correlate (*Hua* VI, p. 151), we confirm anew the necessity of the epoché as an "entrance gate" to Husserlian phenomenology. Indeed, in Chapter III we can see that because the epoché is what makes possible a thematization of the noematic object, the procedure of "bracketing" is crucial not only to Husserl's transcendental phenomenology, but to Heidegger's phenomenological project as well.

5. REDUCTION AND CONSTITUTION

The question we pose here, following Husserl, is a question about how an existing world and mundane entities can be experienced as such. This question is dubbed the question of *constitution*. Since introducing that question, we have been attempting to outline the general way in which one could meaningfully proceed to answer it. In the center of this undertaking stands the so-called transcendental reduction – the "regress" from that whose constitution is to be explained (the "noematic correlate") to the dative of manifestation or constitution. The idea is that such a reduction should reveal – within the subjectivity for whom constitution takes place – the structures that explain constitution.

Yet, what is the exact relation between the notions of constitution and transcendental reduction? Although we have already refuted the objection that constitutional phenomenology would fall prey to the same difficulties as the causal account, it is still as if the "regressive" procedure of reduction goes the wrong way, apparently backing away from the object, to the transcendental subjectivity. It appears as if we must have some kind of positive movement, returning from subjectivity to the object. Accordingly, Gadamer's suggestion regarding the relation between constitution and reduction seems essentially correct: "'Constitution' is nothing but the 'movement of reconstruction' ['*Wiederaufbaubewegung*'] that follows after the reduction has been performed."[41]

But we must tread with caution here. Is the reduction really a "backing away" from the object in favor of the subject, so that the problem of *returning* to the object could arise? I do not think so. Let me substantiate this claim with a few simple considerations.

First, Gadamer seems to place constitution on a par with reduction, whereas the two notions are crucially different in terms of position within the phenomenological framework. "Reducing" is what the phenomenologist does, when she uses the noematic correlates as guiding clues for exploring the experiencing subjectivity. "Constitution" – is this also something that is essentially done by the

---

[41] Gadamer, "Die phänomenologische Bewegung," p. 135.

phenomenologist in her capacity as phenomenologist? On the contrary, world-constitution already happens before there can be any phenomenology, and it continues to happen throughout the phenomenological investigations. World-constitution is not something that we – as phenomenologists – *perform*, or bring about, but something we – as phenomenologists – want to *understand*. In other words, if indeed we did initiate a *Wiederaufbaubewegung*, this would not be constitution itself, but only an attempt on the part of the phenomenologists to "reconstruct" a certain (process of) constitution.[42] It is in fact obvious that phenomenology must "come too late" to initiate constitution as such, because if the world were not already constituted there would be no question for phenomenology to pose. This is also a reason why Husserl never stops emphasizing that one must necessarily begin in the "natural attitude," that it is simply impossible to be a phenomenologist from day one (*Hua* IX, pp. 47, 270).

Second, we must not assume that the epoché, or the reduction, in any way disassembles the world. Rather, the epoché leaves the existing world untouched, while "locking it up" for the purpose of the constitutive investigation. Thus, with no *Abbau* taking place, no *Wiederaufbau* of the existing world can possibly be needed.[43] But what about a *return*, then, in some way or other? Since the noematic correlate is all we have to go by as transcendental phenomenologists, the idea of actually "leaving" the object, or "backing away" from it, seems counterproductive. Indeed, *only by continuing to pay serious attention to the object can we say anything about transcendental subjectivity*. Therefore, no "return" to the world or the objects is needed either.

In contrast to Gadamer's claim, the actual relation between constitution and transcendental phenomenological reduction can be described as one between what we want to understand and the method by which we are able to understand what we want to understand. When we perform the reduction, we see the world (and everything mundane) as *constituted*, as the "result" of a process of manifestation (constitution) (*HuDo* II/1, p. 191). It is precisely the workings of this process of manifestation that we want to unveil in constitutive phenomenology, and in order to do so we must use the constituted as a guide for our *reduction* into the place of constitution. Constitution is therefore no "progressive" movement in contrast to, and as supplement to, the "regressive" movement of transcendental reduction, but rather constitution is that bringing-about of manifestation *that we explore by way of the reduction*. Thus, the reduction is not just *one* of the movements in transcendental

---

[42] In fact, this is what goes on in the so-called *genetic* phenomenology. Thus, in so far as one does not interpret the *Wiederaufbau* as the process of constitution itself, Gadamer's characterization has a certain legitimacy after all.

[43] But again, in his phenomenology of history, and in genetic phenomenology in general, Husserl does have a notion of deconstruction (*Abbau*) in play (cf., e.g., *EU*, p. 47), and thus also the idea of re-construction (cf. *EU*, p. 48). But this re-construction, at least generally, is of something that is already there, as a "finished" product, already constituted. Our "reconstruction" is therefore not the *constitution* of the object, but precisely a *reconstruction* of its genetic constitution.

phenomenology, it is *the* movement – on its shoulders *the universal research assignment* (*Forschungsaufgabe*) of Husserl's phenomenology is placed (cf. *Hua* VI, p. 177).[44]

6. CONSTITUTIVE PHENOMENOLOGY

So far, I have avoided the question of the philosophical status of Husserl's question of constitution. I have established that it is not a question to be answered by any of the sciences of the natural attitude, but no attempt has been made to place it in relation to the traditional questions of philosophy. Of course, nor have I begun to discuss the "contents" of Husserl's constitutive analyses, and I shall not turn my attention to this problematic until Chapter IV. At present, however, let me try to draw some preliminary conclusions regarding the philosophical status of the problem of constitutive phenomenology.

A great number of commentators insist that Husserl's constitutive phenomenology should be considered an *epistemological* project, in contrast to Heidegger's *ontological* project.[45] At times, that claim is substantiated by references to Husserl's explicit appliance of the concept of "ontology" to those eidetic sciences of the natural attitude that study either the essential characteristics of a region of objects ("regional" ontologies – cf. *Hua* III/1, p. 23), or what essentially holds for any object, regardless of region ("formal" ontology – cf., e.g., *Hua* III/1, pp. 26-27). Also, the later Husserl oftentimes speaks of an ontology of the "lifeworld" (*Hua* VI, p. 176), something not unlike what we attempt to develop in Chapter I of this study. Whereas these uses of the notion of "ontology" are perhaps the most common in Husserl's writings, I think it is possible to discern at least one other use – one that will compel us to revise to some extent the standard interpretation of Husserl's project as epistemological.

Husserl is on one important point critical towards the natural attitude, but to be sure not because it is wrong, or in need of "proof." As I argue above, the epoché by no means implies a criticism of any truths, or alleged truths, of the natural attitude, nor does it entail that that attitude is itself somehow "wrong." What Husserl seems to "hold against" the natural attitude lies elsewhere: it has to do with the *ontology* of that attitude being abstract, one-sided, or incomplete (*Hua* IX, p. 297; *Hua* VIII, p. 449). Its incompleteness stems from the circumstance, mentioned earlier, that in the naive natural attitude a transcendental subjectivity is nowhere to be found. Any naive-natural ontology – even formal ontology – is bound to be incomplete, or one-sided, in that it sees nothing but *objects*, although it itself presupposes something

---

[44] Maurice Natanson is therefore perfectly right in emphasizing that "when we speak of phenomenological reduction, we are pointing to philosophy itself rather than some limited technique" (*Edmund Husserl*, p. 75).

[45] See Richard Schacht, "Husserlian and Heideggerian Phenomenology," especially pp. 295, 304; Hubert Dreyfus, *Being-in-the-World*, p. 3. Jean-Luc Marion claims that according to Husserl, ontology simply is not phenomenology (*Reduction and Givenness*, pp. 40, 43, 46).

that is essentially not an object, viz. an experiencing subjectivity. In other words, there "is" something that (naive) natural ontology, whether regional or formal, cannot include, and that is transcendental subjectivity.

As explained above, Husserl maintains that it is only in the constitutive investigation, more precisely in the phenomenological reduction, that transcendental subjectivity can be unveiled as such. Therefore, it is only in and through the reduction, in and through transcendental phenomenological research, that ontology is made complete. Now, since transcendental phenomenology already encompasses all the natural ontologies on the side of that which must be explained, Husserl can say that in fact transcendental phenomenology is *itself* the most concrete and universal ontology (cf. *Hua* I, p. 181; *Hua* VIII, p. 215). Only transcendental phenomenology encompasses all there "is" – both on the side of the world and the mundane, and on the side of world-experiencing subjectivity – thus only it can lay claim to the title of *universal ontology* (*Hua* IX, pp. 251-252, 296-297).

This account, however, only establishes that Husserl's phenomenology ultimately acquires ontological importance; it does not show that the project of transcendental phenomenology is itself an ontological one. In view of our definition of constitutive phenomenology as dealing with the "how" of world-experience, it seems that this project must be conceived as fundamentally *epistemological*. That we must grant to Husserl an awareness of the ontological significance of transcendental phenomenology does not weaken the strong epistemological current in his project as such.

But Husserl is occasionally very sharp in his criticism of traditional (Cartesian) epistemology. Not just because he thinks that it has gone about solving the problem of world-experience in the wrong way, and not just because he thinks that it has been too occupied with "securing" the world and mundane entities, but rather because the very *question* that traditional epistemology raises is *nonsensical* (*widersinnig*) (*Hua* I, p. 116; LV, p. 231). Why does Husserl dismiss traditional epistemology so emphatically? According to Husserl, epistemology has traditionally proceeded by way of drawing attention to the fact that every existing object is known to me only through my experiences (*Hua* I, p. 115). Because these experiences are being interpreted as "immanent" to my consciousness, the problem of *transcendence* arises: "how can this business, going on wholly within the immanency of conscious life, acquire objective significance?" (cf. *Hua* I, p. 116)

One would expect Husserl to demonstrate the misguided nature of this question with reference to his analyses of the *intentionality* of consciousness. The notion of intentionality is one Husserl picks up from his teacher Franz Brentano, and develops in detail in *Logische Untersuchungen*. There, intentionality is defined as a characteristic quality of certain experiences, viz. that they relate themselves, in some way or other, to objects (*Hua* XIX/1, pp. 385, 391-392). For instance, in a perception something is perceived, and in a judgment, something is judged, as Husserl explains (*Hua* XIX/1, p. 380). Let us briefly remind ourselves how this "intentional relation" is to be understood, and how it is *not* to be interpreted. Perceptual intentionality, for example, is not to be interpreted as a relation that occurs when two entities – consciousness and object – are both present, as if this co-presence would give rise to a causal connection, or some other "bond" between the entities (*Hua* XIX/1, p. 389). Rather, intentionality essentially belongs to the perceptual experience itself; it is in the perceptual experience itself that we find the relation to an object (*Hua* XVI, p. 14). This does not mean that perceptual intentionality is a relation that is internal to consciousness, so that one could ask whether an "external" object in fact corresponds to the intentional object. Descriptively, we find no such "internal" object, Husserl claims, but rather only an "external" object (*Hua* XIX/1, pp. 386-387). The "intentional" object, the object intended, is none other than the "real," external object (unless we are the victims of some illusion, in which case there is no "real" object) (*Hua* XIX/1, p. 439). In other words, when I perceive, I am already perceptually "out there" with the external objects; there is no "island of the mind" if the mind is essentially such as to direct itself towards external objects. It is evident that this implies a critique of the traditional epistemological problem of "transcendence."

But in fact, Husserl does not refer to his theory of intentionality at this point. Instead he claims that it is the failure to perform the epoché and initiate the reduction that makes the whole problem absurd (*Hua* I, p. 116). That is to say, it is because traditional epistemology remains in the natural attitude that its question cannot be Husserl's question. Because traditional epistemology poses the question of world-experience from within the natural attitude, it is condemned to the absurdity of the transcendental circle (cf. *Hua* IX, p. 265). If we ask how one could escape the "island of the mind" in order to reach an "object" (*Hua* I, p. 116), surely we have posited two entities – mind and object – whereas the question of world-experience is so universal as to be also a question of how "minds" (one's own as well as those of others) and "physical objects" can manifest themselves in the first place. One might insist that the object precisely is *not* posited, but (at least initially) dismissed so that only the "mind" remains. But the word "remains" illustrates the problem with that objection: it is as if we start out with two entities, then remove one of them, and finally pose the question of how the remaining entity could reach another entity anew.[46] All of this takes place within the natural attitude, "subjectivity" is simply posited as the "little tag-end of the world" (*Endchen der Welt*) (*Hua* XVII, p. 235) that is left when all the other pieces have been cut off. The question of world-experience as such is also a question about the experience of that little end piece, but Cartesian epistemology poses it as if it pertains only to one kind of mundane entity (viz. material objects); hence the absurdity of this epistemology (*Hua* XVII, p. 260).

Let us take this criticism of traditional epistemology one step further. As should be abundantly clear by now, Husserl does not subscribe to the view that the existence of the world is "uncertain," or indeed something that it would be "wrong"

---

[46] Consequently, the later Husserl abandons the notion of "residue" that he uses in *Ideen I* to describe transcendental subjectivity (*Hua* VI, p. 81).

to believe in. Rather, the world and everything mundane is unquestionably there, according to Husserl. The addition that Husserl wants to add to this is that *we do not understand* how the world can be unquestionably there for us, and this understanding is what the phenomenology of constitution must supply. What status will such a phenomenological explanation have? Obviously, it cannot be Husserl's intention to build a bridge from one type of mundane entity to another, nor in fact can Husserl want to describe *any relation* between beings. This type of problem is still not radical enough, since for one to pose the question of a relation between beings, these beings must be given somehow beforehand – and it is precisely this *original* being-given that Husserlian phenomenology is interested in. Any epistemological theory that attempts to account for our way of "establishing" *contact* with the "external world" – whether it thereby posits a mundane "soul" or not – works with an external world that *is already there for us*, already somehow given, so that we could in fact pose the question how this tacitly presupposed *original* givenness comes about. This "original" givenness itself must not be viewed as a relation, since a relation presupposes two (or more) entities that are related (the *relata*), thus it only forces us to pose once again the question of how these entities are manifested in the first place. Clearly, one would face an infinite regress.

Some will probably object that Husserl himself posits the world and everything mundane, since the bracketed world is what he must use as a guiding clue (*Leitfaden*) in the constitutive investigation. While this is essentially correct, we must take care not to misjudge its implications. If the process of constitution is correctly interpreted as a relation between an experiencing consciousness and an experienced object, these two terms of the relation would be presupposed as existing beforehand. But Husserl – as he is presented in the present chapter – does *not posit anything* "beforehand," neither a "subject" nor an "object." What phenomenology needs to "posit" in order to get started is indeed the experienced world and mundane entities, but precisely *only insofar as they are manifested*, i.e., not as being there "beforehand," but only as involved in the process of manifestation. "Before" the original manifestation, or "behind" it, we have posited *nothing* (whether mundane entities, a world, or transcendental subjectivity), thus we have done nothing that would allow for the question of this manifestation to be interpreted as a question about a relation *between* what was thus presupposed. The world is posited as manifest and *only* insofar as it is manifest; and we are inquiring precisely into this manifestation.

Connected with this is Husserl's firm rejection of anything resembling a Kantian *Ding an sich*. Husserl rejects the idea of something "behind" the manifest entities and the manifest world, suggesting this is a completely empty gesture, or pure "mythology" (*Hua* VIII, p. 441). Husserl insists that what there is must be something that can experienced (*Hua* XV, p. 370). We are here touching upon one aspect of Husserl's infamous *idealism*.[47] According to Husserl, the idea of a world "outside" and "independent of," or "behind," this manifest world, while not exactly a piece of logical nonsense, is nevertheless a "factual" absurdity (*Hua* III/1, pp. 102-103; *Hua* I, pp. 32-33, 117). If words such as "world" and "reality" are to have any meaning for us, they must refer to *this* world, the manifest world in which we live and act, Husserl argues (cf., e.g., *Hua* VIII, p. 462; *Hua* VI, p. 258), and thus the suggestion that there might be "things" or a "world" beyond the manifest world, amounts to empty speculation or even nonsense.

To spell out a few implications of the discussion of Husserl's idealism, it might be advisable to briefly consider the debate about the proper interpretation of Husserl's notion of constitution. Some commentators claim that the best translation of Husserl's concept of constitution is "creation,"[48] whereas others insist on interpreting it as roughly equivalent to "restitution,"[49] or even "discovery." As to the first interpretation, Robert Sokolowski directs attention to the fact that Husserl's texts abound with uses of the verb "constitute" in the reflexive form,[50] and argues that "[s]uch an expression is not used for things which are totally caused by something else."[51] Obviously, "we do not say that a manufactured object constitutes itself,"[52] so when Husserl does say such things, it is natural to assume that he wants to indicate that in his phenomenology, constitution does not mean "creation" (cf. *Hua* XVII, p. 258). Besides, constitution is not basically a process in which I am active. The point is not that there is no such thing as active constitution – because there certainly is, according to Husserl – but that all such "active" constitution presupposes underlying *passive* constitution (*Hua* XXXI, p. 3; *Hua* IX, pp. 209-210). In other words, with regard to the most fundamental levels of constitution, it would be wrong to say that *I constitute*.[53] The notion of creation, however,

---

[47] Husserl's idealism is often severely criticized by commentators. But in fact, if one tries to place Husserl within the realism-antirealism discussion of contemporary so-called analytic philosophy, he turns out, on a number of important points, to be rather sympathetic towards the realist view. For instance, with regard to inaccessible regions of space and time, Husserl is – because of his theory of "horizon intentionality" – much closer to the realists than to the antirealists. Ultimately, however, Husserl does belong in the idealist camp if one understands by idealism "the position that what there is must be possibly conceivable by us, or possibly something for which we could have evidence" (Thomas Nagel, *The View from Nowhere*, p. 93).

[48] This seems to be the interpretation of Hans-Georg Gadamer in *Wahrheit und Methode*, p. 252. Similarly, Nam-In Lee, *Edmund Husserls Phänomenologie der Instinkte*, p. 237.

[49] Cf. Walter Biemel, "Die Entscheidenden Phasen der Entfaltung von Husserls Philosophie," p. 200.

[50] For a few places in the early Husserl where "constitute" appears in the reflexive form (*sich konstituieren*), see *Hua* II, pp. 12, 13, 71, 73, 75; *Hua* XVI, pp. 8, 20, 154, 284. For the later Husserl, cf. *Hua* I, pp. 97, 117, *et passim*.

[51] Robert Sokolowski, *The Formation of Husserl's Concept of Constitution*, p. 216.

[52] Ibid.

[53] Thus, Gethmann's analyses of the relation between Husserl and Heidegger are misleading, since the former is constantly accentuated as the one claiming that subjectivity is what constitu*es* (cf. *Verstehen und Auslegung*, pp. 123, 126, and *Dasein: Erkennen und Handeln*, pp. 26, 32). Hubert Dreyfus goes as far as to claim that Husserl attempts to "ground all forms of intentionality in the meaning-giving activity of a detached transcendental subject" (*Being-in-the-World*, p. 141).

undoubtedly carries with it the connotation of an activity, so in this regard, it is also entirely unsuitable to translate Husserl's concept of constitution. But does constitution, then, simply mean "restitution" or "discovery"? This would hardly be compatible with the argument leveled against Cartesian epistemology above. It makes no sense, according to Husserl, to say that constitution is the process that "restitutes" for us an object that *an sich* was there to begin with – rather, constitution is that which originally realizes manifestation; without this manifestation, we could not say that anything "exists."

It has been persuasively argued that the two alternatives of "creation" and "restitution" are in fact false alternatives in that they share a fateful presupposition.[54] Both interpretations are committed to a type of realism that – although appropriate in the natural attitude – cannot be accommodated within Husserl's transcendental attitude. That the "restitution" view is perfectly compatible with realism is obvious, but interpreting constitution as creation seems on the other hand to entail a clear-cut subjective idealism. But as Husserl points out, the notion of "creation," or "making," (*Erzeugen*) is one that normally refers to activities of manufacturing within the mundane sphere (*Hua* XVII, p. 175). Now, on one or two counts – as we have seen – it is indeed too much of a subjective idealism to identify constitution with something like this mundane concept of creation, yet on another count it is not "idealistic" enough. First, "creation" in the mundane sense is never *ex nihilo*, i.e., something new is always created out of something already present. This idea of something "already there" before the process of constitution was rejected above. An even more troubling aspect of the concept of "creation" – because this applies to creation *ex nihilo* as well – is that it carries with it the idea of the created entity being "set free" once the process of making it is completed. That is to say, the concept of creation seems to be accompanied by a commitment to the idea of a reality existing strictly *an sich*. As we have already seen, Husserl ties the notion of reality closely together with the notion of manifestation. The idea of a "world" outside the manifest world is unambiguously rejected, and thus Husserl must also reject the idea that the process of constitution could be one of "making" objects and a world that would subsequently simply exist, whether or not any kind of manifestation of them would be possible at all. If the objects escape the manifest world – according to Husserl – they escape the *only* (meaningful) world, i.e., they no longer "exist." Therefore, the strong notion of existence *an sich* associated with the natural concept of "creation" can have no place in Husserl's phenomenology of constitution. Both "restitution" and "creation", then, must be dismissed, and on grounds that are basically identical. In Rudolf Boehm's words:

These two [...] interpretations of the problem of constitution seem to be opposite extremes. Yet they have a presupposition in common. In both cases, an objective reality, existing in itself, is presupposed, and it is

---

[54] Cf. Rudolf Boehm, *Vom Gesichtspunkt der Phänomenologie*, pp. xvi-xvii; and "Zur Phänomenologie der Gemeinschaft," p. 92. Similarly, Dan Zahavi, *Husserl und die transzendentale Intersubjektivität*, p. 89; and *Husserl's Phenomenology*, pp. 72-74.

with regard to such a reality that they ask whether, according to Husserl, consciousness uncovers the reality, or simply creates it in the first place.[55]

As Eugen Fink argues, Husserl's notion of constitution simply cannot be rendered adequately by *any* "mundane" concepts, including those of "restitution" and "creation."[56] Fink's interpretation is instructive not just because it warns us about using mundane concepts to describe constitution, but also because Fink attempts to say something *positive* about that important notion. Constitution, he tells us, must be seen as *productive* in nature, rather than simply receptive, i.e., it would after all be "better" (but still inadequately) translated as "creation" than as "restitution."[57] This cannot be surprising, given our discussion in the present section. We have stressed already that according to Husserl, one cannot say that "things" or "the world" exist prior to, or independently of the process of constitution. Rather, *constitution is the process of manifestation that brings entities and world into "being" for us* – the process without which none of this would "be there" for us. Constitution does not make new entities from old entities, nor does it *create* entities *ex nihilo*. Rather, it is the process that realizes their being-there-for-us, and since Husserl does not recognize any objective or mundane being-there except that of being-there-*for*-subjectivity, it is the process that realizes *being*. Now, insofar as the task of transcendental phenomenology is to *understand* world-experience, or world-constitution, Husserl is perfectly right to conclude that phenomenology must strive to deliver "an incomparably novel and unsurpassably comprehensible *understanding* of what the real being of the world, and real being as such, *means*" (*Hua* VIII, pp. 481-482).

An important addition that is indicated by this quotation is that constitution not only realizes *mundane* being, as if it would have no relevance for, or leaves out, the being of transcendental subjectivity. Although Husserl is of the opinion that transcendental subjectivity is something that has never been "born" and cannot die (*Hua* XI, pp. 378-381), he at times clearly recognizes that transcendental subjectivity *needs* something constituted in order to exist itself (at least in any concrete sense) (*Hua* XIV, pp. 244, 379). In view of the way transcendental

---

[55] Boehm, "Zur Phänomenologie der Gemeinschaft," p. 92.

[56] See Fink, "Die phänomenologische Philosophie Edmund Husserls in der gegenwärtigen Kritik," in *Studien zur Phänomenologie 1930-1939*. The reference is to p. 143 in that volume. Cf. Fink, *Nähe und Distanz*, p. 201.

[57] Fink, *Studien zur Phänomenologie 1930-1939*, p. 143. It is worth noting that Fink's text "Die phänomenologische Philosophie Edmund Husserls in der gegenwärtigen Kritik" originally appeared (in an issue of *Kantstudien*) with a preface written by Husserl, in which the latter declares that there is no sentence in the text that goes against his own sincere conviction (cf. *Studien zur Phänomenologie 1930-1939*, p. viii). Ronald Bruzina attempts to show that Husserl is not quite right in that assessment (see Bruzina's thorough "Translator's Introduction" to Fink's *Sixth Cartesian Meditation*), but I think he does not succeed. I find it surprising that Bruzina can declare his basic agreement (despite his preference for a less sharp formulation) with Van Breda's claim that the article in *Kantstudien* is an attack on the very foundations of Husserl's thought (cf. "Translator's Introduction," p. lxxxiii, n. 119). My argument in the present chapter follows Fink's reasoning fairly closely at the same time that it contains many references to Husserl; thus it constitutes, in a sense, an attempted refutation of Bruzina's claim.

subjectivity is defined in the present chapter, this must be so. Transcendental subjectivity, we recall, is nothing but the "human" subjectivity, only viewed exclusively as a world-experiencing subjectivity, as the "place" of the manifestation of the world. If no thing and no world is manifest, how can there be a "place" of its manifestation – except in the most empty of senses?

To return to the question posed in the beginning of this section, what is the philosophical status of Husserl's question of constitution? I argue that the problematic of constitution is not identical with the problem of "transcendence," which is traditionally dealt with in epistemology. Constitution cannot be viewed as a "relation" between two *relata* called "subjectivity" and "world," since that interpretation only forces one to pose the question of constitution again. This is the case at least as long as one does not want to take the – according to Husserl – "factually" absurd route of positing entities beyond the reach of manifestation. On pains of basically the same absurdity, one also would have to refrain from identifying the notion of constitution with "creation" or "restitution." Constitution, I conclude, should rather be seen as the process that realizes *being*. Thus, what appears as a clear-cut example of an epistemological problematic in fact turns out to be essentially *ontological*: *what Husserl's phenomenology eventually wants is to understand the being of the world*, or not just that, but rather *being as such*.

Taking the argument of this entire chapter into account, it must be concluded that as a philosophy that wants to ask the fundamental question of constitution, Husserl's transcendental phenomenology in fact poses a *question of being*.[58] Contrary to the claims of some commentators,[59] questions of being are not ignored in Husserl's phenomenology, nor are they ruled out by the methods of epoché and reduction (*Hua* VIII, p. 479). Instead, Husserl is doing little more than asking about being, albeit in a particular sense that should not immediately be identified with Heidegger's question of being.[60] The outcome of this chapter, then, may be illustrated in the following way. At one point in *Sein und Zeit*, Heidegger rhetorically asks if the question of being is a case of free-floating speculation about empty generalities, or if it isn't, rather, "*of all questions, both the most basic and the most concrete?*" (*SZ*, p. 9) Husserl answers: "Yes, as a transcendental-phenomenological question about the constitutive meaning of being [*Seinssinn*]" (RB, p. 12).

---

[58] This is not as original a claim as some might think. Heidegger already interprets Husserl thus (cf. *GA* 20, pp. 136, 157), and Fink consistently claims that Husserlian phenomenology is in fact only interested in the being of the world (cf. *Studien zur Phänomenologie 1930-1939*, pp. 119, 189). Similarly, Rudolf Boehm, "Zijn en tijd in de filosofie van Husserl." Levinas even goes as far as to declare that the problem of constitution is ontological in Heidegger's sense (*The Theory of Intuition in Husserl's Phenomenology*, pp. lvi, 124, 154). A similar view is defended by Timothy Stapleton in his book, *Husserl and Heidegger* (see pp. 88, 115, 117).

[59] See, e.g., James C. Morrison, "Husserl and Heidegger: The Parting of the Ways"; Jacques Taminiaux, "From One Idea of Phenomenology to the Other," p. 36; and Jean-Luc Marion, *Reduction and Givenness*, p. 43.

[60] Indeed, Husserl dismisses the Heideggerian concept of being as "mythical" (RB, p. 59).

CHAPTER III
THE QUESTION OF BEING

1. THE NEED FOR THE QUESTION OF BEING

As seen in the last section of Chapter II, Husserl rejects as absurd the question of transcendence posed by traditional Cartesian epistemology. By "question of transcendence," Husserl means the question regarding the possibility of "escaping" the immanent sphere of consciousness in order to reach an external object (cf. *Hua* I, p. 116). Instead of this question, Husserl poses that of "constitution," which he identifies with the problem of how entities can manifest themselves, i.e., *be* there, for transcendental subjectivity.

In a similar manner, Heidegger wants to dismiss the question of traditional epistemology. He dubs it the problem of the "subject-object-relation" (as we see shortly, he wants a quite different problematic to bear the name "problem of transcendence"), and insists that it disappears if one grasps the Husserlian concept of intentionality properly (*GA* 26, p. 168). One cannot ask the question of how to escape the confines of immanence and establish contact with a "transcendent," external object, once one realizes that consciousness is essentially *intentional*. If intentionality is an essential feature of consciousness, this means that insofar as consciousness *is*, it is already "out there" with the so-called external objects. But, as Heidegger is quick to point out, intentionality itself becomes a problem, then, since we are entitled to ask how this essential relatedness to entities itself comes about (*GA* 26, p. 168). In other words, the problem of the "subject-object-relation" is simply exchanged for the problem of intentionality.

Postponing until Chapter VI an examination of whether this problem of "intentionality" is identical with Husserl's problem of constitution (as presented in Chapter II), I now follow Heidegger's argument explaining why the problem of intentionality, in turn, must be replaced by the question of *being*, and by the problem of "transcendence" in a new sense.

Heidegger grants that the human being is described in one of its essential features by the notion of "intentionality" (*GA* 19, p. 424; *GA* 24, pp. 90, 224). From Heidegger's perspective, one of Husserl's crucial contributions to philosophy resides precisely in the way the latter develops this notion borrowed from Brentano (who found it in medieval Scholasticism) (*GA* 17, pp. 260-261). Although the *word* "intentionality" seems banned from *Sein und Zeit*, one should not think that Heidegger considers the notion itself inappropriate, or even misleading. What Heidegger ultimately wants to point out regarding intentionality is simply that it is *less fundamental* than Husserl thinks. In other words, while Husserl and Heidegger can agree that "intentionality" is the title of a problem rather than any solution,[1] Heidegger wants to add that it is not the title of the *fundamental* philosophical problem (cf. *GA* 26, p. 170).

According to Husserl, there are a great many different intentional relations. I can "intend" the same object – the blooming apple tree, for example – in a number of different ways: I can make judgments about it, silently wish that it was cut down, remember it, perceive it, and so forth (cf., e.g., *Hua* XIX/1, pp. 426-427). And even the perception of the apple tree can take different forms, depending on the "way" I perceive it, my current "interests" in it (purely esthetic, scientific, etc.), and the like. If we stay with the example of perceptual intentionality, one of Husserl's important insights is that different types of objects demand to be perceived in different ways. Every perception, Husserl says, is just "fitted" (*angepasst*) to the object it is a perception of (*Hua* XV, p. 417; cf. *Hua* XVII, p. 169). Obviously, I not only see such things as rocks or trees, I also see other persons, and perhaps I "see" solutions to mathematical problems. All of these acts of "perception," in Husserl's wide sense of the word, cannot have the same structure, since they are perceptions of crucially different types of things. Perceptual intentionality is not simply to be identified with "sense-perception" (whatever that actually means), nor is it – more generally – correctly described as an empty, indifferent "having," that simply relates to every type of object in an identical manner, according to Husserl (*Hua* IX, pp. 238, 280; *Hua* II, pp. 74-75). On the contrary, "*every kind of object has its own mode of self-giving, i.e., self-evidence*" (*EU*, § 4, p. 12).

That we humans are able to perceive both apple trees and other humans is evident. Following Husserl, we must say that this means that our perceptions are "fitted to" these two kinds of objects, that is, that they heed to how each type of object (tree, person) "demands" to be perceived. In the 1927 lecture course *Die Grundprobleme der Phänomenologie*, Heidegger tries to introduce the problematic of being precisely in reference to this:

What is it that belongs to an uncovering of a being, in our case the perceptual uncovering of a present-at-hand entity [*Vorhandenem*]? The mode of uncovering and the mode of uncoveredness of the present-at-hand obviously must be determined by the entity to be uncovered by them and by its way of being. I cannot perceive geometrical relations in the sense of natural sense perception. But how is the mode of uncovering to be, as it were, regulated and prescribed by the entity to be uncovered and its mode of being, unless the entity is itself uncovered beforehand so that the mode of apprehension can direct itself toward it? On the other hand, this uncovering in its turn is supposed to adapt itself to the entity that is to be uncovered. The mode of the possible uncoverability of the present-at-hand in perception must already be prescribed in the perceiving itself; that is, the perceptual uncovering of the present-at-hand must already understand beforehand something like presence-at-hand. In the intention of the perceiving something like an *understanding of presence-at-hand* must already be antecedently present. (*GA* 24, p. 99)

Let me attempt to unpack this compact argument. The first part of the quotation faithfully follows Husserl's insight, viz. that the perception must adjust itself to the

---

[1] *Hua* III/1, p. 337; *Hua* VI, p. 85. See, too, Heidegger's famous preface to Husserl's *Vorlesungen zur Phänomenologie des inneren Zeitbewußtseins* (*Hua* X, p. xxv).

type of entity it is to be a perception of. But, Heidegger asks, how is the perception able to do that – how can it heed to the way an entity must be perceived? An answer that immediately comes to mind is that the type of entity in question must have been perceived before; since the entity is thus known already, it is possible to approach it in the right way. But, as Heidegger points out, this "earlier" perception would have been in similar need of fitting itself to the kind of entity it was to be a perception of. Thus, if one explains the possibility of perception by reference to another perception, an infinite regress seems the inevitable result. Against this type of account, Heidegger claims that a certain preceding *understanding* is the only thing that can render intelligible the possibility of perception. More precisely, one needs to understand *as what* (*als was*) one must perceptually approach an entity, if one is to be able to perceive the entity (*GA 21*, p. 146).

But what does it mean to understand "as what" an entity must be addressed or approached? As explained, it cannot mean that one must already have had some kind of perceptual encounter with the entity, because it is precisely the *as-what*-understanding that first enables one to perceptually approach the entity, so to speak. But perception, we remember, is only one type of intentional relation to entities. Could it not be that some other type of relation – say, some kind of non-perceptual "involvement" or "coping" – makes possible the *perceptual* type of approach to entities? This is certainly the way some commentators understand Heidegger.[2] But in fact, the same problem returns, according to Heidegger, for in order to be able to "cope" with an entity, one must already have understood the entity *as* something-with-which-to-cope in this or that way (cf. *SZ*, p. 85; *GA 27*, pp. 192-193). In other words, when we want to understand how perception can direct itself to different types of objects, it is not specifically the reference to previous *perceptions* that threatens with an infinite regress, but rather the *reference to any relation to entities*. Our knowledge of "as what" to address an entity cannot stem from any kind of previous encounter with an entity of the type, since that account forces us to pose the question of how *that* encounter was possible, and so forth. There must be something that makes encounters with entities possible, something *that is not itself an encounter with an entity*.[3] Yet, obviously, that something can hardly be "unrelated" to the entity, but must precisely be an understanding of an "as what," an understanding of how this entity demands to be approached.

Let me elaborate on this. For example, an apple tree – as what does it demand to be understood? As an apple tree, of course, i.e., *as what it is*. Just as with Husserl, we must not be scared off by the apparent platitudes (*GA 24*, p. 79). An apple tree,

---

[2] Cf. Hubert Dreyfus, *Being-in-the-World*, especially p. 107.
[3] It seems to me that this is where Hubert Dreyfus' pragmatist reading of Heidegger is the most problematic. Basically, Dreyfus never reaches the level of Heidegger's phenomenological-ontological project. Downplaying Heidegger's "ontological difference" (which, it must be admitted, is absent from *Sein und Zeit* itself; cf. the last section of the present chapter), Dreyfus identifies "understanding of being" with a certain non-thematic relation to entities, called "background coping" (*Being-in-the-World*, p. 107). More on this in Chapter VI.

as explained, demands a certain kind of perception, which is different from that of, say, a person. How can my perception direct itself in such a way as to satisfy that demand? No previous encounters with apple trees can help us here, since such encounters would force the same problem upon us once again. Instead, I must already understand "as what" (*als was*) to "take," to approach this entity, this apple tree. Obviously, it cannot be that I should approach the apple tree as something other than what it is – that would precisely make impossible my perception of the apple tree as an apple tree, that is, as something different from, for example, people or mathematical equations. Rather, understanding "as what" a certain entity such as an apple tree must be addressed is understanding "as what" that entity *is*, i.e., which *mode of being* the entity has. Accordingly, Heidegger concludes: "An entity can be uncovered, whether by way of perception or some other mode of access, only if the being of this entity is already disclosed – only if I already understand it" (*GA* 24, p. 102).

Before we flesh out the notion of "mode of being" (*Seinsart*) with some concrete examples, Heidegger's argument is bound to seem somewhat obscure. But for the moment we have to live with that obscurity, since it is by no means clear how one could set about bringing something like a "mode of being" into view. Despite the obscurities, in a quite formal way we understand that an "understanding of being" (*Seinsverständnis*) must essentially belong to the human being, insofar as intentionality is an essential feature of that being. According to Heidegger, relating intentionally to an entity is only possible on the basis of an understanding of the (mode of) being of that entity.

It appears, then, that a simple consideration of the problem of intentionality forces us to pose new questions. The notions of *being* and *understanding of being*, closely connected as they are, make inevitable two similarly closely connected questions, viz. that of the possibility of understanding of being, and that of the modes of being of entities, or of the "meaning" of being as such.

As to the first, Heidegger is quite clear that just as intentionality is no final solution – as if all one needs to do to make every problem vanish is to point out to those discussing the "subject-object-relation" that the subject is essentially intentional – neither is "understanding of being." On the contrary, we obviously need to inquire into how that understanding of being is itself possible (*GA* 24, p. 106). Because the human being has an understanding of being, one can say that the human being "transcends" all entities, all beings – it goes "beyond" them to their "modes of being" (*GA* 27, pp. 206-207). Accordingly, Heidegger identifies understanding of being with "original transcendence" (*Urtranszendenz*, or *ursprüngliche Transzendenz*) (*GA* 26, pp. 20, 170), or simply with "transcendence" (*KPM*, p. 123). The problem of the possibility of understanding of being may then be labeled the *problem of transcendence* (*GA* 26, p. 170). As should be perfectly clear, this is a completely different problem from the one Husserl labels the problem of transcendence (and vigorously rejects). Heidegger does not talk of transcendence in the sense that some "consciousness," initially closed in upon itself, becomes able to "transcend" its borders and reach out into an "external" reality (cf. *GA* 26, p.

212). In fact, "transcendence" in Heidegger's sense is not the transcendence to *any entity*, but rather – as already pointed out – the transcending *of all entities*, the "moving beyond" the entities to their being. Accordingly, one could very well call this a question of being (*Sein*), but for the sake of univocality let us for now retain the name "question of transcendence."

The second question that arises, once we demonstrate that something like an understanding of "being" essentially belongs to the human being, is the question what "modes of being" we find that we understand, i.e., what manners of being "there are," and further, what "being" as such is supposed to mean.[4] This cluster of problems Heidegger refers to as the "question of being" (*die Seinsfrage*) (*SZ*, p. 4), or the "question of the meaning of being" (*die Frage nach dem Sinn von Sein*) (*SZ*, p. 1). This question – according to Heidegger one that has remained un-asked since the times of Plato and Aristotle (*SZ*, p. 2) – is apparently the ultimate, guiding question of Heidegger's phenomenology.

Let me anticipate a possible objection to this discernment. It is claimed, and not unconvincingly so, that in fact the question of "the meaning of being" is none other than the issue above labeled the question of "transcendence," viz. the question of the possibility of *understanding* of being.[5] The argument apparently finds support in Heidegger's definition of "meaning" (*Sinn*) in *Sein und Zeit*: "Meaning is that wherein the intelligibility [*Verständlichkeit*] of something maintains itself" (*SZ*, p. 151). Meaning is that in which the understandability of something "keeps itself" or resides – what does this mean, when applied to the question of the "meaning" of being? The "meaning of being" must be that in which the understandability of being resides – and that, surely, must be the *understanding of being* that essentially belongs to the human being, i.e., to Dasein. We may therefore conclude that "[t]o ask about the meaning of Being is [...] to ask about how Being becomes understandable; it is to ask about Dasein's understanding of Being."[6] In other words, there are not two questions here, but rather only one: the question about the meaning of being.

Instead of attempting to unpack Heidegger's exceedingly difficult definition of *Sinn*, I shall try to counter this objection by pointing out a passage in which Heidegger appears to me to clearly recognize the presence of *two* important questions, rather than one. But first of all, let me acknowledge that there is a partial truth in the objection under consideration. To ask about the meaning of being *is*, in an important sense, to ask about Dasein's understanding of being – since it is

---

[4] I do not think one should take this to mean that Heidegger's question concerns the meaning of the word "is," as Ernst Tugendhat does. His argument that Heidegger's question of being is meaningless is based entirely upon that interpretation (cf. "Heideggers Seinsfrage"), but I think what Heidegger is really asking is whether all entities "exist" in the same way, or whether, e.g., humans and rocks have quite different *manners* of "existing" (as opposed to different "properties," or "attributes," etc.). See Chapter VI.
[5] See John Sallis, *Delimitations*, pp. 91-92. Sallis's argument goes in a slightly different, but still similar direction in *Echoes*, p. 99.
[6] Sallis, *Delimitations*, p. 91.

precisely Dasein's understanding that must guide us in our inquiry into the meaning of being. As phenomenologists, we are not supposed to be "profound" and speculative, but rather to inquire into being only "insofar as it enters into the intelligibility of Dasein" (*SZ*, p. 152).[7] This does not mean, however, that to ask about the meaning of being is to ask about "how being becomes understandable." To pose the question of the meaning of being is quite simply to ask *what* we are to understand by "being," what being means (cf. *GA* 26, p. 171), what manners of being are disclosed to us, and this is hardly identical with the question of *how* an understanding of such manners of being (whatever "being" might mean) is possible. It seems, on the contrary, to be only on the basis of some kind of preliminary analysis of *what* being *means* – an answer to a "what" question, one could say in a not quite apt terminology – that one could proceed to ask how an understanding of something like the analyzed could be possible – a "how" question, to put this in a manner that should be taken with similar caution. In fact, as I hope to show in the course of this study, if Heidegger *would* claim that these two questions are actually only the one question of how being can be understood, he would be closer to Husserl than anyone has ever dared to suggest, and he would lose one of his most weighty arguments against his phenomenological mentor. But I think Heidegger is clear that, however closely related, the problem of being and that of transcendence are not identical: "The problem of being, however, is the basic problem of philosophy as such, and closely connected to it is the guiding problem of transcendence" (*GA* 26, p. 187).[8]

The discussion in the present section shows that there is a need to pose the questions of "transcendence" and of *being*, at least once we adopt Husserl's theory of intentionality. Heidegger does adopt the notion of intentionality – contrary to what a superficial reading of *Sein und Zeit* would lead one to think – only, he insists that the notion of intentionality is not a fundamental one. Intentionality, being an "ontic" relation, a relation to entities, can only be made intelligible by reference to a "relation" that is *not* ontic, but rather "ontological," i.e., a "relation" to *being*. This "relation," this understanding of being, must itself be questioned, along two closely connected lines.

2. PHENOMENOLOGY

Having established the need for a question of being (and of the understanding of being), the next logical step is to ask how such a question should be posed, and perhaps answered in due course. In the early Freiburg lectures, and throughout the

---

[7] Cf. the section on "fundamental ontology" below.
[8] In a similar vein, Walter Biemel, and, following him, David Farrell Krell claim that Heidegger's thinking has a "double leitmotif," viz. that of the "question of being" and the "question of truth" (Biemel, *Martin Heidegger*, p. 35; Krell, *Intimations of Mortality*, p. 77). See *SZ*, p. 154. In his critical commentary on Heidegger's philosophy, *Heidegger's Philosophy of Being*, Herman Philipse distinguishes no less than five "leitmotifs" in the question of being.

Marburg period (with the possible exception of the last lecture course), Heidegger is clear that we must proceed along *phenomenological* lines. To give a first hint as to what phenomenology is, Heidegger refers to Husserl's maxim, "To the things themselves" (*SZ*, p. 27; cf. *Hua* XIX/1, p. 10). There is hardly anything in Husserl's phenomenology that Heidegger is as happy with as this "slogan"; it is referred to again and again in the early lecture courses that profess to be phenomenological. One would naturally presume that the reason why Heidegger is eager to adopt the maxim of "Back to the things themselves" is that it is sufficiently empty to leave room for a phenomenology quite different from the one Husserl has developed. In accordance with this interpretation, it must be noted that while Heidegger seems to be faithful to the phenomenology of his mentor insofar as the *slogan* of phenomenology is concerned,[9] he is also emphatic that the essential thing about phenomenology "does not lie in its *actuality* as a philosophical 'movement'" (*SZ*, p. 38). On the contrary, "[w]e can understand phenomenology only by seizing upon it as a possibility" (*SZ*, p. 38). One should therefore not be surprised if Heidegger's notion of phenomenology turns out to be fundamentally different from the actual (*wirklich*), existing Husserlian phenomenology.[10]

According to Heidegger, the notion of phenomenology designates a *method* rather than any sort of thematic field – it describes the "how" rather than the "what" of an investigation (*SZ*, p. 27). The term "phenomenon," Heidegger explains, derives from the Greek word *phainomenon*, which roughly means "that which manifests itself" (*SZ*, p. 28). *Logos*, on the other hand, means "speech," but in the absence of any adequate analysis of what "speech" itself is supposed to mean, this translation can make us little wiser, according to Heidegger (*SZ*, p. 32). We need to understand that what *logos* fundamentally designates is the "making something manifest," or letting something be seen, viz. making manifest that which is spoken about (*SZ*, p. 32). With these two etymological points in hand,[11] we can develop a formal notion of the method (the "how") we call phenomenology. Phenomenology must "let that which shows itself be seen from itself [*von ihm selbst her*] in the very way in which it shows itself from itself" (*SZ*, p. 34). Since phenomenology is silent regarding the "what" of the investigation, its task can be described as letting that which manifests

---

[9] Eventually, however, Heidegger even rejects this maxim. In a sketchy text from the fifties or sixties, Heidegger claims that the principle of "Back to the things themselves" is "no essential [*prinzipielles*] principle; no primordial principle – neither historically, nor systematically [*sachlich*]" ("Über das Prinzip 'Zu den Sachen selbst,'" p. 5). Apparently, the trouble is that the principle entails that *consciousness* is the "thing itself" (ibid.; cf. *ZSD*, pp. 68-70), but it remains quite dubious how, and even *if*, this is so. In fact, it seems to me that the early Heidegger himself, as well as Husserl, have gone back to "things themselves" different from that of "consciousness."
[10] See Heidegger's careful remarks in "Edmund Husserl zum siebenzigsten Geburtstag." Dermot Moran even claims that "[p]henomenology, for Heidegger, stems from Aristotle not Husserl" (*Introduction to Phenomenology*, p. 228). In the course of this chapter, we see that this claim is too strong.
[11] Of course, regardless of whether or not Heidegger's etymologies are "largely fake" (Richard Rorty, *Contingency, Irony, and Solidarity*, p. 131), the formal definition of phenomenology may capture adequately at least part of what phenomenology is about, as I think it in fact does.

itself – whatever that might be – be seen "in person" just the way it manifests itself "in person." Consequently, it is justified to label any description of beings "phenomenology," insofar as it describes those beings strictly the way they manifest themselves in person (*SZ*, p. 35).

This *formal* notion of phenomenology, however, must be given a more specific direction. A procedure to let what manifests itself be seen in person precisely as it manifests itself – where would something like this be of most use? Obviously, Heidegger says, phenomenology would be most called for with regard to something

> that proximally and for the most part does *not* show itself at all: something that lies *hidden*, in contrast to that which proximally and for the most part does show itself; but at the same time something that belongs to what thus shows itself, and it belongs to it so essentially as to constitute its meaning and its ground. (*SZ*, p. 35)

We demonstrate above the necessity of the question of being. How does that problematic square with Heidegger's attempt to give concrete direction for the method of phenomenology? As explained in Chapter I, examples of things that "immediately" and "mostly" manifests themselves are such things as objects for use, and other persons. In other words, "entities" or beings of various sorts are immediately manifest. And what about "being"? Being is not mostly, or immediately manifest – "[w]e do not simply find it in front of us" (*GA* 24, p. 29) – but it does have a close relation to that which is. For entities to manifest themselves, it is necessary that we have something like an understanding of their "being," as we have just seen. "Being," that which is understood in the understanding of being, therefore in a sense belongs to the entities as the "foundation" or "ground" (*Grund*) for them, insofar as they are manifest. It is not only the case, then, that the question of *being* demands something like a phenomenological method to pave the way to those peculiar "things themselves"; the very definition of *phenomenology* also points to the question of being. The problematic of being – what Heidegger calls the "ontological" problematic, in contrast to the "ontic" problems dealing with being*s*, with entities – and the method of phenomenology refer to each other. They form the twin faces of philosophy, one naming the thematic "object" of philosophy, the other its "method" (*SZ*, p. 38). *Phenomenology is exclusively the method of ontology* (*WM*, pp. 66-67), and *ontology is the science of being that can only be* (scientifically) *carried out as phenomenology* (cf. *GA* 24, pp. 3, 466).

There is thus no contradiction in Heidegger's declaration, on the one hand, that phenomenology is silent regarding the "what" of an investigation, and on the other hand, his claim that being is the phenomenon *par excellence* – contrary to the views of some commentators.[12] Entities of the various sorts are *already* manifest "in person," thus in no particular need of being *made* manifest in or through phenomenology. This, it must be emphasized, does not entail that everything about those entities is perfectly lucid; on the contrary, there is something fundamentally obscure about them, viz. "as what" they are, their modes of being. This obscurity,

---

[12] Frederick Elliston, "Phenomenology Reinterpreted," p. 278.

more than anything else, calls for phenomenological illumination – and thus the notion of phenomenology, formally unattached to any specific type of research, gets wedded to that of ontology.

Phenomenology in this specific sense is the procedure to open and secure access to the *being* of entities; it is the method by which we are able to "see" being in person as it manifests itself in person. Just as Husserl's methods of epoché and reduction are developed to fit the leading problem of constitution, rather than simply forced upon that problematic from the outside (cf. *Hua* III/1, p. 161), so Heidegger wants his phenomenological method to take shape in a confrontation with the matter to be investigated (*GA* 17, p. 45). How are we able to thematize something like being?

3. HUSSERL'S EPOCHÉ

In Chapter I we see how Heidegger, on the one hand, acknowledges that a lifeworldly object, such as a chair, from the viewpoint of everyday Dasein, seems to be something that can be described aptly as a multi-layered thing, while, on the other hand, he also insists that such a description is in fact a distortion. It seems obvious that Heidegger, while describing the everyday Dasein, has to occupy a position *outside* everydayness. What Heidegger wants to thematize, viz. "modes of being," can simply not be brought into view as long as we are submerged in everydayness. Therefore, asking the question about being can hardly be a simple matter.

Some argue that Husserl's epoché is useless to Heidegger, precisely because the latter wants to pose the question of being. As Herbert Spiegelberg formulates the point, "the reduction [or rather, the epoché] consists primarily in suspending, at least temporarily, the question of whether any given phenomenon has being."[13] For the early Heidegger intent on investigating being, the epoché would then obviously be counterproductive, since "it would seem rather strange to approach such a problem by first looking away from it."[14] It is undeniable that Heidegger, at times, expresses views about the epoché and reduction that seem to support Spiegelberg's description of the epoché (or reduction) as primarily "negative," and thus ill-suited to the question of being. In line with some of Husserl's more unfortunate formulations, Heidegger thus characterizes the reduction as a procedure of *Ausschaltung* (*GA* 17, p. 258), and in perfect consensus with Spiegelberg, Heidegger can consequently declare that "[i]n its methodological sense as a disregarding [*Absehen-von*], […] the reduction is in principle inappropriate for determining the being of consciousness positively" (*GA* 20, p. 150). In view of the discussion of the epoché in the last chapter, however, it would seem that Spiegelberg and Heidegger misrepresent Husserl's epoché (or reduction). Neither the reduction, nor the epoché entail looking away from anything, in fact quite the opposite. Although the epoché may be said to

---

[13] Spiegelberg, *The Phenomenological Movement*, Volume I, p. 299.
[14] Ibid. Cf. Bernard Boelen, "Martin Heidegger as a Phenomenologist," p. 100.

"bracket" the being of entities, at the same time it *has to* keep all of this in view, as explained above. Indeed, in complete opposition to Spiegelberg's view of the matter, one can argue that *without the epoché, Heidegger's investigation into being could not possibly be carried out*. In the present section, I shall attempt to substantiate this controversial claim.

In Chapter II, we point out a positive aspect of the procedure of "bracketing." We bring the noematic correlate into view only in and through the epoché, because only when the "natural" knowledge of the encountered objects is bracketed do the *experienced just as experienced* surface undistorted. With the epoché, the descriptions that are supplied by everyday Dasein are not ones we are allowed to employ directly, and as a result we are able to gain a slightly different view of the entities we encounter. My claim is that this "slightly different" view is precisely what Heidegger needs if something like "modes of being" is to surface. If we are to be able to thematize being, the distorting interpretation of everydayness must not exactly be ignored – in fact that would be a fateful mistake – but rather "locked up" so that we can not appeal directly to it. Only in and through the epoché can we view entities precisely the way they manifest themselves, i.e., only then can we see clearly "as what" they actually manifest themselves. In other words, the epoché being the entrance gate to what Husserl calls the noematic correlate, it is in fact also the entrance gate to a possible thematization of the "as what" of entities, that is, of their *mode of being*. If this is the correct way to depict the matter, then Heidegger, in order to get his ontological investigation started, must accept something like the Husserlian epoché, as well as Husserl's notion of the experienced-just-as-experienced.

Of course, Heidegger is committed to Husserl's epoché only insofar as it is in and through the epoché that the noematic correlate surfaces. I do not intend to claim that Heidegger is committed to the notion of the "general thesis of the natural attitude," which, as we have seen, plays a crucial part in the motivation for the performance of Husserl's epoché. Nor is he necessarily committed to the Husserlian question of constitution, although it might be that one of Heidegger's questions is in fact closely related to Husserl's question of "constitution."

But surely, this argument has at least one very weak link. In apparent opposition to the critical remarks noted above, Heidegger actually does, in places, recognize that there is a "positive" side to the epoché or reduction (*GA* 58, pp. 249-250, 254). That is to say, he does not consistently claim that the epoché is only a negative *Absehen-von*. But in contrast to this he severely criticizes Husserl's notion of "noema," or noematic correlate, essentially every time he introduces it. The very concept of noema precisely *distorts* the view of something like modes of being, because of its *theoretical* connotations, Heidegger emphasizes. It is no coincidence that Husserl chooses the concepts of *noesis* (Greek: intellect, thought) and *noema* to describe the two sides of the intentional relation; on the contrary, it gives valuable testimony to Husserl's overemphasis on the theoretical sphere of "knowledge" and "reason," according to Heidegger (*GA* 20, p. 61; *GA* 26, p. 169; *GA* 63, p. 92). However, this does not mean that the notion of noematic correlate, introduced in the last chapter, can have no place in Heidegger's phenomenology. In fact, whatever Husserl's reasons for choosing the concept of "noema" might be, if we understand by that notion nothing but the experienced just as it is experienced, it remains crucial to Heidegger's undertaking.

Heidegger's lecture courses from the twenties, which were only recently published, provide valuable clues to Heidegger's reception of Husserl's phenomenology. In connection with our specific concerns, it is remarkable that Heidegger in the first of his Marburg lecture courses acknowledges his debt to the Husserlian notion of the experienced-just-as-experienced. And it is worth noting that this is done in a lecture course that is generally highly critical towards Husserl's phenomenology, at times clearly unjustly so. In other words, there is close to no reason to assume that Heidegger is attempting to please Husserl – I think, on the contrary, that it is one of the (perhaps rare) occasions where Heidegger reveals something like the true extent of his indebtedness to his phenomenological mentor.[15] The first of the relevant passages reads:

Intentionality must not be considered a special feature of psychical processes; rather, it must be given as a manner, in which something is encountered in such a way that what is encountered comes to the fore together with the encountering: the directing-oneself-at together with its specific at-what. This is the fundamental significance of that which is, from the beginning, meant by intentionality, so that in this attitude, along with the cogitare, the cogitatum is given as the entity in the How of its specific being-encountered in the approach and involvement itself.
With this discovery of intentionality, the path for radical ontological research is explicitly given for the first time in the whole history of philosophy. (GA 17, p. 260)

Phenomenology precisely does not direct itself towards acts in the old sense but, rather, towards the completely new domain: towards the ways of relating-oneself-to [*Sichbeziehens-auf*], in such a way that the to-what [*das Worauf*] of relating-oneself is present. *As long as I do not have this basis, I am not in any sense able, in direct experience of an entity, to see something like a character of being; indeed [I am unable] to practice something like ontology.* (GA 17, p. 262, my emphasis)

Ontology, referring to Heidegger's phenomenology of being, is thus not possible without the foundation supplied by the "new domain" of intentionality we find in Husserl. Without this foundation it is impossible to bring "modes of being" into view. Heidegger elaborates:

The characterization of intentionality is what makes the research method of phenomenology possible in the first place. For the latter is possible when the act which is reflected upon is present, along with the reflection; [i.e.,] that which the reflection is directed towards [is] not the natural object, but the *object in the how of its being intended* [*im Wie seines Gemeintseins*]. To use a trivial example, a table is not placed

---

[15] Von Herrmann acknowledges that Heidegger "takes up" (*aufgreift*) Husserl's discovery of intentionality, but insists that it is at the same time clear that "Husserl precisely does not tread this path, because the care for certainty, which is determining for him, prevents him from doing so" (*Hermeneutik und Reflexion*, p. 110). As I have tried to argue, it is not fruitful to emphasize too strongly the motive of "certainty" in Husserl's philosophy. It seems to me that in his study of Husserl and Heidegger, von Herrmann takes for granted the correctness of Heidegger's dubious portrayal of Husserl, according to which Husserl is fully under the influence of the Cartesian search for certainty. It is too early to say whether Husserl in fact does take the route he has opened for Heidegger, but if it should turn out that he does not, this is hardly because he is determined by any *Sorge der Gewißheit*.

in the thematic field of phenomenology as this specific object; rather, it is *considered in the how of its object-being*. (*GA* 17, p. 263, my emphasis)

If we call forth this directing-oneself at something, then at the same time we have co-given the at-what of directing-oneself, in the way in which it is intended in the act. We experience the intended in the characterizations of its being-intended. Thus, we have the possibility of interrogating the experienced world with regard to its being-there [*hinsichtlich ihres Daseins*]. We can learn to see an entity in its being. In this way the scientific basis is established for the question concerning the being of entities. (WDF, p. 160)

It is, to be sure, the all-important notion of the object-in-its-how-of-being-intended (*im Wie seines Gemeintseins* – an expression of Husserl's) that makes possible phenomenological research in its Heideggerian version,[16] as indeed it is this notion that makes possible Husserlian phenomenology. There is good reason to think this is what Heidegger is referring to when he declares that Husserl is the one who opened his eyes (*GA* 63, p. 5).[17] Now, as pointed out in the preceding chapter, it is only in the epoché that we are able to consider entities in the "how" of their being manifested. This means, for Heidegger, that it is only in and through the epoché that we are able to view the entities in their *being*. Once again, Heidegger himself seems[18] to draw the conclusion unambiguously:

Every phenomenological analysis of acts considers the act in such a way that the analysis does not really go along with the act, does not follow its thematic sense, but rather makes the act itself the theme, so that

---

[16] Cf. the remarks to that effect in Emmanuel Levinas, *Discovering existence with Husserl*, pp. 22-23, 87. In a similar vein, Rudolf Bernet argues that "for Heidegger, the entity considered 'in the how of its being intended' constitutes the proper focus of the new phenomenological ontology" ("Husserl and Heidegger on Intentionality and Being," p. 139).

[17] Heidegger himself often stresses how important Husserl's notion of "categorial intuition" from the sixth of the *Logische Untersuchungen* is to the discovery of the question of being (WDF, p. 161; *GA* 15, 373-381; *ZSD*, p. 86). This point is taken up and developed by Jacques Taminiaux in a number of articles, such as "Heidegger and Husserl's Logical Investigations," "From One Idea of Phenomenology to the Other," and "The Husserlian Heritage in Heidegger's Notion of the Self." Other commentators, such as Jiro Watanabe ("Categorial Intuition and the Understanding of Being in Husserl and Heidegger") and Einar Øverenget (*Seeing the Self*, esp. ch. II), also stress Heidegger's indebtedness to Husserl's notion of categorial intuition. However, it would seem to me that Husserl's problem (cf. *Hua* XIX/2, pp. 657-693) of how, e.g., the "is" in the claim "The paper is white" can find intuitive fulfillment, given that it cannot be intuited through the senses like "paper" and "white," is something very different indeed from Heidegger's inquiry into modes of being. Heidegger's question, or one of them, is more like the question what manner of being something like a sheet of paper has. Related to this is the point that, according to Heidegger, being is something we understand, not something we intuit in Husserl's sense. Husserl's doctrine of categorial intuition might be a source of inspiration to Heidegger, but I find it hard to see how Heidegger could feel truly indebted to Husserl on this point. It seems to me that what is pointed out in the main text is a much more tangible "Husserlian heritage" in Heidegger's phenomenology of being.

[18] In fact, within this apparent praise of Husserl's epoché lurks a fundamental criticism. The quotation does not necessarily show that Heidegger recognizes the epoché as crucial to *his own* approach to the question of being. Rather, the epoché is being described as Husserl's way of making entities present in their mode of being, a way that Heidegger thinks suffers from at least one important difficulty, as we see later in the present study (Chapter VI, Sections 5 and 6). The quotation is, however, important to us, because, insofar as Heidegger already acknowledges the necessity of Husserl's notion of experienced-as-experienced to the question of being, he is forced to recognize that the performance of the Husserlian epoché is exactly an, or perhaps the, entrance gate to the question of being as such.

the object of the act is also thematized in terms of how it is presumed [*im Wie seines Vermeintseins*] in the corresponding intention. This implies that the perceived is not directly presumed [*vermeint*] as such, but in the how of its being. This modification, in which the entity is now regarded to the extent that it is an object of intentionality, is called *bracketing*.

This bracketing of the entity [i.e., the epoché] takes nothing away from the entity itself, nor does it purport to assume that the entity is not. This reversal of perspective has rather the sense of making the being [*Seinscharakter*] of the entity present. This phenomenological suspension of the transcendent thesis has but the sole function of making the entity present in regard to its being. (*GA* 20, p. 136)

Contrary to what the ill-chosen concept of *Ausschaltung* tempts one to think, Heidegger continues, the epoché is only, and "in an extreme and unique way," about the determination of the *being* of entities (*die Bestimmung des Seins des Seienden*) (*GA* 20, p. 136).[19]

Just as Husserl claims that when I cast a happy glance at a blooming apple tree, my noematic correlate is nothing that can "burn," so Heidegger can now claim that when I sit here looking through my books and striking the keys of the keyboard in front of me, what I am encountering are not first and foremost objects that have a "layer" of materiality upon which other layers are built. The keyboard does not manifest itself as somehow "immaterial," as though Heidegger would agree with a Berkeleyan idealist. Heidegger is quite ready to grant that a certain materiality belongs to the keyboard in my interaction with it, but he simply wants to add that we should not assume that this materiality is best described as some fundamental "layer" within the object. If I pay attention to the keyboard *just as it figures in my interaction with it*, i.e., to the keyboard as a noematic correlate, it becomes clear that the most fundamental "level" of it is its *Um-zu*, according to Heidegger (*GA* 24, p. 415). I type on the keyboard, I *use* it, in-order-to write this text; that is to say, most fundamentally, the keyboard manifests itself to me as something-with-which-to-write-texts. Such a shower of hyphens is appropriate here because we are trying to get a mode of being into view, rather than to say something commonplace such as, "The keyboard is something, viz. a material thing that has the property of being useful for this or that purpose." The latter way of describing the keyboard, almost identical as it is to the description with all the hyphens, is still radically *different* from it, since it is more than compatible with the "layer" theory of the object. One should not be mystified by Heidegger's extensive use of hyphens, but one should respect it and understand the hyphens the way Heidegger wants them to be understood: as indications that what is being described is *one*, indivisible and unitary phenomenon (cf. *SZ*, p. 53; *GA* 24, p. 234).

Although these hints concerning an analysis of the "objects" of everyday life are only preliminary, and discussed in greater detail later (Chapter VI), we are now in a position to outline approximately how the notion of noematic correlate achieves

---

[19] A very different discussion of the significance of the epoché to the relation between Husserl and Heidegger is found in Hans Rainer Sepp, "Zeit und Sorge." Sepp argues that a pre- or non-theoretical reformulation of the epoché has critical potential vis-à-vis Heidegger. I, in contrast, argue that Husserl's epoché – without the Cartesian overtones, but by no means purged of all "theoretical" intentions – is an essential methodological tool for Heidegger.

crucial importance to Heidegger's question of being. Also, we are able to appreciate more deeply the difference, discovered in Chapter I, between Heidegger's negative evaluation of the everyday interpretation of encountered entities and Husserl's apparent sympathy with the same. Husserl, it seems, never uses the "noematic correlate" as the starting point of a criticism of the natural attitude; i.e., at every point in the phenomenological analysis Husserl would confirm that no matter how the apple tree appears to me, it still is, *in itself*, flammable, and it still has, *in itself*, the founding layer of materiality. He does not equate, in other words, the entity in its "how" of manifestation with the entity in itself, it would appear. Heidegger, on the other hand, precisely uses the noematic correlate in an effort to launch a "critique" of the everyday interpretation, because as Heidegger sees it, there is every reason to suppose that the entity *as it manifests itself* "in person" is identical with the entity *in itself*. For Heidegger, the "mode of manifestation" of an entity – which Husserl's epoché made visible for the first time – is nothing but the "mode of *being*" of the entity, the "way" it *is in itself*.[20] The discovery of the noematic correlate, then, allows us to see (or rather, it takes the first of a series of steps that will eventually allow us to see) the "modes of being" that entities have, thus it allows us to obtain the vantage point from which the distorted nature of the everyday interpretation of being can be unveiled. In other words, when Heidegger describes everydayness, he does so from within Husserl's epoché.

A necessary first methodological step in Heidegger's ontological phenomenology is thus documented. Before we have any chance of thematizing something like being, or modes of being, we first must perform Husserl's epoché,[21] and bring the noematic correlate into view. So far, at least, Heidegger's phenomenological path does not stray significantly from that of Husserl. But there are many more steps that Heidegger deems necessary, insofar as one aims to open and secure access to the question of being.

4. FORMAL INDICATION

By performing the Husserlian epoché, we are able to gain distance to the everyday interpretation of things. We are able to approach entities in the *"how"* of their manifestation. But "being," Heidegger knows, is not "initially" and "mostly" manifested; in fact, in everyday life, something like "being" is nowhere to be found. An investigation into being goes against the grain of everyday life to such an extent

---

[20] Cf. Bernet, "Husserl and Heidegger on Intentionality and Being," p. 139.

[21] Steven Galt Crowell clearly sees this. His articles on Husserl and Heidegger are now collected in the volume *Husserl, Heidegger, and the Space of Meaning*. On p. 197 of that volume we read: "This being becomes visible as such only through a reflection that first sets aside or reduces the naturalistic thesis about being inherent in everyday life." I think that with the publication of *GA* 17, the textual support for claims such as these is less ambiguous than Crowell feels compelled to admit (ibid., p. 197). The importance of the lectures published as *GA* 17 to the question of Heidegger's indebtedness to Husserl is emphasized as early as 1967 by Ernst Tugendhat, who had access to a student *Nachschrift* of the course. See Tugendhat, *Der Wahrheitsbegriff bei Husserl und Heidegger*, p. 262.

that it calls for extreme caution (cf. *GA* 24, p. 459). The epoché undoubtedly removes severe obstacles from our phenomenological view, but what if the question of *being* – since it is probably the most "unnatural" of questions – can be prejudiced in ways that escape the brackets? Yet, how could any "prejudice" belonging to everyday life, or the natural attitude, escape the epoché? To answer this question, we must take another brief look at Husserl.

One important insight of the early Heidegger is that the way we express ourselves as phenomenologists – i.e., the concepts we employ – is responsible for much of the bad prejudice in phenomenology. Husserl's epoché, while removing obstacles from our view, in no way restricts the language with which we describe our phenomenological findings. What is "bracketed" is the "thesis" of the natural attitude, the "knowledge" and interpretations belonging to that attitude, and not its concepts. As Husserl would no doubt point out, the epoché neither could, nor should purify our language, since no language is available to us apart from the "natural" language (cf. *EU*, p. 58). Even if we invented a "new" language, we would still have to be able, at first at least, to define its concepts using the natural language – so if the natural language were prejudiced, how could we have reason to believe that the "new" language would be less so (cf. *HuDo* II/1, p. 107n)? Insofar as we want to say anything as phenomenologists, we have to employ the "natural" language, although we may only do so together with a complete alteration of the meaning of its concepts (*Hua* VI, p. 214; *Hua* XV, p. 390). Regarding the question of how this "alteration" is supposed to occur, Husserl is conspicuously vague, or even inconsistent, sometimes claiming that the alteration comes about completely "of itself" (*ganz von selbst*) (*HuDo* II/1, p. 83n), once the epoché and reduction are performed, and at other times acknowledging that it takes perpetual struggles (*immer wieder neuer Anstrengung*) to keep the insistent "natural" meanings at bay (*EU*, p. 58), although he does not reveal any details on the execution of these battles.

Although Heidegger does use neologisms, one should not conclude that Heidegger's alternative to Husserl's "struggle" is simply that of inventing a new language. Rather than inventing a new language, Heidegger instead tries in the early Freiburg lectures to develop a method of "formal indication" (*formale Anzeige*) to fend off prejudicial expressions. Concurrently with the publication of the early Freiburg lectures, this notion of "formal indication" has in recent years attracted significant attention in the literature on Heidegger.[22]

---

[22] One of the very first to analyze "formal indication" in any detail is Otto Pöggeler (see especially his "Heideggers logische Untersuchungen," pp. 82-89). But to my knowledge, the first study to be entirely devoted to this notion is Th. C. W. Oudemans's 1989 article bearing almost the same title as Pöggeler's work, viz. "Heideggers 'logische Untersuchungen,'" occasioned by the then recently published volume 61 of the *Gesamtausgabe*. "Formal indication" also plays a major role in Theodore Kisiel's extensive study of the young Heidegger's development, *The Genesis of Heidegger's Being and Time*, as well as in a number of other studies of Heidegger's phenomenology published in the nineties (e.g., John van Buren, *The Young Heidegger*, especially pp. 324-341; and Daniel Dahlstrom, *Heidegger's Concept of Truth*, esp. pp. 242-252, 435-445). Among the most helpful shorter analyses of "formal indication" is Daniel O. Dahlstrom's "Heidegger's Method: Philosophical Concepts as Formal Indications," whereas the very

Formal indication is described by Heidegger as "a particular methodological level of phenomenological explication" (*WM*, p. 29). Nowhere does Heidegger unfold this "methodological level" in sufficient detail,[23] which means that any analysis of it is condemned to a certain degree of reconstruction. The best manner to approach formal indication is by way of the task that this methodological stage is intended to perform. Having gained access to the entity in the "how" of its manifestation (through the epoché), the question is how are we to speak of this "how" in such a way as to remain faithful to it despite the pressure from tradition and everyday "truisms" (cf. *GA* 61, p. 20). Since we do not know in advance the correct way to describe a particular mode of being – indeed, a "mode of being" is something we must first learn to see – separating "bad" prejudices from apt descriptions may be no easy matter. All we have to go by is the entity in its "how," so we must let *it* supply our concepts, somehow: "the conceptuality of the object in the respective definitory determination must be drawn out of the mode *in which the object is originally accessible*" (*GA* 61, p. 20). But how can we shape our concepts according to how the entity originally manifests itself? First, we must somehow rein in our use of "ordinary" concepts, i.e., maintain a certain conceptual "emptiness" that may be given content later (*GA* 60, p. 82). But initially directing ourselves towards the noematic correlate, we must be able to say *something*, i.e., we must approach it with some kind of concepts, only these must be concepts that indicate rather than describe. It seems that we need some initial conceptual "take" on the noematic correlate that both fends off natural prejudices and points the way to a "right" description (cf. *GA* 63, p. 80). Unless something "warns" us against traditional or everyday prejudices, we are liable to fall victim to them, thereby closing ourselves off from the phenomenon uncovered by the epoché. Yet, a warning is not itself enough; to get started, we also need something *positive*, some direction, some "question," so to speak, with which to approach the entity, with which to *make it talk* about its mode of being. These initial "indications" cannot themselves be the full description, since they are the ones that must first guide the description along the proper path. Being thus almost devoid of descriptive content, the initial indications can be called *formal* – they *are* not descriptive, but are more like signposts that tell us where to look for a description. This methodologically necessary beginning stage of phenomenology, this *Ansatzmethode* (*GA* 61, p. 141;

---

recent article "Heidegger's Formal Indication: A Question of Method in *Being and Time*," by Ryan Streeter, is somewhat less lucid.

[23] Theodore Kisiel relates how Heidegger in the lecture course of the winter of 1920-1921 apparently had to break off his extensive treatment of formal indication abruptly due to a complaint from some of the students. It seems that the students convinced the dean of the philosophical faculty that the course had too little religious content to match the advertised title of the course (*The Genesis of Heidegger's Being and Time*, pp. 170-173). Interestingly, the meditations on phenomenological method announced at the beginning of the lecture course of the summer of 1927 (cf. *GA* 24, p. 33) suffered a similar fate, since Heidegger never got round to an exposition more detailed than the one in the introduction to the course. This time, however, the culprit seems to have been simple lack of time, rather than student complaints.

cf. *GA* 60, p. 64) of "pointing the way" while "pushing away," is what Heidegger labels *formale Anzeige*.

First of all, the formal indication is "prohibitive," or negative, as though it issues a warning (*GA* 60, p. 63). Heidegger says: "The *formal indication* [...] possesses [...] a *prohibiting* (deterring, preventing) *character*" (*GA* 61, p. 141). What, precisely, is it that must be warned against? Prejudices, naturally, but what kind of prejudices? These are prejudices regarding the "modes of being" of entities, prejudices built into our philosophical and natural language. But as pointed out above, "being" is nowhere to be found in our everyday world, and according to Heidegger himself, philosophy – in the last two thousand years – has not even asked about being, let alone discussed it. So how can our language be prejudiced regarding being, when we never in fact discuss it? Rather than constituting an objection to Heidegger, this question singles out the peculiar nature of those prejudices Heidegger wants to warn against:

> The formal indication prevents every drifting off into autonomous, blind, dogmatic attempts to fix the categorical sense, attempts which would be detached from the presupposition of the interpretation, from its preconception, its nexus, and its time, and which would then purport to present *an sich* determinations of an objectivity, which has not been discussed with regard to its meaning of being [*Ansichbestimmtheiten einer auf ihren Seinssinn undiskutierten Gegenständlichkeit*]. (*GA* 61, p. 142)

It is precisely our *not discussing* modes of being that has to be prohibited; that is to say, the formal indication prohibits our drifting off into a discussion of "properties" of entities – entities left undetermined with regard to their mode of being. In a way, one could thus say that what the formal indication warns against is drifting away from the *ontological* level, down to an ontic level. More precisely, *formal indication prohibits any ontic discussion for as long as we are doing phenomenological ontology*. It guards us against a very "natural," and thus constantly threatening, *metabasis eis allo genos*. But guarding against a *metabasis*, as noted, is also the principal task of Husserl's epoché within the program of constitutive phenomenology – thus formal indication, at least in its negative aspect, seems quite aptly labeled a specifically "Heideggerian epoché."[24]

The *metabasis* that consists in sliding from an ontological to an ontic problematic constitutes a prejudice regarding the question of being, because we may not assume that "leaping over" the problematic of modes of being ensures "neutrality" in relation to that problematic. On the contrary – as Chapter I illustrates – everyday life tends to "fall off" into an objectifying interpretation of each and every entity. It is because being remains undiscussed in everyday life, or at most becomes "discussed" in empty everyday "gossip," that a specific interpretation (the one according to which everything is "present-at-hand") is so powerful (*GA* 18, pp. 272, 275). If we want to be able phenomenologically to describe modes of being

---

[24] Daniel O. Dahlstrom is one of the few commentators who notices how this negative aspect of formal indication looks a lot like "Heidegger's way of appropriating the Husserlian epoché" ("Heidegger's Method: Philosophical Concepts as Formal Indications," p. 783n).

faithfully, we need first of all to fend off those prejudices that result from a slide into an "ontic" problematic. According to Husserl, we have no language except the "natural" language. The "natural" language is the language with which we refer to mundane entities, processes, relations, and so forth. In Heideggerian terminology, this means that our language is basically "ontic": we have many words for entities, for relations between them, but it seems concepts (and especially the grammar) are lacking for the enterprise of describing the *being* of entities (cf. *SZ*, p. 39; *GA* 20, p. 203). Therefore, *the "negative" aspect of formal indication consists in picking out guiding concepts that make it difficult or impossible to slide into an ontic discussion of entities and their properties.*

Yet formal indication is not merely negative; it has an important *positive* side as well. In order to make the entity "speak" regarding its mode of being, we need a "question" with which to confront it, a "direction." Direction is exactly what formal indication gives us. It *leads* us in our phenomenological investigation (*GA* 60, p. 55); it binds to a certain itinerary:

There resides in the formal indication a very definite bond; this bond says that I stand in a quite definite *direction of approach*, and it points out the only way of arriving at what is proper [*Eigentlichen*], namely, by exhausting and fulfilling what is improperly [*uneigentlich*] indicated, by following the indication. (*GA* 61, p. 33)

Obviously we do not have, from the outset, the adequate concepts at our disposal – these, in particular, are supposed to be supplied by the entity in its "how." Therefore, the formal indication is precisely improper or "inauthentic" (*uneigentlich*),[25] it is "empty" in the sense that no content is found in the formally indicative concepts, but only a direction (*GA* 61, p. 33). This "only," however, should immediately be taken back, insofar as it is absolutely crucial the particular direction that is opted for (*GA* 61, p. 33): the formal indication determines the way we henceforth look at the phenomena (*GA* 60, p. 55).

What "positive" direction does formal indication give us? A first answer to that question can be supplied if we turn our attention, once again, to the "negative" aspect of Heidegger's *Ansatzmethode*. Formally indicative concepts must be concepts that prevent the silentl exchange of an ontological problematic for an ontic one. At the same time that we try to prevent the slide into considerations of entities, we need to keep in focus "the matters themselves," i.e., we must employ concepts that somehow point towards what *is* to be discussed. That, however, is "being."

---

[25] Heidegger's use of the notions *eigentlich* and *uneigentlich* at this point has little to do with his use of the notions in *Sein und Zeit*. One must look, rather, to Husserl to see what Heidegger means. In *Logische Untersuchungen*, Husserl distinguishes between "authentic" and "inauthentic" thought (*eigentliche und uneigentliche Denkakten*) (*Hua* XIX/2, p. 722), i.e., between acts of thought that only signify and lack intuitive fulfillment and thoughts that have fulfillment, or are fulfilling acts. Similarly, Husserl speaks in his 1907 lectures *Ding und Raum* of authentic (or proper) and inauthentic (or improper) manifestation (*eigentliche* and *uneigentliche Erscheinung*), meaning thereby the modes of manifestation attributed to the front side, and the back side, respectively, of the perceived spatial object (*Hua* XVI, p. 50). See, concerning this, Steven Crowell, *Husserl, Heidegger, and the Space of Meaning*, pp. 137-144.

Hence, Heidegger can say, "'Being' is what is indicated formally and emptily, and yet it strictly determines the direction of the understanding" (*GA* 61, p. 61). *The formally indicative concepts, on the one hand, are supposed to prevent a metabasis into an ontic problematic, but, on the other hand, they are also supposed to point the way to the ontological problematic.*

Despite, or rather because of, the immediate lucidity of all of this, it can be hard to shake off the suspicion that it is tautological, or, at the very least, obvious given Heidegger's ontological question. When aiming to do ontology, we should prevent an ontic problematic from interfering, while we strive to focus on the ontological problematic – does this not go without saying? Of course, but let us not forget that the problems we are dealing with in this section are problems of *language*. Since "being" is the subject of neither everyday nor explicit philosophical discussion, according to Heidegger, not only do we need to bring it into view, but we also need to use *concepts* that will further this thematization and allow us to remain focused on it. These cannot be concepts that tacitly carry a specific ontology with them; rather they must be concepts that *awaken us to an ontological problematic*; that point toward it while keeping tacit ontological commitments at bay. Now, any ontic description tacitly harbors ontological commitments; so insofar as we aim to bring an ontological problematic into view, we have to prevent any slide into an ontic problematic. This is not only done by an epoché in Husserl's sense, but also by observing the utmost caution when choosing phenomenological concepts. Indeed, there is something obvious in all of this – it goes without saying that one should always describe something using those concepts that are most suited to such a description – but that does nothing to reduce its importance, and the crucial point is that it is very far from obvious *which* concepts to use in ontological phenomenology.

Although it is certainly not the case that only ontic concepts can be formally indicative, these are nevertheless the ones that are especially needed in the beginning – when we are only trying to clear a path *to* ontology. As an example of a crucial formally indicative concept, one that is ontic in the sense that it denotes an entity, let us consider that of Dasein. The following preliminary reflections on the notion of "Dasein" unavoidably anticipate something that will be discussed in more detail later, but we need at this point to put some flesh on the method of *formale Anzeige*, if we want to understand how it works.

Dasein, Heidegger says, denotes the entities, or the beings, we ourselves are: "This entity which each of us is himself [...], we shall denote by the term 'Dasein'" (*SZ*, p. 7). That entity (*Seiende*), however, is what we usually refer to as the *human being*, that is, Dasein appears simply to be Heidegger's new word for "human being" (*Mensch*). But what is wrong with "human being"? A quite natural understanding of "human being" is that of *animal rationale* (*SZ*, p. 48). A human being is an animal, a living sensing creature who separates him/herself from other animals through the fact that she/he has language, and the ability to think. Or, some would perhaps say that "human being" denotes a particular material entity that has, in addition to a physical body, something like "soul" and "spirit" (*Geist*) (*SZ*, p. 48). In either case, a human being is a kind of entity (*Seiende*) that has a number of essentially different properties, components (body-soul-spirit), or *layers*. But just like the layer theory of the human being – as we saw Heidegger suggesting already in the first chapter of this book – is committed to a certain ontology, viz. the ontology of presence-at-hand, so are the other interpretations of the "human being," Heidegger insists (*GA* 63, p. 21). If we "posit" the human being as a "thing" in the world, it does not matter how much we emphasize that this "thing" has the ever so important "property" or "component" of being able to experience and interact with other things – the notion of presence-at-hand retains its dominance. In other words, the notion of "human being" is problematic in this context insofar as it brings with itself a tacit, completely ignored or "forgotten" ontological commitment (*SZ*, p. 49).

What, then, about the notion of "subject," or "subjectivity"? When we say that we are *subjects*, we are presupposing no foundational layer or component of materiality, thus, it would seem, no particular mode of being. According to Heidegger, however, no matter if the notion of "subject" is wedded to that of "soul" or not, it once again evokes the idea of presence-at-hand (*SZ*, pp. 46, 114). Isolating the sphere of experiences and thoughts and labeling it the "subject," and emphatically contrasting this sphere with that of material things; as ontically noisy as this may be, it still amounts to an ontological silence, and thus does not do away with the ontological presuppositions that such a silence brings along with itself (*SZ*, p. 46). On the contrary, it allows them to work unnoticed.

None of this is intended to mean that Dasein denotes something other than the subject. On the contrary, Heidegger emphasizes that Dasein denotes precisely the subject (*GA* 27, pp. 72, 115),[26] only it does so in a *formally indicative* way. Unlike the notions of "human being" and "consciousness," and perhaps even "subject," Dasein does not entail a commitment to a specific ontological view of the entity in question. Rather than tacitly advancing a certain interpretation of the being of the creatures we ourselves are, it *directs our attention to the being* of those creatures, it *awakens us* to the question of their being. *Da-Sein*, "there-being," "being-there"; what does it mean? That is something we do not know yet, and the important thing is precisely that we do not know yet, i.e., that the concept does not facilitate thinking about this entity in terms of its "properties," "components," or "layers." In fact, not a word has been said about "consciousness," or about "body": where Dasein stands with regard to these concepts – ontologically loaded as they presumably are by being ontologically silent – is as yet left entirely open. But a direction is given; more precisely, our gaze is directed towards the *explicit question* of the being of this entity.

---

[26] Even if one is essentially trying to make the right point, I believe it is a mistake, and one that only serves to give the notion of Dasein a mystical aura, to claim, as von Herrmann does, that "Heidegger's philosophical *beginning in Dasein* is *not a new characterization of subjectivity*, but rather a *departure* from subjectivity" (*Subjekt und Dasein*, p. 10). Heidegger himself stresses that he intends to carry out "a fundamental revision of the hitherto reigning concept of the subject" (*einer grundsätzlichen Revision des bisherigen Subjektbegriffes*) (*GA* 27, p. 115). For him, the essential thing is precisely to make "the subjectivity of the subject a problem" (*GA* 27, p. 72; cf. *KPM*, p. 87).

Obviously, insofar as it denotes an entity rather than a mode of being, Dasein is an ontic notion. However, it is a very special ontic notion, in that it is completely silent regarding the "characteristics" of the entity that it denotes. It is a notion, in fact, that as formally indicative prohibits anything but silence regarding such (ontic) issues – it is an *ontically silent ontic notion*. What it does is direct our attention to the ontological question about the being of the "subject," thus in fact the formally indicative concept of Dasein is diametrically opposed – formal indication is a "counter-movement," it is *gegenruinant*, as the early Heidegger says (cf. *GA 61*, pp. 178, 183) – to the concepts of "consciousness" and "human being." These latter notions are ontologically silent and thereby ontologically prejudiced, whereas Dasein is ontically silent, and ontologically "indicative."[27] In a certain sense, one could therefore say that Dasein is an *ontological* notion – precisely because of the way in which it denotes something ontic (the beings that we ourselves are). With these considerations in hand, it should be clear how Heidegger can claim, on the one hand, that Dasein denotes an entity (*Seiende*), and on the other hand that:

This designation "Dasein" for the distinctive entity so named does not signify a *what*. The entity is not distinguished by its what, like a chair in contrast to a house. Rather, this designation in its own way expresses *the way to be*. (*GA* 20, p. 205)

Dasein is thus an excellent example of the method of formal indication. It prevents sliding off into ontic considerations (and the tacit prejudices that these entail), while positively pointing the way to an ontological investigation of the "subject."

If we hold together the two aspects – negative and positive – of the formal indication, it becomes clear that although the notion of formal indication seems conspicuously absent from significant parts of Heidegger's Marburg production, if not all of it,[28] it still lurks in the background. In Heidegger's methodical *Besinnung* in the lecture course of the summer of 1927 (unfortunately left incomplete, like the one in 1920-21), it even surfaces explicitly, although under different name(s). The method of ontology is described in the lectures as having three main components, two of which cannot but be familiar to us by now.

If we want to thematize something like being, Heidegger says, we have no choice but to initially direct ourselves at some entity. Our phenomenological gaze does not remain fixed on the entity, however, instead it is, "*in a precise way*, [...] *led away* from that entity *and led back to its being*" (*GA* 24, pp. 28-29). This procedure of leading the investigating gaze back (*reducere*) from entity to being Heidegger labels the "phenomenological *reduction*" (*GA* 24, p. 29). He emphasizes that this notion of "reduction" is significantly different from Husserl's reduction, which – as we know – is the reduction (leading back) from noematic correlate to

---

[27] Cf. to this Jean-Luc Marion, *Reduction and Givenness*, p. 102. Van Buren says that formal indications are ontically "non-committal" (*The Young Heidegger*, p. 337).

[28] *Formale Anzeige*, after all, does appear in *Sein und Zeit*, on pp. 114, 116-117, and 313. Furthermore, Heidegger still attributes fundamental importance to the notion of formal indication as late as the winter of 1929-1930, as *GA* 29/30 evidences (cf. especially § 70, pp. 421-435).

experiencing subjectivity (*GA* 24, p. 29).[29] As Heidegger hastens to add, this reduction, as a pure aversion, "is a merely negative methodological measure which not only needs to be supplemented by a positive one, but expressly requires us to be led toward being" (*GA* 24, p. 29). This positive leading-*to*, in contrast to the reductive leading-*away*-from, is what Heidegger calls the "phenomenological *construction*" (*GA* 24, p. 30).

Obviously, both of these tasks, the negative "pushing away" and the positive "pointing the way," are performed in the earlier lectures by *formale Anzeige*;[30] that is, at least insofar as the choice of *concepts* is concerned. Insofar as "*vision*" is concerned, as I attempted to make clear in the previous section, the crucial method for Heidegger is that of the epoché (in both *its* positive and negative aspects). Only in and through the epoché – with its negative "bracketing" of everyday and philosophical "gossip," and its positive unveiling of the entity in the "how" of its manifestation – can something like "being" surface; and only through initially using formally indicative concepts – negatively holding the ontic problematic at bay, while pointing towards being – are we able to *describe* what thus surfaces.

So to return to the question of Heidegger's alternative to Husserl, it is clear that Heidegger recognizes the need to take one's point of departure in the natural, or everyday language (*GA* 58, p. 248). However, the concepts we use must be used in a formally indicative way. Dasein, for instance, is no invention of Heidegger's – such a word does exist in German, and even appears frequently in German philosophical literature before Heidegger (e.g., in Kant and Husserl) (*GA* 24, p. 36). What Heidegger does is to give the word a new direction, so to speak. We cannot invent a new language, but must rather "deform" the language we already have in order to make it formally indicative. In this way, we may eventually be able to carry out a phenomenological investigation of *being*.

5. FUNDAMENTAL ONTOLOGY

As pointed out above, Heidegger has to adopt Husserl's epoché. The epoché is what allows the entity in the "how" of its manifestation to surface, and thus, according to Heidegger, the epoché allows the entity in the "how" of its *being* to surface. So, being is "manifest"[31] somehow in and through the manifestation of the entity. Regardless of which type of entity we are talking about, they all have at least one thing in common, and that is that insofar as they are manifest, they are so *to*

---

[29] Some commentators are highly suspicious regarding Heidegger's claim that his reduction has nothing but the name in common with Husserl's transcendental reduction (cf. Paul Gorner, "Heidegger and Husserl as Phenomenologists," pp. 150-151), whereas others simply follow Heidegger (cf. Oudemans, "Heideggers 'Logische Untersuchungen,'" p. 100). I suspect the truth is somewhere in between, as John D. Caputo argues in his article "The Question of Being and Transcendental Phenomenology."

[30] Oudemans points out this connection between formal indication and phenomenological reduction and construction in "Heideggers 'Logische Untersuchungen'" (p. 100).

[31] The quotation marks, of course, indicate that we may not assume that being (*Sein*) is manifest the way entities (*das Seiende*) are (cf., e.g., *GA* 24, p. 29).

someone – to a "transcendental subjectivity," in Husserl's terminology. In view of the argument in the first section of the present chapter, it is evident that in order for entities to appear to a subjectivity, their being must be understood. Thus, an understanding of being essentially belongs to the "subject," to Dasein, insofar as the possibility of letting entities be manifest essentially belongs to Dasein.

Heidegger is quite clear that the understanding of being that essentially belongs to Dasein need not be formulated explicitly. According to Heidegger, we "move" within an understanding of being, an understanding that allows us to encounter entities, but which is itself in no way thematic (cf. *SZ*, p. 4). This non-objectifying, and pre-conceptual (*vorbegrifflich*) understanding of being is what the "science" of *ontology* must make conceptually thematic. Thus, the understanding in question is not itself already a piece of ontology, is not properly ontological, but rather is a *pre-ontological understanding of being* (*vorontologische Seinsverständnis*) (*GA* 24, p. 398; *WM*, p. 132). That is to say, the tacit understanding of being, which Heidegger argues makes possible our encounters with entities, is *not itself an encounter with any entity*, it is not "ontic." But insofar as ontology is the title of the *thematic* philosophical investigation into being, then the non-thematic understanding cannot properly be labeled "ontological" either (although, to be sure, it is an understanding of that which is the theme of ontology); hence, Heidegger calls it the *pre-ontological* understanding of being.

Being, then, is "manifest" in the understanding of being that essentially belongs to Dasein, the understanding that enables Dasein to relate to entities. The "how" of being "appears" only to a *someone*, more precisely to someone who understands something like a "how" of being. Hence, if we want to thematize being, we have to hook on to that understanding-of-being in which it "appears":

> If, now, we take hold of the *basic problem of philosophy* and ask the question about the meaning and ground of being, then, if we do not wish to work merely imaginatively, we must keep a firm hold methodically on what makes something like being accessible to us: the understanding of being that belongs to Dasein. (*GA* 24, p. 319; cf. *SZ*, p. 372)

Dasein thus becomes the focus of phenomenological ontology. In order to be able to do ontology, we must work out a preliminary analysis of the entity we call Dasein, with specific regard to the understanding of being that belongs to this entity. This preparatory investigation must supply the *foundation* for the "genuine" ontology, and Heidegger consequently labels the "analytic of Dasein" "fundamental ontology" (*Fundamentalontologie*): "*fundamental ontology*, from which alone all other ontologies can take their rise, must be sought in the *existential analytic of Dasein*" (*SZ*, p. 13; cf. *SZ*, pp. 14, 37; *GA* 24, p. 319). It is Heidegger's firm conviction that intentionality, and consequently understanding of being, is so essential to Dasein that an understanding of being *itself belongs to the specific "how" of Dasein's being* (*SZ*, p. 12). Hence, the title of "fundamental ontology" applies with perfect accuracy to the task of an analytic of Dasein. The analytic of Dasein is not only that which supplies the foundation *for* ontology, and in this sense "fundamental ontology," it is *itself* an ontology (*KPM*, p. 232) – viz., the "provisional" analysis of the *being* of a specific entity that itself paves the way for the "full" ontology. These remarks raise some issues that must be addressed at this point.

First, there should be no confusion about the *goal* of fundamental ontology. Although interpretations of this kind are rarely met with sympathy from established authorities on Heidegger, Heidegger's project of a *Daseinsanalytik* is widely interpreted as an "existentialist" project.[32] Even in *Sein und Zeit* itself, however, Heidegger makes it quite clear that he has no interest in the burdens of human existence as such: "the analytic of Dasein remains *wholly oriented towards the guiding task of working out the question of being*" (*SZ*, p. 17, my emphasis). Furthermore, he makes no attempt to weaken this point in the subsequent phenomenological writings (cf., e.g., *GA* 26, pp. 20-21; *KPM*, pp. 234-235). That Heidegger's focus is ontological rather than "existential" is further confirmed by the fact that when composing his magnum opus, Heidegger avoids the then popular existential vocabulary, right up until the very last draft.[33] Heidegger's question is the *Seinsfrage*, and it is only because Dasein is the "place of the understanding of being" (*Stätte des Seinsverständnis*)[34] that we turn our attention to the being of Dasein.[35]

Second, we must understand the *status* fundamental ontology has, and must have. The analytic of Dasein that is to function as a fundamental ontology at first sight seems haunted by a logical difficulty. It is supposed to analyze the *being* of a particular entity, whereas it is only through fundamental ontology that we obtain genuine phenomenological access to being. The objection that immediately comes to mind is clearly anticipated by Heidegger:

But if we are to obtain an ontologically clarified idea of being in general, must we not do so by first working out that understanding of being that belongs to Dasein? This understanding, however, is to be

---

[32] Existentialist readings of Heidegger are not just a thing of the past. For a recent example, see John Richardson, *Existential Epistemology*. Richardson's basic thesis is that Heidegger's *Sein und Zeit* must not be seen in any way as "theoretical," but should rather be viewed as a book, the point of which is to pull its readers out of their inauthenticity – e.g., by way of inducing "breakdowns" in them (p. 203) – and into authentic existence. Indeed a Heideggerian philosophy, so concludes Richardson, can have no other purpose: "In thus guiding us to authenticity, phenomenology makes the only proper exit from everydayness, an exit that does not eliminate the unsatisfactoriness that everydayness flees, in the way traditional philosophy has always attempted to do, but that lives in the world in full acknowledgement of this dissatisfying character. This then is the positive task that Heidegger assigns to philosophy" (p. 208).
[33] Theodore Kisiel's thorough historical work reveals that most of the existential vocabulary in several of Heidegger's lectures before the publication of *Sein und Zeit* is the result of later additions. And in fact, says Kisiel, it is only during a single month's work in Todtnauberg (where Heidegger is struggling to gather his manuscripts together to form a coherent treatise) that "the particular conceptual decisions that are to follow from this central concept of *Existenz* are made, superficially transforming BT [i.e., *Being and Time*] into a book inaugurating *Existenzphilosophie*" (*The Genesis of Heidegger's Being and Time*, p. 419; cf. pp. 7, 275, 316, 394).
[34] *SZ*, p. 439 (Heidegger's second marginal note to *SZ*, p. 8).
[35] Walter Schulz's claim that the question about the meaning of being is the question about the meaning of Dasein and nothing else ("Über den philosophiegeschichtlichen Ort Martin Heideggers," p. 104) thus would seem only to hold true to the extent that it is emphasized that Dasein, or the being of Dasein, is precisely the place where "all" being, also the being of other entities, becomes accessible and articulated.

grasped primordially only on the basis of a primordial interpretation of Dasein, in which we take the idea of existence as our clue. Does it not then become altogether patent in the end that this problem of fundamental ontology which we have broached, is one which moves in a 'circle'? (*SZ*, p. 314; cf. *GA* 20, p. 197)

How can we interpret the *being* of an entity, unless we *already have an articulated understanding of what "being" means*? And yet, it seems that if we want to achieve a philosophical understanding of the meaning of being, we have to plunge ourselves into an interpretation of the being of a particular entity. Heidegger does not attempt to explain away this apparent "circle." He does answer the objection, however, and his answer is twofold. First, he points out that our task as phenomenologists does not consist in developing deductive arguments. Since it is within the latter context alone that "begging the question" is a legitimate accusation, Heidegger cannot rightfully be charged with it (*SZ*, p. 315; *GA* 20, p. 198). The circle in question, moreover, is hardly one that can be avoided, according to Heidegger. Insofar as we want to ask the question of being, we must direct our gaze at that "locus" where being "manifests" itself. That locus is the *Seinsverständnis* that belongs to the being of the entities we ourselves are. So in order to understand being, we must direct ourselves towards the being of this particular entity, in order to unveil the "content" of its understanding of being. To be sure, this *is* circular, but we can see that the project of fundamental ontology deals with the problem in the best possible manner, more precisely, it "leaps into the circle" in the right way (cf. *SZ*, pp. 153, 315). That said, however, Heidegger emphasizes that the analytic of Dasein can be *only preliminary* (*vorläufig*) (*SZ*, p. 17). A genuine phenomenological understanding of the being of this particular entity presupposes, of course, that being as such is understood already. Therefore, the initial investigation of the being of Dasein must be subsequently *repeated* in light of the more elaborate understanding of being (that the analytic of Dasein itself made possible) (*GA* 24, p. 319; *SZ*, pp. 17, 333). Perhaps this may serve as an illustration of Heidegger's claim that every genuine method makes itself obsolete when it has led to true insights (*GA* 24, p. 467): the analytic of Dasein (fundamental ontology) must supply us with the insight into being that makes the initial analytic obsolete and necessitates its repetition on a new and more enlightened level.

In the context of his presentation of the program of fundamental ontology, Heidegger acknowledges that the regress to the "subject" – the path of modern philosophy from Descartes to Husserl – basically is "the only one that is possible and correct" (*GA* 24, p. 103, cf. p. 444). Moreover – although there is little evidence to suggest that he acknowledges this explicitly – Heidegger is in fundamental accordance with Husserl when he emphasizes that it is not the subject *in itself* that is interesting for philosophy, it is the subject only as the "place for the totality of entities" (cf. *GA* 27, p. 360), i.e., as the locus where the totality of entities manifest themselves. For Heidegger, this means by extension that phenomenology is interested in the "subject" qua place of *Seinsverständnis*. But Husserl's regress to the subject as the dative of world-manifestation, we remember, is called the "transcendental reduction." Constitutive phenomenology is a *Forschungsaufgabe* carried out as a series of phenomenological reductions, as a "going back" from the entity in its "how" of manifestation to those structures in the experiencing subject that explain the coming about of manifestation. May we say, then, that Heidegger's project of fundamental ontology is the exact equivalent to Husserl's project of phenomenological reductions? Yes and no. As explained above, Heidegger has not one, but *two* (closely connected) phenomenological questions, viz. the question of transcendence and that of the meaning of being. The question of the meaning of being is a question about the modes of being that "occur," and more generally, what "being" as such means. The question of transcendence, on the other hand, is defined as the question, *which structures make possible the understanding of being* – and that understanding, in turn, is that which makes possible the experience of, and interaction with, indeed any kind of relation to entities. With what is bound to be a very preliminary characterization, we may consequently say that the genuine equivalent of Husserl's transcendental reduction seems to be Heidegger's regress to subjectivity *insofar as it aims to uncover the structures that make possible the understanding of being, and, by extension, the relation to entities*. This question is conspicuously akin to Husserl's question of constitution,[36] and Heidegger's method for approaching the question is almost identical to Husserl's reduction.[37] In fact, the difference seems to reside mainly in the fact that Heidegger makes the question more complicated by arguing that relations to entities must be mediated by something like an understanding of the mode of being of entities. Structurally, it seems obvious that *Heidegger asks a question of "constitution," and proposes to answer it in and through a phenomenological reduction*. Heidegger's other question, the question of the meaning of being, however, seems to have no equivalent in Husserlian phenomenology.

These issues are at the very thematic heart of the present study, and I return to them later. As a preliminary summary of the discussion in this section, it may be said that the *movement* in Heidegger's project of fundamental ontology ("back to the subject") is not significantly different from the movement in Husserl's transcendental phenomenology (the reduction), indeed not significantly different from the movement in transcendental philosophy in general. Moreover, Heidegger's project – or better, one of the two projects – shares the basic interests of transcendental philosophy; correctly understood, the project of decoding our "*mode of cognition* of objects, *as far as* this mode of cognition *is possible* a priori"[38] is Heidegger's project too. Hence it should not surprise one that Heidegger dubs his

---

[36] Carl Friedrich Gethmann argues emphatically that Heidegger's thinking here stands on the foundation of a constitutive transcendental philosophy, in fact *Husserl's* constitutive phenomenology (*Verstehen und Auslegung*, pp. 51, 186, 195). More on the relation between constitution and transcendence in Chapter VI.
[37] See Theo De Boer's convincing argument in "Heideggers kritiek op Husserl," pp. 247-249. Even earlier, Georg Misch argues that Heidegger's analytic of Dasein appropriates Husserl's reduction (*Lebensphilosophie und Phänomenologie*, p. 225). See also Francis Seeburger, "Heidegger and the Phenomenological Reduction."
[38] Kant, *Kritik der reinen Vernunft*, B 25.

phenomenological ontology "the transcendental science" (*GA* 24, pp. 23, 460; cf. *GA* 22, p. 10).[39]

6. THE DESTRUCTION OF THE ONTOLOGICAL TRADITION

In the first section of the present chapter, I present Heidegger's argument that relating to entities, whether perceptually, in using interaction, or whatever, presupposes an understanding of the "as-what," i.e., of the being, of the entities in question. In the section on the Husserlian epoché, I suggest that the "as-what" of an entity, such as the keyboard in front of me, is most aptly described as *Zuhandenheit*. In other words, according to Heidegger, it is evident that it is the understanding of the keyboard as ready-to-hand rather than simply present-at-hand that enables me to interact with the keyboard the way I do. Since it is Heidegger's contention (as it is Husserl's) that most entities we encounter are more similar to the keyboard than to pure, material *things*, it seems reasonable to claim that the being of those entities that we first and foremost encounter should bear the name *Zuhandenheit*. In drawing that conclusion, Heidegger is at odds with the everyday interpretation of being, according to which everything has the being of presence-at-hand. In the previous section, we learn that if we want to pose the question concerning being, we must focus on the understanding of being that essentially belongs to the human being, to Dasein. But when we turn to Dasein's understanding of being, we cannot but notice that these two incompatible "understandings" are equally present: everyday Dasein tends to interpret the being of each and every entity as presence-at-hand (*Vorhandenheit*), whereas immediately, so Heidegger claims, most entities present themselves rather as ready-to-hand, as something-with-which-to… According to Heidegger, it is this latter understanding that makes possible our encounters and interaction with the entities, whereas the former understanding is the *interpretation* we, as everyday Dasein, grow up in, are raised in (*SZ*, p. 20) – the interpretation Heidegger calls the "dominant" interpretation (*herrschende Ausgelegtheit*) (PIA, p. 249).

Although it should be evident by now that Heidegger is very critical towards the prevailing everyday and philosophical interpretations of the being of things and humans, he nevertheless recognizes that there might be some "truth" hidden in that

---

[39] Most Heidegger scholars agree with Heidegger that the project of fundamental ontology fails, and they are generally not unsympathetic to the claim that the reason for its failure is a least partly found in the fact that in *Sein und Zeit* and *Kant und das Problem der Metaphysik* Heidegger gets too entangled in the tradition of transcendental philosophy. Therefore, my presentation of the author of *Sein und Zeit* as a transcendental philosopher is hardly controversial. (For Heidegger scholars who themselves say as much, cf., e.g., Otto Pöggeler, *Der Denkweg Martin Heideggers*, pp. 64, 179-180, and John van Buren, *The Young Heidegger*, pp. 44, 363-367.) It is only if one argues, as does, e.g., Carl F. Gethmann (cf. *Verstehen und Auslegung*, pp. 12, 291, *et passim*), that Heidegger's thinking is transcendental from start to finish that one goes decidedly against the mainstream of Heidegger scholars. The question of Heidegger's thinking after the so-called "*Kehre*," and its relation to "transcendental philosophy," is beyond the scope of the present study, however.

interpretation. It is oversimplifying the matter to claim that the *Zuhandenheit*-interpretation is "right" (period), whereas the *Vorhandenheit*-interpretation is always "wrong." On the contrary, within certain boundaries, some legitimacy can probably be attributed to the notion of *Vorhandensein*, Heidegger emphasizes (*GA* 63, p. 91; cf. *SZ*, p. 55). Heidegger's proposed way for discovering the *positive* aspect of the prevailing interpretation of being is given the apparently negative title of *destruction of the ontological tradition* (cf. *SZ*, p. 22). For the proper understanding of the fundamental ontological project, it is of some importance to understand, at least in outline, the idea of the destruction, and the systematic place it occupies in the project of *Sein und Zeit*. This is what I intend to offer in the present section.

It is a basic assumption of Heidegger's that the prevailing everyday interpretation of being – according to which everything is presence-at-hand – is closely associated with the interpretation of being prevalent in the ontological tradition dating back to ancient Greece. It is the philosophical tradition that dictates that we interpret the mode of being of ourselves and the things around us the way we do. Only, we do not *see* that we stand thus in a tradition (*SZ*, p. 21; *GA* 17, p. 282). In fact, when viewing matters from the viewpoint of everydayness, it is *obvious* that a keyboard, say, is a material thing with certain properties that make it useful for the purpose of writing. Such a description, obviously true as it appears, wears no "tag" or "index" to reveal that it is a description handed down from the philosophical tradition. Stated otherwise, the tradition, in handing down to us such an interpretation of being, *hides* from us the fact that it hands anything down (*SZ*, p. 21). Presently, of course, we occupy a position "outside" everydayness: the epoché has taught us to "see" something like modes of being (and "see" that the dominant interpretation might not be the "right" one), and the method of formal indication has given us an idea of how to conceptually approach the thus seen. In other words, we are able to see the discrepancy between the dominant interpretation and the implicit understanding of being that is manifest in Dasein's interaction with entities.

The interpretation of the being of each and every entity as *Vorhandenheit*, so Heidegger says, is handed down from tradition, but in such a way that we do not see it. To everyday Dasein, it seems the most obvious matter in the world. If the destruction is critical towards anything, it is precisely towards this "attitude-of-perceiving-as-self-evident" (*Selbstverständlichkeit*) (*SZ*, p. 21) the interpretation according to which all entities are taken as present-at-hand; the destruction is not, in fact, a critique of the "content" of the everyday interpretation as such. On the contrary, it aims in a specific way to *appropriate* the dominant interpretation. Heidegger repeatedly points out that the destruction does not criticize "the past," but only the *present* (*SZ*, p. 22; *GA* 17, p. 119; PIA, p. 239). He is even more specific in a recently discovered manuscript dating from 1922,[40] a manuscript that contains

---

[40] This is the so-called *Natorp-Bericht*. For the history of this manuscript – not unimportant for an elucidation of the *personal* aspects of the Husserl-Heidegger relationship – see the "Nachwort des Herausgebers" in PIA, pp. 270-274.

what must be Heidegger's most lucid presentation of the project of destruction. As he writes there, "the critique which simply and already arises from the concrete actualization of the destruction does not apply to the bare fact *that* we stand within a tradition, but applies rather to the *how* [*dem Wie*]" (PIA, pp. 249-250). *As far as the destruction itself is concerned*, the problem is not *that* we are handed down an interpretation according to which every entity is understood as *vorhanden* (although elsewhere, Heidegger offers ample criticism of this interpretation), but rather *how* we stand within this tradition, viz. that we are *in ignorance of the fact that we stand in a tradition*. What must happen under the heading of a destruction of the history of ontology is a "deconstructing" (*abbauenden*) going-back (*Rückgang*) to the original motives and experiences that might have lead to the prevailing *Vorhandenheit*-interpretation (PIA, p. 249); a "going-back" to the "sources" from which the philosophical tradition – "partly" in an "authentic" manner – has shaped its interpretation (*SZ*, p. 21). We must, in other words, begin in the present, with its "blind" adherence to a handed-down interpretation of being, and step by step follow this interpretation back in history, through its stages of "obviousness," or "self-evidentness," until we reach its "source": the "living" and at least partly justified (Greek) experience that gave rise to it (cf. PIA, p. 249).[41] Of course, we shall not be surprised if we discover that the prevailing interpretation is indeed only partly justified, legitimate within certain narrow limits, but this does not change the fact that the destruction is mainly *positive* in relation to the tradition: "But to bury the past in nullity is not the purpose of this destruction; its aim is *positive*; its negative function remains unexpressed and indirect" (*SZ*, p. 23). When we destruct the history of metaphysics, we are precisely re-discovering the domain within which the interpretation of entities as being *vorhanden* is justified, and at the same time we are uncovering the *boundaries* of that domain (*GA* 17, p. 118). In the destruction, then, we put the traditional interpretation in its proper place; far from "negating" it, the destruction is in fact a *positive appropriation* (*positive Aneignung*) (*GA* 24, p. 31) of the tradition. As indicated already, the negativity of the destruction applies only to the "present," more precisely to the blind *Selbstverständlichkeit* with which we accept the interpretation of being as presence-at-hand for each and every entity.

In the present context, it is important to locate the precise position of the "destruction" within the project of fundamental ontology. It is quite natural to assume – in view of Husserl's alleged neglect of history[42] – that the notion of

---

[41] Few will fail to notice how close this comes to Husserl's notion of going back through a tradition of "sedimented" conceptuality to the historical "original instigation" (*Urstiftung*) of the scientific meaning-formations (*Sinngebilde*) and methods, developed in his last great work, the *Krisis* (cf. *Hua* VI, pp. 57, 73). It is very probable that Husserl is under some influence from Heidegger in developing this notion. Even if it could be shown that thoughts such as these are found in Husserl's manuscripts before the publication of *SZ*, the odds are that Heidegger is the main inspiration. It is thus an interesting fact that it was Husserl who sent the *Natorp-Bericht* to Göttingen and Marburg (cf. PIA, "Nachwort des Herausgebers," p. 271). Could he have read it himself?

[42] This is Heidegger's own verdict on Husserlian phenomenology (cf. *GA* 63, p. 75; *GA* 17, pp. 213-214; WDF, p. 176). In his "Vorwort" to William J. Richardson's *Heidegger: Through Phenomenology to*

destruction constitutes an implicit criticism of Husserl more than anyone else. Whatever Husserl's manuscripts might contain on the subject of historicity, the crucial point in connection with our present interest in the question(s) of being is that the "destruction" is *not* an *indispensable* methodological component in any investigation of being, at least the way the Heidegger of *Sein und Zeit* understood such an investigation. In fact, the destruction *presupposes* an investigation already well under way. Let me try to substantiate this claim.

In one of the early Freiburg lecture courses, Heidegger seems at one point to claim that philosophy *begins* with the destruction (*GA* 59, p. 183), only to admit at once that in truth, the destruction cannot get started without a "basic experience" (*Grunderfahrung*), "indeed a phenomenological basic experience" (*GA* 59, p. 187). What Heidegger is forced to recognize is that the project of a destruction of the history of metaphysics needs not one, but two "guiding clues." In order to initiate the destruction, we must have a clear notion of (1) that which is to be "destructed," viz. the dominant ontological interpretation, and (2) the "basic experience" just mentioned (*GA* 59, p. 180). Without our phenomenological *Grunderfahrung* of something like readiness-to-hand, how could the dominant interpretation appear anything but true, even if it had lost its "obviousness"? And without keeping this dominant interpretation in view, how could we proceed to "destruct" it? Both guiding clues seem necessary for the destruction. To begin the destruction of the tradition, we must already have gained enough distance from the latter to see it *as* a tradition. More precisely, we must have had access to some sort of "phenomenological basic experience" that reveals to us both that the handed-down interpretation is an interpretation of *being*, and that it is only *an* interpretation, one that can be questioned regarding its legitimacy. Accordingly, it is only *when we have already learned to "see" something like modes of being that we can begin the destructive appropriation of the tradition.*[43] This has two consequences.

First, the task of the destruction is not to remove the obstacles from our view, so as to enable us to see something like modes of being, and more specifically, *alternative* modes of being to that of *Vorhandenheit*. It is not, then, the destruction which initially "frees" us, or distances us from the traditional interpretation of being; on the contrary, there could be no motive to initiate a destruction, had we not

---

Thought, the old Heidegger confirms this assessment, while apparently sharpening it: "The historicity of thought remained *completely* [*durchaus*] *foreign* to such a position [i.e., Husserl's "philosophical position"]" (p. xv, my emphasis). The question, however, is whether the "*durchaus*" is justified. In his later years, Husserl would not only lay much greater emphasis on historicity in general, he would even refer to a "historical path to phenomenology" as the best way to access transcendental phenomenology (*Hua* VI, pp. 378-382, 495; *Hua* XXIX, p. 426). As mentioned in the introduction above, Husserl scholars thus speak of a "*Kehre*" in Husserl's phenomenology, implying that Heidegger's critique might very well hold for the early and "middle" Husserl that Heidegger knew, but less so for the later Husserl. Cf. Rudolf Bernet *et al.*, *Edmund Husserl: Darstellung seines Denkens*, pp. 10, 213.

[43] Jean-Luc Marion argues along similar lines. Cf. *Reduction and Givenness*, pp. 108-109, 228n.

already distanced ourselves from the traditional interpretation.[44] All of this is in fact implied by Heidegger's own description of the task of destruction in *Sein und Zeit*:

> We understand this task as one in which by taking *the question of being as our clue* [*am Leitfaden der Seinsfrage*], we are to *destroy* the traditional [or "handed-down": *überlieferten*] content of ancient ontology until we arrive at those primordial experiences in which we acquired our first characterizations of being – the characterizations which have guided us ever since. (*SZ*, p. 22)

One cannot begin a destruction of the handed-down stock of classical ontology without first recognizing the handed-down *as* handed-down, and – at least equally important in the present context – one cannot carry out such a destruction following the "guiding clue" of the *Seinsfrage*, without having developed that question (in some rough shape) already.[45] It is as if both the positive and the negative work involved in reaching the thematic of being must be completed before one can launch the project of destructing the tradition. Accordingly, the only sensible task left for that destruction becomes that of discovering what "truth," after all, there is in the handed down interpretation. It therefore makes perfect sense when Heidegger emphasizes the mainly positive nature of the destruction – the destruction is, far removed from anything "negative," an appropriation of the "truth" of the tradition within its proper limits.

Second, insofar as Husserl fails to pose the question of being in Heidegger's sense (which, we should note, has not been demonstrated yet), this cannot be due to his failure to "destruct" the history of ontology. If we must already be awakened to the Heideggerian problematic of modes of being in order to initiate the destruction, then it cannot be Husserl's (alleged) neglect of the idea of a destruction that causes his (alleged) neglect of the question of the meaning of being. The contrary, however, could be the case, i.e., that Husserl's (alleged) neglect of the question of being plays a significant part in his (alleged) failure to destruct the ontological tradition. In other words, the problem of "destruction" is not of crucial importance in a discussion of an explicit posing of the question of being, however crucial it might eventually become in Heidegger's actual ontological investigation. Accordingly, it is perfectly reasonable that in the context of the planned work on *Sein und Zeit*, Heidegger

---

[44] Thus I cannot agree with Philip Buckley's claim that only the destruction "can shake Dasein out of its somnolent life in the standard interpretations of the 'They'" (*Husserl, Heidegger, and the Crisis of Philosophical Responsibility*, p. 183). The destruction is not possible until Dasein has already been awoken from that forgetful sleep.

[45] The suggestion that this basis for the destruction itself becomes accessible only in *another* destruction (so argues Hans Ruin in his *Enigmatic Origins*, p. 84) seems to me not very promising. From the way Ruin introduces the idea, it is clear that no infinite regress is invited – it is not the case that the second destruction presupposes a third, and so forth. Rather, a full circle results, in that the second destruction presupposes the first, while the first destruction could only be launched on the basis of the second destruction. Ruin thinks this "is the circularity with which philosophical thought must now attempt to struggle" (ibid.), but it would seem to me that the Husserlian tool of epoché and Heidegger's own method of formal indication show how it can be possible to thematize being without needing to carry out – at least initially – *any* destruction.

places the problem of destruction in the (never published) second part (cf. *SZ*, pp. 39-40), rather than in the beginning of the work.

The most important insight gained in the present section is that – in contrast to the notions of epoché, formal indication, and fundamental ontology – the notion of destruction seems not to be of crucial importance to the project of phenomenological ontology, at least the way Heidegger conceives of this project in *Sein und Zeit*. To be sure, for a full phenomenological ontology, mapping the domain of legitimacy of the prevailing interpretation is an indispensable task, but it is one that presupposes that much essential work is already done. In an investigation of the basic projects of Husserlian and Heideggerian phenomenology, the destruction does not, therefore, belong to the thematic core.[46]

7. PHENOMENOLOGICAL ONTOLOGY

By now, we have ample reason to suspect that what Heidegger labels ontology is something quite different from the "regional" and "formal" ontologies of Husserl. Seen from the vantage point of Heidegger, these latter "ontologies" – aiming to describe what essentially holds for particular regions of objects, or for any object regardless of region – do not even reach the truly ontological level. In the present section, I attempt to substantiate this claim.

On the surface of things, Husserl's "ontologies" are in at least partial agreement with the ontological claims advanced by Heidegger. After all, what a Husserlian ontology of material substance would reveal might correspond pretty well with a Heideggerian ontology of *Vorhandensein*, and perhaps a Husserlian ontology of the region of consciousness, or of the "person," would correspond with Heidegger's ontology of Dasein. Does not Husserl speak in *Ideen I* of the "most essential"

---

[46] Against my interpretation that the destruction has some positive task within the framework of *Sein und Zeit*, one could argue that in fact it has *no* task left to perform within that framework. Thomas Schwarz Wentzer thus claims that once Heidegger places the project of an analysis of Dasein in the center of *Sein und Zeit* as something that should function as the guiding clue for the subsequent destruction, he realizes that it is, after all, perfectly possible to practice phenomenological ontology *without having set the destruction in motion*, and therefore the destruction is no longer needed within the project defined by the analytic of Dasein (Wentzer, *Bewahrung der Geschichte*, pp. 145-158). Certainly, the task left for it to perform is no longer *crucial* to the Heideggerian undertaking – indeed, the conclusion of the present section is that the destruction does not belong to the methodological "core" of Heidegger's phenomenological project. I am not convinced, however, that there is absolutely *no* task for it to perform within the framework of that project. (In fact, perhaps one should even consider the reduction more important than I do in this section. It could thus be argued that it is precisely a "destructive" confrontation with the tradition that makes Heidegger so attentive to the possible implicit ontological commitments in our philosophical concepts; and that formal indication could thus, in a certain sense, be said to spring from the destruction. I shall be happy to grant that that the destruction has more functions within the program of fundamental ontology than explicitly acknowledged in this section. However, I still believe that the main argument is essentially correct: a destruction *am Leitfaden der Seinsfrage* only makes sense if a lot of work is already done. Obviously, we must already be able to formulate the question of being – we must already see that being is *questionable* – if this question is to function as our "guide" or "clue" in our destructive confrontation with the tradition.)

difference between being (*Sein*) as *Erlebnis* and being (*Sein*) as thing (*Hua* III/1, p. 87)? And does he not add that what we have touched upon here is simply "the essentially necessary diversity among modes of being [*Seinsweisen*], the most cardinal of them all [...]: the diversity between *consciousness and reality*" (*Hua* III/1, pp. 87-88)? The terminology is unambiguously that of an ontological investigation in Heidegger's sense, but does Husserl *explicitly* ask about these "modes of being" *as* modes of being? Heidegger claims he does not (*GA* 20, p. 158). Underneath the surface of apparent agreement with regard to both line of questioning and (at least partially) answers, we find fundamental differences – differences that have to do with what Heidegger immediately after writing *Sein und Zeit* begins to call the *ontological difference* (*ontologische Differenz*) (cf. *GA* 24, pp. 22, 109, 454).[47]

From Heidegger's point of view, Husserl's regional "ontologies" – no matter how sharply they differentiate between the region of material things and the region of "consciousness" – remain naively committed to a particular ontology (in Heidegger's sense of the word). This is because they fail to pose the question of modes of being *in explicit contrast to entities and their properties*. Husserl's regional "ontologies" aim to determine what essentially belongs to particular "regions" of entities, but they do not ask whether these essential traits should be understood as attributes belonging to an entity that, in principle, could be stripped of them, so as to leave the entity a "naked" thing. Stated otherwise, the question that is never explicitly posed by Husserlian regional "ontologies," according to Heidegger, is whether, for example, the essential traits of "consciousness" and "material thing" should be considered *properties* that in principle could be removed from the entities in question, so that the entities would be reduced somehow to "indifferent" objects, or whether the essential differences at stake here are rather differences in *modes of being* (cf. *GA* 20, pp. 158, 178). Heidegger illustrates the point with the examples of "sound" and "color": "When I seek to distinguish the essence of color from that of sound, this distinction can be made *without my asking about the manner of being of these two objects*" (*GA* 20, p. 151, my emphasis). From the perspective of the *Seinsfrage*, then, Husserl's regional "ontologies," failing to explicitly pose the question of modes of being, are dangerously ambiguous. However, they do not

---

[47] Jean-Luc Marion claims that Heidegger has a concept of *ontological difference* in play already in *Sein und Zeit* itself, "contrary to the opinion, to our knowledge without exception, of the commentators" (Marion, *Reduction and Givenness*, p. 116). Has Marion discovered something that escapes all other commentators? I think not. To be sure, Marion is correct in emphasizing that the expression *ontologische Unterschied* appears in *SZ* (e.g., on p. 56). However, it refers, not to the difference between being and entities, but to a difference in modes of being. Marion himself eventually admits that it is only after *Sein und Zeit* (in fact he says after 1927, but that is obviously incorrect given the fact that the notion appears several times in Heidegger's 1927 lecture course, *Die Grundprobleme der Phänomenologie*) that Heidegger uses the notion *ontologische Differenz* to refer to the difference between being and entities (*Reduction and Givenness*, pp. 127-128). However, the *Sache* that is only after *SZ* explicitly *labeled* "ontological difference" is very present in Heidegger's magnum opus, as Alberto Rosales argues in detail (see his *Transzendenz und Differenz*, Part I).

remain ambiguous for long, according to Heidegger. Rather, the regional essences (*Wesen*) are naively interpreted precisely along the lines of "attributes" belonging to "real objects," whose being as a matter of course is understood as *Vorhandensein* (*GA* 20, pp. 151-155). The whole difficulty stems from the circumstance that Husserl (from Heidegger's point of view) fails to see the difference between (modes of) being and (properties of) entities. Husserl, in other words, fails to notice what Heidegger calls the *ontological difference*, viz. "the differentiation between being and entities" (*die Scheidung zwischen Sein und Seiendem*) (*GA* 24, p. 22).[48]

But Husserl has at least one other concept of "ontology." Transcendental phenomenology is itself ontology, in fact the only truly universal ontology. This is because only transcendental phenomenology, with its thematization of transcendental subjectivity and all this subjectivity encompassed (on both the "noetic" and the "noematic" sides), is able to include all there is. However, it seems obvious that these considerations, in Heidegger's terminology, are purely *ontic* – they are considerations of entities rather than of being. The "ontologies" of the natural attitude are abstract precisely because they fail to include an *entity*, viz. transcendental subjectivity. To be sure, transcendental subjectivity is not just any entity, but is it not an entity nonetheless (cf. *Hua* IX, pp. 296-297)? Interestingly, Husserl seems to have to say that it is not, because (as we point out in Chapter II) there are not *two* entities – human (mundane) subjectivity and transcendental subjectivity. But in what sense, then, is only transcendental phenomenology "complete" and "universal" ontology? What "ontological addition" does the discovery of transcendental subjectivity imply? That remains to be seen.

Against all these Husserlian concepts of "ontology," none of which (with the possible exception of the last one), according to Heidegger reach the truly ontological level, Heidegger calls for an explicit distinction between entities and being, and an explicit posing of the question of being. Heidegger is not suggesting that the philosophical tradition, after Aristotle and up to Husserl, is not *about* being, rather he claims it fails to pose the question of being *explicitly*. Husserl – so Heidegger elaborates in a lecture course – not only poses the question of being, he also answers it (*GA* 20, p. 155). Or better, he answers it without explicitly posing it (*GA* 20, p. 158), thereby "dogmatically" taking a particular notion of being for granted throughout, namely the notion we know from *Sein und Zeit* as presence-at-hand (cf. *GA* 20, p. 157). This is no coincidental blunder on Husserl's part, according to Heidegger (*GA* 20, p. 182) – it is the result of a deeper case of neglect. As illustrated by looking at Husserl's notion of "regional ontology," if one does not explicitly discriminate being from entities, one cannot thematically reach the level of *being*. Everything depends upon making explicit the *ontological difference*:

We must be able to bring out clearly the difference between being and entities [*den Unterschied zwischen Sein und Seiendem*] in order to make something like being the theme of inquiry. This distinction is not

---

[48] This point is emphasized by James C. Morrison, "Husserl and Heidegger: The Parting of the Ways," p. 56.

arbitrary; rather, it is the *one by which the theme of ontology and thus of philosophy itself is first of all attained*. It is a distinction which is first and foremost constitutive for ontology. (*GA* 24, p. 22, my emphasis)

The truly ontological thematic, the thematic of being, is only reached when one explicitly contrasts being with entities. Because Husserl's regional "ontologies" are oblivious of the ontological difference, they remain thematically on the ontic level, with unnoticed ontological commitments in play, according to Heidegger.

But what about the question of constitution, which, after all, is Husserl's *real* question? The question of constitution, so I claim in Chapter II, is in some way or other a question about *being* – it is a question about the *being-there-for-us* of the mundane entities and the world. It seems that here, at least, there is a quite explicit discrimination in play between entities and their being. So should we not conclude that Husserl, too, formulates a phenomenological ontology, although he seems to reserve the name "ontology" for a number of *ontic* investigations? Unfortunately, things are more complicated. The Husserlian question of constitution is similar to Heidegger's question of transcendence, and while that certainly entitles us to label the question of constitution a question of "being," it also shows that it is not to be identified with the specific Heideggerian *Seinsfrage*. Is there any such equivalent in Husserl? The immediate answer would seem to have to be negative. What is more, does not Husserl's question of constitution pertain *only to the constituted*, i.e., does it not leave the "entity" *for whom* constitution occurs – transcendental subjectivity – unquestioned regarding its being?

Before these questions can be even partly answered, we must remove the somewhat abstract appearance of this whole discussion. Chapters II and III attempt to present the general outlines of the phenomenological projects of Husserl and Heidegger – the basic questions and the most important methodological notions – which naturally excludes a concrete treatment of the "content" of their respective phenomenological work. This latter task is all the more important since much of the debate surrounding the relation between Husserlian and Heideggerian phenomenology centers on more concrete issues. If we want to be able to discuss freely the problems of constitution, transcendence, and manners of being, then it is necessary to address some of the points that have generated discussion in the literature on Husserl and Heidegger, so that they will not return to haunt us when we reach the matters most central to our theme.

CHAPTER IV
WORLD

1. OBJECT-INTENTIONALITY AND WORLD

Much discussion in the literature on Husserl and Heidegger revolves around the concept of world. It would not be entirely wrong to say that a significant part of that discussion was triggered by a famous passage in *Sein und Zeit*, in which Heidegger charges traditional philosophy with presupposing too little rather than too much when characterizing subjectivity. This passage, which occupies us through Chapter V, runs as follows:

> If, in the ontology of Dasein, we "take our departure" from a worldless "I" in order to provide this "I" with an object and an ontologically baseless relation to that object, then we have "presupposed" not too much, but *too little*. (*SZ*, pp. 315-316, cf. p. 206)

How does Husserl react to this when reading *Sein und Zeit*? Having already read more than three hundred pages of the book that, as Gadamer suggests, must look ambiguous to him, sometimes articulating a transcendental phenomenology, sometimes criticizing the same,[1] Husserl is suspicious that the charge is above all leveled at his phenomenology. In the margin of his copy of *Sein und Zeit*, Husserl notes: "objection 'worldless I'" (RB, p. 37).

Although the criticism of Husserl is veiled throughout the pages of Heidegger's magnum opus – often disguised as a critique of Descartes[2] – it is in this case so thinly disguised that there can be little doubt that Husserl is in fact one of Heidegger's primary targets. But if so, is it a justified criticism? In spite of Husserl's preoccupation with the notion of intentionality, many commentators are willing to grant the legitimacy of the charge.[3] It would be insufficient to reply that these commentators simply fail to pay attention to intentionality, as I argue presently, or that they misinterpret the epoché as involving a command to exclude the world from the phenomenological thematization of a "pure" ego. Rather than rushing to choose sides in this debate, we need to approach the question with care and from two different corners. First, we must examine the notion of "world" phenomenologically – not only Husserl's notion, but also the one Heidegger might have in mind when leveling the charge. Is there any common ground to be found here, or is what

---

[1] Gadamer, *Wahrheit und Methode*, p. 259n.
[2] See Heidegger's own comment to p. 98 of *Sein und Zeit*, *SZ*, p. 442. Indeed, Günter Figal suggests that Descartes basically functions as a pseudonym for Husserl in Heidegger's main work (*Martin Heidegger: Phänomenologie der Freiheit*, p. 18).
[3] Timothy Stapleton simply declares that this charge is "undoubtedly correct" (*Husserl and Heidegger: The Question of a Phenomenological Beginning*, p. 101; cf. p. 103). Friedrich-Wilhelm von Herrmann subscribes to the same view, but with an important qualification (*Subjekt und Dasein*, p. 65). See, too, Jean-Luc Marion, *Reduction and Givenness*, p. 97, and Lilian Alweiss, *The World Unclaimed*, p. 72.

Heidegger labels "world" in fact absent from Husserlian phenomenology, or at least not something that essentially belongs to transcendental subjectivity as understood by Husserl? This last remark suggests the second line of questioning we must pursue here. What is the notion of Dasein we find in Heidegger, and is it perhaps the case that being-in-the-world (*In-der-Welt-sein*) describes more aptly the being of Dasein than the being of Husserl's transcendental subjectivity? These are sizeable questions, and they are given only sketchy and preliminary answers in the present study. But, if we are to be able to locate with some accuracy the differences separating Heidegger's and Husserl's questions of being, we must to a certain extent understand what conceptions of world, mundane entities, and subject are being developed in the two phenomenologies.

Mundane entities are discussed in some detail in Chapter I, and although our focus in that chapter is on the "everyday" or "natural" life and the extent to which there could be any motivation for such a life to question itself, what is said there remains true. It does so for Husserl because he never gives up his "sympathy" with the natural attitude's descriptions of entities (cf. *Hua* XIV, p. 278) – although he does not approve of any "naturalization" of the soul or of cultural objects, and, more importantly, although he contests the claim that any such description in the natural attitude could ever be the whole story. It is also true for Heidegger because he delivers his description of everyday Dasein from a standpoint that is already phenomenological. As far as individual mundane entities are concerned, then, we already have sufficient indications that the Husserlian and Heideggerian accounts are – on the "descriptive" level at least – close to identical. In Chapter VI, we return to a discussion of Husserl and Heidegger's very different ontological interpretations of the description.

As already documented in detail, it cannot be the case that Husserl's epoché and reduction imply that one should ignore the world in favor of some "subjective" sphere of being. On the contrary, the method of reduction demands that we keep the world and everything mundane in view, since this has to function as transcendental guiding clues for our going-back to subjectivity. Also, if what is meant by the charge of "worldlessness" is specifically that the reduction, although in need of a mundane "guiding clue," involves a "retreat" back to a subjective sphere, never to return to the world again, we can dismiss the charge at once, especially in view of the discussion in Section 5 of Chapter II. The regress to subjectivity does not imply an abandonment of the world or the mundane; the reduction does nothing but articulate the being-there-for-us of the world, and it can only do so by never "leaving" the theme of world. However, from the fact that the world does not disappear from the focus of Husserlian phenomenology with the performance of the transcendental reduction, it does not follow that *the subjectivity* reached in and through such a reduction cannot be "worldless" in some precise sense yet to be specified. Surely, Heidegger would never think that Husserlian phenomenology has no interest whatsoever in the world; rather, he must have reason to assume that, in spite of Husserl's insistence on the importance of the world and the mundane as transcendental guiding clues, the transcendental subjectivity that Husserl uncovers nevertheless has to be called "worldless."

But Husserl never tires of emphasizing that – as intentionally directed – transcendental subjectivity *has in itself* a relation to objects. It is essentially object-directed, and were we to take intentionality away from the transcendental subject, it would simply cease to be *transcendental* subjectivity, since it could no longer be the "place of manifestation" of anything. And not having experiences *of* anything, it would in fact also cease to be *subjectivity* in any concrete sense (cf. *Hua* XIX/1, pp. 377-378).

In spite of all this, one commentator – Pierre Keller – claims that Husserl opts "for a theory of intentionality based on acts of consciousness that need have no object at all,"[4] and that this is just what constitutes the crucial difference between Husserl and Heidegger.[5] Certainly, insofar as what is meant is that acts of imagination, memory, or even perception might have intentional objects that turn out, in fact, not to exist in reality (one may, once again, think of the puddles seen on the road ahead on a hot day), then Husserl's theory of intentionality does have a great deal to say about precisely these sorts of acts.[6] But one is left to wonder what types of acts, then, Husserl should study instead. Furthermore, why is it a problem to study acts whose objects *need* not exist? It seems that the commentator's apparent worries – that phenomenology should concentrate on acts whose objects *necessarily* exist – surely cannot be Heidegger's.

However, as we read on in the commentary, it emerges that the real issue is that Husserl allegedly thinks intentionality can be understood "by abstracting from the existence of the very objects to which consciousness is directed in intentionality."[7] It is precisely this view and the resultant "internalist" interpretation of intentionality in Husserl that Heidegger rejects, according to Pierre Keller.[8] Notice that the issue here is not whether the objects of intentional experiences should count "as nothing" to phenomenology, as Husserl originally claims in *Logische Untersuchungen* (*Hua* XIX/1, p. 427), or whether the exclusively "noetic" focus that Husserl later sees as characteristic of that work should be supplemented by a "noematic" focus (cf. *Hua* III/1, p. 298). If anyone accuses Husserl's transcendental phenomenology of "ignoring" the objects of acts, in order to concentrate on the subjective acts themselves, they can be refuted easily; but obviously this is not Keller's contention. Rather, it is the *existence* of the objects that is allegedly ignored by Husserl, and

---

[4] Pierre Keller, *Husserl and Heidegger on Human Experience*, p. 17.
[5] Keller, *Husserl and Heidegger on Human Experience*, p. 116.
[6] Interestingly, however, the Cartesian Husserl would precisely say that his phenomenology or his theory of intentionality *isn't* itself *based* on acts that need have no existing object, although it *describes* such acts in detail. While I perceive, for instance, it is absolutely indubitable that the act of perceiving exists, and thus *the phenomenological act directed at the act of perceiving is precisely the one, for which an object cannot possibly be non-existent*. But clearly, Keller is discussing the types of acts "dealt with" in Husserl's theory of intentionality, rather than the ones in which phenomenologizing itself is effectuated.
[7] Keller, *Husserl and Heidegger on Human Experience*, p. 116.
[8] Ibid.

hence leads him to an "internalism" unacceptable to Heidegger. But in what way *should* Husserl take the existence of the intended objects into account? Certainly, Husserl would be quick to point out that the noematic correlates uncovered by phenomenology – the intended objects just as intended – would be, e.g., for (normal) acts of perception, precisely "real," "existing." When touching the keyboard in front of me, there is no question that the perceived keyboard is perceived as existing, and thus it would simply be bad phenomenology if Husserl were to abstract from the "existence of the object" in this sense. Needless to say, Husserl's works are full of passages that document that he does not make this mistake. I suspect that what the commentator has in mind is a much stronger notion of "existence": not existence as something that belongs to a description of certain noematic correlates, but existence *out there, in reality, in the real world*. In other words, the main difficulty with Husserl's theory of intentionality would then be its failure to take into account the question of whether or not the intended objects *really* exist, and this is a significant difficulty because it might be that the real existence of the objects plays a major part in the "intentional" account of our awareness of them. Husserl ends in an unacceptable "internalist" position because he never even considers the role of the intentional objects, qua existing, in his account of our experience of them.[9]

Brought down to this formula, Keller's criticism is clearly an echo of the "naturalist" objection discussed at some length in Chapter II, Section 2. This reading seems to be confirmed by the definition Keller gives of internalism. An internalist is one who believes

> it is possible to understand at least some contents of the mind in the narrow terms provided by introspection and first-person awareness that does *not appeal to any knowledge of other persons or objects outside of the person in question*.[10]

The difficulty with Husserl's account of intentionality, it would appear, is thus that it tries to account for our awareness of the world and of the mundane without appealing to any knowledge of that world and those mundane entities. But as emphasized in Chapter II, one cannot *explain* our experiences of the world and of mundane entities by reference to the existence of that world and those entities. This

---

[9] It must be pointed out that there is one other way of reading Keller's criticism. Let me quote the passage from p. 116 in full: "The nature of intentionality cannot be understood by abstracting from the existence of the very objects to which consciousness is directed in intentionality." What if "existence" is used here as a synonym for "being," or "mode of being"? Then the passage would reflect Heidegger's view, as presented in Chapter III, Section 1, very well indeed. Apart from the question of why Keller then prefers to say "existence" (which in Heidegger generally means the mode of being specific to *Dasein*) rather than (mode of) being, it is not clear to me how introducing the notion of being, and understanding of being, involves a criticism or a rejection of "Husserl's *internalist* interpretation of intentionality" (ibid., my emphasis), rather than, say, of Husserl's blindness to the question of *being*. It seems to me that if "existence" here means "mode of being," the question would be whether Husserl is not missing something in his account of intentionality, something essential to intentionality, viz. being. But this is not something, the absence of which turns Husserl's account into an "internalist" account. Rather, it makes it an account that fails to reach the level of *ontology*.

[10] Keller, *Husserl and Heidegger on Human Experience*, p. 111; my emphasis.

is because we have no access to "the existence of objects" except through our experience of them *as* existing, which means that the naturalist critic must "live" uncritically in, and in her explanation "make use of," the very type of experience we want to explain. She starts out at the wrong end, assuming as non-problematic the very experience she herself wants to problematize; in a word, she confounds the *explanans* and the *explanandum*, and we have seen in some detail why this cannot amount to any explanation at all. Husserl, therefore, cannot be criticized consistently for understanding intentionality in abstraction from the existence of the intentional objects – because if Husserl does not "abstract" in his account of intentionality from the existence (in the sense discussed) of the intended objects, if he does not refrain from appealing in the natural way to our knowledge of them, he can not succeed in making intelligible our intentional awareness of those objects at all.[11] I do not believe that Heidegger's charge of "worldlessness" has anything to do with Pierre Keller's criticism of Husserl, nor do I believe that Heidegger would make Keller's objection his own under any other heading. In *Grundprobleme der Phänomenologie*, for example, Heidegger rejects emphatically the "natural" account of intentionality according to which intentionality is a relation between two entities, a relation that subsists only insofar as the entities (object and subject) exist. In opposition to such an account, Heidegger insists that the "subject" itself *is* intentionally related (*GA 24*, pp. 83-84; *GA 20*, p. 40). This is hardly compatible with the position that a satisfactory account of intentionality should take into consideration the existence of, or our (non-phenomenological) knowledge of, the intended objects. As should already be clear to some extent, the present study argues that Heidegger (at least the Heidegger of *SZ*) is a transcendental phenomenologist, posing questions of constitution, and not a realist of the type brought to our attention by Keller.[12]

Intentional experiences always have their intentional objects (although these need not exist). There is no intention without an *intended* object, thus insofar as transcendental subjectivity is essentially characterized by intentionality it would be analytically false to call it "objectless." But "objectless," as Heideggerians point out, is not the same as "worldless"; and while Husserlian transcendental subjectivity cannot rightfully be described as having the first mentioned characteristic, one might be justified – precisely because it is *exclusively* object-directed, directed at entities – in giving it the latter label. In other words, Heidegger can accuse Husserl's transcendental subjectivity of being "worldless" because "there is no concept of world in Husserl other than that of a totality of spatio-temporal events regulated by

---

[11] For a similar reply to Keller's internalism charge, see Alweiss, *The World Unclaimed*, pp. 4-21. See, as well, Dan Zahavi, "Husserl's Noema and the Internalism-Externalism Debate."

[12] However, Steven Crowell argues convincingly that Heidegger shifts "toward a transcendental realistic perspective that is not supplemental to, but *inconsistent* with, the phenomenological project" (*Husserl, Heidegger, and the Space of Meaning*, p. 237) shortly after *SZ* (e.g., in the "metontology" of *GA 26*), and that *SZ* in fact already in an inconsistent way incorporates both exclusive perspectives. For Crowell's argument in its entirety, see the cited work, pp. 222-243.

laws,"[13] or other than that of the "totality of real (and ideal) entities."[14] Husserl's only concept of world is that of a *totality* of entities or events, it would seem. This conception of world is one Heidegger briefly mentions in *Sein und Zeit*, and he labels it "world" (in quotation marks) in contrast to his own conception of world (without quotation marks) as that in which Dasein "lives" (*SZ*, pp. 64-65). It is thus with respect to the latter concept of world that Husserlian transcendental subjectivity is "worldless": it is not "world"-less – it precisely has "world," i.e., is intentionally related to entities – but it is worldless, i.e., lacking any essential bond with the *world* in Heidegger's specific sense.

Now, before we discuss whether this in fact must be a problem for Husserl – it might be, after all, that the Heideggerian concept of world is phenomenologically unsound or inferior to Husserl's conception – let us take a closer look at the claims just cited. Is Husserl's sole concept of world really that of a totality of either spatio-temporal events or of real and ideal entities? Do we find in Husserl no other notion of world than that of a totality of beings and events?

2. WORLD AS HORIZON

It is certainly true that Husserl, as Ludwig Landgrebe points out, tends to initiate his analyses of world-constitution by focusing on the individual given entity.[15] But from the beginning, Husserl appears to realize that the individual entity is never given in complete isolation, as if perceiving this computer screen would initially mean seeing it as *everything* there is. Rather, the computer screen is seen as a mere part of a world that extends beyond it. For instance, although my focus is on the computer screen, there is in fact more in my visual field: the table on which the computer screen stands, the curtains behind it, the window pane and, beyond that, trees in autumn colors. These things are part of the non-thematic object-background (*gegenständlicher Hintergrund*) against which the thematically perceived computer screen stands forth (*Hua* VIII, p. 145). But reality, just as it is given to me in my present perception of the screen, does not end there. It extends beyond my present view: I can let my gaze wander on to the door behind me, and behind that door I know a familiar corridor is to be found, and although none of this, under normal circumstances, figures *explicitly* in my awareness, or is co-*thematized* by me as I sit here caught up in writing and philosophizing, it nevertheless "counts" for me, according to Husserl. The perceived "does not count, so to speak, for itself but instead counts as an extract from a broader environment of objects" (*Hua* XVI, p. 210; cf. *Hua* III/1, pp. 56-57). Furthermore, this computer screen and this curtain are perceived as belonging to a world that even extends beyond what I will be able to view in my whole lifetime. The key term with which Husserl attempts to

---

[13] Jacques Taminiaux, "From One Idea of Phenomenology to the Other," p. 34.
[14] Friedrich-Wilhelm von Herrmann, *Subjekt und Dasein*, p. 65; cf. pp. 54, 59. Similarly, Timothy J. Stapleton, *Husserl and Heidegger*, pp. 69-70.
[15] Cf. Ludwig Landgrebe, *Der Weg der Phänomenologie*, pp. 57-58.

conceptualize the being-there of this reality – never as a whole actually perceived, yet somehow always implied in that which is actually perceived – is already introduced in *Ideen I*:

But not even with the domain of this intuitionally clear or obscure, distinct or indistinct, *co-present* – which makes up a constant halo around the field of actual perception – is the world exhausted which is "on hand" for me in the manner peculiar to consciousness at every waking moment. On the contrary, in the fixed order of its being, it reaches into the unlimited. What is now perceived and what is more or less clearly co-present and determinate (or at least somewhat determinate), are penetrated and surrounded by an *obscurely intended horizon of indeterminate actuality*. (*Hua* III/1, p. 57, cf. pp. 101-102)

Whatever I am occupied with, at every moment I find myself surrounded by a *horizon* of undetermined reality. Even when I am caught up in writing a text or arranging my books, an endless reality is, in a non-thematic way, "there" for me (Hua XV, pp. 631, 493). A natural way of understanding Husserl here and the way he himself seems, at times, to understand the idea of the "world as horizon," is the following. The perceived object, say the computer screen, is seen as an object in a more or less intuitively given "object-field" (*Dingfeld*) (*Hua* VI, p. 165), e.g., this office with its various other objects. But what "counts" for me, what "there is" for me, does not end there. Rather, the object-field presents itself as merely a "slice" of the world; "as the momentary field of perception, [it] always has the character for us of a *sector 'of'* the world, of the universe of things for possible perceptions" (*Hua* VI, § 47, p. 165). The world, according to the quotation, is thus the universe of perceivable things – surely, this is precisely the concept of "world" (in quotation marks) that Heideggerians criticize Husserl for positing as the only concept of world. The world-horizon, so it seems, functions for Husserl as the universal "container" for perceivable objects, or is even simply the totality of such objects. The latter notion of world-horizon seems implied, for instance, in Husserl's characterization of the world as the horizon *of* things (*Horizont von "Dingen"*) or realities (*Hua* VI, pp. 369, 167; cf. *EU*, pp. 28-29; *Hua* XV, p. 193), rather than the horizon *for* things, and in the description of the world as the "universal unity" of things (*die Alleinheit von Dingen*) (*Hua* XXIX, p. 296). From the Heideggerian viewpoint, Friedrich-Wilhelm von Herrmann draws the conclusion to this discussion nicely:

Insofar as consciousness is already intentionally alongside the entities, the critique of a "world"less subject that may be directed at Hartmann's subject of knowledge cannot be leveled at Husserl. But if by world, we do not mean the totality of real (and ideal) entities, given horizontally, but rather the disclosedness of world (clearing, openness) as that which ontologically makes it possible for entities to be encountered as inner-worldly (and thus also [makes possible] the givenness of objects for consciousness), then the intentional consciousness of Husserl – both the objectified and the transcendental-constituting consciousness – must also be characterized as *worldless*. It is worldless because it is only intentionally related to life-worldly objects, and to the universal horizon of the life-world that embraces all possible objects – i.e., it is only related to *inner-worldly* [entities].[16]

---

[16] Von Herrmann, *Subjekt und Dasein*, p. 65.

In other words, it seems the introduction of the notion of horizon only brings more clearly to light the essential limitations of Husserl's description of the phenomenon of world, as seen from Heidegger's point of view. By no means does it allow Husserl to redirect his focus away from individual things and their manifestation for a subjectivity to a world *not composed of such things* – a world that allows things to manifest themselves in the first place. Although Husserl insists that we do not perceive things in complete isolation; although he realizes that each individual object is necessarily perceived in a setting that involves other objects, and ultimately the whole universe of objects – his notion of world still remains essentially that of a collection, or a totality of objects. So goes the Heideggerian argument.[17]

But this argument, in my view, overlooks the most important features of the notion of horizon as Husserl develops it in his concrete analyses of perceptual intentionality. As I attempt to show in what follows, the idea of horizon is in fact, if understood correctly, an *alternative* to the conception of world as totality, rather than just another version of it. It must be emphasized, however, that the following account only points out a few facets of Husserl's massive work on horizons and "horizon intentionality" (or "horizonal intentionality").[18] The importance of the notion of horizon to Husserl's phenomenology can hardly be overestimated, and a full treatment of all its aspects is not possible in the present study.[19]

As pointed out above, Husserl is clear that I never perceive any object in complete isolation from other objects. When perceiving a tree, I see it as a tree in a garden, surrounded by other trees, and so forth. But the perceptual horizon of this present act of perception is not exhausted by these "object-surroundings." To the perceived tree itself, independently of its surroundings, belongs a perceptual horizon: the tree presents itself as one that I could view from different angles, thereby bringing different sides (such as the presently "invisible" backside of the trunk) into view, and also as one that I can inspect more closely with regard to the actually perceived side itself (*Hua* XI, p. 7). These multiple different aspects of the tree are co-intended, according to Husserl, in my present perception of the tree – a perception that, strictly speaking, only presents one such aspect:

> The object is not actually given, it is not given wholly and entirely as that which it itself is. It is only given "from the front," only "perspectivally foreshortened and projected" etc. While many of its properties are illustrated in the core content of the perception, at least in the manner which the last expressions indicate, many others are not present in the perception in such illustrated form: to be sure, the

---

[17] Cf. Timothy Stapleton, *Husserl and Heidegger*, p. 101. This is not, however, the argument of C. F. Gethmann. Gethmann is ready to grant that Husserlian transcendental subjectivity "has" a world, is "related" to a world, but maintains that it is worldless in the sense that it does not itself *belong* to the world; that it is not itself *in* the world (cf. *Verstehen und Auslegung*, p. 247). In the next chapter and (especially) in Chapter VI, I return to the question of what it means when Heidegger emphasizes that Dasein is *in*-the-world.

[18] I use "horizonal" and "horizonally," of course, because "horizontal" and "horizontally" have definite meanings that do not fully agree with Husserl's notion of *Horizontintentionalität*.

[19] For a fuller account of horizon and world in Husserl's phenomenology, see Donn Welton, *The Other Husserl*, Part Three (pp. 329-392).

elements of the invisible rear side, the interior etc., are co-intended [*mitgemeint*] in more or less definite fashion [...], but they are not themselves part of the intuitive, i.e., of the [strictly] perceptual or imaginative content, of the perception. (*Hua* XIX/2, Sixth Inv., § 14, p. 589)

The additional sides or aspects belong to the perceived tree precisely as intended in the perception in question (i.e., to the noematic correlate); it is *according to the perception* itself that the tree has "more to offer," Husserl emphasizes (*Hua* XVI, p. 50). If we were we to successfully isolate some "core" of complete perceptual presentation and discard the intentional "surplus," the result would be a disintegration of the concrete perception. In other words, the intentional surplus must *itself* be considered a *perceptual* intentional surplus, rather than some non-perceptual intentionality, e.g., an imaginative intentional complex, always accompanying a perception (cf. *Hua* XVI, p. 56). What I perceive when I perceive a tree is not an aspect of a tree, nor (in most cases) one side of it, but precisely the tree itself, the "whole" tree, according to Husserl – and that means I perceptually co-intend much that is not itself, strictly speaking, manifest. The concrete perceptual manifestation encompasses both "proper" or "authentic," and "improper" or "inauthentic," manifestation (*eigentliche und uneigentliche Erscheinung*) (*Hua* XVI, p. 50), as Husserl expresses it in 1907. Noematically speaking, we may say that to the perceived object just as perceived belongs a *horizon* of co-intended sides and aspects (*Hua* VI, p. 161). Thus, the paradigm of an intuitively "presenting," act, the paradigm of a "fulfilling" act, turns out to be "a complex of full and empty intentions" (*Hua* XVI, p. 57).

But must perception have this "horizonal structure"? In *Ideen I*, Husserl claims that even a god would have to perceive material things this way, if she were to perceive them, *as they are*, at all (*Hua* III/1, p. 89). It is not because we are "finite" creatures that we can perceive mundane entities only in perceptions that exhibit the horizonal structure. Rather, the entities themselves demand this sort of perception; it belongs to their essence that they manifest themselves in that way and no other (*Hua* III/1, p. 88). According to Husserl, a perception that does not have the horizonal structure would simply not be a perception of something like a tree – it would not be a perception of a *transcendent* object, an object not contained in or exhausted by my experience of it (*Hua* XIV, p. 349). A completely or "adequately" perceived tree would be no tree at all. It would be something inseparable from my instantaneous experience. In *Logische Untersuchungen*, Husserl already goes some way towards an account of why this must be so. As he explains there:

If perceptions were always the actual, genuine self-presentations of objects that they pretend to be, there could be only one single perception for each object, since its peculiar essence would be exhausted in this self-presentation. (*Hua* XIX/2, Sixth Inv., § 14, p. 589)

We are to imagine that everything intended in my present tree perception is also *given* in that perception, that all the "intentional terminals" making up the tree-noema are in the strict sense manifest. Now, if I move my upper body just a few inches to either side, then – given that *everything* intended was already given in the previous perception, i.e., that *all* aspects of the tree were fully manifest – we would have to say that my perception could no longer be a perception of the same unaltered object. It could not possibly be the same unchanged tree I would now perceive, because moving my upper body a few inches makes me see new aspects. If these new aspects are new aspects of *the same* tree, then we would have to say that *not all aspects* were after all given to begin with, which by hypothesis they have to be (cf. *Hua* IX, pp. 180-181). But why is it important that we can have several perceptions, different in perceived content, of the same object? As a matter of fact, we certainly can, and it would be factually wrong to claim that a perception of something like a tree can ever give all aspects of its object at once – but why does Husserl think it is a matter of principle that a thing-perception is "inadequate" in this way?

If all aspects of the perceived object are fully manifest, and hence if the perceived object changes whenever the "perceptual content" changes, then the *perceived object would change with the experience*. Every qualitatively different perceptual experience would mean a qualitatively different perceived object. No object could be explored further, no object could be seen from different sides, nor perceived in different ways (e.g., touched instead of watched); there would simply be nothing more to any object than what I would instantaneously have given to me. And if this were so, how could the experiences be experiences *of* something? Would it not rather be the case that experience and object could not be separated, that object and perceptual experience would merge? The experience would seem to absorb the object completely, so that perceived could not be differentiated from the perceptual experience. This is in fact what Husserl concludes:

> If we think of the ideal appearance that is extracted from the nexus of fulfillment and is temporally extended, then we would have a fully concrete appearance as the absolute givenness of a thing. What sort of givenness would this be? It would contain nothing of improper givenness, thus no back side and no interior would be without presentation. It would contain nothing indeterminate; it would be a thoroughly proper [*eigentliche*] and fully determining appearance. Would there still be a difference among appearance, what appears, and the transcendence determined thereby [*Hätten wir noch einen Unterschied zwischen Erscheinung und Erscheinendem und die damit angesetzte Transzendenz*]?[20] The appearance would indeed be no mere adumbration; it would contain no unfulfilled moments of apprehension, moments that, so to speak, point beyond themselves. (*Hua* XVI, pp. 116-117)

> Thus the entire thing coincides, as it were, with its presentation [...]. (*Hua* XVI, p. 120)

Hence a perception *of* something, of a tree as something "out there in the garden," something transcendent in relation to the perceptual experience, is only possible in the way that the "properly" manifest is embedded in a horizon of not-properly-manifest (cf. *Hua* XVI, p. 55; *Hua* XI, p. 6; *Hua* IX, p. 183; *Hua* VI, p. 162). And it should be clear by now that the "core" of proper manifestation is not a potentially independent act, nor alone the "true" perception; rather, the true, concrete perception is the *whole* that has as its ineradicable structural moments the "proper" and the "improper":

---

[20] The English translation strikes me as slightly confusing here. Husserl asks whether there is still a difference between appearance and what appears, and thus whether there can still be the transcendence that is determined by that difference. And his answer, as the following quotation shows, is negative.

Generally speaking, perception is original consciousness. We have, however, a curious schism in external perception: Original consciousness is only possible in the form of an actually and genuinely original conscious-having of sides and a co-consciousness of other sides that are not originally there. (*Hua* XI, p. 4; cf. *Hua* XV, pp. 305-306)

This means in general that no concrete perceptual object – even viewed (artificially) in isolation – can manifest itself without a horizon of intuitive "absence" playing its part, as it were (cf. *Hua* XI, p. 242). A tree could not possibly manifest itself as such to me in an act of perception, if that perception did not both intend intuitively given aspects and intuitively non-given aspects. Thus, object-perception is not such a simple matter, according to Husserl. It is not as though there could be any pure and simple givenness of any mundane entity (cf. *Hua* III/1, p. 89); rather, horizonal givenness is simply the necessary and unchangeable "style" of mundane being (*Hua* XV, p. 500). One cannot even claim that in the absence of the co-intended horizon, what I would have given to me would perhaps not be a "whole" thing, but rather just one *side* or one aspect of a thing, because obviously a "side" is necessarily a side *of* an object, i.e., it refers to other sides, thus it can only be given *as* a side when horizonal intentionality of other sides, or aspects, is in play (*Hua* XVI, pp. 51, 55; *Hua* X, p. 55; *EU*, p. 31).

It is important to note that the co-intended horizon must be there from the beginning, implied in the very first glance I cast at the object. If I am to cast a glance at precisely that, an object, it must be the case that the multiple improperly given aspects are co-intended at once. It cannot be my further inspection that leads to the discovery of "additional" aspects of the object, because if I had not from the beginning anticipated "more" than the strictly given, there would be nothing there to explore (cf. *Hua* VI, p. 382). Obviously, all of this has important implications not only for the Husserlian conception of the world, but also for his notion of subjectivity, and we therefore return to some of these insights in Chapter V.

In Husserlian terms, every perceived mundane entity has by necessity an "inner horizon" (*Innenhorizont*), a horizon of not-yet-manifest and no-longer-manifest aspects of the same entity (cf., e.g., *Hua* VIII, p. 147) – and as we have seen, without such an "inner horizon," we would not perceive any mundane entity at all. We can thus label the object-surroundings in which such a perceived object is always perceived, the "outer horizon" (*Außenhorizont*).[21] The world itself, then, presumably encompassing both inner and outer horizon as well as the "properly" manifest, could be called the *universal* horizon, from out of which what appears appears.

---

[21] It seems to me that Husserl does not always distinguish between inner and outer horizon in the same way. In *Erste Philosophie II* and *Erfahrung und Urteil*, for instance, the inner horizon is all that of an *object* that is not intuitively given (backsides and so forth) (*Hua* VIII, pp. 146-147; *EU*, p. 28), while it seems in *Hua* IX that unseen sides are located in the outer horizon, so that the notion of inner horizon refers to the possible, but not authentically intuitively actualized aspects of the properly manifest side (e.g., those aspects of the thing that would manifest themselves, were I to "move closer") (*Hua* IX, p. 195). Perhaps the best thing is not to distinguish sharply between inner and outer horizon in the first place.

This discussion of object-perception therefore teaches us something essential about the concept of world as horizon. The world is not a totality of entities, but as horizon it is rather the very structure that *allows* entities to come forth (cf. *EU*, pp. 24-25). If the world is the universal horizon, then it cannot be a totality of entities, because entities cannot manifest or constitute themselves in any, so to speak, "horizon-free" manner. If entities are simply and completely given, given without horizons of non-givenness, then it would make sense to say that the (rest of) the world, as world-horizon, is the *totality of those entities not momentarily given*. But, as a matter of principle, there can be no such horizon-free givenness of any mundane entity, according to Husserl. Even when we abstract from all surroundings, and consider the individual perceived entity as if it were given in complete isolation, we are necessarily referred back to perceptual horizons. Hence, if we take seriously the notion of world-*horizon* and take care not to overlook the implications in it, we can appreciate why Husserl remarks that the world is something *in* the things themselves rather than a collection of things (*Hua* XXIX, p. 296). The world, as ("inner") horizon, is certainly part of what makes up the manifest things as they are manifest, and if individual things already imply world in this sense, if they need it, as it were, in order to constitute themselves, then it hardly makes sense to say of the world that it is a collection or totality of things. If we understand by world-horizon the *totality* of entities, this would seem to suggest that the entities are what make the world possible,[22] or at most that world, and individual entities are interdependent (cf. *Hua* VI, p. 146). But our previous discussion of perceptual intentionality shows that the horizon is the condition for the possibility of entities, and not vice versa. To be sure, there can be no horizon present except as a horizon allowing entities to come forth, and in that sense the world-horizon "needs" entities (*Hua* VI, p. 146). But that does not mean that entities make possible the horizon, it means only that an intentional horizon in no way can be other than as a horizon that lets *entities* appear. Since no entity can be given otherwise than in and through co-intended horizons, the idea of the world as a totality implies that *also the world itself* can be given only in and through co-intended horizons. Intentional horizons, such as the multitude co-intended in the present perception and co-responsible for the fact that I perceive this or that thing, would then be something making possible the appearance of the world, rather than themselves constituting the world. The world could not *itself* be the perceptual horizon, but only a collection of entities emerging in and through the perceptual horizon. Hence, the concept of world as horizon is not only non-identical with the concept of world as totality; it is in fact *incompatible* with it.[23] The two would be compatible only if entities could be given "horizon-free."

---

[22] See for instance Husserl's own reflections in *Hua* IX, p. 96.
[23] Cf. Donn Welton, *The Other Husserl*, p. 324 (cf. pp. 87, 326, 331-346). See, too, Burt C. Hopkins, *Intentionality in Husserl and Heidegger*, p. 276, note 7, and Anthony J. Steinbock, *Home and Beyond*, pp. 98-109.

In short, the world is not a horizon of things, but a horizon *of possible experience*, "an infinite horizon of possible experience" (*Hua* VIII, p. 148) or,[24] even more accurately stated, the universe of actual as well as possible experience (*Hua* XIV, p. 312), and this makes all the difference.[25] As a horizon of possible experience, the world has a mode of being (*Seinsweise*) completely different from the mode of being of the individual thing, Husserl emphasizes (*Hua* VI, p. 146). A horizon of possible experience is that in and through which, as we have seen, any individual entity can manifest itself, it is not itself a "container" of such entities, nor is it a totality of them. As *universal horizon, the world is a structure that allows individual entities to manifest themselves* (cf. *Hua* VI, p. 267).[26]

If we return to our discussion of "wordlessness," it becomes evident that the charge is not legitimate if it is based on the assumption that Husserl has no other concept of world than that of a totality of entities. If being-in-the-world means "transcending to the World as the possibility for encountering objects,"[27] then Husserlian transcendental subjectivity is certainly in-the-world. It transcends intentionally to the universal world-horizon, thereby allowing entities to appear. Without the "transcendence" in the shape of horizonal intentionality, Husserl is clear that there can be no transcendence at all.

Although the discussion in the present section seems to suggest it, Husserl does not mean to say that the world is nothing but a world of possible perceptual experience. In addition to being there as a world of perception, he emphasizes, the world is there "with the same immediacy as a *world of objects with values, a world of goods, a practical world*" (*Hua* III/1, p. 58). In fact, the world-horizon is *primarily* (*vor allem*) determined by our everyday practices, Husserl says, and if he restricts himself, at times, to speak of it as if it is just a horizon of possible perception, this is simply because the world as practical world is necessarily *founded* in the world as world of perception (*EU*, pp. 52-53; *Hua* XV, p. 441). Every practical activity, as we already know from Chapter I, presupposes an underlying

---

[24] But is "horizon" not, in fact, a misnomer then? After all, Husserl wants to apply this concept to an *infinite* reality (*Hua* III/1, p. 57) an "infinite horizon," but a horizon is a limit, it is the limit of that which I can see. That is true, but a horizon is not a *rigid* limit, it is precisely not a fence surrounding me, but something that *moves with me* wherever I go, something that continually signals to me that there is more to explore. Cf. to this Hans-Georg Gadamer, *Wahrheit und Methode*, p. 250. See, as well, *Hua* IV, p. 299, where Husserl points out that the "infinity" of the world should be understood to signify the *openness* of the world, and does not mean that it contains an infinite number of objects.

[25] In the words of Ludwig Landgrebe, the world is the possible "and-so-on" ("*Undsoweiter*") of our experience (*Der Weg der Phänomenologie*, pp. 54, 185), a notion of world Landgrebe explicitly contrasts with the conception of world as a totality of entities (p. 185) (cf. *Hua* XV, pp. 200, 523). See also Klaus Held, "Das Problem der Intersubjektivität und die Idee einer phänomenologischen Transzendentalphilosophie," pp. 18-19.

[26] When Husserl says, in opposition to Kant, that the world is an object, viz. the "universal object" (*Hua* IX, p. 95; cf. *Hua* XXIX, p. 300), then he does not mean "object" in the same sense as when he speaks of individual objects. Husserl, as already noted, subscribes to the view that there is a "difference between the manner of being of an object in the world and that of the world itself" (*Hua* VI, § 37, p. 146).

[27] Timothy Stapleton, *Husserl and Heidegger*, p. 109.

"layer" of perception, according to Husserl. I cannot hammer nails into a wall unless I can see the nails and feel the hammer-thing in my hand, and the world cannot be the universal horizon for practical activity unless it is the horizon for perceptual experience. The latter founds the former. But we remember from Chapter I that this need not mean that I primarily *live* in acts of perception, nor does it entail that the concrete world primarily counts for me as a world of perception.

Would Heidegger be convinced, or would he still maintain that the true phenomenon of world nevertheless remains unseen by Husserl? In order to clarify this question, we must give a brief outline of Heidegger's concept of world.

3. WORLD AS A REFERENTIAL WHOLE

When approaching the phenomenon of world as this is developed in *Sein und Zeit* and other of Heidegger's writings from the late twenties, perhaps it is advisable to take our point of departure (as we do when outlining Husserl's notion of world) in the individual, given entity (cf. *SZ*, p. 66). As already indicated a number of times, the entity that Dasein immediately encounters is not a material object that is simply "there," that "occurs"; it is not even an object with certain cultural strata, but rather it is something essentially different, in Heidegger's view. The entity that Dasein finds itself immediately occupied with is what Heidegger labels the *Zeug*. In what appears to be a clear contrast to Husserl, Heidegger insists that the "tool" has a *mode of being* different from that of a "material thing." A tool *is* something-with-which-to...; this *Um-zu* makes up the very being of the tool. Understanding the *um-zu*, understanding *Zuhandenheit*, is what enables me to encounter, for example, a hammer *as* a hammer, that is, enables me to encounter it in a using interaction.

Although this is already mentioned in Chapters I and III, it has wider implications that have thus far gone unnoticed. The hammer is something-with-which-to drive nails into wooden boards. That is, in the structure of "with-which-to" that is constitutive of the hammer lies a reference to something (*SZ*, p. 68). The same holds for all "tools": wooden boards are something with which one – provided additional tools such as hammers and nails are available – can build something, e.g., a house. What is a house? A house is something in which one can live – an "inhabitation-tool" (*Wohnzeug*), as Heidegger puts it (*SZ*, p. 68). One tool necessarily refers to other tools that necessarily refer to yet others, i.e., strictly speaking there can be no *single*, isolated tool. A tool can be what it is as a tool only in a *whole* of tools or equipment (*Zeugganzes*), Heidegger emphasizes (*SZ*, pp. 68, 353; *GA* 24, p. 232). This whole comes "before" and makes possible the individual tool in the sense that the individual tool *can only be as a tool* if it is already placed in a whole of such tools. A hammer can not be as a hammer in the absence of further tools such as nails and boards. If a tribe of Amazon Indians, completely unfamiliar with hammers and nails, came across a hammer by coincidence, they would probably be unable to "uncover" it specifically as a hammer. That does not mean, however, that they would perceive the hammer as a mere occurrent thing – they would most likely see the hammer as an instrument yet to be understood by them, and proceed to find out "what it could be used for" by way of *placing it in their already familiar whole of equipment*. The hammer could not in any way be encountered as what it is – as a tool – except by being embedded in a whole of tools referring to each other.[28]

It is perhaps tempting to conclude that what Heidegger wants to label the world is precisely this whole of equipment, considered as a totality, or the totality of such totalities of equipment. Some might even contend that Heidegger himself at times approaches such an interpretation, e.g., when he remarks that with the whole (*Ganzes*) of the tool-interconnection the world announces itself (cf. *SZ*, p. 75). However, a tool-interconnection (*Zeugzusammenhang*) is ultimately something quite different from a whole of tools, if the latter is understood as a "sum," totality, or collection of entities. And as we already know, Heidegger emphasizes repeatedly that the world (without quotation marks) is not to be identified with the sum of all existing entities (*GA* 20, p. 258; *GA* 24, p. 235; *GA* 29/30, p. 405). When Heidegger's specific use of the notion of world is introduced in *Sein und Zeit*, in contrast to the "world" (in quotation marks) as the "sum total" of entities, he defines it as that *in which* Dasein "*lives*" (*SZ*, pp. 64-65). "In" what, then, does Dasein "live," if not in the totality of entities?

The word "lives" ("*lebt*") is put in quotation marks by Heidegger himself in the passage in question. This is probably because he wants to indicate that in his terminology, it is not strictly correct to say that Dasein "lives"; rather, Dasein *exists* (*SZ*, p. 50; *GA* 27, p. 71). Why use the word "live" at all, then? Could it be that Heidegger means by "live," not the being-mode of animals, or of humans, but rather something akin to what Husserl talks about when he speaks of the acts in which we "live"? As noted in Chapter I, Husserl acknowledges that we do not normally "live" in acts of disinterested perception, meaning that these acts are not the ones we are *active* in. We normally "live" in various practical acts, that is, we are not "attentive" of or interested in the visual appearance of the hammer-thing, but of getting this board nailed down next to that one, and so forth. When Husserl here speaks of "living," he speaks of those acts that we are truly *engaged* in. Could it not be that Heidegger uses "living" in more or less the same sense here? In fact I think he does, with the minor qualification that Heidegger does not mean by world anything "noetic," but rather the "noematic" side of everyday involvement, if one may employ a Husserlian idiom here.

---

[28] Some interpreters of *Sein und Zeit* emphasize that the important thing is not that a tool is used, but that it is used the *proper way* (cf. John Haugeland, "Heidegger on Being a Person," p. 18; Mark Okrent, *Heidegger's Pragmtism*, pp. 31-32, 46-47). Of course, there is a right way to use a hammer as a *hammer*, and a wrong way to use it, but the question is whether this is really an important point for Heidegger. I suspect that what Heidegger would find interesting is that Amazon Indians and Bushmen, too, would relate to a hammer as a *tool*, even if they did not use it specifically as a hammer. I suspect, further, that the interpreters who hold that Heidegger is really trying to direct our attention to what goes on when a hammer is used the "right way" (specifically as a hammer), are somehow misconstruing the *ontological* point that Heidegger is trying to make – that they are making an *ontic* point of it. More on this in Chapter VI.

Let us rephrase the question, then. At what is Dasein for the most part "interestedly" directed, what is the "object" of its involvement? It is surely not the individual tool (cf. *GA* 24, pp. 232-233). When I am busy piecing together a new bookcase, I am not constantly focused on the screwdriver in my hand; in fact I might be so caught up in the project that I completely forget that the screwdriver is there. Nor am I occupied with the screw or the board as such, Heidegger would claim, although it would be wrong to say that I am in no way attentive of the board and screw. I am attentive of and interested in the board, not *as such*, as an individual entity, but as *functioning* in this or that way within the work at hand. What I am occupied with is assembling the base of the bookcase, for instance, and in this activity it would be wrong to say that I am, first and foremost, actively directed at any one entity, and that I am attentive of a number of such entities. Should we say, then, that the idea of the bookcase in its finished state is what occupies me as I assemble the base of the bookcase? Something along these lines seems to be what Heidegger suggests at one point in *Sein und Zeit* (*SZ*, pp. 69-70; *GA* 20, p. 260), but such a claim is hardly phenomenologically sound. For one thing, it would presumably be quite difficult to get the job done properly if one was constantly focusing on that which is to be constructed (*das Herzustellende*). And secondly, this suggestion seems to be too narrowly tied to the process of manufacturing or producing something. What about my use of shoes, say, or the way I "use" my bicycle "in order to" get from A to B? The latter example may appear to support the questionable suggestion, since my use of the bike is precisely intended to "produce" my being at B at a specific time. But conditions of mania aside, it seems simply wrong to say that the future position at B is what I am engagingly "*living*" in. It seems more correct to emphasize that I am "living" in all those references involved in the process of my getting there (turning right at the next light, taking care that this driver has seen me, etc.). What I am "living" in when wearing a shoe, or cycling on my bike, or indeed assembling the base of my new bookcase is the *referential* structure itself, the references themselves and not the entities, Heidegger would ultimately claim (*SZ*, p. 354; *GA* 24, p. 416). What I am "attentive" of is first and foremost something like how (this board) must be fitted to (that block) using (that size of screw) before (that other board) can be put in place, and so forth. *Everyday Dasein "lives" in a system of references*, rather than in any collection of entities, according to Heidegger.

As said above, each individual piece of equipment is in its being something that carries, or is, a reference to other tools. The screwdriver refers to the screw, and so on. But this is not all. The defining characteristic of the screwdriver as a tool is in fact not directly the reference to other entities, but its *usefulness*. This is implied in Heidegger's use of *Um-zu* to describe its being, since *um zu* literally means "in order to." The reference to other tools, the screwdriver's reference to the screw, is a reference to the screw only in and through the *usefulness* of the screwdriver to drive a screw into... Considered thus, one might say that the being of the tool is that of "relevance" or "deployment" (*Bewandtnis*) (*SZ*, p. 84),[29] and that the references that Dasein "lives" in are references of relevance, and furthermore, that they make up a totality or whole of relevance (*Bewandtnisganzheit*).[30] Obviously, this nexus of relevance must eventually end up in something that is no longer *itself* useful for something else, but rather the *telos* of the whole system of references. This *telos* – the ultimate "for the sake of" (*Umwillen* or *Worumwillen*) that the whole structure of "in order to" presupposes – can be nothing but the being of the human being, Heidegger claims (*SZ*, p. 84; *GA* 24, p. 418).

Although it is not a matter of great importance to the present investigation, Heidegger apparently dodges what might be seen as the true question entailed in the indication of the world as that in which Dasein "lives," since he never in fact positively says what everyday Dasein is mainly *thematically aware* of. Above, I use both "attention" and "interest" in an attempt to capture what Heidegger might mean by Dasein's "living" in this or that, but admittedly attention is not the same as interest. I might pay attention to something that I have no interest in, e.g., because other interests dictate that I should do that. What I "live" in – given such an example – would still be the actually uninteresting conversation, not the (interesting) future fruits to be reaped by engaging in the conversation. In other words, "engagement" or "attention" perhaps capture more adequately what Heidegger (following Husserl) would label "living in." The question about interest aside, then, one might want to press Heidegger for an answer to the question regarding everyday Dasein's attentive focus. He uses such terms as "focus" and "theme" only when aiming to point out critically what Dasein cannot be, in the strict sense, attentive of (e.g., this or that tool, the finished work). Consistently, he almost always prefers to say what Dasein "*moves in*" or what it "*resides in*," and that is then identified with the web of references as such:

When I am completely engrossed in dealing with something and make use of some equipment in this activity, I am just not directed toward the equipment as such, say, toward the tool. And I am just as little

---

[29] The German word *Bewandtnis* is close to untranslatable, as Ernst Tugendhat points out (*Der Wahrheitsbegriff bei Husserl und Heidegger*, p. 290n). But clearly, as Tugendhat indicates, *Bewandtnis* is here closely related to the "for what purpose" (*Wozu*) (p. 290). See Theodore Kisiel's many suggestions for English equivalents in *The Genesis of Heidegger's Being and Time*, p. 493. I am following Kisiel here, since I think "relevance" (for what purpose?) and "deployment" (putting something to use) preserve at least some of the connotations that Heidegger's use of *Bewandtnis* carries, in a very plain and lucid manner.

[30] Hubert Dreyfus suggests that we understand the relation between the notions of "referential whole," "equipmental whole" and "involvement whole" (the latter being what I call a whole of "relevance") in the following way: "The *equipmental whole* [...] describes the interrelated equipment; the *referential whole* its interrelations; and the *involvement whole* adds human purposiveness" (*Being-in-the-World*, p. 97). (I see no reason to disagree, and add only that "relevance" fully captures the element of "human purposiveness.") While Dreyfus seems to think all of these wholes are (aspects of) the world, Paul Gorner, in "Heidegger's Phenomenology as Transcendental Philosophy" (p. 25), argues for a sharp distinction between the referential whole and the whole of "relevance," arguing that only that latter should be labeled "world." I am inclined to agree with Dreyfus on this particular point.

directed toward the work itself. Instead, in my occupation I move *in* the relevance-relations [*Bewandtnisbezügen*] as such. (*GA* 24, p. 416; cf. *SZ*, p. 354)

It thus becomes clear that the references are precisely the *involvements* [*Wobei*] in which the concernful occupation dwells; it does not dwell among isolated things of the environing world and certainly not among thematically or theoretically perceived objects. (*GA* 20, p. 253)

What Heidegger wants to say is that the terms "directedness," "theme," and "focus" are not adequate to capture what goes on in everyday involvement (*Umgang*) at all. Assembling a bookcase is a "practical" activity, and as involved in this way with its surroundings, Dasein has no clearly discernible thematic focus. What happens is simply that Dasein *"lives"* or *moves in* the relations of "usefulness," thereby not thematically aware (though usually by no means unaware) of the various tool-entities as such, nor thematically directed at the to-be-constructed bookcase, nor indeed reflectively thematizing its own activity as such (*SZ*, p. 354). *But nor should we say that the referential web is thematic as such*: "Dwelling in it [i.e., in the "relevance"], that is, having the tool in use, means precisely not having the reference itself objectively" (*GA* 20, p. 260; cf. *SZ*, p. 75). We should not approach everyday practical life in terms of thematic awareness, Heidegger argues. Our usual interaction involvement with the world, though by no means deprived of circumspective vision, is as such *unthematic* (cf. *SZ*, pp. 76, 353). Thematic awareness is something I have when I am involved in theoretical observation – itself a kind of involvement, though by no means the most ordinary – not something that necessarily characterizes the type of involvement attributable to everyday Dasein, let alone all types of involvement (see *SZ*, p. 363).

What a Dasein "lives" in, then, is not for Heidegger the same as what a Dasein is thematically aware of. Still, the best way to approach Heidegger's use of "living," "moving," or "residing" in or by must surely be by taking one's point of departure in Husserl's idea of acts in which we "live" – and let us note in passing that Husserl perhaps expresses himself the way he does precisely to avoid invoking the narrower idea of (theoretical) "theme" or "focus." Following Heidegger, we can say that involved everyday Dasein is not necessarily "thematically" aware of anything – neither individual tools, nor the to-be-constructed, nor in fact the web of references – but it *moves in* or *resides by* the *web of references* and not the individual tools or anything of that sort.

Nevertheless, Heidegger is not claiming that the references in which Dasein "lives," "moves," or "resides" cannot in any way become "thematic" in an everyday context, but only that they are hardly ever thematic as objects of a neutral, purely theoretical investigation. Although consistently maintaining that tools, work, and even the referential web itself remain inconspicuous (*unauffällig*) in the normal context of unproblematic use (*GA* 24, pp. 439-440), he considers a number of ways in which the referential web can nevertheless become highlighted in the everyday using *Umgang*. Among these are the well-known examples of disturbances – as when a tool is missing or broken – in the using involvement. What happens, Heidegger asks, if for instance a tool malfunctions? Since the most apt way of encountering a tool as a tool is the using interaction with it, and since this interaction is made impossible by the tool's malfunctioning, the tool now presents itself to its would-be user in a certain "unhandiness" (*Unzuhandenheit*), Heidegger observes (*SZ*, p. 73). One could even say that the useless, broken tool announces itself in a certain presence-at-hand, as merely another occurrent entity, as it lies there unsuited for anything (ibid.). And yet Heidegger maintains that "[t]his presence-at-hand of something that cannot be used is still not devoid of all readiness-to-hand whatsoever; equipment which is present-at-hand *in this* way is still not just a thing which occurs somewhere" (ibid.). Although it literally loses its handiness, or rather because of the way in which it loses it, the tool accentuates its readiness-to-hand in a "farewell," as it were (*SZ*, p. 74). When I discover that the needed tool is broken, its "in order to" is precisely highlighted in a way it is not in the unproblematic use. Now I am suddenly painfully aware that I needed this tool in order to make that thing that I needed for that project, and so forth. With the disturbance of the reference, the reference itself becomes explicit (*ausdrücklich*), Heidegger says (ibid.). Moreover, as the example just given shows, it is in fact not only the individual malfunctioning tool, so to speak in its isolated *Um-zu*, that is accentuated, because "[w]hen a reference to some particular 'towards-this' [*Dazu*] has been thus circumspectively aroused, we catch sight of the 'towards-this' itself, *and along with it the work-connection* [*Werkzusammenhang*] [...] as that wherein concern always already dwells" (*SZ*, pp. 74-75, my emphasis).[31] Not only the keyboard in its "in order to" or "with which to" is accentuated when the keyboard malfunctions, but a whole *web of references*, as well: I needed the functioning keyboard in order to write that text, which in turn had to be finished by that date, so that it could be submitted to that conference, etc.

Another way that the web of references can be accentuated for everyday Dasein is in the encounter with the *sign*. A sign such as an indicator on a car – to use Heidegger's own example – is itself characterized by "in order to," i.e., it is itself a tool of some kind (*SZ*, p. 77). In contrast to most other tools, the indicator has the job of making itself noticed – it is of the utmost importance that pedestrians, bicyclists, and other drivers notice the signal (cf. *SZ*, p. 80). But notice how? The point is of course not that other road users should notice the indicator as just another tool belonging to the car, like the radio antenna. Rather, the indicator has the specific function of giving the other road users an orientation within their surroundings, Heidegger claims (*SZ*, p. 79). What the indicator accentuates is, e.g., that this car will turn right at the next junction, and thus it also highlights the further references of my needing to make sure the driver has seen me in order that I may safely proceed to cycle straight ahead. In other words, the indicator is a special tool in that it accentuates neither the indicator itself as a tool, nor in fact any other entity

---

[31] Once again, Heidegger uses an important Husserlian term in his phenomenological description, viz. that of *Weckung* or *wecken* (literally "waking" or "arousing"). This is perhaps *the* key term in Husserl's *Analysen zur passiven Synthesis* (*Hua* XI). Interestingly, in Heidegger's lectures of the summer of 1925, he employs the equally Husserlian term "appresenting" (*appräsentieren*) in a similar context (*GA* 20, pp. 258-259).

– instead it highlights a *web of references*. Heidegger concludes: "Signs always indicate primarily 'wherein' one lives, where one's concern dwells" (*SZ*, p. 80).

Encountering a malfunctioning tool or a sign are unique situations in that they both involve an accentuation of the web of references "in which" Dasein lives, or by which Dasein resides. This web of references, following Heidegger's initial formal definition of world, constitutes the *world*. Accordingly, it should come as no surprise that Heidegger concludes that both the broken piece of equipment and the sign have the important function of making explicit to everyday Dasein its environing *world* (cf. *SZ*, pp. 75, 82).

The world is the referential whole that I must have uncovered somehow in order to grasp the reference constituting the being of the equipment, which, in turn, allows me to encounter the equipment as equipment. In order to uncover the tool as a tool, Dasein should first of all understand the reference constituting the mode of being of the tool. This reference, of course, is a reference to something, and that something (usually) itself has a mode of being defined by its reference *to*. In other words, a whole web of references (e.g., hammers referring to nails referring to wooden boards, etc.) must be understood in order for Dasein to be able to interact with the individual entity (e.g., use the hammer for hammering):

> The world itself is not an entity within-the-world; and yet it is so determinative for such entities that only in so far as "there is" a world can they be encountered and show themselves, in their being, as entities which have been discovered. (*SZ*, p. 72)

On Heidegger's account, then, the world is *a whole of references* that, as such, allows for individual entities to present themselves. Without an understood world, there can be no encountered entities (*SZ*, pp. 365-366; *GA* 24, p. 235).

Some commentators point out that this conception of the world seems to exclude certain modes of being. Especially the phenomenon of *nature*, as it originally presents itself, seems to find no place in the account of *Sein und Zeit*, it is argued.[32] The relations of "in order to" and "for the sake of" are what constitute the world, according to the text of the magnum opus (cf. *SZ*, p. 364). The question is not only what place is left for the encounter with something present-at-hand within this whole of "usefulness," but also whether, for instance, nature really falls within the Heideggerian alternatives of presence-at-hand and readiness-to-hand. Nature may be used as a paradigm case here, to discuss the more general charge that the early Heidegger's conception of the world is ontologically narrow. There are at least three concepts of nature brought into play in *Sein und Zeit*. Let us briefly consider them in turn.

As for the first manner in which nature can manifest itself, here we clearly find it encountered as something with the being of readiness-to-hand. Nature appears in the materials needed for the making or constructing of whatever Dasein makes or constructs, e.g., the wood and iron that are needed if a hammer is to be

---

[32] See Otto Pöggeler, *Der Denkweg Martin Heideggers*, p. 208; and Hans-Georg Gadamer, "Die Wahrheit des Kunstwerks," pp. 251-252.

manufactured. Materials are, as the example shows, tools that distinguish themselves from most other tools by the fact that they need not themselves be manufactured in order to be the tools they are. Materials are "entities [...] which are *always already ready-to-hand*, but which, in themselves, do not need to be produced" (*SZ*, p. 70, my emphasis; cf. *GA* 20, p. 262). The iron is always already something with which to... Moreover, Heidegger emphasizes that even when it is not directly encountered as material for some product, the nature that surrounds us is still essentially encountered as something "with which to": "The wood is a forest of timber, the mountain a quarry of rock; the river is water-power, the wind is wind 'in the sails'" (*SZ*, p. 70; cf. *GA* 20, p. 270). Nature is here just as much ready-to-hand as hammers and nails are.

Another concept of nature is briefly brought to light as Heidegger mentions the public world. He writes:

Along with the public world, the *environing nature* is discovered and is accessible to everyone. In roads, streets, bridges, buildings, our concern discovers nature in a particular way. A covered railway platform takes account of bad weather; an installation for public lighting takes account of the darkness [...]. (*SZ*, p. 71)

How is nature encountered here? At first, one might be inclined to think that this is an instance where nature appears *outside* the relational whole of "in order to." After all, the roof that covers the platform is there "in order to" shelter persons waiting from the rain, but the *rain* itself is surely not "in order to." Yet the rain does not appear here as something merely present-at-hand; it appears, rather, to the circumspection of Dasein as something that might possibly interfere with or disturb Dasein's *Umgang*. With the readiness-to-hand of the roof, the rain is present as something "taken into account specifically with regard to its detrimental character, insofar as it is threatening, obstructive, unserviceable, resistant" (*GA* 20, pp. 269-270). The rain appears, in other words, as something possibly *in the way* of Dasein's activity, and it is for that reason the roof is needed. Nature is here encountered, not as straightforwardly ready-to-hand (along the lines of material or "wind in the sails"), but as a certain *unhandiness* that by no means reduces it to something merely present-at-hand. There is precisely an enormous difference between taking caution to protect oneself from the rain and simply recording the fact that water is falling from the sky. The unhandiness of nature is, so to speak, a deficient mode of readiness-to-hand, and thus it still belongs within the nexus of references.

Finally, Heidegger mentions nature as a limit case (*Grenzfall*) of possible innerworldly entities (*SZ*, p. 65). In a marginal note added subsequently, he remarks that nature is here understood in the sense of modern physics (*SZ*, p. 441) – thus presumably as something present-at-hand. But Heidegger not only assigns this concept of nature the place at the limit of what can be encountered within the world, he even contends that the *way* to encounter nature in this sense is in and through a "deworlding" (*Entweltlichung*) of the world (*SZ*, pp. 65, 112; *GA* 20, pp. 227, 266), a process in which the "worldliness" of the world is made to fade.

The problem that Pöggeler and Gadamer bring to our attention, it should be emphasized, is not solely that the Heideggerian conception of the world seems to exclude anything present-at-hand. As Husserl himself points out, purely "occurrent" entities play a very little part in our everyday life, if any at all (cf. *Hua* IV, pp. 27, 182). The problem is rather that the dichotomy of "presence-at-hand" and "readiness-to-hand" seems to dominate Heidegger's account of the world to such an extent that the original phenomenon of nature gets lost in the process. The flowers on the hillside are either the flowers of the botanist (*Vorhandenheit*) or a possible gift to a beloved (*Zuhandenheit*); there is nothing in between, or beyond these alternatives (cf. *GA* 20, p. 50; *SZ*, p. 70). The freshness of the air on a clear winter morning is either a simple fact of physical nature, or it is something I "make use of" in order to improve my health. But this is hardly convincing. My experience of the freshness of the morning air is neither an encounter with something *Um-zu*, nor is it something I simply register as a present-at-hand fact. Rrather, it is something that will *color* all the activities I engage in that morning. Yet, in a world more or less exclusively defined by webs of "in order to" and "for the sake of," there seems to be no way to accommodate a phenomenon of this type.

According to Otto Pöggeler, this problem emerges because in *Sein und Zeit*, Heidegger describes the world almost exclusively in terms of the existential of understanding, forgetting the other (equiprimordial) existentials, most notably that of "affectivity" or "disposedness" (*Befindlichkeit*).[33] The original phenomenon of nature is supposedly primarily uncovered in my *mood*, not in my understanding of something as "useful" or "relevant," yet as uncovered affectively or "mood-wise," it co-determines my understanding interactions with equipment.

However, in the wake of *Sein und Zeit*, Heidegger appears to rethink the phenomena of world and nature. If in the magnum opus the world was a referential web given to the understanding of Dasein, the world is now described as "worlding" (*welten*) (*GA* 26, pp. 219-221; *GA* 27, p. 336; *WM*, p. 164),[34] and even "governing" (*walten*) (*WM*, p. 164; *GA* 29/30, p. 510). More importantly, *nature* is explicitly

---

[33] *Der Denkweg Martin Heideggers*, p. 208. If *Sein und Zeit* displays a shortcoming on precisely this point, it is very surprising indeed given the remark Heidegger makes on p. 138 of that work: "Indeed, *from the ontological point of view* we must as a general principle leave the primary discovery of the world to 'bare mood.'" For a careful analysis of Heidegger's notion of "moods," see Hans Ruin, "The Passivity of Reason – On Heidegger's Concept of Stimmung."

[34] The expression is from Heidegger's early Freiburg years. As early as in the so-called "war emergency semester" of 1919, the young Heidegger exhibits extraordinary terminological inventiveness, introducing to his students not only the phrase "it worlds" (*es weltet*) (*GA* 56/57, pp. 73, 88-89, 94), but other unusual expressions as well. For instance, the later Heidegger's key term *Ereignis* appears as well – both with and without a hyphen (cf. ibid., pp. 69, 75, 78). Hans-Georg Gadamer, himself a student of the early Heidegger, therefore suggests that Heidegger's much discussed "turn" or "reversal" (*Kehre*) should actually be understood as a *return* (*Rückkehr*) to his earlier intentions (Gadamer, "Erinnerungen an Heideggers Anfänge," pp. 10-11) – a suggestion many Heidegger scholars welcome (cf. David Krell, *Intimations of Mortality*, pp. 98, 111; Theodore Kisiel, *The Genesis of Heidegger's Being and Time*, pp. 3, 458; John van Buren, *The Young Heidegger*, pp. 137, 367).

introduced as something beyond the alternatives of presence-at-hand and readiness-to-hand,[35] something intimately connected with Dasein's affectivity:

> Dasein is corporeality, and body, and life [*Körper und Leib und Leben*]. It [Dasein] does not only, or primarily, have nature as an object for contemplation; rather it is nature. But not in the way that it constitutes a conglomerate of matter, body, and soul; it is [rather] nature qua transcending entity, [qua] Dasein – through and through governed and attuned [*durchwaltet und durchstimmt*] by nature. By way of a moodedness [*Gestimmtseins*], Dasein in each case finds itself [*befindet sich*] in the midst of the entities that govern it through and through. (*GA* 27, pp. 328-329)

Nature is what attunes the human being "through and through," and what Dasein cannot master, according to Heidegger (ibid., p. 329). Some seven years later, in the lecture "Der Ursprung des Kunstwerkes," Heidegger approaches a similar phenomenon, by introducing the notion of "earth" (*Erde*) as a complementary to "world" (*HW*, p. 34). In this lecture, the concept of "thing" – in *Sein und Zeit* synonymous with the ontology of presence-at-hand – is both strictly separated from that of the tool, and held at a far distance from the notion of present-at-hand objects. The thing, so Heidegger now claims, is something we essentially must understand on the basis of "earth," rather than either of the former alternatives (*HW*, p. 56). Taking these later lectures into account, it is clear that if the conception of the world in *Sein und Zeit* is ontologically narrow (defined more or less exclusively in terms of relations of "relevance"; cf. *SZ*, p. 364), then Heidegger attempts to improve on that situation in the decade that follows.

4. THE PHENOMENON OF WORLD

Some argue that one of the most fruitful ways of approaching the question of the possible affinities between Husserlian and Heideggerian phenomenology is through the concept of world.[36] Given the debate in the literature – especially the criticism of Husserl's conception of the world – surrounding precisely the concept of world, that suggestion may at first appear unconvincing. Yet, as I hope to show in this section, there are certain structural similarities between the two accounts, as these have been presented in this chapter.

First, the conception developed by Husserl of world as horizon is eventually unearthed as incompatible with the notion of world as a totality of entities. As horizon, the world is precisely a structure without which entities could not possibly present themselves, a pre-condition for the manifestation of entities rather than

---

[35] Already in *Sein und Zeit*, however, Heidegger mentions (though without elaborating on it) nature as something that "encompasses" us. Nature in this sense is neither something present-at-hand, nor is it ready-to-hand, Heidegger says (*SZ*, p. 211; *GA* 21, p. 314). Daniel Dahlstrom speculates whether this leaves open the possibility of a nature that somehow – being neither present-at-hand nor ready-to-hand – converges with Dasein (*Heidegger's Concept of Truth*, p. 266). Judging from Heidegger's Freiburg lecture course from the winter of 1928/29, quoted in the main text, Dahlstrom's hunch appears to be close to the mark.

[36] See Richard H. Holmes, "The World According to Husserl and Heidegger," p. 373, and Donn Welton, *The Other Husserl*, p. 347. Cf. also Welton's article "World."

something itself consisting of such entities. The Heideggerian concept of world as whole of references exhibits the same features. It is not itself to be conceived as a totality of entities, whether with the being of "occurrent" things or equipment. Rather, the world is the referential structure allowing such entities to be encountered. If the world is an entity or a collection of entities, presumably it itself would have to be placed in a referential whole, i.e., *in a world,* in order to be encountered; or, using the Husserlian model, it would itself have to be given horizontally, i.e., *in a world*. Husserl and Heidegger thus appear to agree on one perfectly tangible, if only negative point – viz. that the world cannot phenomenologically be described as a totality of entities – and on one positive, if less palpable point – viz. that the world should in some way or other be conceived as a structure that allows entities to come forth.

Second, according to both authors, the world is experientially "present" in roughly the same way. Husserl, as we have seen, emphasizes that the world is something I am conscious of in a "dim" manner (*Hua* III/1, p. 57). The world is, "no matter what else we are conscious of, in a certain manner also given to consciousness [*bewusst*], although not 'objectively,' not as the theme of an act directed at it" (*Hua* XV, p. 425; cf. pp. 439, 631). Although it can be thematized (by phenomenology), the world is no theme for the naturally attuned subject (*Hua* VI, p. 300). It is there in a non-thematic, "background" kind of way, making possible our thematic awareness of whatever we are thematically aware of (*EU*, pp. 24-25). Yet, exactly the same could be said of Heidegger's notion of world. The world is something that does not, normally at least, announce itself, and as present in this "background" manner, it makes possible our unproblematic interaction with individual (inconspicuous) entities (cf. *SZ*, p. 75).

Third, in spite of the fact that the two notions of world seem, from a Husserlian perspective, to refer to two different "levels" of concrete life (namely, the concrete practical-understanding level on which we live, and the founding level of perceptions "in serving function"), if one probes a bit deeper, further structural similarities are uncovered. These will be revealed if we pay attention to the way in which both conceptions of world are developed. In both instances, the initial focus is on the individual entity, rather than any collection or configuration of such entities. Even with this initially limited focus, Husserl and Heidegger are both driven to the insight that the individual entity is not given as a simple matter, but rather, according to both accounts, it gives itself only by, as it were, dragging something more along with it. How does that happen? In Heidegger's view, the individual tool can only present itself as such insofar as it is understood in its being, that is, in its *reference* to… A referential structure must be understood if there is to be any encountered entity. In Husserl, the situation appears significantly different; after all, not a word has been said about references in our presentation of Husserl. But what, for instance, is a perceptual "inner horizon"? The horizon of "improperly" manifest that the "properly" manifest is embedded in is not unrelated to the authentically manifest. How could it be, if the properly manifest aspect is to be *an* aspect of the same as the continuum of improperly manifest aspects are aspects of? The properly given aspect cannot be self-sufficient, as it were, but must – as a dependent moment – refer to other aspects, if it is to be an aspect *of...* (*Hua* XV, p. 306). We might say, accordingly, that is in its *reference to* a continuum of other aspects that the authentically manifest aspect becomes an aspect of a thing. Clearly, then, nothing in principle prevents us from interpreting the Husserlian conception of world as itself a "referential structure," along the lines of Heidegger's concept of world (cf. *Hua* XV, p. 308).[37] What is more, this reading seems to be partially confirmed by certain passages written by Husserl himself. In *Cartesianische Mediationen*, for instance, he uses the term "reference" (*Verweisung*) to describe the phenomenon of horizonal intentionality (*Hua* I, pp. 82, 97; cf. *EU*, p. 27), and in an early lecture course he formulates the relation between proper and improper manifestation thus: "Actual appearance 'refers' ['*weist hin*'] to such and such possible appearance, and actual perception in a harmonious perceptual nexus refers to these or those possible perceptions that are in accord with the elapsing perceptual nexus" (*Hua* XVI, p. 291). In conclusion, perhaps Husserl may after all be said to agree with Heidegger's characterization of the world as a whole of references.

However, Heidegger's conception of the world in *Sein und Zeit* is not, as we have seen, a merely formal idea of a referential whole, but that of a very specific referential system – viz. a system of references of "in order to" and "for the sake of." We have already mentioned that Heidegger's analysis of the phenomenon of world seems, in the magnum opus at least, a bit too closely tied to the specific situation of the craftswoman in her workshop – it is, more than anything else, a "work-world" (*Werkwelt*) (*SZ*, p. 352). But a similar point could apparently be made concerning Husserl. The world-horizon, for Husserl, is first and foremost a horizon of possible *experience* (*Hua* VIII, p. 148), even if he emphasizes that in its full concretion, it is much more than that.

Still, although this is a large claim that cannot be properly substantiated in the present study, it seems to me that the notion of world-horizon has more descriptive potential than the conception of the world as a referential web. It appears, e.g., that "horizon" can capture not only perceptual phenomena, but "practical" phenomena as well. One can make intelligible a Dasein's moving about in its referential web in terms of "practical horizons," or horizons of "practical possibilities" (see, e.g., *Hua* XIV, p. 215), just as the continuous co-presence of the unperceived office wall behind me can be made intelligible in terms of "perceptual horizons." This becomes evident when we look at an unpublished manuscript. In "Ms. A VI 14 a" from the beginning of the thirties, Husserl repeats his contention that, no matter what we are

---

[37] This is indeed the interpretation Welton develops, using the Heideggerian notion of *Verweisungszusammenhang* (*The Other Husserl*, pp. 85, 332; "World," p. 736). Heidegger uses this term, e.g., in *SZ*, pp. 87-88, 123; *GA* 20, pp. 252-253, 268. It might be objected that this is stretching Husserl's conception of the world too far in the direction of Heidegger. But my point is simply that the Husserlian conception of world as horizon seems able to encompass that which Heidegger is trying to bring to light under the heading of *Verweisungszusammenhang*; i.e., I am claiming that the conception of world as horizon *can* be stretched in such a way, not that Husserl actually develops it along those lines.

caught up with, "the whole world is always in this connection the implicit background, the constant universal horizon."[38] He continues: "In addition, a 'practical horizon,' a horizon of that which I can do in my horizonally given situation, belongs to every activity, every praxis."[39] The individual references are ordered somehow in relation to the practical "goal" of the activity, something Husserl (like Heidegger) does not describe as thematically in focus, but rather as placed in the horizon: "in the praxis I am directed towards a goal as the end of a praxis-path, and it [the goal] lies in the horizon as the practical towards-which."[40] Furthermore, we have – once again, in case this point has not been emphasized enough in the present chapter – Husserl's unambiguous assurance that this practical horizon has a very special status within the world-horizon: "What is called a 'practical horizon' here thus has a distinctiveness, in terms of 'liveliness,' within the universal horizon 'world.'"[41] The "practical horizon" is precisely the one in which we mainly "live," according to Husserl. Moreover, let us note in passing that Heidegger himself uses the concept of horizon when he tries to account for the relation between the "relevance" of the individual piece of equipment and the "referential whole" that constitutes the world. In *Sein und Zeit*, he writes:

Relationships of involvement [or of "relevance": *Bewandtnisbezüge*] are intelligible only within the horizon of a world that has been disclosed. Their horizontal character, moreover, is what first makes possible the specific horizon of the "whither" of belonging-somewhere regionally. (*SZ*, p. 368)

Now the crucial point is that even the phenomenon of nature – precisely one of the phenomena that do not fit well into the account of the early Heidegger – as something uncovered in moods, can apparently be captured by this Husserlian notion. In fact, Husserl himself develops, if not a full-blown theory, then at least sketches for a theory of mood along precisely these lines. Mood, according to Husserl, is something that relates, in a background kind of way, to the horizon more than any particular objects. In this way it "colors," so Husserl explicitly says, not

---

[38] "[…] stets ist dabei die ganze Welt der implizite Hintergrund, der ständige Universalhorizont" (Ms. A VI 14 a, 19a).
[39] "Dabei gehört wesensmässig zu jedem Tun, zu jeder Praxis ein 'praktischer Horizont', ein Horizont dessen, was ich in meiner horizontmässig bewussten Situation kann" (Ms. A VI 14 a, 24b).
[40] "[…] praktisch bin ich auf ein Ziel gerichtet als Ende eines praktischen Weges, und das liegt im Horizont als das praktische Woraufhin" (Ms. A VI 14 a, 25a).
[41] "Was hier 'praktischer Horizont' heisst, hat also innerhalb des Universalhorizontes 'Welt' eine Auszeichnung in der Weise der 'Lebendigkeit'" (Ms. A VI 14 a, 26a). Here it is also worth quoting the following passage from a manuscript to which Husserl himself attaches the remark "that is against Heidegger" (*Das ist gegen* Heidegger), and in which he explicitly mentions Heidegger more than once: "What comes first, or can come first, for an awakened theoretical interest? Is the structure of the practical environing-world, and the I or the we as practical, not something that comes very late here? – Although the practical world is doubtlessly the most concrete, in correlation with the practically interested subjectivity, living a practical life of consciousness" (*Hua* XXXIV, p. 260). Certainly, not everything is opposed to Heidegger. As we emphasize repeatedly since Chapter I, Husserl is just as emphatic as Heidegger that the concrete world is mainly a "practical world."

only whatever we might happen to look at, but essentially the whole world as well.[42] Is it not very plausible to explain all of this in terms of horizons? Or, to put it more cautiously, is there any reason to think that Husserl's notion of world-horizon should *not* be able to capture this?

The conception of the world as world-horizon is so illuminating and at the same time strangely "neutral" to ontological issues in Heidegger's sense of the word that there is no reason why it should not be able to capture the practical and "mood-related" dimensions of the world as well as the "theoretical" dimensions. World-horizon, one might perhaps say, is an *ontologically non-committal* concept of the world, i.e., one that does not prejudice the being of intra-mundane entities. It stands in no opposition to the specific notion of a whole of references, and at the same time it is not essentially tied to the idea of readiness-to-hand, nor is it committed to an ontology of presence-at-hand.

In this way, the characterization of the world as horizon appears to be the phenomenologically most fruitful approach to the world. The conception of the world as world-horizon seems at once able to capture the practical, referential nexus the importance of which Heidegger (rightly, I believe) emphasizes, and to capture some of what appears to escape the early Heidegger's somewhat ontologically narrow account.[43]

---

[42] See Nam-In-Lee, "Edmund Husserl's Phenomenology of Mood." I base this entirely on Lee's article, especially pp. 114-115. Notice the excellent quotations from the manuscript M III 3 II 1.

[43] The descriptive and hermeneutic *power* of the notion of "horizon" is perhaps greater than any of Husserl's other key concepts (maybe even including "intentionality" and "lifeworld"). As Levinas writes in *Totality and Infinity*, "[s]ince Husserl the whole of phenomenology is the promotion of the idea of *horizon*, which for it plays a role equivalent to that of the *concept* in classical idealism" (pp. 44-45). In fact, "horizon" is not only an essential concept within what is normally regarded as the phenomenological movement. Where, for instance, would Gadamer's *Wahrheit und Methode* – with its all-important idea of "fusion of horizons" – be without it?

CHAPTER V

SUBJECTIVITY

1. INTERSUBJECTIVITY

In the preceding discussion of the world and intra-worldly entities, other subjectivities remain conspicuously absent. This is by no means because Husserl and Heidegger have nothing to say about intersubjectivity, but rather because other subjects are precisely subjects, and thus demand a separate discussion. Still, the best way to introduce intersubjectivity is to return briefly to the phenomenon of world. In both Husserl and Heidegger, the phenomenon of world is intimately connected with intersubjectivity.[1]

How is the world related to intersubjectivity? One can easily document that, for both Husserl and Heidegger, other subjects (or Dasein) are entities that appear *in* the world. As Husserl acknowledges, I experience the others as mundane objects (*Weltobjekte*) (*Hua* I, p. 123), and Heidegger states that the other Dasein is encountered as something "within the world" (*innerweltlich*) (*SZ*, p. 118). Yet, they are both emphatic that this particular type of intra-mundane entity is very different from tools and mere perceptual objects. The others, Husserl adds, I experience "at the same time as subjects for this world, as experiencing this world" (*Hua* I, p. 123), and as Heidegger observes, the other Dasein is, "in accordance with its kind of being *as Dasein*, itself 'in' the world in the manner of being-in-the-world" (*SZ*, p. 118). In the present section, I attempt to show how it is careful analyses of the phenomenon of the world that leads both phenomenologists to attribute *transcendental* status to intersubjectivity.

Let us consider the perceptual noema "blossoming apple tree." How does the tree present itself to its perceiver? Recalling our discussion of the world-horizon in the previous chapter, we can certainly say that the tree presents itself in and through "inner" as well as "outer" *horizons*. The authentically manifest aspect is embedded in a multitude of other aspects of the same apple tree, and at the same time an open horizon of aspects not of this entity is vaguely, unthematically intended. Without the latter, the perceived entity would be co-extensive with the world; without the former, there would be no transcendent perceived entity at all. Now, as I perceive the apple tree from my window, the co-intended backside of its trunk is "improperly" manifest. That is, it is co-intended horizontally in the perceptual act itself, yet strictly speaking I do not see it. I might have inspected it previously, and it is certainly possible for me to view it subsequently, but while I perceive the tree

---

[1] See Klaus Held, "Das Problem der Intersubjektivität und die Idee einer phänomenologischen Transzendentalphilosophie," p. 29, and Günter Figal, *Martin Heidegger: Phänomenologie der Freiheit*, p. 135.

from my present position, the other side of the trunk is not, in the strict sense, given. That, however, does not mean that what for me is the backside of the trunk is not available to perception now at all, but only that it is not so *for me*. While I am still viewing the tree from my window, I have no perceptual access to the improperly manifest sides, but that does not mean that these sides are not there "yet," but only come into being as I leave my room in order to investigate the tree further. As emphasized in Chapter IV, if the intended object is not from the beginning "more" than the properly given, then there would be no possibility of "investigating further." Similarly, we must refrain from speculating whether the multiple aspects are perhaps already "there," but not yet possible properly *given* aspects, as if they are invisible up to the very point when I set out in my attempt to discover them. If we stick to describing the perceived tree *just as it is perceived*, we must say that it gives itself as perceivable from all sides at once, despite the fact that it is not possible for me to perceive all sides of it except in an infinite continuum of perceptions. What this indicates is that while *I* cannot perceive the tree from all sides at once, there might be other subjects perceiving the sides that are at the moment inaccessible to me (cf. *Hua* XIII, pp. 377-378).[2]

Thus, our example shows that merely perceptually given things, even things of "nature" such as apple trees, refer to other experiencing subjects (*Hua* IV, p. 86; *Hua* XIV, p. 421; *Hua* XV, p. 110). The same case can of course be made just as easily for cultural objects. A tool, for instance, is not only something with which *I* can do this or that; it is also of possible use to others (*Hua* IV, p. 188; *Hua* IX, p. 118). Furthermore, it refers as a "reminiscence" to someone who has made it, Husserl says (*Hua* XV, p. 505; *EU*, p.55); it "tells of man as worker, as inventing, as executing, etc., however ambiguously, however indeterminately, still worker as working subject for this work, etc." (*HuDo* II/1, pp. 200-201).

The same holds for the world-horizon as a whole. I do not know what is happening right now in Times Square in New York City. I cannot see it, nor do I necessarily think about it at all, and yet it is implied in that dim, unthematic way in my present perception – implied as something that *can* be witnessed, right now, as it takes place. It cannot be witnessed by *me*, but by others. Just as the person who originally invented a specific piece of equipment might have died a long time ago, without this affecting the fact that the thing still carries a reference, no matter how vaguely, to its inventor; in a similar sense, the experienced world refers to other subjects also when none are present. Even a universal plague leaving me as the sole survivor would not do away with the intersubjective meaning of the experienced world, Husserl claims (*Hua* I, p. 125). In other words, the noematic world disclosed by the epoché is simply one that, just as it presents itself to *my* experience, bears traces of other subjects.[3] And this is not only or even primarily in the sense that

---

[2] See, concerning this, Dan Zahavi, *Husserl und die transzendentale Intersubjektivität*, pp. 32-40, and Manfred Sommer, "Fremderfahrung und Zeitbewußtsein. Zur Phänomenologie der Intersubjektivität."

[3] This is precisely the realization that necessitates, in Husserl's eyes, the introduction of the so-called "primordial reduction." It is not because I initially find myself as a solipsistic subject that it becomes

other subjects are among the entities that I encounter in that world, but in the sense that the world I experience, and in which I act, I experience as a world that others experience, and act in, as well:

> In any case then, within myself, within the limits of my transcendentally reduced pure conscious life, I experience the world (including others) – and, according to its experiential sense, not as (so to speak) my private synthetic formation but as something other than me [*mir fremde*], as an *intersubjective* world, actually there for everyone, accessible in respect of its objects to everyone. (*Hua* I, p. 123; cf. *Hua* XV, pp. 5, 64-65; *Hua* XVII, p. 243; *Hua* VI, p. 469)

For Husserl's transcendental phenomenology, this is a crucial insight. It brings Husserl to the realization that if the world is to have the meaning it does have, viz. "present-for-everyone" (*Für-jedermann-da*) (*Hua* I, p. 124), then I cannot alone be responsible for its transcendental constitution. Rather, the world, including all its natural and cultural objects, must be the product of an "intersubjective constitution" (*Hua* VI, p. 171). If I pretend that no others are there then the world loses its "meaning of being" (*Seinssinn*), Husserl observes (*Hua* XXIX, p. 198; cf. *Hua* XV, p. 46). Therefore, he explicitly draws the remarkable conclusion that only as part of a community of transcendental subjectivities can I be the place of world-constitution that I am (*Hua* I, p. 166; *Hua* VI, p. 175). Transcendental subjectivity is ultimately transcendental *inter*subjectivity.

Obviously, not only the structure of the noematic world is affected by this. As part of a transcendental community of subjects, I am there for others, as they are there for me – and this is something I realize (cf. *Hua* I, pp. 157-158). In other words, the noetic side of the transcendental-phenomenological field of research bears traces of intersubjectivity, just as the noematic side does. Not only is the world the noematic correlate of an open community of subjects, but each single one of these subjects must know itself as part of such a community, i.e., know that it not only has its others, but is itself an other to them. Each subject, therefore, is also *to itself* "an other to its others" (*Hua* XIV, p. 421; *Hua* XV, p. 645).

Turning to Heidegger's discussion of other subjects, one immediately notices that he frequently introduces the problematic of others in the context of an analysis of the "tool." In accordance with Husserl, Heidegger emphasizes that "along with the equipment put to work, those others for whom the 'work' is destined are 'encountered too'" (*SZ*, p. 117). In fact, it is not only the case that the tool carries a reference to its user – and, for the industrially produced tool, a vague or "average" one (*SZ*, p. 71; *GA* 20, pp. 260-261) – it also refers to a manufacturer, a distributor, and so forth. Even the field that we pass when we are out for a walk refers to others, viz. the farmer that neglects it or manages it well (*SZ*, pp. 117-118; *GA* 20, p. 330).

---

necessary for the phenomenologist to reduce to the "sphere of ownness" – indeed, if I were a solipsistic subject, such a reduction would be impossible (and, if it were possible, utterly pointless) – but because I discover a noematic world completely permeated with intersubjectivity. On this point, cf. Søren Overgaard, "Epoché and Solipsistic Reduction." Another question is whether Husserl's "primordial reduction" is possible, whether one can imagine a "world" that is not shared with others. For an argument that one cannot, see James G. Hart, *The Person and the Common Life*, pp. 184-186.

Yet, in a great many domains of our everyday lives, we are not ourselves completely familiar with the tools that surround us. Heidegger considers the example of a visit to a shoemaker's workshop. I personally would be unable to name many of the tools that I would encounter in such a workshop, and, with my lack of routine, would be very clumsy with my handling of the tools – for many of them, I would even have no idea what they are used for. I would thus not know how to begin to put them to use (*GA* 24, p. 431). That does not mean, however, that these unfamiliar things would present themselves to me as merely occurrent entities, but rather, they precisely present themselves as *unfamiliar* tools (*GA* 24, p. 432), tools that *I* cannot uncover in their proper *Um-zu*. This should make it evident that although the other Dasein announces itself in and through the ready-to-hand entities, it is not announced as *itself* an entity of that type. The other Dasein that is encountered in and through the well-managed field or the shoemaker's shop is precisely encountered as one who takes care of the field, one who understands how to use these tools – one who moves concernedly in the references of fertilizing and removing weeds in order to let the barley thrive, or in those references vaguely anticipated by me as somehow ending up in a finished pair of shoes (cf. *GA* 20, p. 330). That is to say, the other is by no means encountered as a thing, but the other way around: "such 'things' are encountered from out of the world in which they are ready-to-hand for others – a world which is always mine too in advance" (*SZ*, p. 118). Here I therefore encounter, not a some*thing*, but a some*one* who is "with me" in the world – a *Mitdasein* (ibid.; *GA* 20, p. 326).[4]

As the references that constitute the being of individual tools are shared with others – and in many cases are more properly "their" references than mine (as when I do not understand the "in order to" of the tool) – so the whole web of references is something that I essentially share with others. In Heidegger's words, the world is "always the one that I share with others. The world of Dasein is a *with-world* [*Mitwelt*]" (*SZ*, p. 118; cf. *GA* 24, p. 421).[5]

---

[4] Emmanuel Levinas, albeit without explicitly mentioning Heidegger, criticizes this approach in his book *Totality and Infinity*. When one approaches the other through his work, so Levinas objects, one "has penetrated into his interior, but in his absence. He has been understood like a prehistoric man who has left hatchets and drawings but no words" (p. 181). This, according to Levinas, amounts to startling or surprising the other (p. 178), instead of addressing him or her *face to face* (cf. pp. 182-183). A similar criticism is found in Michael Theunissen's *Der Andere*, where Heidegger is charged with considering the other *Dasein* only to the extent that it "can be read off the ready-to-hand [entities]" (p. 172; similarly, Bernhard Waldenfels, *Das Zwischenreich des Dialogs*, p. 241). Whether or not this is a trenchant critique of Heidegger (and it may not be), it certainly seems not true of Husserl. In volumes XIV and XV of the collected works, there are several manuscripts dealing with the act of "turning towards the other" in genuine dialogue (cf. *Hua XIV*, pp. 166-168, 211; *Hua XV*, pp. 471-479; and Søren Overgaard, "On Levinas' Critique of Husserl").

[5] The expression "co-world" or "with-world" (*Mitwelt*) is one Heidegger uses from very early on, together with the expressions "environing-world" (*Umwelt*) and "self-world" (*Selbstwelt*) (cf., e.g., *GA* 58, pp. 33, 56; *GA* 59, p. 59; *GA* 61, p. 94). In the summer of 1925, Heidegger explicitly criticizes this terminology, because, as he now says, it gives the false impression that the other Dasein has an intramundane mode of being (*GA* 20, p. 333). As the term *Mitwelt* is used in *Sein und Zeit*, however, it clearly

The individual Dasein is therefore no isolated subject occupied with its equipment. As the environing world is not originally a world in which only one Dasein lives concernedly with its stock of tools, so the individual Dasein is not exhaustively defined by its "being-amidst" ready-to-hand entities. Just as originally and essentially, Dasein is "being-with": "Dasein is equiprimordially being-with others *and* being-among intraworldly entities" (*GA* 24, p. 421; cf. *GA* 20, p. 328; *GA* 27, p. 118). In fact, it is only because the individual Dasein, in its own being, is "being-with" that it can encounter any "co-Daseins," Heidegger claims (*SZ*, p. 120). This indicates that "being-with" is not constituted by, nor dependent on, the actual presence of other human beings (*GA* 20, p. 328; *GA* 24, p. 414, WDF, p. 163), but the other way around. Others can actually be there with me, as well as be absent and missing, only insofar as I am already, in my own being, constituted by "being-with" (*SZ*, p. 120). The possibility of my being completely alone constitutes a proof rather than a refutation of this claim, because only someone who is determined by "co-being" could possibly be alone (ibid.).

In a certain sense, social existence even tends to dominate all aspects of Dasein's being-in-the-world. As already briefly mentioned in Chapter I, Heidegger describes everyday life as ruled by convention:

We take pleasure and enjoy ourselves as *one* [*man*] takes pleasure; we read, see, and judge about literature and art as *one* sees and judges; likewise, we shrink back from the "great mass" as *one* shrinks back; we find "shocking" what *one* finds shocking. The "one" [*Das Man*], which is nothing definite, and which all are, though not as the sum, prescribes the kind of being of everydayness. (*SZ*, pp. 126-127)

Although this dictatorship of the "(every)one" can be modified, it can never really be extinguished, Heidegger claims (*SZ*, pp. 169, 179). Moreover, the publicity constituted by the rule of *das Man* is not "only" responsible for our habits and moral and aesthetic judgments: it "proximally controls *every way in which the world and Dasein get interpreted*, and it is always right" (*SZ*, p. 127, my emphasis). The only available interpretation of oneself and others, as well as of the world and intra-mundane things, is the one supplied by the "(every)one." Indeed, being to this extent ruled by the social institution that is all of us, though no-one in particular, the everyday Dasein is simply not itself, according to Heidegger. The self that we proximally and for the most part are, is the "one-self" (*SZ*, p. 129).

For both Husserl and Heidegger, then, the world is essentially one that I share with others. It is not only my world, the one I experience, but rather, the world is precisely experienced by me as *our* world, the one we all experience, the one in which we all act.[6] Thus, both Husserl and Heidegger ultimately attribute

---

gives no such impression. Here it only refers to the world, not to the other Dasein as such – it refers to the world precisely as *one I share with others*. The term *Mitdasein* (that Heidegger himself introduces as the better alternative in 1925 – cf. ibid.) is reserved for the being of the others.

[6] Hence, Sartre's observation that Heidegger's account of intersubjectivity is modeled on the idea of a *crew*, rather than a situation of conflict (*Being and Nothingness*, p. 246), partly fits Husserl as well – even if Husserl emphasizes more than does Heidegger the transcendence of the other, and the possibility of "turning to the other," face to face (cf. note 4 above). This claim can be substantiated by reference to the

transcendental status to intersubjectivity. I alone do not constitute the world; I alone do not understandingly project references of "in order to" – I essentially do it together with others. As transcendental subjectivity is essentially intersubjectivity, so Dasein is essentially *Mitsein*.

Having thus touched on the theme of intersubjectivity, we can conclude that this is not an instance where significant differences between the two phenomenologists' analyses are encountered. Whatever may be the differences between the being of Heidegger's Dasein and the being of Husserlian transcendental subjectivity, they both essentially bear the mark of – possible, if not necessarily actual – community. We must look elsewhere to discover what, if anything, Heidegger may legitimately object to in Husserl's characterization of transcendental subjectivity. If that subjectivity is "worldless," then it must be unveiled in a careful analysis of the structures of the individual transcendental subject.

2. TRANSCENDENTAL VS. MUNDANE SUBJECTIVITY: SOME INITIAL CONSIDERATIONS

In this study, it is argued that transcendental subjectivity is simply defined by Husserl (though not in so many words) as the "dative of manifestation" of the world and everything mundane, or as the one *to whom* the world is present. It is further argued that transcendental subjectivity is accessed only in and through the phenomenological reduction, i.e., only in and through a regression from the "experienced just as experienced" (the noema) to experiencing subjectivity. Since the transcendental subject is initially defined as a viewpoint on the world, a *point* where a world is disclosed, we cannot subject it to direct scrutiny, and we thus only learn about its structures by attending phenomenologically to its "noematic correlate." On its concrete structures, we have so far been silent; this silence must now be broken.

In the preceding chapter, the charge of worldlessness is taken as a guiding clue. There we investigate whether Husserl has an alternative to the conception of the world as a totality, and more generally to what extent the Husserlian conception of world differs from Heidegger's. Far from justifying Heidegger's charge of worldlessness, the two accounts of the world are unveiled as similar in a number of important respects – in fact, we seem eventually to have to grant a slight superiority to Husserl's notion of world-horizon. But let us now approach the question of "worldlessness" from another angle: subjectivity. To what extent might transcendental subjectivity be said to "lack" the world? And – to put the ball back

---

very frequent use of such expressions as *Mitsubjekte, Mitmenschen, Miteinanderleben*, and even *Mitsein* and *Mitdaseiende* in Husserl's analyses of transcendental intersubjectivity (cf. *Hua* VI, pp. 166-167, 260; *Hua* VIII, p. 137; *Hua* IX, pp. 489-490; *Hua* XIV, p. 419; *Hua* XV, pp. 134-135, 163, 342, 386, 456). As Husserl declares, "against" is a mode of the (original) "with" (*Hua* XIV, p. 409). For more on the similarities and differences, agreements and mutual critiques, within the most significant French and German phenomenological accounts of intersubjectivity, see Dan Zahavi, "Beyond Empathy: Phenomenological Approaches to Intersubjectivity."

into Heidegger's court – what does it actually mean when Heidegger emphasizes Dasein's "being-in-the-world"? The issue of subjectivity will continue to occupy us beyond the present chapter, but before we can deal in any adequate manner with the *ontological* question of subjectivity, we must shed some "ontic" light on the topic.

Saying that the transcendental subject is the subject considered insofar (and only insofar) as it is the place of the manifestation of the world, already, in a functional manner, separates subject and world. It might be the case that the subject is defined exclusively in terms of the world, but it is precisely defined as what lies "outside" the world or, as Sartre would put it, the "negation" of the world.[7] The transcendental subject is functionally defined as the place where the world appears, and that means that it is not – *in its capacity of transcendental subject* – one of the entities appearing in the world. Functionally defined as the dative of manifestation, transcendental subjectivity must be separated from the world functionally defined as the "genitive" of manifestation.

But some clarifications are in order at this point. For instance, one might be inclined to think this entitles one to describe Husserlian transcendental subjectivity as "detached."[8] Such a claim could be substantiated in roughly the following way. The "natural" subject is precisely not detached; it is involved in the world and the mundane, submerged in this or that project, or activity, and so forth. Transcendental subjectivity, however, is "withdrawn" from such projects and activities; the only "activity" it engages in is that of "constituting" the world (from which it keeps itself aloof) in acts of theoretical "contemplation." But this division of labor – the naturally attuned subject as the "practical," involved subject, and the transcendental as the "theoretical," detached subject – is hardly found in Husserl. The transcendental subject is, for Husserl, also the subject involved in this or that activity, engulfed by this or that project, but considered *just as the place where* such activities can take place, where such projects can be carried out. And conversely, it is not the case that the natural attitude is simply "practical" (although Husserl and Heidegger agree that this is mainly the case) – there is such a thing as theoretical activity in the natural attitude. More importantly, transcendental subjectivity is, we should note, none other than the naturally attuned subject (*Hua* I, p. 75), namely considered exclusively as *subject*. The naturally attuned subject, in other words, is precisely the transcendental subject studied by constitutive phenomenology. As pointed out earlier, the subject living in the natural attitude is already the transcendental subject, only it does not yet know itself as such (ibid.; *Hua* VI, p. 209).

But perhaps the critics want to raise a different issue. What about the one who *studies* the naturally attuned subject in its capacity of transcendental subject, what

---

[7] Jean-Paul Sartre, *Being and Nothingness*, pp. 181-185.
[8] There are some remarks to that effect in Hubert Dreyfus, *Being-in-the-World* (esp. pp. 47, 141). It also seems implicit in comments made by Carl F. Gethmann (*Dasein: Erkennen und Handeln*, p. 27), Walter Biemel ("Husserls Encyclopaedia-Britannica Artikel und Heideggers Anmerkungen dazu," p. 277), and even Emmanuel Levinas (*Discovering Existence with Husserl*, pp. 71, 106).

about the *phenomenologist*? Is she not precisely detached from the world? We phenomenologists, surely, are posing theoretical questions; we are approaching the subject with the question of "constitution." More importantly, as posing such a question, we are already slightly distanced from the world; we are detached, to a certain extent, from the process of constitution that we are inquiring into. Phenomenologists are spectators, not participants. While this is certainly true, we must not lose sight of the fact that the subjective life to which we are "spectators" is not detached in this way: "The non-participating, the abstaining, of the phenomenologically attuned ego is *his* affair, not that of the naturally perceiving ego that the former reflectively observes" (*Hua* I, p. 73, emphasis deleted).[9] This "double life of the subject," as Rudolf Bernet labels it, is an ineradicable component of Husserlian phenomenology. One can therefore say that Husserl's transcendental subjectivity (considered as the "spectator") indeed *is* detached from the world. On the other hand, though, one would still have to acknowledge that transcendental subjectivity (as considered *by* the spectator) is precisely *not* detached. And for those who would argue against the idea that the subject has, or could have, such a "double life," the question is whether Heidegger in fact presents an attractive alternative, or whether we find the same structure in his own phenomenology of Dasein.[10]

I shall not pursue this point, however. The crucial point in the present context is that it is far from obvious that the "spectator" is completely detached from the world. After all, what we phenomenologists cannot allow ourselves to lose sight of is precisely the world and everything mundane – as emphasized repeatedly. The phenomenological "spectator," in other words, does not cut off all ties to the world, nor does she cease to be interested in the world. Her interest pertains precisely to the *constitution of the world* and everything mundane. To call to mind the words of Merleau-Ponty, we might say that the transcendental "spectator" "slackens the intentional threads which attach us to the world and thus brings them to our attention."[11] Although Husserl keeps returning to a description of the transcendental "spectator" as "uninterested" in the world and in being (cf., e.g., *Hua* I, p. 73; *Hua* VIII, p. 92; *Hua* VI, p. 160), at other times he clearly recognizes that the phenomenologist does not lose all such interest, nor denies herself every statement about the world (*Hua* XV, p. 366). In fact, transcendental phenomenology, so Husserl declares at one point, is *radikale Welterforschung* (*Hua* XXVII, p. 178). For

---

[9] These motifs remind one of Fichte more than they do of Descartes. Indeed, it might be much more fruitful to compare Husserl's phenomenological reduction with Fichte than with Descartes. Fichte's idea that the philosopher should "abstract from being" in order to clarify the "ground of all being," and his insistence that it is precisely the philosophizing ego, rather than the ego that the philosopher studies, that should undertake this abstraction, seem much more closely related to Husserl's notion of the phenomenological reduction than does Cartesian doubt. Cf. Johann Gottlieb Fichte, *Versuch einer neuen Darstellung der Wissenschaftslehre (1797/98)*, pp. 33-38.

[10] The latter is in fact what Bernet argues in his article "Phenomenological Reduction and the Double Life of the Subject."

[11] Maurice Merleau-Ponty, *Phenomenology of Perception*, p. xiii. Cf. Merleau-Ponty, *The Primacy of Perception*, p. 49.

this reason, Husserl eventually wants to abandon the notion of "spectator" (*Zuschauer*) – hence my quotation marks all along – and replace it with the notion of the "phenomenologizing" subject (*HuDo* II/1, p. 192).

In view of the discussion of the world in the preceding chapter, we are in fact able, at this point, to assess the charge of worldlessness as such. Transcendental subjectivity, functionally defined as a viewpoint on the world, cannot be "without" the world in any significant sense. It is true, to be sure, that Husserl believed that transcendental subjectivity could continue to exist – although not completely unaltered – even if the world is "annihilated." Yet, we should take care to understand that position – which might not even be Husserl's last word on the matter – in the right way. What Husserl always has in mind is the possibility of all experiences dissolving into what Kant calls a "confusion of appearances" (*Hua* XVI, p. 288).[12] A situation, in other words, where all horizonal intentions are continuously disaffirmed; where I cannot explore any object further, because every object already ceases to be experientially present as soon as I make perceptual contact with it, etc. In short, this is a situation in which I am no longer able to *experience* a world (*Hua* III/1, p. 103). But since intentionality is what defines me, even then I would have to be directed towards something, even then I would have my intentional objects (even if I could never, in the strict sense, separate them from me). That is to say, even given this extreme hypothetical scenario, I would continue to be an *openness towards*…(*Hua* XIV, pp. 244-245). This conclusion follows directly from Husserl's insights into the intentional nature of the subject. As he puts it in *Cartesianische Meditationen*, it is clear from the outset "that the transcendental ego […] is what it is solely in relation to intentional objectivities" (*Hua* I, p. 99). Without its intentional "world" subjectivity is not *concrete* (*Hua* I, p. 102). Ultimately, Husserl therefore emphasizes that "[w]ithout a realm of pre-given things [*Vorgegebenheiten*], a realm of constituted units, constituted as not-I [*Nicht-Ich*], no I is possible" (*Hua* XIV, p. 379). Its intentional directedness towards…, its openness to…, are essentially what *define* transcendental subjectivity: its "mode of being" is nothing but its continuous life in world-constitution (*Hua* VI, p. 275). Hence, to call Husserlian transcendental subjectivity "worldless" would seem completely unjustified.

So although a clear functional distinction can be made between the transcendental subject and the constituted world, the transcendental subject is by no means detached, or aloof, from the world. Nor can it lose its intentional openness to a world; on the contrary, that openness defines it. But is it not outside the world, extra-mundane? This question is one that continues to occupy us through the rest of this chapter, and it cannot at present be answered. But let me just reemphasize that transcendental subjectivity thus far has been *functionally* defined, but only functionally. Therefore, we may do well to pay heed to Husserl's reminder in the "Londoner Vorträge" that he refrains from claiming that the transcendental

---

[12] *Kritik der reinen Vernunft*, A 111.

subjectivity is "outside" the world, and "separated" from it, just as he refrains from claiming that it is a "piece" of the world (LV, p. 212).

A mere piece of the world, an object among objects in the world, is what I am as a "human being," according to Husserl (*Hua* VI, pp. 149, 457). Although this "mundane subject" is also me – that is, it is not an other – it is radically different from the transcendental subject (*Hua* VIII, pp. 71-72). Roughly stated, although the naturally attuned subject is the transcendental subject, as considered by the phenomenologizing subject (transcendentally attuned), the *mundane* subject, the human being, is one of the worldly entities manifest to the naturally attuned transcendental subject.[13] The mundane subject, one might say, is the naturally attuned subject's self-description: it is itself, insofar as it is found in the constituted world. In other words, whereas the transcendental subject is me, functionally defined as the place of the manifestation of the world and of worldly entities, then the mundane subject is me considered as one of the worldly entities thus manifested. When I cycle to work in the morning, I may consider myself as the place where this bicycle, this street, this city, and this dimly co-intended world-horizon is experientially anchored, or I may look upon myself as just one more worldly object (albeit of a special sort, in that this object has something like a mind, a psyche) changing position in the world.

Strange as it may seem, this latter mentioned subject, the "mundane" subject, is the one that could, with some legitimacy, be called "worldless."[14] Although it is "in" the world, it is in it as just another object. Chairs and houses are "in the world" in just this sense, but chairs and houses are precisely eminent examples of *worldless* entities, according to Heidegger (*SZ*, p. 55; *GA* 21, pp. 213-214). Matters are not significantly changed by the attribution of "mental states" to the "human" objects, since such states can be studied independently of whether or not they are "related" to any objects. According to Husserl, the science of psychology in fact studies this realm of "mental states" in abstraction from the physical, external world (cf. *Hua* IX, p. 248). Indeed, not only *can* one study the "mental states" independently of their possible relation to objects and a world; this is even the context in which the problem of the "external world" arises and continues to thrive. How do I know that there is a computer screen in front of me? I know it because I am wide awake and I see the screen there, right in front of me. I can stretch out my hand and touch it as well. But what is here supposed to justify my certainty that there is an object "out there," and that it is more or less the object I think it is, is nothing more than *my experiences*, that is, *states in me*, and far from serving to refute any skeptic, the reference to such states only aggravates the problem. How do I know that the thing

---

[13] In the *VI. Cartesianische Meditation*, Eugen Fink thus distinguishes between *three* egos (that are nevertheless one and the same): the mundane or human ego, the transcendental-constituting ego, and the phenomenologizing spectator (*HuDo* II/1, pp. 45-46).
[14] So Burt Hopkins argues. See his article "The Husserl-Heidegger Confrontation and the Essential Possibility of Phenomenology," esp. pp. 138, 148, note 31. See, as well, Steven Crowell, "Does the Husserl/Heidegger Feud Rest on a Mistake?"

out there corresponds to the states in me, indeed how do I know that there is *anything* out there corresponding to these states? Clearly, the introduction of the realm of the "mental" does little to prevent the label of "worldlessness" from being attached to the "human" object (cf. *SZ*, p. 60). The contrary is rather the case: if one describes the subject as an object in the world, then the addition of what Ryle would call states of a "ghostly" nature does not remove the isolation, and consequent worldlessness, of such an object.[15] Adding objects of one kind to objects of another kind makes no intentional and world-disclosing subject. Therefore, whereas transcendental subjectivity cannot be conceived without its objects and its world, the mundane subject can.

The notion that the subject is both a mundane subject, an insignificant entity *within* the world, and the subject *to* which the world is manifest, so Husserl realizes, appears paradoxical. He himself refers to this as the "paradox of subjectivity" (*Hua* VI, pp. 182-183). But with his distinction between the transcendental and the mundane subject, Husserl thinks he has dissolved the paradox. Whereas the position that the mundane subject, an object among objects in the world, is what constitutes the world amounts to nonsense (*Hua* V, p. 154; *Hua* VI, p. 183; *Hua* XV, p. 483), it makes perfect sense to say that the same subject can be viewed both under the aspect of its transcendental function (in which case it is *not* one of the objects in the world), and under the aspect of its worldly existence (in which case it is *not* the place of the constitution of the world) (*Hua* IX, p. 292). Thus, Husserl's solution is to maintain the identity between mundane and transcendental subject, but at the same time to claim that it is the subject viewed under radically different aspects. There are not two subjects, not even two closely connected ones (*Hua* VIII, p. 71; *Hua* IX, p. 294), but only one subject, viewed from two different angles, as it were. A mere "change of attitude" is, once I have become acquainted with the transcendental stance, all it takes for me to view one instead of the other (*Hua* IX, p. 294).

Husserl further believes he can show it to be a necessity that transcendental subjectivity "mundanizes" itself, becomes an entity within the world: "It is apodictic that <the> ego must occur in the world as a human being" (*Hua* XXIX, p. 260; cf. *Hua* VI, pp. 115-116). Transcendental subjectivity can neither avoid becoming one of the worldly objects, nor can it choose to withdraw itself from this mundane existence. As Husserl puts it, the human being "is an object in the world and at the same time subject for the world, and because it is the latter it cannot cease being the former" (*Hua* XXIX, p. 152). This is clearly not in any tension with what is

---

[15] The mention of Gilbert Ryle here is quite appropriate. Although the *positive* message of *The Concept of Mind* is very different from the argument of the present study, some of Ryle's negative points are very much in accordance with it. Ryle's objections to the "dogma of the ghost in the machine" are not only that "[m]en are not machines, not even ghost-ridden machines" (*The Concept of Mind*, p. 79), and that there are no ghosts (ibid., p. 154). In addition to that, he continuously returns to the observation that minds, according to the dogma, are themselves things or machines, only different sorts of things or machines. That is, the "ghosts" themselves are conceived "para-mechanically" (ibid., pp. 20-21, 62, 112, 177, 211). As Heidegger would put it, the idea of mental states is the idea of something with the being of presence-at-hand, and can therefore never make intelligible the human "being-in-the-world."

presented in the previous paragraph. *In its capacity of transcendental subject*, the "human being" is not one of the objects in the world; yet, as it constitutes the world, it cannot avoid constituting itself as an "object" in the world (cf. *Hua* I, p. 130; *Hua* XV, p. 287). I return to this characterization of the "mundane" subject in Chapter VI.

But we have not yet made the charge of "worldlessness" disappear altogether. There is one possibility we have not considered. Carl F. Gethmann thus claims that what the charge of "worldlessness" really means is that Husserl's transcendental subject is not conceived, and cannot be conceived, as *in* the world, although it is doubtlessly "related" to the world.[16] Our next task is therefore to try to understand what it actually means when Heidegger emphasizes Dasein's "being-in-the-world." Is this, as Gethmann would have it, something that cannot possibly characterize Husserlian transcendental subjectivity?

3. DASEIN: SOME INITIAL CONSIDERATIONS

In view of Husserl's distinction between the subject considered as *in* the world (the "human being") and the subject considered as the place of the manifestation of the world, it is hardly surprising that he finds Heidegger's *Sein und Zeit* methodologically inadequate. He interprets Heidegger's introduction of the concept of Dasein, and the characterization of Dasein as "being-in-the-world" as a clear indication that the phenomenological reduction is abandoned or neglected, and thus the whole account can only be viewed as one that remains stuck in the "natural attitude." In Husserl's eyes, then, the subjectivity analyzed in Heidegger's magnum opus could be none other than the "mundane" subject, the "human being." The "anthropology" that Husserl contrasts with his own transcendental phenomenology in his 1931 *Kantgesellschaft* lecture is thus first and foremost Heidegger's phenomenology.[17] Let us take this "anthropology charge" as our guiding clue in the following discussion. Can Heidegger's insistence that Dasein is being-in-the-world legitimately be interpreted as an indication that Heidegger abandons the transcendental attitude, or remains in the natural, mundane attitude?

The first thing to note is of course that neither "epoché," nor "reduction," nor indeed "transcendental ego" and "constitution," are concepts that Heidegger explicitly uses in *Sein und Zeit*. He does hint, a few times, at his undertaking being "transcendental," but always in ways that would not seem entirely familiar to Husserl (e.g., "being" is described as the "transcendental"; *SZ*, pp. 208, 38). However, as documented in detail, Heidegger could not develop his

---

[16] Gethmann, *Verstehen und Auslegung*, pp. 247-248. See, too, Levinas, *Discovering Existence with Husserl*, p. 85: "In a certain sense intentionality is an *Ausser-der-Welt-sein* rather than the *In-der-Welt-sein* of consciousness."

[17] See *Hua* XXVII, pp. 164-165. The other main target is Max Scheler, whom Husserl even mentions by name (ibid., p. 180). For other places where Husserl criticizes (explicitly or implicitly) Heidegger's allegedly "anthropological" phenomenology, cf. RB, pp. 13, 56; *Hua* V, p. 140.

phenomenological analyses without the aid of Husserl's method of epoché. At least in some of his lectures, Heidegger admits that without the Husserlian notion of "the experienced in its 'how'" – something we do not have access to, as long as we have not performed the epoché – no ontological research would be possible (*GA* 17, pp. 262-263; WDF, p. 160). Also, we have some indication that a question not unlike Husserl's question of constitution is present in Heidegger's work. Both these points would suggest that although the epoché and reduction are not explicitly introduced in Heidegger's magnum opus, they are nevertheless performed.[18]

The most important point, however, is that Heidegger sometimes describes Dasein in ways that are almost identical to the ways in which Husserl characterizes transcendental subjectivity. In his October 1927 letter to Husserl, for instance, Heidegger implies that "Dasein" is his name for the "place" of the transcendental (*Hua* IX, p. 601). As already mentioned, Heidegger remarks in a marginal comment to *Sein und Zeit* that "Dasein is not an ontic case for an imaginative [*vorstellende*] abstraction of being, but rather the *locus of the understanding of being* [*Stätte des Seinsverständnisses*]."[19] And finally, in the lecture course *Einleitung in die Philosophie*, Heidegger even refers to Dasein as the "peculiar place for the totality of entities" (*eigentümliche Ort für die Ganzheit des Seienden*) (*GA* 27, p. 360). These summarily presented remarks provide evidence for a close structural kinship between Heidegger's notion of Dasein and the Husserlian conception of transcendental subjectivity. Just as the transcendental subject is the subject considered qua the "place" where the world and everything mundane manifests itself, so "Dasein" indicates the "place" or the "site" of the understanding of being – the understanding, as we recall, without which entities could not manifest themselves, according to Heidegger.

But Heidegger also characterizes Dasein – the entity "we ourselves are" – in terms that seem to indicate that he is describing something very different from Husserl's transcendental subject. As early as the first pages of *Sein und Zeit*, Heidegger states: "But to Dasein, being in a world is something that belongs essentially" (*SZ*, p. 13). Or, as he also puts it, "[b]eing-in-the-world is an essential structure of Dasein's being" (*GA* 24, p. 241; cf. *SZ*, p. 53; *GA* 20, p. 214; *GA* 21, p. 212). However, Heidegger is very eager to specify how this is *not* to be understood.

First, as something that essentially (*wesenhaft*) characterizes Dasein, "being-in-the-world" is not a property that Dasein can ever lose, nor is it something that is only constituted whenever some other thing is present outside Dasein (*SZ*, p. 57; *GA* 20, p. 214; *GA* 21, p. 212). Just as "intentionality" is not a relation that occurs when two things (subject and object) are placed in near vicinity of each other, but rather something that essentially characterizes the subject as such, and something without which no "things" could be there in the first place – so "being-in-the-world" is an

---

[18] Tugendhat suggests that Heidegger has no need to explicitly introduce the epoché, since he "stands within it" from the beginning (*Der Wahrheitsbegriff bei Husserl und Heidegger*, p. 263). This squares very well with our findings in Chapters I and III.
[19] *SZ*, p. 439 (marginal note to p. 8). My emphasis.

essential structure of (the being of) Dasein. Therefore, it would be simply absurd to imagine a Dasein without its "relatedness" to a world – it would be a conception of a Dasein that was no Dasein (*GA* 20, pp. 222-223). Likewise, there can be no world if there is no Dasein, Heidegger emphasizes (*SZ*, p. 365; *GA* 24, pp. 241, 420, 422; *GA* 26, p. 251). The world is the referential whole that "must already have been ecstatically disclosed so that in terms of it innerworldly entities can be encountered" (*SZ*, p. 366), but as such it is not something that can "be" in the absence of an understanding subject, a world-disclosing Dasein. Just like a human being cannot be conceived without its "relation" to the world, so the world "is" only as disclosed to a human being.

Secondly, Heidegger's "being-*in*" should be carefully distinguished from any "spatial" or even "non-spatial" being *contained* in (e.g., as the soul might perhaps be conceived as being "contained" in the body, though not occupying a specific space of the body) (*SZ*, p. 54; *GA* 20, p. 213).[20] The model of "being-in" that Heidegger is here trying to counter is of course the model of "presence-at-hand," the idea of merely occurring things inside other merely occurring things (*SZ*, p. 54). It is important to note that the reason why Heidegger objects to this idea of "being-contained-in" is not that he thinks something crucial is missing in the account, viz. something like the attribution of "experiences" to the human being occurring "inside" the world (cf. *SZ*, p. 56). On the contrary, this notion – which would place Dasein on a par with what Husserl calls the "mundane subject" – is emphatically rejected by Heidegger: "Dasein is not also present-at-hand among things with the difference merely that it apprehends them. Instead, Dasein exists in the manner of *being-in-the-world*" (*GA* 24, p. 234). In other words, Heidegger is clearly trying to distance himself from the Husserlian account of the "human being." One of the reasons for his doing so is evidently that he perceives the danger we pointed out in the previous section. When one emphasizes that the "inner" states of "cognition" of all the other things belong to the "human thing" (*Menschending*), then the question naturally follows, to what extent, then, this "human thing" can know that an external world corresponds to these states (*SZ*, p. 60). If this is what being-in-the-world means, then being-in-the-world in principle is compatible with "worldlessness."

Negative clarifications such as these play a crucial part in Heidegger's attempt to shed light on the phenomenon of being-in-the-world. This is because just as Husserl's naturally attuned subject has its self-interpretation, so does Heidegger's everyday Dasein. As already mentioned, everyday Dasein has the tendency to

---

[20] Alweiss concludes from this that we "should never confuse Dasein's existential structure of Being-in-the-world with the way in which a body is in space" (*The World Unclaimed*, p. 83). She takes this to mean that Heidegger must be describing a "*disembodied* Dasein" (ibid., p. 87), and indeed that *Sein und Zeit* "throughout refuses to return to the body, sensibility, or any corporeality" (ibid., p. 124). What Alweiss seems to overlook completely is that Heidegger is precisely struggling to reveal how Dasein has a manner of being-in-the-world, which cannot be reduced to mere "onhandness" within the world, but which is nevertheless a very bodily and corporeal situatedness *in* the world. See the next section of the present chapter, as well as Chapter VI.

interpret its own being (as well as the being of the encountered entities) along the lines of present-at-hand entities (*SZ*, pp. 58, 201) – a tendency that must be countered by phenomenology if it is to be able to approach its subject-matter in an unbiased manner. But obviously, saying what being-in-the-world is *not* is insufficient. By way of an etymological consideration, Heidegger indicates the more proper interpretation of his use of "in":

> Being-in [...] is a state of Dasein's being; it is an *existentiale*. So one cannot think of it as the presence-at-hand of some corporeal thing (a human body) "in" an entity which is present-at-hand. Nor does the term "being-in" mean a spatial "in-one-another-ness" of things present-at-hand, any more than the word "in" primordially signifies a spatial relationship of this kind. "In" is derived from *"innan"* – "to reside," *"habitare,"* "to dwell." *"An"* signifies "I am accustomed," "I am familiar with," "I look after something." (*SZ*, p. 54)

"Being-in-the-world," then, characterizes the being of Dasein, but it does not have the meaning of "being-inside," "being-contained-in." Rather, it means that Dasein "inhabits" the world, is "familiar" with it (*GA* 20, p. 213). The nature of this inhabitation and familiarity is discussed in the previous chapter. The world, so it was argued, is the *referential whole* that Dasein "lives" or "moves" in, and on the basis of which Dasein is able to interact with the individual piece of equipment. So "being-in-the-world" would appear to mean nothing more than understandingly "moving around" in the web of references, a relation to the world that is denied other types of entities.

The same point is underscored by Heidegger's observation that, although in-the-world, Dasein is no "inner-worldly" entity (cf. *SZ*, pp. 43, 104). To be more accurate, one would in fact have to say that the "although" in the preceding sentence is misleading, since in Heidegger's terminology being-in-the-world means something entirely different from being-intra-mundane:

> Presence-at-hand and occurring within the world must be sharply distinguished from being-in a world [*In-Sein in einer Welt*]; [i.e.,] from that which belongs to the essential manner of being of Dasein. A stone or a table is present-at-hand within the world, i.e., a world-thing; but it never "is" in a world in the sense of being-in and being-alongside a world. A human being, in contrast, is strictly speaking never present-at-hand within the world. (*GA* 21, p. 240n; cf. *GA* 24, p. 240)

Typical intra-mundane entities such as chairs and hammers are precisely not in-the-world, but worldless, Heidegger says (*SZ*, p. 55). These entities have the mode of being of readiness-to-hand. Hammers and chairs are encountered within the world (therefore they are intra-mundane) as suited for the job, as comfortable, etc., and they are encountered as such by an entity that "inhabits" the world, moves understandingly about in the world's more or less familiar references – but the chairs and hammers do not themselves inhabit the world in this sense. They are located at this or that place *within* the world, whereas Dasein "is 'in' the world in the sense that it deals, concernfully and with familiarity, with the entities encountered within-the-world" (*SZ*, p. 104; cf. *GA* 17, p. 105). Dasein's "being-in-the-world," then, seems to be its essential and ineradicable possession of – or even better: its being nothing but – a relation (*Bezug*) to the world (cf. *GA* 20, p. 223), an *openness* to the world (*GA* 21, p. 143). As Heidegger puts it in his 1924 lecture on the concept of time:

Dasein as being-in-the-world means: being in the world in such a way that this being means: dealing with the world; tarrying alongside it [*bei ihr verweilen*] in the manner of performing, effecting, and completing, but also contemplating, interrogating, and determining by way of contemplation and comparison. (*BZ*, p. 12)

What these considerations seem to suggest is that Dasein's being in-the-world, yet not within-the-world, hardly differs significantly from the transcendental subject's being related-to-the-world, yet not an object in-the-world. Even in the period following the publication of *Sein und Zeit*, where Heidegger describes Dasein as being "in the midst" of what there is (*GA* 27, p. 328; *GA* 29/30, p. 403), he still insists that it does not mean that Dasein simply occurs among other entities (*WM*, p. 166). Thus, if our discussion of *In-der-Welt-sein* has been adequate then we can now answer both questions posed above. First, if what Heidegger means by emphasizing Dasein's being "in" the world is nothing but its being *related* in practical and theoretical ways to the world, then one obviously cannot make intelligible the sense in which Husserlian transcendental subjectivity is "worldless" by reference to its being "related" to the world, yet not "in" the world. Heidegger's distinction between the human "being-in-the-world" and the "innerworldly" being of such things as tools is so sharp that it seems to annul any critical potential that his characterization of Dasein at first appears to have vis-à-vis Husserlian transcendental subjectivity. But with the same stroke, Husserl's charge is also annulled. One clearly cannot accuse Heidegger of doing "anthropology," in the sense that he remains uncritically in the "natural attitude," if his characterization of Dasein has nothing in common with Husserl's notion of the "human being." What Heidegger attempts is precisely to uncover the structures of something very akin to transcendental subjectivity – something that "inhabits" the world, is "familiar" with it, and is no object *within* the world.

Whereas the second of these two points is indisputable, the first is less so. In the above discussion, we remain on an abstract level, ignoring Heidegger's concrete elaboration of the being of Dasein under the heading of "care" (*Sorge*). Now if we leave for a moment the abstract level of discussion and turn to Heidegger's description of the structure of care, we can give some indication that "being-in-the-world" is not just another way of expressing the subject's "relatedness" to the world. On the contrary, Dasein is literally *in* the world – which must not be taken to imply that Heidegger abandons, in the course of his analyses, the distinction between being-in-the-world and being intra-mundane.

The aspect of "being-with" aside, the being of the human being has three equiprimordial and interdependent moments. First of all, Dasein is always occupied with this or that, interacting with this or that piece of equipment. It is always already "amidst" or "alongside" (*bei*) certain intra-mundane entities (cf. *SZ*, pp. 61, 164; *GA* 20, p. 222). That this aspect of the being of Dasein should not primarily be understood along the lines of perceptual *Erfahrung* scarcely needs to be repeated here. As Heidegger unequivocally puts it, "[p]roximally, this already-being-alongside [*Schon-sein-bei*] is not just a fixed staring at something that is purely present-at-hand" (*SZ*, p. 61), but rather a concerned "being-involved-with" (*Zu-tun-haben*) the "world" (ibid.).

The second aspect of care is what Heidegger dubs "being-ahead-of-oneself." As pointed out in the previous chapter, Heidegger describes the world as a web of references of the type "in order to," anchored in references of the type "for the sake of." The *telos* of Dasein's activities is ultimately its own being, "namely in each case the being that it is not yet, but can be" (*GA* 21, p. 235). Our "being amidst" ready-to-hand entities is aimed at our own potential for being (*Seinkönnen*), i.e., as involved with inner-worldly entities we are already essentially "ahead of ourselves" (*SZ*, p. 191). This is not to say that Dasein always has plans for the future, but rather, according to Heidegger, it is this essential openness to one's potential for being that underlies and makes possible all specific projects and plans (as well as any "indifference" towards the future) (*SZ*, p. 145).[21]

Our present interest in Dasein's being-in-the-world concerns neither of these aspects of the care-structure, however. What is important in the present context is the circumstance that they are co-determined by a third: the *facticity* of human existence (*SZ*, p. 56). This is where the "worldliness" of Dasein becomes accentuated. The human being is not only not able to sever its bonds with the world, but rather, it finds itself "thrown" into the world, already placed in the world, and placed amidst a certain range of intra-mundane entities, Heidegger claims (*SZ*, pp. 135, 192, 221; *GA* 21, p. 217). Just as Dasein is "being-amidst" (*Sein-bei*) and "ahead-of-itself" (*sich-vorweg*), so it is equiprimordially "already-in" (*Schon-sein-in*) a world (*SZ*, pp. 249-250). To add to this, "not of its own doing," would obscure things rather than clarify them, because its seems to imply that it is, at least, imaginable that Dasein *had* thrown itself into the world – which would mean that Dasein could, after all, be imagined "before" or "independently of" its being-in-the-world. And Heidegger precisely wants to deny the latter notion (*SZ*, pp. 57, 116). Thus, what "facticity" formally indicates is that being-human simply is being-already-given-over-to a world and having to pick it up from there: "Dasein, in so far as it *is*, has always submitted itself already to a 'world' which it encounters, and this *submission* [*Angewiesenheit*] belongs essentially to its being" (*SZ*, p. 87; cf. p. 135; *GA* 21, p. 213).[22] After *Sein und Zeit*, Heidegger sometimes expresses this point by saying that Dasein is "abandoned" (*preisgegeben*) in the midst of the world (*GA* 27, pp. 326-328). This strongly suggests that being-in-the-world cannot adequately be translated with "being-related-to-the-world." Although I am not one of the present-at-hand or ready-to-hand intra-mundane entities, I find myself intimately connected with them in my "destiny," as Heidegger puts it (*SZ*, p. 56). As they are what they

---

[21] The systematic importance of this difference between the openness to one's indefinite potential for being and particular options and projects is unfolded in great detail in Günter Figal, *Martin Heidegger: Phänomenologie der Freiheit*.

[22] Though obviously not as an *act*, as something *Dasein* literally *does*. Cf. Heidegger's subsequently added marginal remark to the quoted passage (*SZ*, p. 442).

are only in the equipmental whole, so I am what I am as thrown into the midst of this whole.[23]

In the following chapter, I argue in more detail for the claim that there is more to "being-in-the-world" than just being "related" to a world. As for now, let me just draw one preliminary and "formally indicative" conclusion. When Heidegger argues that Dasein is not "within" the world, what he is saying is in fact *not* that Dasein is not literally *in* the world; rather, he is denying that Dasein has the mode of being of "things" or "objects" in the world. He is denying that Dasein has the mode of being of presence-at-hand or readiness-to-hand, but not that Dasein literally exists in the midst of such entities. To put it differently, Heidegger is not only not assigning Dasein to some extra-mundane observation post, but positively assigning it to a *mundane* one. But the crucial point is just that *this* mode of mundane being must be strictly separated from the kind of mundane being that characterizes ready-to-hand entities.[24] As Heidegger puts it in his Kant-book, with the existence of Dasein, the world is "broken into" in such a way that it is thereby opened up, manifested (*KPM*, pp. 228-229). So, with an expression that may sound paradoxical at first, one can say that Dasein is *in the world*, though not as a thing or as an object, but *as a "subject" for the world*. This is simply *how* the human being is *in* the world.

Once again, then, we are referred back to Husserl and the question of how his conception of the transcendental subject is ultimately placed in relation to the world. Is it an extra-mundane subject, or is it, *as transcendentally functioning* subject, "in-the-world"?

4. TRANSCENDENTAL SUBJECTIVITY AND THE BODY

The world and everything intra-mundane is what constitutes itself for, or in, transcendental subjectivity. The latter is therefore itself nothing intra-mundane, but a "viewpoint" upon the mundane. Functionally, this is how transcendental subjectivity is defined. For this reason it has no "content" immediately available for phenomenological inspection, but is only discovered in the "transcendental reduction," the method that takes us back from the manifest world to the experiencing subject.

What these recapitulations indicate is that we should take care not to proceed to transcendental subjectivity with too firmly cemented notions of what we will find. It is the *reduction* that must guide the attempt to reveal the structures of the "place of the manifestation of the world," not our ever so reputable and generally accepted

---

[23] The idea of exposedness that is quite naturally associated with the notion of "thrownness" is captured by Heidegger with the concept of *Befindlichkeit* (disposedness, affectivity) (*SZ*, p. 340). As facticity is related to affectivity, so being-ahead-of oneself is related to the existential of understanding, and being-amidst is related to "falling" (*SZ*, pp. 175, 336). Such three-part structures abound in *Sein und Zeit*.

[24] As one recent commentator puts it, "while the traditional modern interpretation seems to adhere to a notion of subjectivity as a thing that is not in the world, Heidegger introduces an interpretation according to which subjectivity is a Being-in-the-world that is not a thing" (Einar Øverenget, *Seeing the Self*, p. 2).

assumptions about the nature of the "subject." Before the reductive work is set in motion, "transcendental subjectivity" is a point with no extension – a *functional placeholder* for whatever structures we might discover that can make intelligible the constitution of the world. This follows immediately from our presentation of Husserl in the previous chapters. In the present section, I argue that, in spite of his use of such phrases as "the region of pure consciousness" (*Hua* III/1, p. 99), Husserl persistently holds on to this principle of following the reductive investigation wherever it might lead – also if it leads to a radical redefinition of transcendental subjectivity. In the concrete phenomenological analyses, if not in statements of a more programmatic nature, Husserl would even follow his guiding clue if it meant characterizing the transcendental subject in terms that made highly questionable the appropriateness of the identification of transcendental subjectivity with "pure consciousness."

Taking the perceived object as his guiding clue, Husserl asks what the noetic counterpart to the noematic "horizon" might be. If the mundane object is never given other than in a play of authentic givenness and horizonal co-givenness, then how must the subject that is to be the subject experiencing such an object be structured? As always, one must focus closely on the noematic correlate to get the first hints of what the answer might be. In other words, the first thing to ask about is how the perceptual horizon *appears*, how it is experienced.

We have touched on the issue of the status of the horizonally intended a few times. In the first section of this chapter, it is thus argued that the co-intended backside of the apple tree I see from my window has – for me, in my present perception – the status of perceivable right here and now, although I can not possibly be the subject of that perception. The perceptual horizon, in other words, is essentially a horizon of possible authentic givenness *to others*. But if we consult our tree-noema a little more closely, we realize that this obviously cannot be all there is to say about the status of the horizon. For me, too, the co-intended backside is perceivable, as is in principle the whole, essentially open-ended, outer horizon. The world-horizon is presented to me as a horizon of possible experience (*Hua* VIII, p. 148; *Hua* VI, p. 167), not only an other's possible actual experience, but my and her possible *future* (and past) experiences as well, namely what she or I *could* experience if a certain continuous series of perceptions were set in motion (or what we *did* experience back when...) (cf. *Hua* VIII, p. 148). Furthermore, the perceptual horizon is not just presented to me as a horizon of possible givenness to me (as well as to others) in the sense that it could "happen" to me at one point in time that I had (what is presently) the backside of the tree authentically manifest instead of the side that is now authentically given. Rather, the perceptual possibilities that we noematically express when we refer to the strictly speaking unperceived backsides of things are possibilities that *I can* realize. Focusing on the "inner horizon," Husserl expresses the point thus:

Every experience has its *experiential horizon* [...]. This implies that every experience refers to the possibility – and it is a question here of the capacity [*Ver-möglichkeit*] of the ego – not only of explicating, step by step, the thing which has been given at first glance, in conformity with what is really self-given of it, but also of obtaining, little by little as experience continues, new determinations of the same thing. (*EU*, § 8, p. 27)

The possibility (*Möglichkeit*) of perceiving in the strict sense the improperly manifest aspects of the apple tree is a possibility, for which the realization lies within my capability (*Vermögen*); it is thus a *Ver-möglichkeit*. Husserl is well aware that it is not *in fact* possible for me to experience, say, the surface of the sun from close range; but he nevertheless insists that if the surface of the sun is to count for us as belonging to our world, then it must, *in principle*, be perceivable, and that perceivability must, *in principle*, be something I could realize (cf. *Hua* XIII, pp. 294-296). To put it differently, the surface of the sun must be vaguely anticipated and "sketched" (*vorgezeichnet*) along these lines, even if we all know that it is a factual impossibility ever to realize the perception of the aspects so sketched.

Yet these reflections give rise to another question. How can I realize these possibilities? If the backside of the perceived tree trunk is something *I* can bring to proper manifestation, then Husserl must give some indication of *how* I am able to do that. Husserl takes this question very seriously and dedicates detailed analyses to it from as early as 1907. Until the end of his life, he continues to refine these analyses and reconsider their ultimate consequences, but he seems never to have doubted the original answer.

The manifold improperly given aspects are, at the most fundamental level, aspects that I can turn into properly manifest aspects by *moving* myself, according to Husserl. In other words, the improperly manifest aspects are possible authentically given aspects because they are *correlated* with a system of subjective potential for *movement* (*Hua* XI, pp. 14-15). Since we are here dealing with structures of the transcendental subject, the movements in question can clearly not be objective movements "out there" in perceived space; rather, the subjective potential for movement that we are uncovering here is a precondition for the constitution of a perceived space. As we see in the previous chapter, horizonal intentionality is what makes possible the constitution of mundane entities, so if horizonal intentionality itself can be made intelligible only by reference to self-movement, then self-movement, too, is something that makes possible the appearance of mundane objects. The self-movement at stake here is not the "mundane subject" changing position in the world, but a self-movement that essentially belongs to the transcendental subject. Husserl therefore introduces the terms "kinesthesia" and "kinesthetic sensations" to denote this immediate subjective awareness of one's own bodily position and movement (*Hua* XVI, p. 161). The horizonally co-intended, Husserl can then say, is co-intended as correlated with a system of "kinesthetic" *Vermöglichkeit* (*Hua* VI, p. 164; *Hua* XV, pp. 284-285).

Thus, according to Husserl, a "constitutive duplicity" is found in every perception (*Hua* XI, p. 15). There is, on the one hand, the proper and improper object-manifestation, and on the other hand, the system of realized and not-yet-realized kinesthetic possibilities. Husserl is not only saying that both "kinesthesia" and "appearances" must "be there" to make a perception; he is claiming that they must stand in a special kind of relation to each other (*Hua* XI, p. 14). They must be related in such a way that the present appearance of the tree is experienced as an appearance under certain circumstances, viz. the kinesthetic situation I have, ideally speaking at least, chosen to realize.[25] The "distribution" of proper and improper givenness I have while perceiving the apple tree in the garden is thus the result of my having realized this possible kinesthetic situation instead of another belonging to my open-ended system of kinesthetic possibilities. I could choose to get up and walk out there to inspect the tree from a closer range, or from other angles, whereby other aspects would be properly given (and the previously properly manifest aspects would now be emptily co-intended). The horizontally intended aspects of the tree are precisely intended as *correlates* to the "kinesthetic horizon" (cf. *Hua* XI, p. 15; *Hua* XVI, pp. 190-191), the horizon of possibly realizable kinesthetic sequences and situations. The two are correlated in such a way that "if" this particular sequence of kinesthetic activities is realized, "then" that sequence of properly given aspects follows (*Hua* IV, pp. 57-58; *Hua* VI, p. 164).

This is, according to Husserl, how the subject perceiving something like an apple tree must look. It must be a *kinesthetic* subject. The horizon of emptily intended aspects – without which no object could manifest itself – has the status of "would-be" proper manifestation, namely "would be" *if* this or that sequence of kinesthetic activities was set in motion. As Husserl concludes in *Krisis*:

Clearly the aspect-exhibitions of whatever body is appearing in perception, and the kinestheses, are not processes <simply running> alongside each other; rather, they work together in such a way that the aspects have the ontic meaning [*Seinssinn*] of, or validity of, aspects of the body only through the fact that they are those aspects continually required by the kinestheses [...] and that they correspondingly fulfill the requirement. (*Hua* VI, § 28, pp. 108-109; cf. *Hua* IV, p. 310; *Hua* XI, pp. 14-15)

As Dan Zahavi emphasizes, it is important not to underestimate the significance of this correlation.[26] It should already be clear that it is not as if the interplay between kinesthesia and aspects is relevant only for perceptions that involve a perceiver that actually moves about. My kinesthetic sensations are not only relevant for my perception of the apple tree when I actually get off my chair, setting the kinesthetic sequences in motion that will lead me to perceive (in the strict sense) the other aspects of the tree. The horizon of kinesthetic *potential* makes intelligible the potentiality of the emptily co-intended horizon when I remain seated and just cast an absent-minded glance at the tree. Just as the properly manifest aspect is the aspect under these actual kinesthetic circumstances, so the horizontally intended aspects are

---

[25] Obviously, I can also be kinesthetically aware of my moving or being moved without having *chosen* to do so. If someone pushes me, I am immediately aware that my limbs change position (although I by no means chose to move them), and similarly I am, or can be, aware of my breathing. On the basis of examples such as these, Husserl in one manuscript distinguishes between "foreign" or "compulsory" kinesthesia (someone pushes me), passive, but "allowed" kinesthesia (my breathing – which I *could* hold back), and "active" kinesthesia (I lift my glass to drink) (cf. *Hua* XIV, p. 447).

[26] Dan Zahavi, *Self-Awareness and Alterity*, p. 95. My account of Husserl's phenomenology of the body owes a great deal to Zahavi's discussion (*Self-Awareness and Alterity*, pp. 91-109), as well as to Donn Welton's article "Soft, Smooth Hands: Husserl's Phenomenology of the Lived Body."

aspects under other, potential, kinesthetic circumstances – *and that is how they figure in this present perception,* when I just cast a glance at the tree in the garden.

Needless to say, Husserl is not suggesting that I am constantly thematically aware of the system of kinesthetic possibilities (or of the correlated object-aspects). When I am sitting here caught up in writing, I am of course neither thematically aware of the series of kinesthetic activities that would take me home, nor am I aware of the aspects that would in that case be given to me. If I were thematically occupied with either of these, it would have a damaging effect on my ability to concentrate on writing. In fact, even when I am actively performing certain movements, I am usually not thematically occupied with them. When I am moving my fingers across the keyboard, I am not thematically aware of the kinesthetic activities that I am thus willfully engaged in. I am "living" in the philosophical problem I am trying to grasp, and the kinesthetic sensations are only there "in the background of attention" (*Hua* IV, p. 128).[27]

With the introduction of kinesthesia, Husserl is clearly entering the domain of the *body*. Kinesthetic activities are activities of the body; my kinesthetic potential is my potential for bodily movement. But, as Husserl himself points out, this account appears to beg the question (*Hua* V, p. 121; *Hua* IX, p. 197). The body, surely, is one of the mundane entities constituted, so how can we refer to the body when we are precisely trying to account for the constitution *of* things like the body? This would precisely be a transcendental "circle" of the type outlined in Chapter II above.[28] Husserl, however, emphasizes "that the body is both thing and function" (*Hua* IX, p. 197), and that the apparent circularity disappears when the relation between these two senses of the body is phenomenologically elucidated. His solution is thus to claim that the kinesthesia – the transcendentally functioning body – are what constitute mundane things, including the body considered as such a thing: "It is in virtue of these free acts [the kinesthesia] that [...] there can be constituted for this ego, in manifold series of perceptions, an object-world, a world of spatial-corporeal things (*the body as thing included*)" (*Hua* IV, p. 152, my emphasis; cf. *Hua* XVI, p. 282; *Hua* XV, p. 285). My kinesthetic, functioning body genuinely belongs to me in my capacity of transcendental subject, whereas the physical, spatial body-thing belongs to the realm of the constituted world. To be sure, the kinesthesia are "located" in the body-thing (*Hua* XVI, p. 282; *Hua* IV, p. 56), but according to Husserl this is something secondary in relation to (and made possible by) the originally experienced kinesthesia. In order to accentuate the difference between the body as a subjective-kinesthetic functioning body and the body as a physical object in space, Husserl introduces the distinction between *Leib* ("lived body") and *Körper* ("physical body") (*Hua* VI, pp. 109-110).

---

[27] For more on kinesthesia and their function in perception, see John J. Drummond, "On Seeing *a* Material Thing *in* Space," as well as Ulrich Claesges, *Edmund Husserls Theorie der Raumkonstitution*.
[28] See, regarding this, Ulrich Claesges, *Edmund Husserls Theorie der Raumkonstitution*, pp. 99-115.

Even considered as a mere material object, my body has a number of peculiarities. In relation to all the other perceived objects (computer screens, apple trees, and mountains), which appear in various orientations of left or right, near or far, etc., the body is special in that it has "the unique distinction of bearing in itself the *zero point* [*Nullpunkt*] of all these orientations" (*Hua* IV, p. 158). My body is, or carries in itself, the ultimate *here* that all the other perceived objects – in their various degrees of "there" – refer back to (ibid.). In this context, Husserl also notes how this particular thing is one I cannot remove from me, one I cannot distance myself in relation to, and consequently a thing that I only have very limited perceptual access to: "certain of my corporeal parts can be seen by me only in a peculiar perspectival foreshortening, and others (e.g., the head) are altogether invisible to me" (*Hua* IV, p. 159). Although I can to some extent move my hands out in perceived space, they remain very closely tied to my zero point of orientation, and my body as a whole cannot possibly be moved out into perceived space, nor can I perceive it continuously from other angles, etc. (*Hua* XV, pp. 650, 654). My body – even considered as a mere thing – is something like a "zero-thing" (*Nullkörper*), an object so near, and so immutably and necessarily near, that the predicate "near" can hardly even be applied to it (*Hua* XV, pp. 513, 309).

Husserl, as we have seen, argues that the transcendental subject must constitute itself as a mundane entity. With *all* its characteristics, the transcendental subject enters the realm of the mundane objects, i.e., the subjective life in which a world manifests itself, now becomes "mental states" in this particular human being, the kinesthesia are now "located" in the physical body, and so forth (*Hua* XV, p. 546). In other words, the problem of circularity has only helped us to concretize the complex relation of identity and difference between "mundane" and "transcendental" subjectivity: it is not as if the kinesthesia referred to in the constitutive account necessarily presuppose the constituted body; rather, the kinesthesia help constitute the physical body in which they are *subsequently* necessarily "localized." With a slight paraphrase of a passage quoted above, we may say that because the subject is a kinesthetic viewpoint *on* the world, it cannot help constituting itself as physically-bodily (*körperlich*) *in* the world (cf. *Hua* XXIX, p. 152).

Although this particular account of Husserl's theory may at first appear compelling, as it stands it nevertheless seems to suffer from an ambiguity. To be more specific, it is as if two very different conceptions of this self-mundanization are possible here. Let us look at them in turn.

The one that Husserl seems most clearly to subscribe to is, as we see above, the one where the mundane subject is simply constituted as an object among objects in the world. In this model, the self-constitution of the transcendental subject is a self-objectification in which, first, some mere material thing (the physical body) is constituted; and second, this material thing becomes the target of the transcendental subject's mundanizing self-projection (cf., e.g., *Hua* XV, p. 295).[29] When trying to account constitutively for this, we take the mundane subject as our guiding clue and proceed to unearth – in the non-worldly transcendental subject – the structures that account for the constitution of this particular objectivity. The human being as a whole, then, is a mundane, constituted *Vorhandenheit*, albeit a unique one (cf. *Hua* IX, p. 603; *Hua* VI, p. 149).

However, there is another way in which one could imagine the transcendental subject "entering" the world. Above, we uncovered the kinesthesia by asking the reductive question of what structures should be attributed to a subject that is to be a subject of a transcendent, perceptually given object such as an apple tree. What if such a reductive inquiry eventually leads to the conclusion that in order to be a transcendental subject, the subject has to be bodily in a strong sense, viz. in the sense that it has to be placed *in* the world? It is important to notice that such an account would not proceed by way of demonstrating how the subject constitutes itself *as an object* in the world, but quite the contrary. It takes no such "mundane subject" as its guiding clue, but an intra-mundane perceptual object (or for that matter a tool), and it simply proceeds to establish which structures would have to be attributed to the correlative subject as a transcendental, functioning subject. Such an account would precisely attempt to uncover what would have to be said of a subject that is to be a world-experiencing *subject*; it would lead us to the conclusion that the transcendental subject should be conceived as *in* the world, but in a sense very different from the sense in which a perceptual object is "in" the world. If such a phenomenological argument could successfully be made, it would force us to radically reconsider the concepts of "subject" and "object."

It seems to me that both types of accounts are found in Husserl, without being clearly distinguished from each other. There are places where the transcendental subject seems to be simply "extra-mundane" and the mundane subject seems just to be another object, and there are other places where Husserl describes transcendental subjectivity in ways that seem to indicate that it is *in* the world, though precisely as a transcendental subject, and not as an object. The latter type of account, in my view, holds the true potential of Husserlian phenomenology, and I concentrate on this type in the following discussion. (The "mundane" subject is discussed in Chapter VI.) Let us turn, once again, to the perceiving subject.

If I let my fingers run gently across the keys on my keyboard, I have certain tactile sensations, according to Husserl. Under normal circumstances, these give me information about the touched object (a number of keys, all slightly curved on the surface, with some space between them, etc.). I can, however, direct my focus in

---

[29] In fact, it is a bit more complicated, as Dan Zahavi has reminded me. This is because, according to Husserl, the mundane subject is not the result of an isolated subjectivity's self-mundanization, but rather the result of an intersubjective constitution. To myself, I am not an object in the world; but to others, I am a "subject-object" – and it is in and through identifying myself with the "object" I am for others, that I become an object in the world (*Hua* XIV, p. 86). But this has no consequences for the argument in the main text: subjectivity still enters the world as a constituted object.

such a way as to be aware of these tactile data, not as providing information about the touched object, but as *my* data, as "located" in my hand. That does not mean that these sensations now inform me about the object "hand" instead of the object "keyboard," but that they now appear as *subjective sensations* located in the *touching* hand (*Hua* IV, p. 146). In other words, the same tactile data can both present an object to me and present to me my touching hand as precisely that: *my touching* hand.[30]

The situation becomes considerably more complicated – as well as more interesting in the present context – if we turn to the phenomenon of one part of the body being touched by another part of the body. In *Ideen II*, Husserl writes:

> Touching my left hand [with my right hand], I have touch-appearances, that is to say, I do not just sense, but I perceive and have appearances of a soft, smooth hand, with such a form. The indicational sensations of movement and the representational sensations of touch, which are objectified as features of the thing, "left hand," belong in fact to my right hand. But when I touch the left hand I also find in it, too, series of touch-sensations, which are "*localized*" in it, though these are not constitutive of properties (such as roughness or smoothness of the hand, of this physical thing). If I speak of the *physical* thing, "left hand," then I am abstracting from these sensations (a ball of lead has nothing like them and likewise for every "merely" physical thing, every thing that is not my body). If I do include them, then it is not that the physical thing is now richer, but instead *it becomes body, it senses [es wird Leib, es empfindet]*. (*Hua* IV, pp. 144-145)

Husserl does not simply want to emphasize that I cannot touch my body without one part of the body functioning as *touching* (*Hua* XV, p. 296). Rather, the situation where one part of the body touches another part is precisely so unique because the "objectified" part of the body is still experienced as functioning as well (*Hua* XIV, p. 57). In other words, the left hand might be an "object" for the right hand, but as I touch it as such it reveals itself as subject – it *feels* it is being touched. Furthermore, it is even possible for me – by a mere change of focus – to let the touching hand become touched and vice versa (cf. *Hua* XV, pp. 298, 302).

These considerations suggest something very important. Experiences of this kind are obviously not possible for a subject that remains "aloof" from the constituted world. Rather, in order to be the *subject* experiencing these things, it must be a subject that can not only touch things, but itself can *be touched* as well. Yet as some might point out, the experience of touching oneself is a very specific kind of experience, and it could perhaps be imagined that a subject would have all kinds of perceptual experiences except this one. Are we not in fact referring, here, to an experience the impossibility of which would not significantly change the perceived world? However, instead of speculating what impact the absence of a body that could make itself an object would have on the perceived world, let us turn to a different kind of perception.

---

[30] Husserl calls sensations considered as functioning in perceptions of objects *Empfindungen*, and in order to stress the radically different function they have when considered as located in the body (in which case they present no object) he introduces the neologism *Empfindnisse* (*Hua* IV, p. 146).

In some manuscripts, Husserl contemplates what it means that an entity is perceived "out there" in perceived space. When the tree manifests itself as "there in the garden," what does that say about me as the perceiving subject? If the tree is perceived as "there," it refers, of course, to a "point of view," to a "here" – which might seem to indicate that I must be placed in the world together with the perceived object.[31] Yet as long as we consider the example of a motionless perceiving subject, this subject is clearly not "in" perceived space; it is more like the point where the perceived space or world opens up. Suppose, however, that I am immobile, that I have no or only a very limited kinesthetic potential; suppose that I do not have the "locomotion" kinesthesia – what status could the perceived object "over there" have? According to Husserl, there simply would be no "over there" and thus no object over there, if I did not have the ability to move closer, that is, if I did not have the ability to make the "there" into a "here." If I do not have that ability, the "object" remains an ambiguous spectacle, no more "external" than "inner." Only when my kinesthetic potential is such as to allow me to *approach* the spectacle (and eventually touch it) is it pulled out of its ambiguity and into perceived space. As Husserl puts it, "the perception of far-reality [*Fernrealität*] in rest and in motion has as its precondition an awareness of being able to get over there, etc." (*Hua* XIV, p. 551).[32] In other words, perceived mundane objects can only have the meaning and status that they do have for me, if I am able – with my kinesthetic activity – to approach them, to make their "there" into a (relative) "here," and so on. It is, to be sure, not the case that by initiating a certain series of kinesthetic activities I *enter* perceived space, since I cannot change the fact that I remain "here" (*Hua* IV, p. 159). But we can certainly say that if we consider perceived mundane entities just as they are perceived, then they refer back to a subject that can make their perceived "place" its own, and thus must somehow be connected in its "destiny" with the world of perceived entities.

In this context, Husserl also considers the tactile interaction with, or handling of, objects. What sense could it have for a subject to take a thing in its hands at one place, carry it along, and drop it at another place – what sense could we make of all this, if the subject's kinesthetic activities were "extra-mundane"? We would certainly have to say that the thing changes position in the perceived world, but we would also have to say that the subject does not. Husserl does not accept that conclusion, but insists, rather, that the kinesthetic-tactile subject must itself change position in space (cf. *Hua* XV, p. 281). Clearly, if any handling of things is to make sense, then my "handling" activities cannot be understood as kinesthetic activities taking place in some "extra-mundane realm," but must be understood as activities

---

[31] This is, e.g., what Sartre argues in *Being and Nothingness*, p. 318.

[32] Is there then, according to Husserl, no "there" that cannot possibly be made "here"? What about the stars in the sky? Husserl himself considers these things, and appears to reach the conclusion that the stars are precisely not mundane things, perceptually given things, in the same sense as apple trees and the like (*Hua* XV, pp. 262-263). As he writes in Manuscript E I 5: "Stars are not a type of reality such as birds." "Sterne sind nicht ein Typus von Wirklichkeiten wie Vögel" (Ms. E I 5, 34a).

"in" this world in some sense. Husserl sometimes underscores this point by saying that the kinesthetic movement brings *its* "external" side with itself, and indeed that the kinesthetic movement *is* a "spatial" movement (*Hua* XV, pp. 279, 290, 652).

What these considerations show is that visual and tactile interactions with mundane entities are not conceivable without a subject that somehow "belongs" to the same realm. I could not perceive anything "there" if I did not have the possibility, in principle at least, of making such "theres" into "heres." Likewise, I could not move things around if I did not myself move around. Not that we should say that the subject must be in the world in the very same sense as the objects with which it engages are in the world; rather, the point is that it cannot possibly be a transcendental subject without somehow entering the world as an embodied subject. To express the point in Husserl's words, the subject must be a subject "that bodies and lives [*leibt und lebt*] in the world" (*Hua* XV, p. 287).

With the introduction of the body, then, something completely new enters the stage (*Hua* IX, p. 198). The body is no "thing," Husserl emphasizes (*Hua* XIV, p. 238; *Hua* XV, p. 309), but precisely something without which there would not be "things," a condition for the possibility of the manifestation of all things (*Hua* XIV, pp. 238, 456; *Hua* IX, p. 107; *Hua* XV, p. 643). Although Husserl maybe never says it in so many words, the body is an essential structure of the *transcendental* subject. What Husserl's analyses again and again seem to return to, however, is the insight that this body (this transcendental subject) does not easily fit into either of the traditional categories of "subject" and "object," or "inner" and "outer." The body stands at the *borderline* between these (*Hua* XIII, p. 410),[33] or as Husserl prefers to put it, it is "subject-object" (*Hua* XIV, pp. 6, 457). To be a world-constituting subjectivity is not to be a "pure" subjectivity, but to be bodily in such a double sense:

> In this way, *as ego of the body*, I am *an ego for the world* [*als Ich des Leibes bin ich Ich für die Welt*] – an ego that is in one moment in this position in space, and in the next moment in that position in space, and thus has its spatiotemporal position. However, I am not in space in the same way as a thing is in space, nor in the same way as my body is in space; I am not in motion the way a thing is in motion. I don't have a place as a thing – my lived-and-physical body [*Leibkörper*] has that – but insofar as I am bodily active [literally "governing": *leiblich walte*], and only exist as active in that way – like the body only exists as body – then *I am one with the body, I am bodily* [*bin ich mit dem Leib eins, ich bin leiblich*], just like the body is body as an organ of the ego. (*Hua* XV, p. 283, my emphasis)

Though it would hardly be correct to say that the passage is unambiguous, it does give certain clear indications about the bodily nature of transcendental subjectivity. It is as a bodily ego that I am a world-experiencing subject. A bodily ego, moreover, that must be "in" space, "in" the world – yet not as a thing, not as a *Körper*. In its capacity of *transcendentally* functioning "body," the body I am "one with" obviously cannot be a *Körper* in the usual sense. But Husserl still does not want to

---

[33] As Paul Ricœur says in his study of Husserl, the animate body that Husserl describes is a "quasi-reality" with "traits that almost cancel its intra-mundane status" (*Husserl*, p. 64). The crucial thing is precisely how to interpret this "almost."

succumb to the *quasi*-Cartesian dualism that one might easily draw as a conclusion; he does not want to replace a *res cogitans-res extensa* dualism with a *Leib-Körper* dualism. In other words, the constituting subject must not merely be "inner-bodily," but essentially also (in some sense) "out there" as well.[34] As Merleau-Ponty later expresses it – far more unambiguously than Husserl, but in basic accordance with him – our body is not "in" space and time the way mere things are, but rather "*inhabits* space and time."[35] Although not really an external physical thing like any other, the very body that is the constitutive precondition for all physical things, including itself as such an external thing, is already in some sense "in the world." In Husserl's own words:

As for my body, it should be mentioned that <it> is not, from the outset, constituted as a physical body [*Körper*] among physical bodies. Rather, more primordial in themselves are outer bodies [*Aussenkörper*], and the own body as an inner-body [*Innenkörper*], which in the walking-kinesthesis is not yet apperceived as moved in space, moved like an outer body. *This inner body already has a double-sidedness*; it is a unity of organs, each of them moved kinesthetically and sensorily [*sinnlich*]. (Hua XV, p. 643, my emphasis)

This conclusion indicates both the fundamental strength and the fundamental weakness of Husserl's approach. On the one hand – and this point can hardly be emphasized too much – the passage clearly documents how Husserl realizes that the transcendental subject cannot be a pure "consciousness" in any traditional sense. Husserl's transcendental subjectivity is not a pure *res cogitans*, but has to be conceived as embodied, and not just in some "intellectual" sense that avoids placing this "bodily" subject *in* the world, *in* space, but rather in a quite literal sense.[36] The transcendental subject does not have a present-at-hand body; it has a body that is its kinesthetic and tactile "organ," its potential for moving and sensing. Yet as such an "inner-body" it is *already double-sided*, as Husserl points out. It is already in some sense "out there."

The weakness, as we see in the next chapter, is that Husserl never successfully disentangles himself from the dichotomies of "inner" and "outer," *Leib* and *Körper*, and therefore cannot view the perceptual subject's bodily "being-in-the-world" in any terms other than that of a "double-sided" bodily being. From one perspective, this may appear as precisely the right conclusion. But Heidegger argues that it is problematic insofar as we aim to understand our manner of being.

As I emphasized, however, Husserl's detailed phenomenological work on the body is also a fundamental strength. In fact, in comparison with Husserl's extensive treatment of the body, Heidegger's few scattered remarks seem almost not worthy of

---

[34] If the "transcendental body" is only a "pure" "inner-body," then "it seems that all we have is a replication of Cartesian dualism in another register, for now it becomes not so much the mind-body problem as the body-body problem" (Donn Welton, "Soft, Smooth Hands: Husserl's Phenomenology of the Lived-Body," p. 48). See, too, Dan Zahavi, *Self-Awareness and Alterity*, p. 168.

[35] Maurice Merleau-Ponty, *Phenomenology of Perception*, p. 139. Cf. *The Primacy of Perception*, p. 5.

[36] Perhaps the real strength of Husserl's account is not only and not primarily that it emphasizes the importance of the body as such, but rather that it stresses the importance of bodily *movement*. For a fruitful development of this Husserlian insight, cf. Maxine Sheets-Johnstone, *The Primacy of Movement*.

mention. Instead of concrete analyses of hands touching each other, of a moving body functioning in perception, we find the more general assurances that Dasein is essentially "in-the-world," and abstract reflections on the nature of the *Da*.[37] Indeed, Heidegger completely refuses to discuss the body in *Sein und Zeit* (*SZ*, p. 108), something even sympathetic commentators find deeply problematic.[38]

Nevertheless, it might be fruitful to briefly review some of the places where Heidegger does have something to say on the phenomenon of the body. Already in 1919, Heidegger emphasizes that what he then calls *Lebenserfahrung* has a necessary relation to embodiment, and he concludes: "This is of fundamental significance" (*GA* 56/57, p. 210). Against the background of this unambiguous statement, the fact that Heidegger uses very little paper in the course of the following ten years to actually analyze this phenomenon of fundamental importance is striking. It is made even more striking by the fact that at least in some of the places where he does have something to say on the body (or embodiment), Heidegger seems to reaffirm his initial verdict.[39]

In the recently published volume 18 of the *Gesamtausgabe*, we find what must be the early Heidegger's most extensive treatment of embodiment.[40] The context is an account of Aristotle's concept of *pathos*, and the terms *Leib* and *Leiblichkeit* appear frequently in the course of approximately ten pages. Heidegger is trying to make it clear that a mood or emotion such as fear cannot be equated with a state of the soul or the mind, but must be conceived as something that affects the *whole* Dasein, including its body. We must understand "that something living as being in the world is, insofar as it is affected by the world, *also affected with regard to its embodiment*; that everything aims at the living *in its full being-there*" (*GA* 18, p. 202). This point is not only uttered once, but in slightly different formulations repeated a number of times (*GA* 18, pp. 203, 206-207). Indeed, in what must be the most approving use of the word embodiment that we will ever get from Heidegger,

---

[37] In the words of Daniel O. Dahlstrom, "Husserl's account of the kinesthetic movements of the body clearly indicates a *tangible* level of transcendence that can be squared with neither a pure and isolated consciousness nor a sense of being as sheer presence – indeed, a level of transcendence, in relation to which, Heidegger's talk of "being-in-the-world" or "being-there" has an oddly abstract, even gnostic ring" (*Heidegger's Concept of Truth*, p. 164).

[38] See, e.g., Hubert Dreyfus, *Being-in-the-World*, p. 137. See Alweiss, *The World Unclaimed*, for an elaborate critique of Heidegger's refusal to discuss the body.

[39] Heidegger seems to have considered the problem of the body extremely hard to come to grips with. In a 1966/67 seminar, he said: "The phenomenon of body is the most difficult problem" (*GA* 15, p. 236). For an argument that Heidegger's thinking is very much concerned with the problem of embodiment, see Søren Overgaard, "Heidegger on Embodiment." Other, and different, discussions of this important issue are found in David Michael Levin, "The Ontological Dimension of Embodiment"; and David R. Cerbone, "Heidegger and Dasein's Bodily Nature."

[40] Thedore Kisiel reveals in *The Genesis of Heidegger's Being and Time* (p. 293) that Heidegger had treated the problem of "corporeality" in great detail in the summer semester of 1924. The lecture course in question, bearing the title *Grundbegriffe der aristotelischen Philosophie*, unfortunately remained unpublished for almost ten years after Kisiel's book saw the light of day. It was published in the summer of 2002.

he even declares that the being of the human being as such is "characterized in such a way that it must be grasped as the *bodily being-in-the-world* [*leibmäßige In-der-Welt-sein*] of the human being" (*GA* 18, p. 199). In other words, Heidegger himself, in this, his second Marburg lecture course, emphasizes that when he speaks of being-in-the-world, what he has in mind has everything to do with embodiment.

A number of more sporadic remarks on embodiment are also worth noting. In *Sein und Zeit* and the Marburg lecture course of the summer of 1925, Heidegger points out how the world of Dasein is oriented in "there" and "here," "left" and "right," and so forth. This, so he emphasizes, is intimately connected with Dasein's being-in-the-world as embodied (*SZ*, p. 108; *GA* 20, p. 319). Although only very briefly, Heidegger refers in this context to Dasein's self-movement: "Every bodily movement is an '*I move*' and not 'it moves itself,' if we disregard certain well-defined organic movements" (*GA* 20, p. 320). Apart from the speed with which this theme (for Husserl the subject of thousands of pages) is brushed aside, it is striking how Heidegger says nothing new in relation to Husserl. On the contrary, he could have simply extracted the passage from *Ideen II*. Like Husserl, he emphasizes that moving the body is *self*-movement and not some external thing-movement out there in perceived space. A few years later, we find Heidegger expressing what seems to be a very different point: "Dasein is thrown, factical, *thoroughly amidst nature through its bodiliness*" (*GA* 26, p. 212, my emphasis). Similarly, he mentions in his first lecture course after the return to Freiburg that although the human being "exists" rather than "lives" (the latter being the mode of being of plants and animals), then that which is referred to as "life" nevertheless "attains a completely different meaning of its own within the existence of the human being, insofar as the latter has a body" (*GA* 27, p. 71). In a passage quoted in the previous chapter, Heidegger also states that Dasein is "corporeality, and body, and life [*Körper und Leib und Leben*]" (GA 27, p. 328). In other words, although moving one's body is not like the movement of an intra-mundane entity – i.e., although it is precisely Dasein's *self*-movement – then the body is what places Dasein "in the midst" of such entities, and even – in a sense not further specified – connects Dasein with those intra-mundane entities that have the mode of being of "life." Although the body is not a *Vorhandenheit*, but an essential structure of Dasein itself, it is precisely a structure that literally places Dasein *in* the world, and connects its "destiny" with that of intra-mundane entities.

This discussion shows very clearly how Heidegger's casual remarks on the body are in basic accordance with Husserl's position. It seems that everything Heidegger positively says about the body or embodiment could be said by Husserl as well, and probably has been said by him. But so far, we have only considered some of the passages where Heidegger attributes *positive* significance to the phenomenon of embodiment, and as any careful reader of *Sein und Zeit* knows, the "body" is mainly the title of something ontologically very problematic. Heidegger often refers to it when he is trying to present an outline of the kind of interpretation of the being of the human being that he holds inadequate. However, these problems concern the question of *being*, and hence properly belong to the theme of the following chapter.

For now, let me try to accentuate the most important insights into subjectivity that follow from our discussion in the present chapter.

5. SUBJECTIVITY

Neither Heidegger, nor Husserl is interested in subjectivity for its own sake. Husserl investigates subjectivity because it is the place where the world and everything mundane constitutes itself. His interest pertains precisely to this constitution, and thus to subjectivity to the extent that it helps to account for it. Similarly, in the Marburg years, Heidegger turns to Dasein, but he does so under the heading of a "fundamental ontology" that is only interested in Dasein because it is the place where the topic of ontology, viz. "being" is accessed. Therefore, Heidegger only attempts to account for the structures of Dasein to the extent that they illuminate that theme. Both phenomenologists are thus mainly interested in the subject (or Dasein) as *functioning*, as the "place" where the world, or entities, or being, somehow "manifests" itself, that is (in a Husserlian terminology that cannot be completely misleading given the strictly functional definition we have given of it), they are both mainly interested in unveiling the structures of the *transcendental* subject.

The present chapter shows that not only are the settings in which Husserl and Heidegger turn to the subject structurally similar, the two phenomenologists even seem to agree on how to characterize the subject on a number of important points. They agree that the world is essentially a world I share with others, and consequently they both emphasize that the transcendental subject can only be what it is as part of a community of subjects. More fundamentally, however, both Husserl and Heidegger are uncovering a subject that can neither be "without" its world, nor can be "related" to it *without entering it*. Not that the subject enters the world as one more object, but rather, according to Heidegger – and ultimately to Husserl as well – the subject enters the world as *inhabiting* it. Heidegger tries to capture this by saying that Dasein is "in-the-world" (as opposed to "intra-mundane"), and for Husserl it appears to be the semi-explicit conclusion to his ever deepening analyses of the kinesthesia and the embodied subject. Both Husserl and Heidegger are thus attempting a fundamental revision of the notion of the transcendental subject, a revision that ultimately involves the idea of a subject whose existence is "in" the world rather than extra-mundane, but "in" the world as precisely "inhabiting" it, "involved with it," or "experiencing" it.

Let me at this point anticipate a possible objection. The transcendental subject, or the world-disclosing Dasein, one might claim, cannot be *in* the world, if this subject is precisely what is to account for the constitution or disclosing of the world. This would be Husserl's transcendental "circle" once again. Though it is perhaps tempting to echo Heidegger's standard reply to this type of objection – that, since we are not attempting to prove anything by deductive argument, this circularity need not trouble us (cf. *SZ*, p. 315; *GA* 20, p. 198) – this reply will not do here. To be sure, we are not arguing deductively, but the "transcendental circle" is not a *petitio principii* of this kind anyway. It is, rather, a situation in which one is trying to *account* for something by reference to that which is to be accounted for; a situation, in other words, where something that essentially belongs to the *explanandum* enters into the *explanans*. Heidegger is in fact in basic accordance with Husserl on this point, since the former himself states:

> We are in agreement on the fact that entities in the sense of what you [i.e., Husserl] call "world" cannot be explained in their transcendental constitution by returning to an entity of the same mode of being. (*Hua* IX, p. 601)

That Heidegger not only states this to indulge Husserl is evident from the Marburg lectures courses where Heidegger emphasizes the radical difference between the dimension of philosophy and the dimension of "positive science." Positive sciences as sciences of entities presuppose the "being" of the studied entities, and thus they cannot meaningfully deal with questions of being, Heidegger points out (*GA* 22, pp. 5-8). Indeed, Heidegger claims (in sentences that could almost have been written by Husserl) that it is simply absurd to expect positive science to be able to assist in the solving of any philosophical problem (*GA* 24, p. 76).[41] In other words, the kind of absurdity that Husserl labels the "transcendental circle" is something Heidegger is just as determined to avoid as Husserl.[42] So the objection would seem to be equally an objection to both phenomenologists.

But clearly, the objection only holds insofar as the only possible kind of "mundane" being is "objective," "constituted" being or, as Heidegger puts it, *intra-mundane* being. And this is precisely the reason why Husserl's analyses of the embodied subject are so fascinating: he is not attempting to account for the constitution of the subject as one more "object" in the world, but only to account for the necessary structures of a subject that is to be the subject perceiving such objects – *only to discover that such a subject must itself, somehow, "enter" the world*. It does not enter the world, I repeat, as yet another constituted object, but rather as the subject realizing the constitution of such objects. Phenomenologizing reductively in this way, we are clearly not begging the transcendental question, for we are not uncritically employing any "natural" knowledge of the constituted world on the side of the *explanans*. One could in fact ask those who would raise the objection why they would assume in the first place that the (transcendental) subject has the characteristics of "pure consciousness" rather than body or Dasein. Why should it *not* be possible for the viewpoint on the world to emerge as a viewpoint that finds itself *in* the world? Why must it be a "supernatural" subject? Is it not as if it is tacitly assumed that the transcendental subject must be, if not precisely the "mind" or the "soul," then at least the properly *purified* "mind" or "soul" – and is that not, once again, a version of the mistake Husserl accuses Descartes of committing: assuming

---

[41] Heidegger therefore even feels entitled to claim that the positive sciences "dream" (*GA* 24, p. 75), a remark that clearly anticipates Heidegger's later contention that science does not think, and indeed cannot think (*Was heißt Denken?*, p. 4).

[42] The interpretation, that it is an important difference between Husserl and Heidegger that Husserl wants to avoid "begging the question" while Heidegger does not (cf. Gethmann, *Verstehen und Auslegung*, p. 242), is therefore, in my view, too superficial.

that the transcendental subject must be some *thing* along the lines of those things we normally accept as existing in the world (and since it cannot be *res extensa*, it must be a properly purified *res cogitans*)? Does *that* not, in fact, look suspiciously like a "transcendental circle"? In any case, it should be evident that the objection is misguided. It assumes that the only way to be *in* the world is to be there as something constituted, i.e., the very assumption that both Husserl and Heidegger are ultimately arguing against.

As far as the analysis has taken us in the present chapter, then, we have unveiled profound similarities between Husserl's and Heidegger's conceptions of the subject. But we have also indicated at least one significant difference. Heidegger's talk of "being-in-the-world," so it is argued, gives the impression of being rather abstract and speculative in comparison with Husserl's phenomenological descriptions of the body. Husserl's phenomenology of the lived body seems to reach a level of concretion that Heidegger's analyses of Dasein do not, and in view of those passages where Heidegger seems clearly to acknowledge the fundamental status of the body, it is remarkable the extent to which he economizes with positive statements on the issue. However, we have still not explicitly posed Heidegger's question regarding the manner of *being* of the "subject." In fact, the most fundamental issues in the relationship between Husserl's transcendental phenomenology and Heidegger's phenomenological ontology – those concerning the problems of constitution, transcendence, and modes of being – are still to be discussed. What we have done in Chapters IV and V only amounts to clearing the ground for a discussion of all the questions we have grouped under the heading of "being" in Chapters II and III. In the next chapter, we must enter that ground.

CHAPTER VI
CONSTITUTION, TRANSCENDENCE, AND BEING

1. UNDERSTANDING OF BEING AND INTENTIONALITY

So far in this study, the notion of *unity* within phenomenology seems to prevail almost completely over plurality. But along the way, I refrained from answering many urgent questions. On more than one occasion, I postponed a question, sometimes with the remark that, as a question of *being*, or of *ontology* (in Heidegger's sense), the thematic treatment of the question properly belonged to a later chapter. Indeed, most if not all of the questions, postponed in this way, are questions that somehow involve the relation between the issues concerning constitution, "transcendence" (in Heidegger's sense), and *being*. In the present chapter, the attempt must be made to tie up some of these loose ends.

I claim that there are two central questions posed in Heidegger's phenomenology, rather than one; and one of these questions I (following Heidegger) call the question of "transcendence." This question, of course, has little to do with what Husserl calls the problem of "transcendence." The latter is the problem of traditional epistemology – the problem of how, or indeed whether, it is possible for the mind to transcend its boundaries and reach some external reality – and Husserl rejects this problematic just as emphatically as Heidegger does. Heidegger's problem of transcendence is rather a problem not unlike Husserl's problem of *constitution*. Heidegger realizes that insofar as relating to entities presupposes understanding something like their modes of being, then two closely connected problems present themselves to phenomenology. First, the different modes of being have to be phenomenologically analyzed, and second, Heidegger explicitly recognizes the necessity of posing the transcendental question of "how an understanding of being is possible in Dasein" (*GA* 24, p. 106; cf. *GA* 26, p. 177). This latter is precisely what we call the problem of *transcendence* (cf. *GA* 26, pp. 169-171, 187, 236-237).

Because of the obvious kinship with Husserl's problem of constitution, a number of questions can be raised about the significance of Heidegger's introduction of the problem of transcendence. Is it intended to replace Husserl's constitutive problematic? *Can* it replace it? If the problem of transcendence is a problem of something ("understanding of being") that appears to be missing in Husserl's phenomenology, then does that disqualify Husserl's approach altogether, or does it rather open up for a peaceful co-existence? To what extent *is* something like the "understanding of being" missing in Husserl's account of world-constitution?

At the heart of these questions, I believe, is the issue of whether Heidegger's account of the necessity of the question of being is satisfactory. In a 1927 Marburg lecture course, as we noted, Heidegger explicitly introduces the problematic of being in the context of *intentionality*, indeed even taking up Husserl's favorite theme of perceptual intentionality. Heidegger claims that intentionality is an "ontic" relation, a relation to an entity, and given Husserl's own emphasis on the essential plurality of "ways of perceiving" (I cannot perceive another human being the way I perceive a mountain – each entity demands a different perceptual "approach," as it were), he argues that the intentional relation must be founded in something that is *not* an intentional relation, not an *ontic* relation. I cannot possibly know, so Heidegger reasons, how to approach any entity perceptually (or in any other intentional way) unless I *understand* "as what" this entity must be taken – an understanding that cannot itself be construed as an intentional relation, since that would result in an infinite regress (cf. *GA* 24, p. 99). As Heidegger puts it in his book on Kant, "at no time […] can ontic knowledge itself conform 'to' ['*nach*'] the objects because, without the ontological [knowledge], it cannot even have a possible 'to what' [*Wonach*]" (*KPM*, § 2, p. 13). The reference to "knowledge" here should be taken with a grain of salt, since what Heidegger ultimately argues is that knowledge is made possible by *understanding* (*SZ*, pp. 147, 315). The "hermeneutic" and the "ontological" strands are deeply interwoven in the early Heidegger, so it would be better to stay with the formulation that (ontic) knowledge is made possible by an understanding of "as what" something should be approached, an understanding of modes of being. If an apple tree, as Husserl claims, demands a kind of perception essentially different from the kind of perception another person demands in order to be seen precisely as a person, then I cannot possibly direct my perception at either of these entities unless I have already understood their different modes of being, so Heidegger's argument goes.

To the best of my knowledge, the validity of this argument has never been thoroughly discussed by commentators. Yet precisely for our purposes, it would appear to be of immense importance to discuss it, since it is an argument that cuts right into the heart of Husserl's constitutive phenomenology. After all, if Heidegger is right that perceptual intentionality presupposes understanding of being, then Husserl's constitutive analyses are incomplete, to say the very least. If intentionality is founded in an understanding of being that Husserl never discovered, then there is a fundamental constitutive dimension that Husserl has overlooked completely.[1]

What would Husserl reply to Heidegger's line of reasoning? For Husserl, the world we move around in is a world of typical familiarity. Even without explicitly categorizing things, I immediately experience them as things of this or that type

---

[1] Husserl scholars would probably want to know at this point whether the priority claimed for the "understanding of being" is a "static" or "genetic" priority. It seems to me that Heidegger wants to say that it is both. That is, temporally we must have *understood* "as what" to approach tools before we are able to use them, and as a matter of "logic," too, relations to entities presuppose an understanding of their modes of being. This suggestion is hardly refuted by Heidegger's emphasis that understanding of being is "not prior in the order of measured clocktime" (*GA* 24, p. 100). The claim that it makes no sense to say that understanding of being precedes an experience of an entity by a certain number of minutes does not necessarily exclude all kinds of temporal priority (cf. ibid., p. 462).

(*Hua* XV, p. 96). I cannot know what I will experience when I pass the next corner, but whatever it is, it will probably, at some level, be familiar to me: cars, trees, houses, humans, and animals – although the individual entities might be thoroughly unknown to me, I am familiar with their *type* (*Hua* I, p. 141) or general *style*, Husserl says (*Hua* XV, pp. 429-430). What is the "origin" of this familiarity? According to Husserl, all the experiences of typically familiar objects genetically refer back to a first experience of an entity of this type, to the original or primal "instituting" of the entity:

Every apperception in which we apprehend at a glance, and noticingly grasp, objects given beforehand – for example the already-given everyday world – every apperception in which we immediately understand their sense and its horizon, points back to a *primal instituting* [*Urstiftung*], in which an object with a similar sense became constituted for the first time. (*Hua* I, p. 141)

According to this account, it would indeed be true that my ability to perceptually "approach" an apple tree refers back (temporally, as well as in terms of logical foundation) to something that is not just another perception of an apple tree, but the creative experiential event that *establishes* things like apple trees for me.

But clearly, Husserl's account in terms of *Urstiftung* is precisely the kind of account liable to generate an infinite regress. How is *that* "original" experience itself possible, given Husserl's claim that each type of entity demands its own particular perception? How can that first experience get started, as it were, unless I already "know" or understand something, viz. *how* to approach this type of entity? However, let us ask what it is that makes this objection convincing. It could be argued that the objection relies heavily on a "realist" interpretation of Husserl's claim that different things have different ways of being perceived (*EU*, p. 12). To be sure, Husserl says that the perception of a person is "fitted" to precisely that type of entity, while the perception of rocks is "fitted" to that type of entity, and so forth (*Hua* XV, p. 417), but knowing Husserl's insistence that there "is" nothing prior to the process of constitution, we cannot take this to mean that there are these types of things lying around waiting for humans to stumble across the right way to "approach them." And it is precisely from something like the latter scenario that Heidegger's argument seems to borrow its strength. The infinite regress results only if we accept the realist assumption that the entities are there, whether or not we humans happen to discover how to experience them. For Husserl, however, the constitutive process, as seen in Chapter II, is the process that *realizes* the being-there of entities – it is not a process in which a subject establishes contact with things that were already there to begin with. The notion of things existing "outside" the reach of constitution makes no sense, according to Husserl. This means that the originally instituting experience must be thought of as an experience that *adds something new to the world*: "Through the *original* realization [*Verwirklichung*] an object of this *kind* [*Art*] can for the first time become existing for me [...] – thus it can exist for me at all, and become an object" (*Hua* XIII, p. 358). We cannot meaningfully ask how this experience was able to "approach" its entity – and thus we cannot generate the infinite regress – since it would not make sense to say that there was any entity there to be approached before it had been "originally instituted." The original instituting at once establishes the being of an entity and the "rules," as it were, for its perception.

Hence, we are now in a position to answer a question mentioned (but postponed) in the first section of Chapter III. What Heidegger calls the problem of "intentionality" should not immediately be identified with Husserl's problem of constitution. Although it looks as if there is nothing like Heidegger's *Seinsverständnis* in Husserl, it would not be right to say that constitution is an ontic event, process, or relation. "Constitution" is not a relation between two entities, nor is it a process where an already existing entity receives new properties and features – it is the process that realizes the being-there of entities, the process without which there would be no entities for us. The problem of constitution is, broadly speaking, a problem of *being*.

But even if the argument that any account that does not refer to something like an understanding of being leads to an infinite regress cannot be used against Husserl, this does not settle the issue. Rather, the problem becomes one of determining which account is phenomenologically the more convincing one. What Heidegger claims is that *Urstiftung*, the "instituting" of a new type of entity, is not at the deepest level an "ontic-intuitive" event, but an *ontological-hermeneutic* event, an event having to do with a changing *understanding of being* (see, e.g., SZ, pp. 361-362; GA 27, pp. 193-195). Do I learn to experience logical relations *as logical relations* in a primordial, "first" experience of them, or would such a primordial experience itself presuppose some *understanding* of the "status" or "manner of being" of such things? The example of logic is quite illuminating, since there are significant differences in the speed with which different people learn to "see" logical relations *as logical relations*. Instead of considering the validity of argument structures, some people continue for a long time to dispute the truth of premises, etc., apparently not yet having learned to "see" the logical relations as such. What happens when they do? It seems to me that the more plausible explanation is that of Heidegger: at some point, one begins to *understand* "as what" one has to take these propositions written on the blackboard and this makes possible one's "ontic" experience of logical relations. When one understands not to take the sentences as statements up for debate regarding their truth, but rather as statements proposed as forming an *argumentative* structure, a structure in which some of the statements are proposed as *implying* another statement – when one understands that this is how the sentences written on the blackboard are to be taken – then one can "perceive" the logical relations as such. Perhaps there is a "first" such experience, rather than a gradual realization, but in any case, it seems a plausible claim that this is made possible by some sudden or gradually dawning understanding of an "as what." Logical relations are not mountains, nor are they claims, and they demand their own kind of "perception," one that is indeed only possible when it has been understood "as what" (*Als-Was*) these things are to be "taken" (cf. GA 21, p. 146). As Heidegger convincingly exemplifies his point in a Freiburg lecture course:

We would never be able to recognize a thing that we correctly call a knife as a thing to cut with – nor would we ever be able to use it – if we did not understand something like: a thing with which to... [*um zu...*], a tool for cutting. (*GA* 27, p. 192)

The really interesting thing is that Husserl himself, in giving an example of the way *Urstiftung* works, comes extremely close to Heidegger's position. Not long after Heidegger had pondered what it means to be able to use a knife, Husserl writes: "The child who already sees physical things understands, let us say, for the first time the purposive sense of scissors; and from now on he sees scissors at the first glance *as* scissors" (*Hua* I, p. 141). Is it a coincidence that Husserl refers here to an *understanding* rather than a perception? Is it not precisely the understanding of something like readiness-to-hand that makes it possible for the child "from now on" to see scissors *as scissors*? Therefore, not only should one take care not to identify Husserl's question of constitution with an "ontic" question (about entities and their properties, and relations between such entities); it even seems that Husserl is on the verge, if one may put it thus, of admitting that something like Heidegger's "understanding of being" finds its place among the primary constitutive events.

Some argue, however, that the claim that intending an entity presupposes an understanding of it (or its being) is quite implausible. This would mean, so the argument goes, that I could not intend a car without understanding it, that is, "without knowing how to use or fix it as a car."[2] Indeed, if this is really what Heidegger means, then it is not very plausible, since it is quite possible to know how to drive a car, and yet to have absolutely no clue how to fix it if it breaks down. Moreover, the position would imply that when a person takes her very first driving lesson, she would not be able to intend the car *as a car* until after having finished the lesson (with at least some rough knowledge of how to steer, etc.). But clearly, this is not what Heidegger says; he does not tie his notion of *Seinsverständnis* that closely to what Ryle has dubbed "knowing how." It is not that I have to know how to drive the car to be able to perceive the car as a car, but that I must *understand* that it is "something-with-which-to-drive" – a necessary, but obviously not sufficient condition for "knowing how" to drive. Understanding an "as what" is equally the precondition for knowing how to use the car, and for perceiving it as the kind of thing it is, and Heidegger nowhere states that knowing how to use it is a precondition for being able to intend it in other ways, e.g., perceptually. On the contrary, Heidegger insists that when visiting the shoemaker's shop, I see her tools as tools, even when I have no idea how to use them myself (*GA* 24, p. 432). In other words, Heidegger does claim that understanding the being of the entity is the precondition for intending it, but understanding the *being* of something is not equivalent to knowing how, *ontically*, to use it properly, and this latter ontic know-

---

[2] Mark Okrent, *Heidegger's Pragmatism*, p. 24. Okrent continues (same page): "But Heidegger doesn't claim that there can be no intentions directed toward a thing unless we understand *it*." Given our many references in Chapter III, Section 1, and in the present section, this claim of Okrent's can hardly be confirmed. The question to be discussed, then, is only whether Okrent is right that Heidegger's view is "wildly implausible."

how is certainly no precondition for being able perceptually to "intend" the entity as what it is.[3] Thus, the objection only gains its appearance as justified from construing Heidegger's understanding of being as a special kind of ontic knowledge.

2. CONSTITUTION AND TRANSCENDENCE

As the preceding section attempts to show, Heidegger's argument for the introduction of the understanding of being has some plausibility. We must now ask what this means for Husserl's project of constitutive phenomenology.

It is important not to overestimate what Heidegger establishes. Saying that every intentional relation to an entity must be founded in an understanding of the being of this entity is not claiming that all there is to say about the manifestation of the entity is uncovered by looking at the structures that make possible that understanding of being. Obviously, there is more to my perceiving an apple tree than the understanding of being that makes possible such a perception, and hence there is more to the transcendental investigation of how an apple tree can "be there" for me than the discovery of the structures that account for the possibility of the understanding of being. Heidegger is well aware of this: "There exists no comportment to entities that would not understand being. No understanding of being is possible that would not root in a comportment toward entities" (*GA* 24, p. 466). It seems, however, that Heidegger thinks what is "left" to explain can only be strictly "ontic" relations between two or more entities, and thus a topic of study for empirical science rather than for philosophy (cf. ibid.; *GA* 26, p. 170).[4] In other words, although Heidegger admits that understanding of being is only a necessary and not a sufficient condition for my present perception of a computer screen, he seems to claim that it cannot be the job of phenomenology to explain more than the condition for the possibility of the understanding of being, and that the rest must be dealt with by other sciences.[5] How should we reply to this? It seems to me that

---

[3] As Daniel Dahlstrom says, "pragmatic readings" such as the one Okrent offers "tend to ignore or at least misconstrue the significance of the difference between ontic, preontological, and ontological levels" (*Heidegger's Concept of Truth*, p. 428). See Section 3 of the present chapter.

[4] This is intimately connected with Heidegger's ambiguous relation to idealism. He consistently maintains that although being would not "be" if Dasein did not exist, nevertheless entities would not be affected by Dasein's non-existence (*SZ*, pp. 183, 212). This has led some commentators to conclude that Heidegger contributes to Husserlian phenomenology a realist impulse. See, e.g., Henry Pietersma, "Husserl and Heidegger"; John D. Caputo, *Heidegger and Aquinas*, p. 27; and Joseph Margolis, "Phenomenology and Metaphysics," p. 166. David R. Cerbone, "World, World-Entry, and Realism in Heidegger," attributes a more sophisticated realism to Heidegger, a realism that only concerns entities, and in fact ultimately places Heidegger beyond the realism-idealism-debate. But since, according to Heidegger, we can have absolutely no relation to entities except in and through an understanding of their being – which means that no entities could ever reveal their *an sich* being, indeed could not be said to have any being, if a Dasein did not exist – then the kind of "realism" that Heidegger defends would seem to be a very thin one that cannot, in the last analysis, be all that different from Husserl's transcendental "idealism" (cf. *SZ*, p. 212; *GA* 26, pp. 194-195). However, I cannot argue this point here.

[5] Thus, this must be what Heidegger would reply to Sartre's criticism that Heidegger can never make intelligible the concrete ontic relations with others (or things). Cf. *Being and Nothingness*, pp. 248-249.

Heidegger himself implicitly demonstrates that this view is untenable, e.g., when he declares that "[p]ositive sciences are sciences for which that which they deal with, that which can become their object and theme, *is already at hand [schon vorliegt]*" (*GA* 22, p. 6; cf. *GA* 24, p. 17). Positive sciences deal with entities that are *already there,* entities that are *already manifest* (*WM*, p. 48; *GA* 27, p. 180), and we see in detail in Chapter II that this is why such sciences cannot meaningfully answer the question of constitution that Husserl poses. Hence, here is a legitimate task for philosophy. The important thing to remember is that Heidegger's *Seinsverständnis* alone cannot make intelligible that entities are "already there," although it might be a necessary condition for their being there. Even if intentionality "needs" the "directional sense" (*Richtungssinn*) that can only be supplied by the understanding of being (*GA* 24, p. 447), then something like *intentionality must be there if any entities are to manifest themselves.* No entities can *schon vorliegen* unless intentionality has already entered the stage.

Consequently, "understanding of being" might be more basic than intentionality, *but it cannot replace it.* Correspondingly, the problem of "transcendence" (in Heidegger's sense) might be more basic than Husserl's problem of constitution, *but it cannot replace it* (cf. *WM*, p. 135). Given the tendency of some Heidegger scholars to assume that Heidegger has made Husserl's phenomenological legacy obsolete more or less *in toto*, this can hardly be overemphasized. Heidegger uncovers a level of "constitution" that does not seem to surface in Husserl, yet that can never invalidate Husserl's constitutive phenomenology as such, but only provide it with a new foundation. On the other hand, however, it is clear that Husserlian intentional analysis cannot completely explain "constitution" (used here in a sense broad enough to encompass all that is needed to make intelligible the manifestation of a world and mundane entities). If Heidegger is right that intentionality is founded in *Seinsverständnis*, then "radical world-research" in Husserl's sense (cf. *Hua* XXVII, p. 178), that is, constitutive phenomenology, cannot be truly radical without also trying to explain the possibility of the understanding of being.

In other words, the relation between "constitution" and "transcendence" is, it would seem, one of mutual dependence. If the project of making transcendental sense of the world and of everything mundane is to be carried out, then both the level of Husserlian constitutive analyses and the (deeper) level of Heidegger's probing into the conditions for the possibility of understanding of being are needed. Although one level – if Heidegger is right – is more fundamental than the other, neither level alone can tell the whole story. And clearly, there is not much constitutive phenomenology in Husserl's sense to be found in *Sein und Zeit*, which can therefore be seen as just as one-sided as anything Husserl writes. Hence, Husserl's disappointment with Heidegger's magnum opus is partly justified. When Heidegger emphasizes that Dasein is already "out there," alongside some encountered entity, rather than something that first has to be dragged out of its confinement to some "immanent sphere" (*SZ*, p. 62), it is thoroughly understandable that Husserl should reply: "But how can all this be clarified except through my doctrine of intentionality [...]? What is said here is my own doctrine, but without its deeper grounding" (RB, p. 20). Husserl's problem, as noted, is not the problem of how a mind can escape its initial confinement and establish contact with an external object. Rather, Husserl recognizes that the subject is intentional, the subject is already experientially directed at "external" objects, but he insists that there is nevertheless some explaining to be done here by philosophy. The intentional openness to the world is undeniable, but does that mean that we understand *how* this is possible? Husserl would reply in the negative, and he sees the main task for phenomenology to be precisely that of making intelligible, through constitutive analysis, this intentional being-alongside things (*Hua* V, pp. 152-153; *Hua* VI, p. 191). And surely he is right. Similarly, however, Heidegger is right in pointing out that, before him, phenomenology had neglected the question of how an understanding of being belongs to intentionality (*GA* 24, p. 447). In other words, if it is correct that Heidegger's account needs something that Husserl's constitutive phenomenology supplies, then it is equally true that Heidegger supplies what is missing in Husserl's constitutive account.[6]

A further point is that the transcendental investigations conducted by Husserl and the early Heidegger seem equally centered on the *subject*. As we have seen, Husserl's transcendental reduction is both what makes intelligible the constitution of the world and of everything mundane, and the method by which the structures of the transcendental subject are discovered. In fact, the being-there of the world is made transcendentally intelligible *by* the regress to the subject. Similarly, Heidegger's project of "fundamental ontology" implies a regress to subjectivity (Dasein), insofar as being is "given" nowhere except in the understanding of being that belongs to the human subject (*GA* 26, p. 177). When we want to understand how being can "manifest" itself, it is to the understanding Dasein that we must turn (*GA* 24, p. 21). In his 1927 lectures *Die Grundprobleme der Phänomenologie*, Heidegger therefore explicitly declares his sympathy with the efforts of modern philosophy to turn to the subject (*GA* 24, pp. 103, 444). Another, very interesting point that I shall here only note in passing is the following: as Husserl and Heidegger proceed to unearth the very deepest constitutive level underlying both perceptual intentionality and *Seinsverständnis*, they both discover that it is, in some sense, *temporality*. To be sure, in neither account is it temporality in a normal, "objective" or "mundane" sense (*Hua* X, p. 75; *SZ*, p. 329), but the very structure that allows for such temporality (as well as everything else) to appear. Heidegger mostly expresses this difference by calling the temporality that is the condition for the possibility of understanding of being "*Zeitlichkeit*" or "original time" in contrast to "*Innerzeitigkeit*" (cf. *SZ*, pp. 329, 333; *KPM*, p. 195; *GA* 24, p. 334), whereas

---

[6] It is truly astonishing how clearly Eugen Fink sees this. As is well known, Fink is of the opinion that "[n]either Heidegger nor Husserl sees the other without a certain 'foreshortening'" (Dorion Cairns, *Conversations with Husserl and Fink*, p. 25). In an unpublished manuscript quoted by Ronald Bruzina, Fink specifies this relationship in a way that is relevant to our present discussion, in observing that "Husserl is blind to transcendence, Heidegger to constitution" (*Husserl ist blind für die Transzendenz, Heidegger für die Konstitution*) (Bruzina, "Gegensätzlicher Einfluß – Integrierter Einfluß," p. 142).

Husserl emphasizes that this deepest, time-constituting level is itself not temporal if we thereby understand something that falls *within* time (*Hua* X, pp. 334, 369-371). According to both Husserl and Heidegger, then, it is ultimately some "ecstatic" three-forked time-constituting structure that allows for intentionality (*Hua* XI, pp. 322-324) and understanding of being (cf. *GA* 24, pp. 377-379, 429). Significant differences are unmistakably there – e.g., about whether this temporality should really be called "inner" or "time-consciousness,"[7] about whether the original mode of time is the future or the present, about whether this original temporality should be considered finite or rather infinite, and so forth – but still the convergence on this particular point in Husserl's and Heidegger's transcendental investigations is remarkable. It also deserves to be noted that Heidegger declares in his last Marburg lecture course that what Husserl dubs "inner time consciousness" is indeed, despite Husserl's ill-chosen name for it, nothing but the phenomenon of original time (*GA* 26, p. 264).[8]

Yet having accepted Heidegger's view that every intentional directedness presupposes some understanding of the mode of being of the entity intended, we are naturally lead to the other question Heidegger poses: the question of (modes of) being. If we always understand the modes of being of things, then is it not an important phenomenological task to describe these modes of being, as they "appear" in our understanding? Heidegger thinks this is probably the most important task for phenomenology, all the more so because this question, so he alleges, has not been explicitly raised for the last two thousand years (*SZ*, p. 2). Perhaps there is no single point that is as troubling for a commentator on Husserlian and Heideggerian phenomenology as the question of Husserl's relation to Heidegger's question of being. So let us turn to this issue. Let us ask whether the real "being" of the tool is that of *Zuhandensein*, or whether the better phenomenological interpretation is the one according to which the tool is an entity consisting of a number of strata, the most basic being the one of "material reality." And what can we say about the being of the subject? These are the questions that will occupy us in the final four sections.[9]

---

[7] Many commentators argue that Husserl's "inner time-consciousness" should never have been named thus, since the phenomenon Husserl describes is not "inner," but prior to the distinction between inner and outer. See Thomas Prufer, "Heidegger, Early and Late, and Aquinas"; Robert Sokolowski, "Ontological Possibilities in Phenomenology"; and James G. Hart, "Being and Mind."

[8] As already emphasized in the introduction, a comprehensive study of being and subjectivity in Husserl and Heidegger would have to deal in much greater detail with the question of temporality. In the present study, the accent is on subjectivity's bodily embeddedness or situatedness in the world, not on the temporal dimensions of subjective life. Good accounts of both differences and similarities between Husserl's and Heidegger's accounts of temporality are found in Rudolf Bernet, "Die Frage nach dem Ursprung der Zeit bei Husserl und Heidegger," and in Daniel Dahlstrom, *Heidegger's Concept of Truth*, pp. 149-159.

[9] These two kinds of entities – equipment and *Dasein* – are not, of course, the only ones Heidegger recognizes. Although there is no reason to assume that it is intended as an exhaustive list, it is worth noting the inventory of entities and their modes of being that Heidegger presents in the 1928/29 lecture course *Einleitung in die Philosophie*: "So, with regard to these different kinds of being of entities, we can differentiate: the existing: the humans; the living: plants and animals; the present-at-hand: material things;

3. UNDERSTANDING THE BEING OF EQUIPMENT: SOME CLARIFICATIONS

Throughout the present study, it is emphasized that the kind of critique that charges Husserl with "the theoretician's narcissism"[10] – projecting upon the natural subjective life studied only one's own theoretical interests – does not hit the mark. Questions of tone and accent aside, Husserl is as clear as Heidegger that normal, "natural attitude" life is mainly practical, not theoretical. Consequently, Husserl never claims that the kinds of things we find in our environment are "pure things," merely "occurrent" entities, or anything of the sort. Rather, he consistently maintains that they are primarily useful things of various sorts (*Hua* IV, pp. 27, 182; *Hua* IX, p. 111). So what separates the two accounts? To put it bluntly, Heidegger insists that "in order to" characterizes the very *being* of the intra-mundane entity (*GA* 20, p. 259), whereas Husserl interprets this usefulness as something like a "layer" of the thing. Husserl is clear that this "layer" of practical utility indeed has priority in the sense that this is the layer we mostly "live" in, when we move around in the lifeworld, but nevertheless it is just a layer, and a *founded* layer at that (*Hua* IV, p. 214). I cannot use a hammer unless I have a visual and tactile perception of it; that is, the layer of "materiality" must be given before the layer of "in order to" can manifest itself, and not vice versa. This is not so, according to Heidegger. The reference of *Um-zu* is what constitutes the *being* of the hammer (*SZ*, p. 83; *GA* 24, p. 415); it is not just another layer on top of others. In the present section, we must try to reveal what this Heideggerian alternative actually amounts to.

It is important to note that Heidegger – unlike many Heidegger scholars, perhaps – recognizes that the Husserlian account is not a clearly false one maintaining that the life-world is a world of pure materiality. Indeed, Heidegger points out that Husserl's description of the practical world seems, if one looks at the final result, an authentic description (*GA* 63, p. 89). In Heidegger's eyes, however, this is hardly a mitigating circumstance, since the "layer ontology" misconstrues precisely the point that, according to Heidegger, is the most important one. It "leaps over" the real being of the thing (*GA* 20, p. 247), and in so doing uncritically posits the being of the encountered entity as presence-at-hand:

When we speak of material thinghood, have we not tacitly posited a kind of being – the constant presence-at-hand of things – which is so far from having been rounded out ontologically by subsequently endowing entities with value-predicates, that these value-characters themselves are rather just ontical characteristics of those entities which have the kind of being possessed by things? Adding on value-predicates cannot tell us anything at all new about the being of goods, *but would merely presuppose again that goods have pure presence-at-hand as their kind of being.* (*SZ*, p. 99; cf. *GA* 20, p. 247)

the ready-to-hand: things for use, in the widest sense; the subsisting [*das Bestehende*]: number and space" (*GA* 27, pp. 71-72). I cannot possibly deal with all of them in the present context, however. Besides, from the beginning, Heidegger's explicit critique of Husserl centers precisely on the question of the modes of being of the two kinds of entities singled out for discussion in this chapter (cf. Søren Overgaard, "Heidegger's Early Critique of Husserl").

[10] See Barbara Merker, *Selbsttäuschung und Selbsterkenntnis*, pp. 79, 194. See, too, Heidegger's own remarks in *Prolegomena zur Geschichte des Zeitbegriffs* on this "basic phenomenological illusion" (*GA* 20, p. 254).

What is this notion of presence-at-hand, occurrentness, or onhandness? Heidegger often writes as if presence-at-hand should be identified with "material being," or "thing-like" being (*SZ*, p. 201), and yet he also insists that the traditional notions of "consciousness" and "subjectivity" are committed to the ontology of presence-at-hand (*SZ*, p. 46).[11] The idea Heidegger seems to have is that we tend to think of things as being there in an undifferentiated way (*GA* 24, p. 396; *GA* 29/30, p. 515). We are well aware that there are all kinds of differences between things, of course, but they are differences that we tend to articulate as differences of "properties," "attributes," "layers," and so forth – hence differences that do not concern the way in which things are there (*GA* 29/30, p. 399). All entities have something in common, namely, that they "occur," i.e., that they are "things." The manner of being there is the same for a rock, a hammer, and a human being: we all occur, we are all here, "on hand," in nature, or in the world, in the same way. It is precisely this "indifferent" mode of being, supposed to be common to all entities whatever their differences, that Heidegger calls *Vorhandenheit*. Presence-at-hand, then, is the notion of "thing-like" being: "This is the name for the way of being of natural things in the broadest sense" (*GA* 24, p. 36). It is the notion of a closed, isolated, and inert manner of being that precisely has to be equipped with certain special features – which are typically also interpreted as closed and isolated, as "observable features" – in order to be "more" than that. Heidegger further contends that this interpretation of the manner of being of entities is anchored in a certain mode of time, namely the present. All being is precisely interpreted as *presence*-at-hand (*Anwesenheit*), he claims (*SZ*, p. 26).[12]

Husserl's description of the perceptual givenness of a thing does not present an alternative to presence-at-hand. Husserl's analyses of perception clearly show that perceptual givenness is no simple matter, that it is something that essentially involves references, and indeed references to "absent" aspects. Nevertheless, they do not leave the level of a thing on hand – on the contrary, they explain precisely the manifestation of a thing, like this computer screen, as an object simply present before the eyes of a perceiving subject. They explain, in other words, the manifestation of the fundamental "layer" of nature that all perceptual experience of things must "move through," even if the interests of the perceiving subject do not "terminate" there. Whatever we encounter in our world, Husserl says, it is "always given, at bottom, as a natural body, endowed with natural properties accessible to simple experience" (*EU*, § 12, p. 54; cf. Hua III/1, p. 354), and it is precisely the

---

[11] Husserl appears to have been troubled by Heidegger's notion of *Vorhandenheit*: "What kind of meaning does presence-at-hand take on? <That of> mere things <had> in the corresponding external observation? But even that is not entirely understandable" (RB, p. 22). In her article, "Phenomenologizing with a Hammer: Theory or Practice?", Gail Soffer also argues that the concept is "poorly defined."

[12] In the winter of 1924/1925, Heidegger develops in great detail how this interpretation of being has its roots in the Greek understanding of *ousia* (*GA* 19, p. 466, *et passim*). For discussions of whether Husserl, too, is an exponent of "metaphysics of presence," see Jacques Derrida, *Speech and Phenomena*, Rudolf Bernet, "Die ungegenwärtige Gegenwart," and Robert J. Dostal, "Time and Phenomenology in Husserl and Heidegger."

constitution of this foundational structure that Husserl's analyses of perception attempt to account for (*EU*, pp. 67-69; *Hua* XIV, p. 390). Husserl even occasionally claims that although objects might have "layers" of practical significance, they do not lose their "style" as objects of nature (*Hua* XV, p. 323).[13] Undeniably, then, Husserl's way of conceiving of mundane things remains committed to the idea of *Vorhandenheit*, in Heidegger's sense.

Heidegger's negative point should thus be reasonably clear by now. Husserl's description of the cultural object as consisting of a number of strata commits itself to the view that, at the most fundamental level, the cultural object is a material thing that is simply there, "on hand." The additional strata or predicates attributed to the thing, since they are necessarily founded in the layer of materiality, do not change the ontological status of the object, though they may be ontically important. First and foremost, the cultural object *is* just as any purely material thing is – even if "value predicates" or strata of practical usefulness essentially belong to the former in contrast to the latter. Heidegger agrees with the ontic result, so to speak, of Husserl's description, but emphatically and repeatedly rejects the ontology that he believes it tacitly advances.

It is perhaps tempting, at this point, to speculate that what Heidegger's claim amounts to is the view that since the perceptual givenness must not be construed as corresponding to some fundamental layer of the keyboard, then it is precisely the other way around. Consequently, the material presence of the keyboard (corresponding to my visual perception) would somehow be secondary in relation to the presence of the keyboard as "useful" (corresponding to my using "interaction" with it).[14] Yet this seems to entail the claim that I could *use* the keyboard even if I could neither see it nor feel it, a claim that, as Husserl would no doubt point out, can hardly be correct. Clearly, however, this is not what Heidegger wants to say. In fact, the first important thing to note about Heidegger's account is that it does not primarily oppose Husserl because the latter deems the "material" layer the founding layer and the "practical" layer the founded (although it may sometimes appear as if this is the point of his criticism), but *because Heidegger rejects the idea of a "layer ontology" altogether*. Or to put it differently, it is not Heidegger's project to change the relation of priority between predicates of "usefulness" and of "materiality" in the

---

[13] Elsewhere, however, he emphasizes that the founded layers of value, practical usefulness, etc., contribute a new "ontological sense" to the object (*Hua* III/1, pp. 267, 355), as Jim Jakobsson has reminded me. But I do not think this changes anything essential: Husserl remains committed to the layer ontology, and that is ultimately the problem.

[14] Dagfinn Føllesdal seems to come close to this view in maintaining that "Heidegger regards our practical ways of dealing with the world as more basic than the theoretical" (Føllesdal, "Husserl and Heidegger on the Role of Actions in the Constitution of the World," p. 371). However, much depends on how this statement is interpreted. As we see shortly, there is indeed a way in which Heidegger does want to claim priority for "practice."

conception of the being of equipmental things, but to replace this whole *manner* of conceiving the being of an entity with an entirely different account.[15]

If we now return to the question of the perceptual presence of the tool, we can indicate how perception enters into Heidegger's account. To be sure, I do see the keyboard here in front of me, but this seeing must be understood as "circumspection" (*Umsicht*) guided by an understanding of the keyboard as something "with which to." It is not as if we can isolate the perceptual part, as it were, of my experience of the keyboard, as I sit here writing; on the contrary, the perception is melted together (*eingeschmolzen*) with my having-to-do-with (*GA 21*, pp. 212-213). I do not see in order to see, Heidegger says, but in order to "find my way" or "make my way" (*GA* 20, pp. 37-38), or perhaps to avoid something threatening (in which case we clearly see the existenti*ale* of "affectivity" in play) (*SZ*, p. 141). In Heidegger's interpretation of them, these points are not as trivial as one might think. He is not just saying that my interests are not active on the perceptual level, but only on the practical one (as Husserl presumably would); he is saying that there *is no* such merely "perceptual" level.

"Practical" behavior is not "atheoretical" in the sense of "sightlessness." The way it differs from theoretical behavior does not lie simply in the fact that in theoretical behavior one observes, while in practical behavior one *acts*, and that action must employ theoretical cognition if it is not to remain blind; for the fact that observation is a kind of concern is just as primordial as the fact that action has *its own* kind of sight. (*SZ*, p. 69, cf. p. 358)

My *seeing* things cannot be attributed to some perceptual act standing "in serving function" (cf. *Hua* VIII, pp. 100-101), but is rather a seeing that originally belongs as an integral moment to my (practical) *Umgang*. As such an *Umsicht*, indeed, perception plays a very significant part in everyday life, according to Heidegger, and the crucial thing is just not to misconstrue this phenomenon of circumspection.

Heidegger defends the same view when it comes to the "material" and "spatial" presence of things. The "hard" physical and spatial presence of things is undeniable, but it is a presence to a circumspection, i.e., as we have seen, a perception that uncovers them as "in the way," as "immobile," as "right for the job," as "dangerous," and so on and so forth. The presence of things to my immediate perception is a presence in an "*as*" (*Als*),[16] and an "*as*"-free perception, if at all possible, demands a certain modification of the original having-to-do-with (*GA* 21, p. 145; *SZ*, p. 149). In other words, it is not that a bicycle, say, does not have a

---

[15] When Heidegger says that "knowledge" is a *founded* mode of being-in-the-world (*SZ*, p. 61; *GA* 20, p. 222), then this must not be understood as a testimony to the secondary nature of all kinds of perception. What is "founded" is only the purely theoretical observation of things – a kind of practice that, as Husserl himself says in *Krisis*, is only one among others, and historically a quite late one at that (*Hua* VI, p. 113).

[16] There are obvious affinities between this Heideggerian account of perception and Wittgenstein's notion of "aspect-seeing." A good account of the convergence is found in Stephen Mulhall, *On Being in the World*, although Mulhall's presentation of Heidegger is not entirely free from problematic claims. Thus, Mulhall seems simply to take for granted that the "baroque metaphysical structures" supposedly construed by Heidegger are really "grammatical" structures "seen through a glass darkly" (*On Being in the World*, pp. 159, 3).

certain weight, color, hardness, solidity, spatial extendedness, etc., and it is not that these things are not experienced by me. But these features mostly only manifest themselves in some circumspective "as": the weight, often something that does not directly manifest itself to me at all, presents itself as "too great" when I am forced to lift my bike; the color is "beautiful," or it is a matter of "indifference" to me, and so on. Although in *Sein und Zeit*, Heidegger only mentions spatial extension, what he says could and should be extended to the other kinds of qualities as well:

> Within certain limits, the analysis of the *extensio* remains independent of the failure to provide an explicit interpretation of the being of extended entities. There is some phenomenal justification for regarding the *extensio* as a basic characteristic of the "world," even if by recourse to this neither the spatiality of the world nor the proximally discovered spatiality of the entities we encounter in the world, nor even the spatiality of Dasein itself, can be conceived ontologically. (*SZ*, p. 101)

This passage is similar to the passage quoted above about the "vision" of practice, even if it seems to concede more to the Husserlian view. It is not as if Heidegger wants to deny that spatial extension is a basic feature of intra-mundane entities; he rejects only the notion that the *mode of being* of such entities can be correctly characterized by reference to something like their spatial extension. In other words, Heidegger is once again denying that the most fundamental description of the tool is the one that characterizes it as spatial and material – not to turn this description upside down, as it were (e.g., claim that the layer of "practical value" is the more fundamental one), but to emphasize that the very idea of such an "*Aufbau*"-ontology is misguided (cf. *SZ*, p. 442). Spatiality does describe the tool in an essential aspect, but the *being* of the tool is its readiness-to-hand, and if we want to understand how spatiality enters into our everyday experience of the tool, then we have to disclose, among other things, how that experience is made possible by an understanding of the tool precisely as ready-to-hand.

The tool, consequently, is not something that we can ultimately make intelligible by reference to its presence in space and time and the addition of value-predicates, strata of "usefulness," or whatever, to the mere spatial object, according to Heidegger. The tool *is* its reference, and the presence it does have in space is itself uncovered in a concerned circumspection of a Dasein that understands the tool as something with-which-to. The hammer is in the toolbox, or it is "missing," or it is "lying around," "in the way," i.e., disturbing me in some other activity (*SZ*, p. 102; *GA* 20, p. 311; *GA* 24, p. 440). None of the tools that we encounter are primarily experienced as simply occupying some position in space; rather, their "position" is "too far away," "in the wrong parking lot," "on the table," etc. (*SZ*, p. 103; *GA* 20, p. 315). Possible perceptual givenness, materiality, spatial extension, a spatial position – all of these things belong to Heidegger's *Zeug*, but precisely to the tool *as tool*, as something whose being is *Zuhandenheit*; that is, these features do *not belong to it in virtue of some "layer" that the tool shares with other types of entities*.

It is important that these claims are interpreted the right way. The main point Heidegger is trying to make is an *ontological* one. We repeatedly stress that Heidegger does not want simply to "reverse" the foundational relationship between "practice" and "theory," as if he is retaining some sort of inverted "layer ontology."

He rejects this way of conceiving the encountered intra-mundane entity altogether. But there are obviously other means for claiming that one way of relating to entities should be considered more original than others, means that are more consistent with Heidegger's notion that practical *Umgang* should not be conceived as in itself "blind" and in need of the help of "theoretical inspection." Insofar as the normally encountered intra-mundane entity is a *tool*, Heidegger, in fact, does want to maintain (so does Husserl himself, as we see in Chapter I) that mere "staring" at this thing can hardly be the most original way to approach it (*SZ*, p. 69). Instead, Heidegger holds that the activity of hammering with the hammer "has appropriated this equipment in a way which could not possibly be more suitable" (ibid.), and indeed "[t]he genuine relation to it is to be occupied with it in using it" (*GA* 20, p. 259). Again, this is not claiming that the practical activity could take place without any kind of perception (which would seem to follow from the "inverted layer ontology"), because this activity has its own *Sichtart*, as we noted.

Admittedly, then, it would be false to claim that Heidegger posits no hierarchy whatsoever between ways of relating to entities. The question, however, is whether this is really his main point. There are plenty of remarks in Heidegger's opus that suggest that it is not. Repeatedly, Heidegger emphasizes that the using involvement with a tool, no less than the theoretical inspection of a thing, is itself made possible by an understanding of its being (*SZ*, p. 85; *GA* 24, p. 390; *GA* 26, pp. 236-237; *GA* 27, p. 192). It is on this *ontological* level that Heidegger's talk of *Zuhandenheit* becomes truly significant.[17] But is it obvious how this "understanding of being" is to be interpreted? According to Hubert Dreyfus' pragmatic reading of *Sein und Zeit*, Heidegger is certainly not just "reversing the priority of theoretical to practical intentionality."[18] Nevertheless, Dreyfus insists that what Heidegger calls understanding of being:

> is not something radically different from ontic transcending (transparent coping with specific things, discovering); rather, it is *the same sort of coping* functioning as the holistic background for all purposive comportment. [...] One needs to be finding one's way about in the world in order to use equipment, but finding one's way about is just more coping. Any specific activity of coping takes place on the background of more general coping. [...] Our general background coping [...] is our understanding of being.[19]

Dreyfus has several illuminating examples to back up this interpretation. He refers, for example, to the necessity, when entering a workshop, of being able to "avoid chairs, locate and approach the workbench, pick out and grasp something as an instrument, etc.,"[20] if one is to be able to use a specific hammer for hammering. Precisely background activities such as these are what, according to Dreyfus, Heidegger calls "understanding of being." However, it should first of all be noted

---

[17] Thus, Okrent is precisely wrong at the point where he identifies existenti*al* understanding with "practical" understanding (cf. *Heidegger's Pragmatism*, p. 131).
[18] Hubert Dreyfus, *Being-in-the-World*, p. 53.
[19] Dreyfus, *Being-in-the-World*, pp. 106-107.
[20] *Being-in-the-World*, p. 104.

that the reference to "background" here is slightly confusing. As seen in Chapter IV, if there is anything that remains inconspicuous, i.e., remains completely in the background, it is the individual tool itself (e.g., *GA* 20, p. 259). The referential whole, to be sure, is not thematic either, but in any case, one cannot make intelligible the difference between the coping with "specific things" and "general coping" by reference to the "background" character of the latter. Second, it is not obvious that the activities of avoiding chairs, locating things, and the like, can be called "hermeneutic" activities at all. Locating the workbench, surely, is an act of "vision," though clearly not (necessarily) a theoretical one, and Heidegger's point is precisely that "all sight is grounded primarily in understanding" (*SZ*, p. 147). However, the third and most important problem with Dreyfus' interpretation is simply that it construes what in Heidegger's view is still essentially an *ontic* relation as the underlying, *ontological* relation. It is important not to overlook the fact that, from Heidegger's perspective, an involvement can be quite latent and unthematic and still be an involvement with *entities* as opposed to *being* (*GA* 24, pp. 232-233; *GA* 26, p. 158). What Heidegger calls understanding of being is what makes possible "background coping" as well as any other type of practical or theoretical coping:

If, for instance, we perform an action which *we do not particularly notice at all* [*eine weiter gar nicht beachtete Handlung*], like opening a door – something we do several times during a day – then this involves grasping the doorknob. If we did not understand in advance what a thing-for-use [...] signifies [*besagt*] then we would not be able to use the doorknob as such. (*GA* 27, p. 192, my emphasis)

Clearly, this is not an example of a "transparent" coping with a specific tool; it is much more like the background activity of picking out and grasping something. And yet, Heidegger does not say that this is what he means by *Seinsverständnis*. Rather, this is precisely offered as an example of an (unthematic) *ontic* involvement that itself "needs" the light of the *ontological* understanding. In other words, Dreyfus' interpretation, though not committing the error of the "inverted layer ontology," still fails to reach the ontological dimension that Heidegger is ultimately trying to unearth.[21]

Heidegger's main point, then, is neither that the "used" entity is more primary than the "observed" entity, nor that entities as undifferentiated background phenomena should be considered primary in relation to "specific" entities as used in a "transparent" coping. It lies at a "deeper" level than any of these issues. Let us now try to take a closer look at the ontological problem that Heidegger wants to raise, to see if we can elucidate what it amounts to and what consequences it has.

---

[21] For a penetrating critique of the pragmatic reading of Heidegger, see Daniel Dahlstrom, *Heidegger's Concept of Truth*, esp. pp. 199-200, 233n, 305-306, 423-433. A somewhat different critique of the pragmatic interpretation is found in William D. Blattner, "Existential Temporality in *Being and Time*." Since the pragmatic reading fails to reach the level of ontology that really interests Heidegger, it is very difficult for advocates of such a reading to argue for the originality of Heidegger's thinking vis-à-vis Husserl, and at the same time present a fair account of the latter's phenomenology. See Dagfinn Føllesdal's response to Dreyfus (Føllesdal, "Absorbed Coping, Husserl, and Heidegger").

4. THE BEING OF EQUIPMENT

Heidegger, as he himself admits on more than one occasion, finds in Husserlian phenomenology the notion of the intended *as* intended, and this notion opens up the possibility of a previously unimaginable, radically "scientific" type of ontology. To quote, once again, from Heidegger's 1925 Kassel lectures, with Husserl's notion of "the intended in the characterizations of its being-intended [*in den Bestimmungen seines Gemeintseins*]" (WDF, p. 160), we have established "the scientific basis for the question concerning the being of entities" (ibid.; cf. *GA* 17, pp. 262-263). When Heidegger claims that the mostly encountered entity (which Husserl agrees is some kind of "cultural object") should be conceived as having the mode of being of *Zuhandenheit*, he is trying to appropriate what Husserl would call a noematic investigation in a radical way. He is asking himself whether, with the "scientific basis" provided by Husserl's notion of the noematic correlate, we can question the standard philosophical interpretation of *all* being as being-on-hand, as presence-at-hand, as occurrentness – *Vorhandensein*. The questions Heidegger is trying to raise, then, are something like the following: Is it phenomenologically verifiable that all being is "occurring," and that the differences between different regions of entities should be interpreted as difference of properties, layers, or the like? What if these differences were instead differences in *modes of being* (*GA* 24, p. 24)? What if there "are" radically different ways for entities to *be*, and these different ways can be discovered in an unprejudiced noematic investigation? Before we try to answer these questions, it might be a good idea to recall Husserl's "principle of all principles," viz. "that *everything originarily* [...] *offered* to us *in 'intuition' is to be accepted simply as what it is presented as being*, but also *only within the limits in which it is presented there*" (*Hua* III/1, p. 51; cf. *GA* 56/57, pp. 109-110; *GA* 63, p. 71). This principle sets the standard by which we can attempt to evaluate Heidegger's and Husserl's accounts.

Heidegger thinks a strictly phenomenological noematic investigation will precisely reveal that a tool *is not* as a rock is. Readiness-to-hand, Heidegger says, is the proper ontological characterization of the tool (*SZ*, p. 71). Husserl, on the other hand, would maintain that at the most fundamental level a tool, too, is a thing of "nature." Interestingly enough, Husserl and Heidegger introduce similar examples to substantiate their quite different views. According to Husserl, our Western life-world contains much that we immediately experience, but which cannot immediately be experienced by people from a different culture. What is German literature, or Michelangelo's *David* to an uneducated stranger, Husserl asks (*Hua* IX, p. 497). It is clear that such a person, "faced with any one of our works of art, sees a thing, to be sure, but does not see the object of our environment, the work of art" (ibid.). Indeed, we do not even have to take our example that far, according to Husserl:

The Bantu would "see" our "park," our houses, churches, etc.; and there would be spatial things there for him, and perhaps even things that to him would have the character of buildings and gardens. *But there is a difference. With respect to the spatiotemporal characterizations, with respect to mere nature, there must be commonality* [*Gemeinsamkeit*]; but what the entrepreneur wanted to do with this building and, correlatively, what sort of "meaning" – esthetic and practical – this building has as such, is something the Bantu can not understand. (*Hua* IX, p. 498, my emphasis)

The practical and esthetical purpose of a park might escape this stranger, but certainly he or she would see things there in those same spots where we Westerners would see things. On this level of space and time, or "nature," we must all be in agreement. For Husserl, this is an indication that there must be some universal structure of the world, the structure of "nature," underlying all the concrete life-worldly differences (*Hua* IX, pp. 498-499, cf. p. 119). How would Heidegger respond to this? In the war emergency semester of 1919, Heidegger considers what he experiences when he enters the auditorium to give a lecture. I immediately perceive the lectern "from which I speak," Heidegger claims. So far, Husserl would certainly agree. But, Heidegger contends, we cannot phenomenologically discover some sort of relation of foundation here, as if I could (at least in principle) separate some dark, box-shaped object as that which "I, as it were, glue the lectern-characteristics [*das Kathederhafte*] onto [...] like a label" (*GA* 56/57, p. 71). All this is faulty interpretation; it is not describing the experienced as it is actually experienced (ibid.). However, imagine a farmer from the remotest parts of the Black Forest, or better yet, a scientifically unschooled native of Senegal suddenly transported from his or her hut to the auditorium. Surely, he or she would not see a "lectern" at all, but rather "a mere thing [*Sache*]; a something that is simply there" (*GA* 56/57, p. 72)? The Senegalese would certainly see something there where we also see something, thus is that not a testimony to the presence of some "layer" or basic structure that we all have in common? According to Heidegger, the crucial point is precisely that just as "we" do not see a dark, cubic "something," nor would anyone else. The Senegalese would presumably see the lectern "as a something 'which he doesn't know what to do with.' The significance of 'equipmental foreignness' ['*zeuglichen Fremdseins*'] and the significance 'lectern' are *completely identical with regard to their essential core* [*ihrem Wesenskern nach absolut identisch*]" (*GA* 56/57, p. 72, my emphasis). In other words, there is no essential difference between our experience and the experience of the complete stranger: we all see something, we all see this something *as* some sort of equipment, and none of us see any merely material-spatial thing. These are the *phenomenological* facts of the matter, and Heidegger seems to indicate that any attempt (such as Husserl's) to extract some notion of a basic layer of "materiality" or "nature" out of it is constructive and prejudiced (*GA* 63, p. 89), i.e., a violation of the "principle of all principles."

Which is the more convincing account? At this point, it becomes clear that there are good reasons for discussing at some length the role of perceptual givenness, materiality, and the like, because it allows us to single out exactly what is at stake here. Both Heidegger and Husserl, of course, would say that the total stranger would see something where we see something, and bump her head against things just as we bump our heads against them. The question is one of how to interpret this. Husserl himself admits, or at least comes quite close to admitting, that the stranger would not see "pure materiality" instead of the church that "we" see, but would probably see some sort of building, the purpose of which might be a mystery to her. But if neither the complete stranger nor we have immediate perceptual access to this "basic structure," how does it enter into Husserl's account? Since none of us actually see this merely material-spatial object, why should we assume that it *is there*? It seems that Heidegger's objection, that Husserl takes recourse to construction here instead of paying heed to the phenomenon, is justified. If we subject any perceptual experience of what Husserl calls a "cultural object" to noematic analysis, then we will find, to be sure, something that has color and hardness as well as "usefulness" and "beauty" – *but we will not discover any stratification of these elements*, and certainly not in the way Husserl imagines. Rather, if I consult my normal perception of the keyboard it is as if its "material" ("primary" and "secondary") qualities are themselves *penetrated* by the usefulness, i.e., are qualities that appear in the light, as it were, of the keyboard as something-with-which-to-write. If we pay close phenomenological attention to the keyboard in the "how" of its manifestation in everyday *Umgang*, we discover that it does not manifest itself as something "on hand," with whatever "additional qualities," but rather as something *Um-zu*; and its spatial position, hardness, color, shape, and so forth, so to speak emanate from this "in order to." The noematic phenomenological analysis, if we conduct it without succumbing to the temptation to construct, forces us to confirm Heidegger's claim that the being of the tool is *Zuhandenheit* rather than *Vorhandenheit*. The tool is not, first and foremost, something that occurs at this or that spatial position, but rather a *reference* of "in order to."

If our findings in this section are correct, then Heidegger's characterization of the being of the tool is phenomenologically more convincing than Husserl's theory of stratification. In fact, there seems to be no phenomenological basis for Husserl's "layer ontology" at all. Although Husserl is saying, on the level of noematic "description," much the same as Heidegger, he nevertheless interprets his descriptive findings in a way that does not have any phenomenological corroboration. If I consult my perception of this computer screen in front of me, then on the side of the experienced-just-as-experienced, *I cannot discover any hint of a stratification*, and yet Husserl insists that "in the world of experience, nature is the lowest stratum [*Schichte*], that which founds all others" (*EU*, § 12, p. 54; cf. *Hua* VIII, p. 260; *Hua* III/1, p. 354).

It deserves mention here that there are other, more fruitful models in Husserl, as Heidegger probably knew given his acquaintance with Husserl's *Ideen II*. In that manuscript, Husserl remarks, for instance, that when I read a book there is a sense in which I do not really *see* the physical object, since I am *attuned* differently, I "live" understandingly in the meaning of the book (*Hua* IV, p. 236). In this context, Husserl even emphasizes that the "physical" presence of the book is not independent of the book as a "cultural object." Rather, the cultural meaning, "*in 'animating,' penetrates* the physical whole in a certain way" (*Hua* IV, p. 238). The same, so Husserl explicitly states, holds for other tools and pieces of equipment: their physical properties are "penetrated" and "animated" by spiritual significance, and we can only really see these entities as "things of nature" if we change our attunement (*Einstellung*) (*Hua* IV, pp. 239, 183). Clearly, this view of "penetration" and of the need to perform a complete change of attitude (*Umstellung*, as Heidegger calls it) to gain access to any "thing of nature" is in some tension with Husserl's theory of the foundational "layer" of nature. The account in *Ideen II* is indeed very close to Heidegger's position, and one may wonder why Heidegger does not mention it, given his detailed knowledge of the manuscript.[22] But these matters aside, it seems that Husserl chooses to stick to the view of the *Gebrauchsobjekt* as a multi-layered thing, even though he has himself conducted noematic investigations that seriously question the adequacy of that view. If this is indeed so, then Heidegger's critique is still trenchant.

The description of the being of equipment, or tools, is not one Heidegger seems to attribute fundamental importance to, however – at least not in the years following the publication of his magnum opus. Whereas he insists in *Sein und Zeit* that "[w]hen one designates things as the entities that are 'proximally given,' one goes ontologically astray" (*SZ*, p. 68, cf. p. 201), Heidegger begins in the semesters immediately preceding and following his return to Freiburg to describe Dasein as "being in the midst of nature," and even "in the midst of the present-at-hand" (cf., e.g., *GA* 26, p. 212; *GA* 27, p. 134). It is interesting to note that in the lectures in which Heidegger seems willing to compromise on the ontological description of the mostly encountered intra-mundane entity, he maintains, as unequivocally as ever, his ontology of human Dasein. If the critique of the ontology of *Vorhandensein* as applied to intra-mundane entities appears softened, his critical assessment of the traditional way of characterizing the *subject* does not undergo any change whatsoever. It seems that if there is anywhere Heidegger continues to believe he has made a significant advance in relation to all previous philosophy (including Husserlian phenomenology), it is in the ontological characterization of the entities "we ourselves are." We now turn to this type of entities.

5. THE "MUNDANE" SUBJECT

In one of the Marburg lecture courses, Heidegger surprisingly remarks that Husserl is interested precisely in answering the question of being (*GA* 20, p. 157). The epoché, so Heidegger points out, has the sole of purpose of making entities present with a view to their being (*GA* 20, p. 136). As the context makes clear, Heidegger is again referring to the circumstance that the epoché makes possible a "noematic" investigation, an investigation of the object "in terms of how it is presumed [*im Wie seines Vermeintseins*] in the corresponding intention" (ibid.). However, it is obvious that what Husserl, in Heidegger's eyes, accomplishes is only part of the groundwork for a truly scientific ontology, since it pertains to the noematic side only. According to Heidegger, the problem of being cannot be restricted to the object-side, but is

---

[22] We have already several times referred to Theodore Kisiel's claim that Heidegger studies *Ideen II* intensively while preparing the detailed Husserl-critique to be presented in the lecture course of the summer of 1925 (*GA* 20). Kisiel, "On the Way to Being and Time," p. 195.

"related – all-inclusively – to what constitutes and to what gets constituted" (*Hua* IX, p. 602). And whereas Husserl is described as having at least been close to posing the question of the being of intra-mundane entities, Heidegger insists that the being of subjectivity is something Husserl never attempts to determine (*GA* 17, p. 270; *GA* 20, pp. 157, 160; *GA* 24, p. 174; *GA* 26, p. 167; WDF, p. 177; *GA* 15, p. 382).

This criticism sets the stage for the present section as well as Section 6 below. Is it true that Husserl does not investigate the mode of being of subjectivity? What can be extracted from Husserl's account about the being of the subject? And how does it square with Heidegger's analyses of the mode of being of Dasein? These are the issues that must be elucidated before we can conclude anything in general about the question of being in the phenomenologies of Husserl and Heidegger.

First, let us look more closely at Heidegger's criticism. Heidegger grants that Husserl not only poses, but also answers the question of the mode of being of intra-mundane entities. Heidegger believes, however, that Husserl asks the "question of being" in a very special way, as the following quotation demonstrates:

> But it has become quite clear that the being of the psychic, the intentional, is first suspended in order to allow the pure region of consciousness to be reached. On the basis of this pure region it now first becomes possible to define the suspended being, reality. *The question of being is thus raised, it is even answered.* We have to do solely with the genuine *scientific way of answering it*, which attempts to define the sense of the reality of something real insofar as it manifests itself in consciousness. (*GA* 20, p. 155)

This interpretation is conspicuously close to Husserl's own view of the matter, viz. that constitutive phenomenology makes the being or meaning of being of the world and the intra-mundane things intelligible (*Hua* I, pp. 173-174; *Hua* VIII, pp. 481-482), viz. their "being-there" for an experiencing subjectivity. This is done, of course, in the reduction that leads the phenomenologist's gaze from the noematic world to the subjectivity for which the world manifests itself. It is Heidegger's contention that it is precisely this reduction that makes impossible the posing of the question of being of subjectivity: "In its methodological sense as disregarding, then, the reduction is *in principle inappropriate for determining the being of consciousness* positively" (*GA* 20, p. 150, my emphasis). Heidegger mentions that Husserl would probably object that he only "initially" abstracts from reality in order to observe it and determine its being so much the better, but Heidegger seems to think this reply is insufficient; he expresses serious doubts "whether this can be sufficient for the question of the being of the intentional" (*GA* 20, p. 151). As Heidegger points out later on in the lecture course, the question of the mode of being of the "pure consciousness" that the reduction reveals is even dismissed as "nonsensical" by Husserl (*GA* 20, p. 157).

It might be argued at this point that it is of little consequence whether Husserl positively characterizes the being of subjectivity or not, as long as he does not at least misconstrue it. This is where Heidegger's third main point is apparent. He contends that Husserl's theory becomes "dogmatic" precisely due to the fact that Husserl follows the tradition in not asking what structure the intentionally directed entity has (*GA* 20, p. 63). Husserl does not, according to Heidegger, reach the "region of pure consciousness" by attending to the matters themselves, but rather by uncritically relying on a traditional (Cartesian) notion of philosophy (*GA* 20, p. 147). Consequently, Heidegger thinks Husserl uncritically adopts the Cartesian ontology of the subject as well, that is, conceives "Dasein as a thing with particular properties" (*GA* 17, p. 241, cf. p. 254; *GA* 20, p. 139). This result is indeed an ontologically prejudiced view of the being of the "subject," namely one according to which the subject, despite the ontic resistance against the "thingification" (*Verdinglichung*) of consciousness, is implicitly conceived as something present-at-hand (*SZ*, pp. 46, 114).

The Heideggerian critique thus consists of three essential steps that must be spelled out carefully. First, it is Heidegger's opinion that Husserl's question of being is about "real" being, i.e., the being of intra-mundane things, insofar as they manifest themselves to (a theoretical) consciousness.[23] Second, he claims that it is in and through the method of reduction that this question of being is answered, while this very reduction at the same time prevents the question of the being of *consciousness* from receiving a positive answer. Third, by not giving a *positive* answer to the question of the mode of being of the subject, Husserl tacitly adopts the traditional ontology of presence-at-hand. The two last points will occupy us on the following pages. We must attempt to determine whether the transcendental reduction is an obstacle to the question of the being of the entity that has intentionality, and whether, explicitly or implicitly, we find in Husserl a commitment to the view that the subject is something merely "on hand."

The very first thing to note is that Heidegger's critique appears to jumble what for Husserl are two issues to be kept strictly apart. One concerns what Husserl calls the "mundane" subject, and another the transcendental subject. When Heidegger first charges that the phenomenological reduction makes impossible the question of the mode of being of consciousness, he is explicitly referring to the "reality of the consciousness given in the natural attitude in the factual human being" (*GA* 20, p. 150; cf. *GA* 26, p. 167). For Husserl, it is one thing to say that the question of the being of the mundane subject is not posed, and quite another to claim, as Heidegger also does, that the question of being is not posed with regard to "pure" consciousness (*GA* 20, p. 157) or transcendental subjectivity. This latter type of criticism is the one that manifests itself in Heidegger's claim that Husserl thinks "ontology" only concerns the object, and not the subject (*GA* 26, p. 190). In other words, we must both consider whether and, if so, how Husserl poses and attempts to answer the question of being of transcendental subjectivity, and ask the same questions about Husserl's account of the mundane subject. Let us start with the latter.

The mundane subject and the transcendental subject are not, as noted above, two beings. There are not two entities, but only one entity that – strange as it may seem – can be described in two quite different ways. In the one description, I am the subject *for* the world and everything mundane, and in the other I am just one, relatively

---

[23] Eugen Fink is of the same opinion in *Nähe und Distanz*, pp. 286-287.

small and insignificant intra-mundane entity. Insofar as the two descriptions, then, describe the same, numerically identical entity, a quite natural question is what it is that they each describe. What about this entity can be the subject of two very different descriptions (cf. *Hua* IX, p. 602)? Interestingly enough, Husserl seems to want to capture the difference by distinguishing between my "human" and my "transcendental" *being*:

> Thus, if we now return to our pure philosophical meditation, there is no doubt that we have to distinguish – indeed, as a beginning philosopher I must distinguish – between my human existence [*Dasein*], originally and perceptually given to me in mundane self-experience, and my transcendental being [*transzendentales Sein*], originally given to me in transcendental self-experience [...]. (*Hua* VIII, p. 73)

In other words, there is one entity only, but this entity must be conceived as having two different modes of being. As a "human being," I have the mode of being of something intra-mundane, and as a transcendental subject, I have a completely different mode of being. When we are describing the transcendental "being," we are – in comparison with the natural, mundane concept – dealing with a reformation (*Umbildung*) of the concept of being, Husserl says (*HuDo* II/1, p. 137n). Thus, when Husserl (as we see in Chapter II) claims that only transcendental phenomenology can lay claim to the title of "universal ontology," he appears to use the word "ontology" in something like its Heideggerian sense. But the question Heidegger would want us to raise and attempt to answer phenomenologically, is whether one of these ontological descriptions might be more in accordance with actual experience than the other. If it is correct, as David Carr recently claims, that Husserlian (and Kantian) transcendental philosophy "hesitates" between two incompatible descriptions of the human subject,[24] then what Heidegger does is to push for a phenomenologically based decision.

It is true, of course, that we find something like both these descriptions in Heidegger. As Heidegger points out more than once, it is not only the case that one "can" interpret one's own being as presence-at-hand. Rather, everyday Dasein almost *always* interprets both the encountered tools and itself and other Dasein as something merely on hand within the world (*SZ*, pp. 58, 130). And yet Heidegger also maintains that "Daseins, we ourselves, are never present-at-hand; Dasein exists" (*GA* 24, p. 37; cf. *SZ*, pp. 42-43; *GA* 21, p. 240n). This leads Carr to surmise that the early Heidegger himself hesitates between the two incompatible descriptions of subjectivity,[25] but I think it is evident from Heidegger's work in the twenties that he does not consider the everyday interpretation adequate. He thinks it is simply a misinterpretation, and that an important part of what phenomenology has to do is precisely to refute such "disguises and concealments" (*SZ*, p. 58).

---

[24] Carr, *The Paradox of Subjectivity*, p. 137.
[25] *The Paradox of Subjectivity*, p. 140: "Like Kant and Husserl, Heidegger in this work [*Sein und Zeit*] essentially leaves us suspended between these two incompatible views of ourselves, as if the alteration between them were simply and descriptively an inescapable part of human experience."

Let us consider, then, what it is that Husserl calls our "mundane" being. According to Husserl, as we have seen, the "human being" or the mundane subject is a type of entity in the world. Husserl appears to change his view more than once on the question whether the human being is really a "double reality," an entity consisting of two "layers" (*Hua* IV, p. 162; *Hua* IX, pp. 106, 109), or whether this way of conceiving mundane subjectivity in fact cannot do justice to the fundamental *unity* of this entity (*Hua* IV, p. 240; *Hua* VI, pp. 222, 227),[26] but this is not the crucial issue at present. The important thing is not even whether, according to Husserl, the subjective aspect or side – the "soul" or the "psyche" – of the human being is *itself* nothing but a worldly thing, a "reality." Whereas in *Ideen II*, Husserl emphasizes that matter and soul have the same "ontological form," viz. the form "substantial reality" (*Hua* IV, p. 125), then he explicitly rejects this view in *Krisis* (*Hua* VI, pp. 216, 236). But as I said, this is not the point. The point is rather that Husserl apparently maintains throughout his career the position that the mundane subject *as a whole* is nothing but a thing in the world:

In one attitude [viz. the "mundane" attitude] my ego [*Ich*] and the ego-acts are characters of a real human being – a type of object [*einer Objektart*] or, more precisely, a type of thing [*Dingart*] in the world [...]. (*Hua* VI, p. 457; cf. p. 149)

The human being in the world; belonging to the world, on hand [*vorhanden*] for one another, like things are on hand for everyone. But it is characteristic of these onhandnesses [*Vorhandenheiten*] that they are ego-subjects that are conscious of the onhandnesses, have ideas and knowledge of them [...].

These special properties [*besonderen Eigenheiten*], however, are properties of real things [*Realitäten*] in the world. And so are my properties, too, as I am a human being and encounter myself as such. (*Hua* IX, p. 603)

Husserl believes that, considered in the natural attitude, *whatever else I might be*, I am first of all some real object or thing at this or that place in the world. Whatever we might say about me, and whether or not it makes sense to say that my soul belongs to me as a "layer," even regardless of whether or not my psyche and its states and qualities can be called realities in the same sense as mere material things and their properties – regardless of all of this, I discover myself as well as others as *things*, as *Vorhandenheiten* in the world.

Heidegger is undoubtedly right that this is because I have a physical body, and that this body is the founding layer – according to the natural mundane interpretation, as portrayed by Husserl – for all other qualities I might have (cf. *GA* 20, p. 172). Heidegger is also right that in conceiving the "human being" in this way, Husserl displays a strong commitment to the ontology of presence-at-hand:

---

[26] If we could take the latter as Husserl's last word on the matter, then the question would remain to what extent this is in fact an advance beyond Descartes. After all, Descartes knew very well that I am not in the body "as a sailor is present in a ship, but [...] I am very closely joined and, as it were, intermingled with it, so that I and the body form a unit" (*Meditations on First Philosophy* [*The Philosophical Writings of Descartes*, Vol. II, p. 56]). However, when Husserl emphasizes that he is no longer talking about "substances" in any sense, but about *abstract* moments (*Hua* VI, p. 232), or indeed even dismisses that conception in favor of the view that we are dealing only with two different "perspectives" (*Blickrichtungen*) (*Hua* XXIX, p. 159), then he seems to leave the Cartesian view behind.

here, the human being as a whole is certainly conceived as a "thing of nature in the widest sense." But, Heidegger asks, is this really a "natural" way of conceiving the human being, or is it not rather a *naturalistic* interpretation (*GA* 20, p. 155)? Is it in fact natural to experience oneself and others as "objects" or "things" in the world?

In *Being and Nothingness*, Sartre describes the strange experience of seeing his own vertebrae displayed on a screen. Watching these pictures of intra-mundane objects, "it was only through a reasoning process"[27] that he could link them with himself. Seeing x-ray pictures of one's insides (or those of others) is of course already a strange experience, because one does not normally have visual access to them; but there is more to it than that. For Sartre, the process of reasoning is necessary because in such a situation, I see myself (or my body) as I am for others, rather than for myself. However, the question I want to raise here is whether part of the reason why an intellectual activity must be unfolded here couldn't be that in the kind of situation Sartre mentions, I experience myself (or parts of myself) as *present-at-hand* objects – a very unusual way to experience not only myself, as Sartre thinks, but in fact others too. If a friend has something in her eye, and we have to help her get it out, there sometimes comes a point where we suddenly see her eye as an "object." One hardly ever relates to anyone entirely, or unequivocally, as present-at-hand, but nevertheless there is a sense in which one may sometimes *almost* see the eye of another as some curved, whitish thing with a certain colored pattern, and *almost* see its movements as mere mechanical movements. Obviously, it is not that we then all of a sudden see something that we do not normally see, because we perceive the very same eye that we have seen so many times before (though perhaps watched less intensively). What seems to have changed is only the *way in which* we perceive the eye of our friend. The situation, in other words, is strange because all of a sudden we have a different approach to this eye, we now understand it as something on-hand rather than as the eye of our friend. It is highly unconvincing, I believe, to attempt to capture what goes on here by claiming that we normally "live" experientially at a higher constitutive level than the one we are here suddenly somehow arrested at. It seems to be my pre-ontological approach that changes, rather than the "stratum" of being of which I am attentive. In fact, if we carefully consult our experiences of each other, we will find not so much as a trace of "stratification" on the noematic side. My friend is not normally experienced as a *Körper* plus something more, and what happens when I suddenly experience her eye as an "object" is not that this "something more" momentarily disappears from the experience. And of course, neither do I experience myself in any of these ways. There seems, rather, to be a fundamental divide between the "as what" of my normal approach to others and myself, and the "as what" of our example – a divide that seems very adequately captured by Heidegger's notion of *Seinsverständnis*.

Again, the issue is not whether I experience others or myself as having some kind of physical presence in the world. Nobody wants to deny that I do. When I am

---

[27] Sartre, *Being and Nothingness*, p. 304.

faced with an opponent on the soccer field, there is no question of her or my physical presence in space, but the dispute concerns the proper way to interpret this. The question is whether the "physical" and "spatial" presence of my opponent and myself warrant the view that we are both some sort of thing or object, some sort of *Vorhandenheit* in the world. Husserl claims that when I encounter the body of the other, I can choose to focus on "the sensorily perceivable, that is, the pure materiality [*Körperlichkeit*], or I can attend to the other person" (*Hua* XV, p. 496). Yet as he himself admits, even when I do the latter, the understanding intentions directed at the person remain "there" (*mit da*), in the background, and do not disappear (*Hua* XV, p. 506). But if this is so, if there really is no way (in an everyday context at least) to see the body of the other *purely* as a physical body, as something "on hand" (cf. *GA* 21, p. 240n), why assume that the best way to explain the other's "bodily" presence is by reference to a foundational, physical body, on which then the layers that constitute her person are built? Is this not an example of the kind of philosophical "construction" that phenomenology precisely has to free philosophy from?

Perhaps it is tempting for Husserl scholars to reply at this point that what we are here referring to as "normal," "everyday" life is what Husserl would call the "personalistic" attitude. As mentioned in Chapter I, this attitude is only one of the sub-attitudes within the natural attitude. Although Husserl agrees that the personalistic attitude is the one we mostly live in (*Hua* IV, p. 183), he insists that it is also possible to assume what he calls the "naturalistic" attitude. In this latter attitude – which is presumably the attitude in which, for example, a physicist or a chemist works – we abstract from the higher levels of spiritual meaning and direct ourselves towards the purely physical aspect of the world. So here, at least, we do have access to the human being as something "on hand," as a thing within the world. Obviously, however, Heidegger is precisely critical of Husserl's way of construing the difference between the naturalistic and personalistic attitudes. Husserl's view of the difference between everyday experience and the experience of the chemist in the laboratory relies completely on the layer ontology: although the world is much more than a world of pure physical objects, we can, as it were, remove abstractly the layers of cultural significance, etc., and reach the founding layer of physicality (the naturalistic attitude). But what if this is not so; what if the "personalistic," everyday, attitude is one in which we have activated a completely different pre-ontological understanding of being than the one the chemist lives in when she is observing fluids in a test tube? This is, we should note, a dispute *internal* to the "personalistic" attitude, internal to "everyday experience." The issue is whether something like Husserl's "layer ontology" can make intelligible the things we experience – *as we experience them* – in "personalistic," everyday life. With regard to subjectivity, the question concerns whether we really experience each other and ourselves as physical things with certain "additional" characteristics when we are outside the laboratory and the operating theatre, or whether something quite different is going on.[28]

Interestingly enough, there seem to be occasions when Husserl tries to distance himself somewhat from the notion of the "mundane subject." There are occasions, in other words, when Husserl no longer seems to "hesitate" between the two descriptions of subjectivity, but decides in favor of the transcendental subject. One might reply that this is hardly surprising given the circumstance that, according to Husserl, it is the *transcendental* subject that constitutes itself as a human being in the world – it is *because* it is the former that it cannot help being the latter. But I think there are places where Husserl goes considerably further than that, claiming that only one "being" truly belongs to the subject, namely its transcendental being. For instance, Husserl remarks in *Zur Phänomenologie der Intersubjektivität III* that the mundane subject is like a "role" that the transcendental subject plays (*Hua* XV, p. 372), thus indicating that it might not be the true being of subjectivity. Another passage is even clearer: "The soul is only alongside and within [*an und innerhalb*] nature in an improper sense. In its proper and true being the soul is transcendental subjectivity" (*Hua* XXIX, p. 183). Husserl, it seems, after all, does not think that my mundane being is a being that belongs to me as authentically as my transcendental being does. In fact, the quotation comes very close to conceding that there *is* no such thing as a "soul" in nature – indeed, that all there is is the transcendental subject. The "authentic and true being" of the "soul" is not its being-a-soul (being something constituted) at all, but being a transcendental subjectivity.

6. THE BEING OF THE SUBJECT

If our findings in the previous section are correct, then Husserl's notion of the mundane subject is in fact something we hardly ever experience (although it might be a quite natural way to *interpret* oneself). We are thus left with the two issues of Husserl's characterization of the being of the transcendental subject and Heidegger's conception of the being of Dasein.

According to Husserl, the transcendental reduction is the method intended to take us back from the experienced world to the experiencing subject (*Hua* IX, p. 340). Indeed, in Chapter II we quote Husserl saying that a real presentation of the transcendental subject only takes place in the phenomenological reduction (*Hua* VIII, p. 80). In the reduction we receive an answer to the question concerning how a subject that is to be the subject experiencing the (bracketed) world "looks, and must

---

[28] One therefore cannot, in my view, claim that Husserl is more "accurate" with reference to the fact that we do, sometimes, experience something present-at-hand, as Dermot Moran claims in his article "Heidegger's Critique of Husserl's and Brentano's Accounts of Intentionality." The *main* issue is whether one can make intelligible entities such as other subjects and tools the way Husserl attempts it, not whether we ever experience something merely on-hand, nor in fact whether these latter experiences necessarily presuppose a switch from some other, and more original, pre-ontological mode of understanding (as Heidegger often claims) (e.g., *SZ*, p. 61).

look" (*Hua* I, p. 86). The issue, however, is not whether the phenomenological reduction uncovers a transcendental subjectivity – because Heidegger recognizes that this is what it does (*GA* 20, p. 150) – but whether it allows the specific question of its *mode of being* to surface, or simply implies the positing of properties of an entity left undiscussed regarding its being (cf. *GA* 61, p. 142). As emphasized in the last section of Chapter III, Heidegger attaches great importance to the explicit grasping of the "ontological difference," as that by means of which the theme of ontology is brought clearly into view (*GA* 24, p. 22). Without explicitly contrasting entities to being, one is almost certain to take a certain inherited notion of being for granted, according to Heidegger. So let us look more closely at what goes on in Husserl's transcendental reduction, to see if we can find some sort of "ontological difference" in play there.

A number of times, we have stressed the fact that, before the onset of the reductive "detective work," the transcendental subject is defined by Husserl as a "point with no extension," as the "point" where everything manifests itself. Transcendental subjectivity, in other words, is not posited as any kind of object, but is defined as the dative of manifestation of each and every object, as well as the world-horizon in which objects are manifest. The question is whether it makes any sense to say that the characteristics we unveil in the transcendental reduction as characteristics of this subjectivity are "properties" of some entity. Properties must be properties of something, but is the transcendental subject really something that may function as a bearer of properties? Husserl's own answer to this question is quite illuminating:

> The ego [*Das Ich*] is not a substrate, not a "bearer," but rather an ego, a source point [*Quellpunkt*] – yet all images are actually inapplicable. (*Hua* XIII, p. 457)

> [T]he ego-pole [*Ichpol*] is what it is, not a bearer, not a substrate for affections and actions, etc.; but precisely ego, point-of-inward-directed-radiation [*Einstrahlungspunkt*], functional center [*Funtionszentrum*] for affections, point-of-outward-directed-radiation [*Ausstrahlungspunkt*], activity-center [*Tätigkeitszentrum*] of activities, of acts. (*Hua* XIV, p. 30)

In this context, Husserl explicitly states that the ego has no properties whatsoever, that it is completely empty in terms of "*sachhaltige*" characteristics (*Hua* XIV, p. 23; cf. *SZ*, p. 12). This all makes perfect sense as an elaboration of the initial, "functional" definition of the transcendental subject, but what about the full, concrete transcendental subjectivity, as this is gradually unveiled by phenomenology? What about all those characteristics we discover in the reduction, e.g., the kinesthetic potential discussed in the preceding chapter? What are these characteristics, if not precisely some sort of properties or "attributes"? Husserl's intuition, I think, is that the reduction approaches the subject in a radically new way. Transcendental phenomenology initially defines the subject as "empty," as "nothing," as the *point* where all content, all "something," manifests itself, thus *not as a possible "substrate" for, or "bearer" of properties at all*. A point with no extension can have no content, can be the bearer of no properties – the only "content" we initially find "in" the transcendental subject is on the side of the experienced world, whose dative of manifestation the subject is.[29] This functional definition and the reduction that Husserl envisions as the method to characterize the subject function, I submit, more or less like an explicit introduction of the "ontological difference." All recourse to ontic considerations (of entities and their properties, layers, etc.) is made impossible, and only the possibility of discovering characters of *being* remains. The transcendental subject is nothing but the "for whom" of world-manifestation, and thus the reduction is nothing but the method to unveil what it means to "be" the "for" (cf. *GA* 21, p. 331). Husserl may never explicitly formulate a principle of "ontological difference," but his "functional" definition of transcendental subjectivity and the reductive method for disclosing it ban ontic considerations so efficiently that nothing but the question of the being of the subject is left. The characteristics discovered in Chapter V cannot be viewed as properties that the transcendental subject could in principle be stripped of. Rather, they are the very structures that *make* transcendental subjectivity transcendental subjectivity, and if we "remove them," then no "naked thing," or essentially altered thing, remains. On the contrary, the kinesthetic *Vermöglichkeiten* are structures in the *being* of the transcendental subject, structures in the absence of which *nothing* would "be there." In his reductive investigations of transcendental subjectivity, then, Husserl does not "present *an sich* determinations of an objectivity, which has not been discussed with regard to its meaning of being" (*GA* 61, p. 142). On the contrary, it makes perfect sense to say that he is precisely uncovering the manner of being of subjectivity.

Therefore, Heidegger's charge that the reduction is fundamentally inadequate for giving a positive answer to the question of the being of the subject seems not entirely justified. If there is any mode of being (as opposed to "properties," "layers," etc.) that is being investigated in Husserlian phenomenology – investigated precisely in and through the reduction – it is the being of the transcendental subject.[30] The subject is functionally defined in such a way that one cannot consider it a bearer of properties, but only ask how it has to *be* in order to be a transcendental subject, i.e., a "place" where the world and everything mundane appears. In the phenomenological reduction, Husserl posits no "*an sich*" properties of an entity left undiscussed regarding its being, because he posits no "entity" and no "properties" at all. Instead, the reduction is intended to do nothing but unveil the *mode of being* of the subject, insofar as it is to be the subject of the world described noematically.

---

[29] Cf. David Carr, *The Paradox of Subjectivity*, p. 94.
[30] Cf. Rudolf Bernet, "Phenomenological Reduction and the Double Life of the Subject," p. 255: "by revealing the correlation between constituting consciousness and the constituted world, the phenomenological reduction makes manifest precisely the (pre)-being of this consciousness and the being of this world as well as the difference between them." See, too, Klaus Held, "Heidegger und das Prinzip der Phänomenologie," p. 121.

Heidegger claims in general that the notion of the "subject" remains committed to the ontology of presence-at-hand (*SZ*, pp. 46, 114, 320).[31] But is that in fact the mode of being that Husserl attributes to transcendental subjectivity? This is a question we should be able to answer given the discussion in the present chapter. The concepts of "thing," "substance," "nature," and the like, as well as such concepts as "property," and "attribute," are precisely the sort of concepts that we cannot apply to transcendental subjectivity, as it is defined above. Transcendental subjectivity is the "source" (*Quellpunkt*) of all that these concepts apply to; it is the place that allows for things of nature, for substances with properties, to manifest themselves. Clearly, then, to accuse Husserl of being committed to the view that the subject *itself* is something present-at-hand is absurd.

Our discussion in Chapter V points in the same direction, although giving more concrete information about the being of the subject. As noted, Husserlian transcendental subjectivity is defined by its intentional openness towards or directedness at the world. The mode of being of transcendental subjectivity is its continuous life in world-constitution (*Hua* VI, p. 275), according to Husserl – something that hardly seems compatible with the notion of merely "occurring," "on hand." Indeed, as we conclude in that chapter, there is a remarkable convergence of Husserl's reflections on the embodied transcendental subject and Heidegger's ruminations on Dasein's "being-in-the-world" though not "inside" the world. In fact, Husserl's descriptions appear to have the advantage of being somewhat more concrete than Heidegger's. Clearly, if our findings in Chapter V are correct, then Husserl's conception of the transcendental subject is not committed to the notion of presence-at-hand. Rather, it looks as if Husserl introduces the notion of a completely different mode of being; a mode of being that seems at once anything but the being of a "thing," or an "object," *and* seems to be an awkward candidate for the traditional title of "subject."

It would appear, then, that Heidegger's critique of Husserl's phenomenology of the subject is misguided. In Husserl's description of transcendental subjectivity, we find no commitment to *Vorhandenheit*, nor does Husserl neglect the task of giving a positive characterization of the mode of being of the subject. However, despite our acknowledgement of the fundamental merits of Husserl's phenomenology of the lived body presented in the previous chapter, we also suggest a weakness in Husserl's approach. Although Husserl successfully redefines subjectivity in a revolutionary way, he continues to move around in the dichotomies of "inner" and "outer," "lived body" and "physical body," and even "subject" and "object." The question I want to raise here is whether this might be more problematic than it perhaps seems at first sight, and whether Heidegger's seemingly "abstract" reflections on Dasein might after all be phenomenologically more adequate. In other words, we must ask ourselves the following question: which is the more adequate

---

[31] Cf. Husserl's protest against the generality of that claim (RB, p. 37).

way to *conceptualize* the being of the entity we ourselves are – Husserl's references to the embodied subject, or Heidegger's reflections on the *Da* of Dasein?

In Chapter III, we emphasize two things about Heidegger's concept of Dasein. First, we point out that Heidegger never intends with his notion of Dasein to refer to anything other than what is traditionally called subjectivity (cf. *GA* 27, pp. 72, 115). Heidegger, however, wants to carry out a "fundamental revision of the hitherto reigning concept of subjectivity [*des bisherigen Subjektbegriffes*]" (*GA* 27, p. 115). Precisely in order to revise or redefine the notion of the entity we ourselves are, Heidegger chooses to replace the traditional notions of "human being" and "subject" with that of Dasein (*GA* 63, p. 21; *GA* 24, p. 90). Second, we suggest that the concept of Dasein is a "formally indicative" concept, i.e., a concept that is intended both to fend off undesired connotations – more precisely to prevent any slide into ontic considerations – and to direct the phenomenologist's gaze towards the theme of being. Both these points taken together, we may say that Heidegger introduces the notion of Dasein in an attempt to capture more adequately the peculiar *mode of being* that the subject has.

Etymology aside, "Dasein" is, in Heidegger's use of it, to be read as a conjunction of the two concepts of "*Da*" and "*Sein*." Neither of these is supposed to be interpreted in any even remotely profound manner; in fact they can be perfectly adequately translated "here" or "there" and "being."[32] Being human, Heidegger claims, is being (*sein*) a "there" (*Da*) (*GA* 20, p. 349). Indeed, one gets the impression that this is *all* Heidegger intends to say with the concept of Dasein: "Dasein is the entity that is something like a 'there'" (*dasjenige Seiende, das so etwas wie ein "Da" ist*) (*GA* 27, p. 136; cf. *SZ*, pp. 132-133). The first thing Heidegger points out to elucidate this somewhat odd characterization is that a "there" is something "in which" something can manifest itself. A "there" is a place, a locus, something that can be occupied by someone or something; for instance, "there" where my writing desk now stands, there used to be an armchair. A *Da*, in other words, is a sphere of dis-closedness (*Erschlossenheit*) into which something like desks and armchairs can enter in some way or other. Strange as it may seem, this is Heidegger's point: "In the expression 'there' we have in view this essential disclosedness" (*SZ*, p. 132).[33] A human being is a sphere of disclosedness in the sense that other entities, whether with the mode of being of equipment, or mere

---

[32] See Daniel Dahlstrom's remarks on the proper translation of the concept of Dasein in *Heidegger's Concept of Truth*, pp. xxiii-xxv.

[33] For reasons that need not concern us here, Heidegger feels entitled to call this disclosedness of Dasein "original truth" (*SZ*, pp. 220-221), a decision that has spawned a lively discussion in the literature on Heidegger. Ernst Tugendhat provides a detailed critique of Heidegger's identification of disclosedness with truth in *Der Wahrheitsbegriff bei Husserl und Heidegger* (esp. pp. 259-405), a critique that is by and large seconded by Cristina Lafont, *Sprache und Welterschließung* (esp. pp. 148-231). For two very different attempts to defend Heidegger against Tugendhat's critique, see Carl F. Gethmann, *Dasein: Erkennen und Handeln*, pp. 115-168, and Daniel Dahlstrom, *Heidegger's Concept of Truth*, esp. pp. 394-423. Dahlstrom's attempt (and implicitly also Gethmann's) is criticized in Søren Overgaard, "Heidegger's Concept of Truth Revisited."

present-at-hand things, or indeed other human beings, are manifest *to* the human being. In other words, being a "there" first of all means being the "peculiar place for the totality of entities" (*GA* 27, p. 360), or being-in-the-world in the sense of being an *openness* towards the world (*GA* 21, p. 143). As we see in detail in the first section of the present chapter, entities cannot manifest themselves unless something like their being is understood, thus Dasein may also be described as the place of understanding of being (*SZ*, p. 439). Hence, *Da-Sein* seems to indicate nothing but the "place of being," the place (*Da*) where something like modes of being (*Sein*) are understood, and where entities therefore manifest themselves.[34] It is of the utmost importance to keep in mind that this is an indication of the very *being* of the subject, according to Heidegger, i.e., it is not some property or feature that Dasein could in principle do without.

Clearly, if the mode of being of subjectivity is its being the place where something like "being" is understood, and where a world and intra-mundane entities are manifest, then it is hardly surprising that Heidegger should also refer to Dasein as the place of the "transcendental" (*Ort des Transzendentalen*) (*Hua* IX, p. 601). The "*Da*" of Dasein formally indicates precisely the functional definition that we, quoting Klaus Held, give for transcendental subjectivity: "[the] place of the appearance of the world."[35] Dasein, that is, appears to be nothing but Heidegger's new label for transcendental subjectivity, insofar as it is investigated with regard to its manner of being.

But Heidegger wants to extract more from the concept of Dasein. The "there" does not only indicate the manifestness of a world and intra-mundane entities. As Heidegger says, our "being amidst... [*Sein bei...*] itself, we ourselves as being amidst... in this way, is, together with the manifestness of the present-at-hand, 'also' manifest [*offenbar*]" (*GA* 27, p. 134). In other words, the "there" that the human being is, is a sphere of disclosedness of "being," world, and intra-worldly entities (the place of the transcendental), but it is at the same time a "there" that is *itself disclosed*. As Heidegger puts it in his first Marburg lecture course:

We also say of a stone that it is there – but the stone is there within the circumference of my world, my being, and the latter is in the world in the manner of *having-the-world-visible* [*die Welt Sichtig-habens*]. Having-visible means the co-visibility [*Mit-sichtig-sein*] of *that* entity that is in the world. This *co-visibility* is expressed in the *there*. (*GA* 17, pp. 288-289)

There are two aspects here to be addressed. The first, which I will not discuss in detail, concerns what – with a term Heidegger explicitly warns against using (*GA* 27, p. 135) – may be called self-awareness. Being a "there" is being co-visible, or disclosed to oneself, Heidegger claims: "The world is at any given time not only *disclosed*, [...] but Dasein is itself there relative to its in-being, *itself there for itself*" (*GA* 20, p. 348; cf. *SZ*, p. 132). As Heidegger emphasizes, this is so quite

---

[34] For some corroboration of this reading, see Otto Pöggeler, *Der Denkweg Martin Heideggers*, pp. 259-260, and John Sallis, *Delimitations*, pp. 112-118.
[35] Held, "Einleitung," p. 41.

independently of whether or not Dasein reflects upon itself, or notices itself, at all (*GA* 27, p. 134).[36]

The second important aspect of the disclosedness of the "there" itself is the manifestness to *others*. As a sphere of disclosedness or openness, Dasein has, as Heidegger puts it, "also already entered into the manifestness of the others" (*GA* 27, p. 138). How this naturally leads Heidegger to a discussion of being-with-others need not concern us here; as Heidegger himself emphasizes, the human being is as such disclosed, independently of whether or not another is actually there to watch it (*GA* 27, p. 129). Indeed, we should not tie this openness or manifestness – as Sartre presumably would – so closely to the (potential or actual) gaze of others at all. Dasein is disclosed *von sich aus*, thus "it does not first become unhidden because another Dasein tears it out of its hiddenness. Insofar as Dasein exists, it has torn itself out of hiddenness – or brings its unhiddenness with itself, as it were" (*GA* 27, p. 130). The entity that is something like a "there" is always already unhidden, manifest, disclosed; this is not the result of some encounter with another subjectivity, not even of a potential such encounter. The "there" of Dasein conveys not only the disclosedness of a world, and modes of being, and the uncoveredness of intra-mundane entities *to* the human being; nor is the scope of its significance exhausted when the disclosedness *of* the "there" to itself is mentioned. In addition to all this, being "there" also means being *exposed*. This exposedness is not merely the exposedness to a possible external *perceiver*, but to a world that surrounds and overpowers Dasein, a world in relation to which Dasein is powerless (*GA* 26, p. 279). The exposedness indicated by the *Da*, Heidegger says, is the exposedness of a subject thrown into, or abandoned in, a world it cannot master (cf. *GA* 27, pp. 326, 329).

It is therefore no surprise that Heidegger links the "there" with the spatiality of the human being. In Heidegger's own words from *Sein und Zeit*, spatial significance "is also implied in the 'there' of Dasein" (*SZ*, p. 299). As Heidegger emphasizes, when being-in-the-world is contrasted with "being-contained-in," this is not intended to mean that every kind of spatiality is denied Dasein: "On the contrary, Dasein itself has a 'being-in-space' of its own; but this in turn is possible only *on the basis of being-in-the-world in general*" (*SZ*, p. 56; cf. *GA* 20, p. 307). Dasein has, Heidegger explains, a peculiar *existential* spatiality (*SZ*, p. 56). Dasein is *in* space, rather than extra-spatial, but clearly it is Heidegger's intention that this being-in-space should be interpreted in a very different way from the way stones and tables are in space:

Neither may Dasein's spatiality be interpreted as an imperfection which adheres to existence by reason of the fatal "linkage of the spirit to a body." On the contrary, because Dasein is "spiritual," *and only because*

---

[36] For a discussion of Heidegger's account of self-awareness, see Steven Crowell, "Subjectivity: Locating the First-Person in *Being and Time*." That Husserl, too, has a theory of pre-reflective self-awareness is argued by Dan Zahavi in *Self-Awareness and Alterity*.

of this, it can be spatial in a way which remains essentially impossible for any extended corporeal thing. (*SZ*, p. 368)[37]

As a preliminary indication of how the human being is "in space," Heidegger says that it literally "takes space in" (*nimmt* [...] *Raum ein*) (*SZ*, p. 368), and that it "arranges" or "furnishes" it for itself (*Sicheinräumen*). The human being does not just occur at some spatial position; it does not just "fill up space," but *in-vades* or *in-habits* space.

The exposedness and disclosedness that Heidegger extracts from the "there" is thus anything but abstract speculation. Indeed, it must be understood in a very concrete sense. As already mentioned, Heidegger begins in the wake of *Sein und Zeit* to lay greater emphasis on this point, now describing Dasein as completely "in the midst of what is" (*inmitten des Seienden*) (*WM*, p.139; *GA* 27, p. 328; *GA* 29/30, p. 403), but in fact this is just an accentuation of the position in the magnum opus, not a change of position. The exposedness of Dasein is its thrown being "out there," *in* the world that surrounds it and overpowers it, the world in which Dasein is concretely, physically and spatially present, though not present-at-hand (cf. *GA* 20, pp. 307-308). Although Heidegger rarely says it in so many words, it is clear from one of the passages quoted in Chapter V that Dasein's unhiddenness and disclosedness in the midst of what is has everything to do with its "being-embodied:" "Dasein is thrown, factical, *thoroughly amidst nature through its bodiliness*" (*GA* 26, p. 212, my emphasis). This is the essence of the third formal indication that Heidegger's concept of Dasein carries.[38]

The being of the subject, then, is the disclosedness of being and world, and the uncoveredness of entities, as well as self-disclosedness and bodily exposedness in the midst of the world. To be sure, Dasein never has the mode of being of something present-at-hand within the world (*SZ*, p. 43), but on the other hand, it is quite literally *in* the world and not just "related" to the world. Subjectivity is a "there" that both *lets* the world and everything mundane be manifest, and *is itself* manifest, exposed. *I am the point where the world opens up, but in such an amazing way that I am myself essentially manifested as well*, according to Heidegger.

But still, would Heidegger's account not benefit from the use of more concrete and familiar terms, e.g., a more unhesitating use of the notion of body? It probably would. However, we must try to look at the matter with *ontological* eyes. Is Husserl's phenomenology of the embodied subject really an ontologically adequate way to approach the entity that we ourselves are? Is it not rather the case that for this

---

[37] The strange circumstance that Heidegger should use the concept of "*geistig*" here – one of the terms that, according to *Sein und Zeit*, is precisely to be *avoided* (*SZ*, p. 46) – is noticed by Jacques Derrida, who devotes an entire book to tracing this concept through Heidegger's works. Cf. Derrida, *Of Spirit: Heidegger and the Question*.

[38] One misses Heidegger's point completely, if one assumes that Heidegger refuses and "*resists* [...] the return to an embodied Dasein" (Alweiss, *The World Unclaimed*, p. 90; cf. pp. 103-104, 124, 142, 165), and as a consequence ultimately describes a Dasein that has to be characterized as disembodied and devoid of spatiality (ibid., pp. 87, 107, 125).

type of approach to yield a proper understanding of subjectivity, an ontological elucidation of subjectivity must have been carried out in other terms already? The problem with Husserl's phenomenology of embodiment, so I claim, is that the "dualistic" terms used in the analysis continue, as it were, to haunt the analysis, precisely also when the analysis in fact seems to indicate the inadequacy of such terms. This difficulty in the Husserlian approach may very well appear harmless and insignificant on the "ontic" level of discourse of Chapter V. But it is Heidegger's contention that, precisely for an *ontology* of subjectivity, it has fateful consequences.

Apart from the claim that such an approach tacitly remains committed to the ontology of presence-at-hand (a claim we have already rejected), Heidegger's major objection to the phenomenology of the body concerns precisely the tendency of the latter to remain stuck in inadequate traditional terminology. The critique is found in various places in *Sein und Zeit* and in lecture courses from the twenties, and it turns on the conception of the "body" as one of the "elements" making up the human being. As pointed out above, the "there" of Dasein means both the disclosedness of a world, of being, and of intra-mundane entities, and Dasein's own manifestness and exposedness. According to Heidegger, it is tempting to construe the first of these characteristics as belonging to something like a "soul," and the latter (the exposedness) as having to do with the bodily "side" of the subject. The result is that the mode of being of the thus *composed* entity as a whole becomes obscure, Heidegger claims:

Hence being-in is not to be explained ontologically by some ontical characterization, as if one were to say, for instance, that being-in in a world is a spiritual property, and that man's "spatiality" is a result of his bodily nature (which, at the same time always gets "founded" upon corporeality). Here again we are faced with the being-present-at-hand-together of some spiritual thing along with a corporeal thing, while the being of the entity thus compounded remains more obscure than ever. (*SZ*, p. 56)

Even if this does not necessarily mean that the subject becomes construed as something present-at-hand, it certainly means that the ontological question of how to understand the being of the *whole human being* becomes utterly perplexing (*SZ*, p. 48; *GA* 20, p. 173). The human being is cut in pieces, as it were, it is viewed as composed of a number of very different elements, and it becomes very hard to understand the entity that we ourselves are in any unitary way (WDF, pp. 161-162). Do I have the mode of being of my body, or of my soul, or does the composition of these have its own mode of being (and if so, then which)?

It would be easy to reply that this cannot count as an argument against Husserl, who, as we have seen, attributes bodily existence to the subject *as subject*. It is only insofar as I am a kinesthetic subject that a world can be presented perceptually to me. When Heidegger refers to the division of subjectivity into various domains, is it not in fact he who displays a very traditional view of the body, a view that Husserl has precisely overcome? I do not think this is entirely correct. To be sure, the way Heidegger presents this objection – with reference to "soul-things" and their connection with "body-things" – Husserl goes scot-free. However, Heidegger's deeper concern seems to be that the notion of "body," even if it has been used to radically conquer the Cartesian conception of the subject, is a Trojan horse that carries, if not exactly a Cartesian dualism, then at least some type of *composition* view in its belly, just waiting to leap out. As the volumes *Zur Phänomenologie der Intersubjektivität* document, Husserl keeps attempting to make my body and bodily movement intelligible in terms of such pairs as *Leib* (the kinesthetic and tactile, *subjective* body) and *Körper* (the physical, spatial body). These manuscripts illustrate both Husserl's second-to-none ability to do thorough phenomenological analyses, even to the point where the conclusions of such analyses would prove questionable the very terms and distinctions employed in the analyses, and his inability, nevertheless, to abandon completely those terms and distinctions. For example, Husserl seems to reach the conclusion that the "transcendental" body is at the same time neither a present-at-hand external entity nor something completely "immanent" or "internal" to the subject – *and yet he continues to speak of this body as "double-sided."* What Husserl's phenomenology of the lived body shows is precisely that I originally experience my body as something that fits neither the category of "outer" presence-at-hand nor the category of "inner," purely subjective being. Yet, he apparently cannot make sense of what he finds except in terms of just such "dualistic" expressions. This is the position the founder of phenomenology ultimately arrives at: I *am* bodily, and not just in some "inner," "intellectual" sense, but in a "double" sense that both covers the "inner" aspect and has some sort of "outer" significance as well. Husserl realizes that my kinesthetic activities can not (except, so he thinks, through the eyes of another) be seen as strictly physical (*körperlich*), so they have to be "inner." But that does not fit entirely well either – given, among other things, the fact that my locomotion kinesthesia can bring me in close contact with most entities perceived "out there" – so they have to be "inner" activities that are already somehow "double sided" (cf. *Hua* XV, p. 643). As Husserl's continuous efforts demonstrate, the tendency to split up subjectivity in parts or "sides" always seems to accompany the "body" terminology. The constant setting is that of "subject" and "object," "inner" and "outer," and to the extent the body is correctly recognized as fitting neither of these categories, it is immediately characterized as both at once, as "subject-object" (cf. *Hua* XIV, pp. 6, 457). To the extent that the subjective, transcendentally functioning bodily movements are recognized as not completely "internal" happenings, then Husserl persistently concludes that they must "also" somehow be "objective [*dingliche*], externally constituted movements" (*Hua* XV, p. 652). In this way, the mode of being peculiar to subjectivity is broken down into ontic fragments that are simply mutations of the traditional alternatives that the phenomenological analysis has in fact already shown to be false alternatives. Consequently, there is ultimately little hope of making the mode of being of subjectivity properly intelligible after all: what is correctly seen as a mode of being quite different from the traditional either-or of "subject" and "object" is cut in pieces and forced into refinements of these very categories.

Indeed, one may even speculate whether the notion of "body" doesn't also nourish a tendency to conceive subjectivity as something different from *its* body (as if the body after all is a thing "belonging" to me), a tendency that seems manifest in the very notion of an "embodied subject." Despite his realization that we *are* bodily

(*Hua* XV, p. 283; *Hua* XXIX, p. 159), Husserl clearly continues to express himself in ways that seem, after all, to strictly separate subject and body, as, e.g., when the body is referred to as the "primordial tool" of the subject (*Hua* XIV, pp. 77, 541). It is as if the concept of "body" is too intimately linked with the idea of a (non-bodily) subject, which through its connection with or inhabitation of a body becomes anchored in the world, to be an appropriate concept for a phenomenology that intends precisely to contest that idea.[39]

As should be more than obvious by now, Heidegger does not avoid the topic of the body in order to deny the bodily existence of subjectivity, as if he after all conceives of the subject as a pure "intellectual" being. In fact, if anyone objects to Heidegger along these lines, they are demonstrating why the concept of "body" is best avoided. This type of objection appeals to the view that the subject is somehow composed of mind and body, wherefore the refusal to take the latter into account can only be interpreted as a commitment to the view that subjectivity can be defined more or less exclusively in terms of the former – and it is precisely this view of the subject that Heidegger is bent on overcoming. Similarly, one should not assume that Heidegger deems the topic of body uninteresting or insignificant. On the contrary, from Heidegger's perspective the problem simply is that this kind of topic needs a phenomenological-ontological *grounding* in an analysis using different concepts, concepts less burdened by tradition (cf. *SZ*, p. 207). He thinks that if we want to be able to grasp adequately what our body is, then we have to first work out an ontology of the human being, attempting to determine in which way this type of entity *is*, without relying on such concepts as "body," "consciousness," etc. Only when having done so may we understand adequately what it means to be "embodied," and the extent to which such terms are both illuminating and misleading. That is why Heidegger introduces the "neutral" (or formally indicative) concept of Dasein (*GA* 26, p. 173).[40]

These, I submit, are the genuine problems that prompt Heidegger to avoid the issue of the body in *Sein und Zeit*. He thinks the notion of the body furthers all kinds of divisions of the entity that we ourselves are, notably the divisions of subjectivity into its "inner" and "outer" aspects or sides, into "spirit" and "body," etc. (*SZ*, p. 56; *GA* 24, p. 90). In this way, it serves to obstruct any attempt to provide an adequate ontological characterization of the human being (*GA* 63, p. 81).

With the notion of Dasein, Heidegger believes he has the conceptual means to make sense of how the human subject *is*. The concept of Dasein is precisely

---

[39] Even Merleau-Ponty, who more than anyone else emphasizes that we *are* our body (*Phenomenology of Perception*, p. 206), sometimes speaks of consciousness as "having" a body (e.g., ibid., p. 351). The notion that the body is my "anchorage in the world" is also found in Merleau-Ponty (ibid., p. 144). Is this not at bottom a quite Cartesian way of expressing oneself?

[40] Compare to this, Otto Pöggeler, *Der Denkweg Martin Heideggers*, p. 260. Similarly, Steven Crowell, *Husserl, Heidegger, and the Space of Meaning*, p. 212: "With Dasein described as being-in-the-world, some have found it strange that Heidegger does not offer a phenomenology of embodiment in *Being and Time*. The primary reason for this is that Heidegger is trying to conceptualize the being of human being prior to the traditional distinction between mind and body."

introduced in an attempt to capture with *one single word* "all" that we are, our "whole" being (cf. *WM*, p. 372), viz. our being-in-the-world *as* the "place" where the world appears. Without such an ontological foundation, we can only make these things intelligible by reference to different aspect, sides, or parts of the subject, thus losing in the process the hope of grasping in an ontologically adequate way the kind of entity we are. This is also the fate of the phenomenology of the embodied subject, according to Heidegger. It remains entangled in dichotomies, and must engage in endless struggles to make intelligible how I experience myself as *one* entity, with one mode of being. As Heidegger recognizes (*GA* 20, p. 37), phenomenology must always struggle not to lose the phenomenon, but when it employs such concepts as "subject" and "object," and also to some extent "body" – concepts that tend to bring a host of other traditional, literally *analytical*, concepts along – then it becomes an uphill struggle, to say the least (cf. *GA* 63, p. 81; *GA* 24, p. 90).

It should hardly be necessary to emphasize that none of this is intended to mean that Husserl's phenomenology of embodiment is "wrong." On the contrary, Husserl is absolutely "right." The problem is just that the terms with which Husserl attempts to describe his findings are not adequate. The mode of being of subjectivity is correctly seen, but scattered by the concepts used to describe it. Constant refinements and specifications (e.g., not "outer," yet not completely "inner" either, etc.) only accentuate that in order to say what he actually wants to say, Husserl would have to begin his analyses anew, in a different terminology. The route he strikes out on only leads to ever more distinctions and specifications, because the inadequate terms of "consciousness," "body," "inner," "outer," and a host of similar dichotomies, set the stage for, and continue to haunt, his analyses.

In conclusion, not only does Husserl pose the question of the mode of being peculiar to transcendental subjectivity; there are even substantial points of convergence between Husserl's descriptions of the being of the transcendental subject and Heidegger's characterization of the being of Dasein. The question, however, is whether Husserl's vocabulary can do justice to the phenomenological discoveries he makes. Here, the concept of Dasein – at first sight abstract and speculative in comparison with Husserl's notion of the kinesthetic, bodily subject – gains a considerable advantage. In any case, it is clear that the agreement we have discovered between Husserl's and Heidegger's descriptions of subjectivity refers to Husserl's characterization of the transcendental, rather than the mundane subject. If there is anything Heidegger unambiguously rejects it is the notion that the human being is something present-at-hand "inside" the world (*GA* 24, p. 37) – that is, precisely Husserl's conception of the "mundane subject."

CONCLUSION

In the introduction to this book, I said that I hoped to accomplish four things in this study. First, I wanted to shed new light on the relation between the phenomenologies of Husserl and Heidegger. Secondly, I wanted to develop in detail their respective phenomenological methods. Thirdly, I wanted to discuss and evaluate some of the concrete phenomenological analyses provided by the two phenomenologists. And finally, I hoped to be able to say something general about the task of phenomenology. Let me now take a step back from the detailed analyses and try to provide an overview of what has been accomplished in the study.

The first objective – to throw new light on the Husserl-Heidegger relation – can really not be separated from the other aims; rather, it is precisely in terms of method, concrete analyses, and phenomenological projects that the relation between the philosophies of Husserl and Heidegger should be elucidated. Therefore, there are three issues to be considered in this conclusion.

I have argued above that Husserl's method of epoché should be conceived as a procedure of "bracketing" or "locking up," not as a procedure of "excluding" or even "ignoring." In particular, it makes no sense to claim that Husserlian phenomenology should "exclude" the world and intra-mundane entities from its thematic field, since – as we saw – these latter (in their "how" of manifestation) are precisely what must function as "guiding clues" for the "phenomenological reduction." The latter we identified as the "regress" from the noematic correlates to the experiencing subject, the regress without which we could say nothing about the subject. In Chapter III, I argued that Husserl's method of epoché is crucial to Heidegger's undertaking. "Bracketing" the natural interpretation of (the being of) entities, the epoché makes possible viewing the entity exclusively in its "how" of manifestation; this, so Heidegger explicitly acknowledges, is precisely what makes it possible phenomenologically to investigate the entity in its mode of being. Heidegger, however, supplies an "epoché" of his own; a "terminological" epoché, as it were. With his method of "formal indication" he struggles to provide expressions suitable for an "unnatural" undertaking such as that of phenomenological ontology, an effort that seems to have no equivalent in Husserl. Finally, we also concluded that under the title of "fundamental ontology" some kind of "phenomenological reduction" – i.e., a regress to "subjectivity" considered as the "place of manifestation of the world" – could be attributed to Heidegger.

Of the phenomenological analyses found in Husserl and Heidegger's writings, we considered in detail those of world, subjectivity, and intra-mundane entities. In opposition to the claims of a number of commentators, we find important points of convergence between the Husserlian and the Heideggerian accounts of the world.

Husserl's conception of world-horizon, just like the Heideggerian conception of the world as a referential whole, is not to be identified with a collection or totality of entities. In both accounts, the world is a "transcendental notion," something that *allows* entities to manifest themselves. Whereas the notion of "referential whole" appears to be too closely tied to the being of equipment, Husserl's concept of world-horizon, so I argued, seems somehow "ontologically neutral" – and perhaps for that reason has more phenomenological potential.

Mundane entities were discussed at some length. I raised the question whether Husserl's account of the "being" of intra-mundane things, the "layer" theory, could be phenomenologically confirmed, when confronted with an unprejudiced "noematic" investigation. Both when it concerned equipment and the so-called "mundane" subject, the answer was negative. Heidegger's account of the being of equipment – that these are understood primarily as "something-with-which-to" – we found to be more convincing than Husserl's account. Similarly, we had to conclude that Husserl's conception of the "mundane" subject – an entity present-at-hand within the world – finds little support in the way we actually experience others and ourselves.

It thus seems that Heidegger appropriates what Husserl would call a "noematic" investigation in a more radical way than Husserl. Husserl, it would appear, never uses the epoché and the noematic research it makes possible to launch a critique of the natural attitude's interpretation of mundane entities. When he says that the natural conception of the world is in no need of correction (*Hua* XIV, p. 278), this should be taken very seriously indeed. Husserl's initial sympathy with the interpretation of the natural attitude is, as it were, reactivated whenever Husserl wants to give an account of the "being" of mundane things. That is yet another reason why the expression "lock up" captures so well what Husserl's epoché does to the natural attitude: it locks it and all of its "knowledge" up, preserves it, without ever subjecting it to critique. If one should try to give an answer to the question whether Husserl actually *poses*, as a *phenomenologist*, the question about the modes of being of intra-mundane entities, the answer would have to be negative. He appears simply to refer to the naturally attuned subject's *interpretation*, without ever using the means of phenomenology to examine whether that interpretation actually squares with what the naturally attuned subject *experiences*. Heidegger, in contrast, has a critical agenda. His radical appropriation of something like a Husserlian noematic investigation allows him to conclude that the standard (everyday and philosophical) interpretation of being – the interpretation according to which the mode of being of all entities is presence-at-hand – does not match our implicit pre-ontological way of *understanding* the modes of being of entities. We hardly ever understand ourselves to have the mode of being of a thing, nor do we experience tools and equipment as present-at-hand entities.

As far as subjectivity is concerned, we found a remarkable similarity between Husserl's analyses of the transcendental subject and Heidegger's phenomenology of Dasein. Neither subject stands above the world; according to both accounts, the subject can only really be the subject *for* the world by entering *into* the world. This is the semi-explicit conclusion to Husserl's analyses of the embodied nature of the transcendental subject. Likewise, Heidegger's concept of Dasein formally indicates a subject that is only the place of world-disclosure by being itself disclosed and placed in the midst of the world. In both accounts, then, transcendental subjectivity is given an important re-interpretation: the world only really opens up and becomes manifest to a subject that itself emerges in the midst of it, encompassed by it. If one should raise the question whether Husserl poses, as a *phenomenologist*, the question of the mode of being of subjectivity, then the answer would have to be positive. Husserl – less explicitly perhaps than Heidegger, but in basic accordance with him – uncovers a subject whose mode of being is in-the-world-*as*-subject-for-the-world, a mode of being radically different from that of *Vorhandensein*.

However, as we discussed these matters in detail, it became clear that Heidegger's formally indicative concept of Dasein has the advantage of being able to capture, in one word, the mode of being of subjectivity. Husserl's terminology (body, consciousness, subject, object, inner, outer, etc.), so I argued, has the tendency to break the phenomenon down into ontic fragments, instead of allowing us to grasp the *ontological* phenomenon, the peculiar mode of being that we have. With the notion of Dasein, the hyphens in the expression "in-the-world-*as*-subject-for..." are *strengthened*, as it were, whereas the Husserlian terminology tends to *erode* the hyphens surrounding the "as." None of this diminishes Husserl's achievement, but it does suggest that Heidegger was wise to worry more about terminology than his mentor.

What has the argument of the present study shown us about phenomenology? Is it, in the last analysis, meaningless to speak of "phenomenology" in the singular, or are there substantial concerns common to both Husserl and Heidegger? This study would indicate that the latter is true. At least three points of convergence are evident.

In a broad sense, Husserlian as well as Heideggerian phenomenology is "hermeneutic" phenomenology. As we saw in Chapter II, even from Husserl's perspective it is never the business of phenomenology to "deduce" or "prove," but always only to "interpret" and "understand." For both Husserl and Heidegger, the task of philosophy is to make the world and ourselves *intelligible*, to help us *understand* these things – and they think this is a task for which deductive reasoning is completely useless (cf. *Hua* XV, p. 115; *GA* 20, p. 78).

But what is it that we must understand? According to the argument of the present study, phenomenology is always about understanding "being."[1] This, however, is in

---

[1] The argument of the present study thus seems to be directly opposed to that of Steven Crowell, who argues, both in his book *Husserl, Heidegger, and the Space of Meaning*, and in a recent article, that the topic of phenomenology "is neither consciousness nor being, but meaning" (cf. Crowell, "Does the Husserl/Heidegger Feud Rest on a Mistake?", p. 123). Crowell does grant that "there is no real objection to invoking 'being' as Heidegger does" (ibid., p. 127), but he insists that there is no good reason to do so either. Instead, he claims, the best term for the *Sache* of phenomenology, and as he says "one that belongs neither to ancient nor to modern philosophy" (ibid., p. 126), is meaning (*Sinn*). I wonder whether that

two different ways: phenomenology poses not one question of being, but two essentially distinct *kinds* of questions that are, broadly speaking, questions of "being." One might perhaps say that Husserl and Heidegger each pose a *transcendental* and a more distinctively *ontological* "question of being."

The first, the "transcendental question," concerns the conditions of possibility of the manifestation of things. Husserlian constitutive phenomenology aims to understand how a world, and intra-mundane entities, can "be there," can be manifested to subjectivity. This question, as we have seen, is not an "ontic" one, but concerns, rather, the realization of the "being-there" of world and intra-worldly things. A similar type of question, so I argued, is found in Heidegger, under the heading of the "problem of transcendence." What Heidegger pursues under this heading are the conditions for the possibility of the understanding of being, the latter being itself something that in Heidegger's account constitutes a necessary though not sufficient condition for constitution. The two questions of constitution and transcendence, I have argued, are not only questions of a similar type – they are questions that *supplement* each other.

The other question of being that is posed by phenomenology concerns the *modes of being* peculiar to different entities. There seems to be significant differences between Husserl and Heidegger in terms of how universally they raise this question. Although Husserl recognizes that, being in need of transcendental "guiding clues," transcendental phenomenology must be in a certain "alliance" (*Bundes-genossenschaft*) with ontology (*Hua* XI, p. 222), he apparently does not think that phenomenological (noematic) analysis should itself *be* ontological, as Heidegger claims. As we have just concluded, only Heidegger consequently poses the question of the modes of being of intra-mundane entities. But, on the other hand, both he and Husserl have a lot to say on the manner of being peculiar to *subjectivity*.

Even though the two questions are closely connected with each other, they should be carefully distinguished. It is one thing to ask about the mode of being a chair has, and quite another to try to reveal how an entity with that mode of being can manifest itself to subjectivity. Consequently, it is misleading to claim, as some commentators do, that Husserl's constitutive analyses inquire into the *mode* of being

---

term is really as unburdened as Crowell seems to think. Would Crowell, e.g., say that the *Sinn* which is the topic of phenomenology is the *drittes Reich* – between the realm of things and the realm of *Vorstellungen* – that Frege speaks of (cf. "Der Gedanke," p. 43; "Über Sinn und Bedeutung," pp. 41-47)? Would Crowell say that the meaning Husserl and Heidegger speak of has to do only with the way things are given to us – with the "telescope" through which we see them – and not with these things themselves? Would he not, rather, agree that the kind of "meaning" that Husserl and Heidegger are interested in is very much *ontologically* relevant? That it is the meaning of *being* of the world, everything mundane, and ourselves? Crowell's discussion with McDowell, and his persuasive critique of the inconsistent transcendental realism of Heidegger's "metontology," for example, seem to me clear indications that Crowell would agree with me on this point (cf. *Husserl, Heidegger, and the space of Meaning*, pp. 14-19, 222-243; see also p. 89). Thus, I doubt that there is much disagreement when it comes to the point. So, to reverse Crowell's statement, if one clarifies that meaning is to be understood as "meaning of *being,*" then there is no real reason why one should not be allowed to invoke the term.

of the constituted entities.[2] Husserl's constitutive phenomenology inquires into the structures that make possible the manifestation of entities, on the basis of a noematic investigation of their "how" of manifestation. It is Heidegger's deep insight that this noematic investigation can be used to carry out a radical phenomenological ontology, an inquiry into precisely the modes of being of entities. This is not, it seems, something Husserl does. Husserl uses the noematic description only as a springboard to launch his constitutive investigation; he does not seem to attach any fundamental ontological significance to the entity in the "how" of its manifestation. Heidegger, on the other hand, thinks this is precisely what one should do; indeed he believes the ontological investigation is the most important as well as the most urgent phenomenological task (*GA* 20, p. 158). From a Heideggerian perspective, then, the constitutive investigation, if it is to provide a genuine understanding of the constituted entity, should be preceded by an investigation of the mode of being of that entity.

Using terminology that is probably not entirely adequate, one may perhaps say that the twofold task of transcendental phenomenology is, on the one hand, to ask a "what" or an "*as-what*" type of question and, on the other, to ask a "*how*" type of question. The question of modes of being is a question that aims at an ontological understanding of the "as-what" of entities and world, whereas the problems of constitution and transcendence both concern the attempt to explain how entities with such modes of being can be there, given to subjectivity. When Husserl claims that, although there is nothing wrong with investigating the concrete life-world, it is only the constitutive analysis that grants us a true philosophical understanding of the life-world (*Hua* I, p. 165), then this is at most partly correct. One might just as well claim that it is only when the manner of being of life-worldly entities is properly understood that the constitutive explanation of their being-there is genuinely illuminating. Neither task should be neglected, because neither can, on its own, provide that ultimate intelligibility that phenomenology aims at, viz.:

an incomparably novel and unsurpassably comprehensible *understanding* of what the real being of the world, and real being in general, *means*; what it means in natural life itself, whose essence has become the universal transcendental theme. (*Hua* VIII, pp. 481-482)

---

[2] This is, e.g., Timothy Stapleton's claim (*Husserl and Heidegger: The Question of a Phenomenological Beginning*, p. 115).

BIBLIOGRAPHY

WORKS BY HUSSERL

Husserliana, Vol. I. *Cartesianische Meditationen und Pariser Vorträge*. 2nd edition. Edited by Stephan Strasser. Dordrecht: Kluwer Academic Publishers, 1991. *Cartesian Meditations: An Introduction to Phenomenology*. Translated by Dorion Cairns. Dordrecht: Kluwer Academic Publishers, 1995. [Translation of *Hua* I, pp. 43-183.]

Husserliana, Vol. II. *Die Idee der Phänomenologie: Fünf Vorlesungen*. Edited by Walter Biemel. The Hague: Martinus Nijhoff, 1950. *The Idea of Phenomenology*. Translated by Lee Hardy. Dordrecht: Kluwer Academic Publishers, 1999.

Husserliana, Vol. III/1. *Ideen zu einer reinen Phänomenologie und phänomenologischen Philosophie. Erstes Buch: Allgemeine Einführung in die reine Phänomenologie*. Edited by Karl Schuhmann. The Hague: Martinus Nijhoff, 1976. *Ideas Pertaining to a Pure Phenomenology and to a Phenomenological Philosophy. First Book: General Introduction to a Pure Phenomenology*. Translated by F. Kersten. The Hague: Martinus Nijhoff, 1983.

Husserliana, Vol. IV. *Ideen zu einer reinen Phänomenologie und phänomenologischen Philosophie. Zweites Buch: Phänomeoologische Untersuchungen zur Konstitution*. Edited by Marly Biemel. The Hague: Martinus Nijhoff, 1952. *Ideas Pertaining to a Pure Phenomenology and to a Phenomenological Philosophy. Second Book: Studies in the Phenomenology of Constitution*. Translated by Richard Rojcewicz and André Schuwer. Dordrecht: Kluwer Academic Publishers, 1989.

Husserliana, Vol. V. *Ideen zu einer reinen Phänomenologie und phänomenologischen Philosophie. Drittes Buch: Die Phänomenologie und die Fundamente der Wissenschaften*. Edited by Marly Biemel. The Hague: Martinus Nijhoff, 1952. *Phenomenology and the Foundations of the Sciences*. Translated by Ted E. Klein and William E. Pohl. The Hague: Martinus Nijhoff, 1980. [Translation of *Hua* V, pp. 1-137.]

Husserliana, Vol. VI. *Die Krisis der europäischen Wissenschaften und die transzendentale Phänomenologie: Eine Einleitung in die phänomenologische Philosophie*. 2nd edition. Edited by Walter Biemel. The Hague: Martinus Nijhoff, 1976. *The Crisis of European Sciences and Transcendental Phenomenology*. Translated by David Carr. Evanston, Ill.: Northwestern University Press, 1970. [Translation of *Hua* VI, pp. 1-348, 357-386, 459-462, 473-475, 508-516.]

Husserliana, Vol. VII. *Erste Philosophie (1923/24). Erster Teil: Kritische Ideengeschichte*. Edited by Rudolf Boehm. The Hague: Martinus Nijhoff, 1956.

Husserliana, Vol. VIII. *Erste Philosophie (1923/24). Zweiter Teil: Theorie der phänomenologischen Reduktion*. Edited by Rudolf Boehm. The Hague: Martinus Nijhoff, 1959.
Husserliana, Vol. IX. *Phänomenologische Psychologie: Vorlesungen Sommersemester 1925*. Edited by Walter Biemel. The Hague: Martinus Nijhoff, 1962. *Psychological and Transcendental Phenomenology and the Confrontation with Heidegger (1927-1931)*. Translated by Thomas Sheehan and Richard E. Palmer. Dordrecht: Kluwer Academic Publishers, 1997. [Translation of *Hua* IX, pp. 237-349, 517-526, 598-599, 600-602.]
Husserliana, Vol. X. *Zur Phänomenologie des inneren Zeitbewußtseins (1893-1917)*. Edited by Rudolf Boehm. The Hague: Martinus Nijhoff, 1966. *On the Phenomenology of the Consciousness of Internal Time*. Translated by John Barnett Brough. Dordrecht: Kluwer Academic Publishers, 1991.
Husserliana, Vol. XI. *Analysen zur passiven Synthesis: Aus Vorlesungs- und Forschungsmanuskripten 1918-1926*. Edited by Margot Fleischer. The Hague: Martinus Nijhoff, 1966. *Analyses Concerning Passive and Active Synthesis: Lectures on Transcendental Logic*. Translated by Anthony J. Steinbock. Dordrecht: Kluwer Academic Publishers, 2001.
Husserliana, Vol. XIII. *Zur Phänomenologie der Intersubjektivität: Texte aus dem Nachlass. Erster Teil: 1905-1920*. Edited by Iso Kern. The Hague: Martinus Nijhoff, 1973.
Husserliana, Vol. XIV. *Zur Phänomenologie der Intersubjektivität: Texte aus dem Nachlass. Zweiter Teil: 1921-1928*. Edited by Iso Kern. The Hague: Martinus Nijhoff, 1973.
Husserliana, Vol. XV. *Zur Phänomenologie der Intersubjektivität: Texte aus dem Nachlass. Dritter Teil: 1929-1935*. Edited by Iso Kern. The Hague: Martinus Nijhoff, 1973.
Husserliana, Vol. XVI. *Ding und Raum: Vorlesungen 1907*. Edited by Ulrich Claesges. The Hague: Martinus Nijhoff, 1973. *Thing and Space: Lectures of 1907*. Translated by Richard Rojcewicz. Dordrecht: Kluwer Academic Publishers, 1997.
Husserliana, Vol. XVII. *Formale und transzendentale Logik: Versuch einer Kritik der logischen Vernunft*. Edited by Paul Janssen. The Hague: Martinus Nijhoff, 1974. *Formal and Transcendental Logic*. Translated by Dorion Cairns. The Hague: Martinus Nijhoff, 1969. [Translation of *Hua* XVII, pp. 1-335.]
Husserliana, Vol. XVIII. *Logische Untersuchungen. Erster Band: Prolegomena zur reinen Logik*. Edited by Elmar Holenstein. The Hague: Martinus Nijhoff, 1975. *Logical Investigations. Volume One*. Translated by J. N. Findlay. London: Routledge and Kegan Paul, 1970.
Husserliana, Vol. XIX/1. *Logische Untersuchungen. Zweiter Band: Untersuchungen zur Phänomenologie und Theorie der Erkenntnis. Erster Teil*. Edited by Ursula Panzer. The Hague: Martinus Nijhoff, 1984. *Logical Investigations. Volume One*. Translated by J. N. Findlay. London: Routledge and Kegan Paul, 1970. [Translation of *Hua* XIX/1, pp. 5-226.] *Logical*

Investigations. Volume Two. Trans. J. N. Findlay. London: Routledge and Kegan Paul, 1970. [Translation of *Hua* XIX/1, pp. 227-529.]
Husserliana, Vol. XIX/2. *Logische Untersuchungen. Zweiter Band: Untersuchungen zur Phänomenologie und Theorie der Erkenntnis. Zweiter Teil.* Edited by Ursula Panzer. The Hague: Martinus Nijhoff, 1984. *Logical Investigations. Volume Two.* Translated by J. N. Findlay. London: Routledge and Kegan Paul, 1970. [Translation of *Hua* XIX/2, pp. 531-775.]
Husserliana, Vol. XXIV. *Einleitung in die Logik und Erkenntnistheorie: Vorlesungen 1906/07.* Edited by Ullrich Melle. Dordrecht: Martinus Nijhoff, 1984.
Husserliana, Vol. XXV. *Aufsätze und Vorträge (1911-1921).* Edited by Thomas Nenon and Hans Rainer Sepp. Dordrecht: Martinus Nijhoff, 1987. *Phenomenology and the Crisis of Philosophy: Philosophy as Rigorous Science and Philosophy and the Crisis of European Man.* Translated by Quentin Lauer. New York: Harper & Row, 1965. [Translation of *Hua* XXV, pp. 3-62.]
Husserliana, Vol. XXVII. *Aufsätze und Vorträge (1922-1937).* Edited by Thomas Nenon and Hans Rainer Sepp. Dordrecht: Kluwer Academic Publishers, 1989. *Psychological and Transcendental Phenomenology and the Confrontation with Heidegger.* Translated by Thomas Sheehan and Richard E. Palmer. Dordrecht: Kluwer Academic Publishers, 1997. [Translation of *Hua* XXVII, pp. 164-181.]
Husserliana, Vol. XXIX. *Die Krisis der europäischen Wissenschaften und die transzendentale Phänomenologie. Ergänzungsband: Texte aus dem Nachlaß 1934-1937.* Edited by Reinhold N. Smid. Dordrecht: Kluwer Academic Publishers, 1993.
Husserliana, Vol. XXXI. *Aktive Synthesen: Aus der Vorlesung "Transzendentale Logik" 1920/21. Ergänzungsband zu "Analysen zur passiven Synthesis".* Edited by Roland Breeur. Dordrecht: Kluwer Academic Publishers, 2000. *Analyses Concerning Passive and Active Synthesis: Lectures on Transcendental Logic.* Translated by Anthony J. Steinbock. Dordrecht: Kluwer Academic Publishers, 2001.
Husserliana, Vol. XXXIV. *Zur phänomenologischen Reduktion: Texte aus dem Nachlass (1926-1935).* Edited by Sebastian Luft. Dordrecht: Kluwer Academic Publishers, 2002.
Husserliana Dokumente, Vol. II/1. *VI. Cartesianische Meditation. Teil 1: Die Idee einer transzendentalen Methodenlehre.* Edited by Hans Ebeling, Jann Holl, and Guy van Kerckhoven. Dordrecht: Kluwer Academic Publishers, 1988 [Main text by Eugen Fink, comments and appendices by Husserl.] *Sixth Cartesian Meditation: The Idea of a Transcendental Theory of Method.* Translated by Ronald Bruzina. Bloomington: Indiana University Press, 1995.
Husserliana Dokumente, Vol. II/2. *VI. Cartesianische Meditation. Teil 2: Ergänzungsband.* Edited by Guy van Kerckhoven. Dordrecht: Kluwer Academic Publishers, 1988 [Main texts by Fink, comments and appendices by Husserl.]
Erfahrung und Urteil: Untersuchungen zur Genealogie der Logik. 7th Reprinting. Edited by Ludwig Landgrebe. Hamburg: Felix Meiner Verlag, 1999. *Experience*

and Judgment: Investigations in a Genealogy of Logic. Translated by James S. Churchill and Karl Ameriks. London: Routledge and Kegan Paul, 1973.
"Randbemerkungen Husserls zu Heideggers *Sein und Zeit* und *Kant und das Problem der Metaphysik.*" Edited by Roland Breeur. *Husserl Studies* 11 (1994): 3-63. *Psychological and Transcendental Phenomenology and the Confrontation with Heidegger.* Translated by Thomas Sheehan and Richard E. Palmer. Dordrecht: Kluwer Academic Publishers, 1997.
"Phänomenologische Methode und phänomenologische Philosophie: <Londoner Vorträge 1922>." Edited by Berndt Goossens. *Husserl Studies* 16 (2000): 183-254.
Ms. A VI 14 a (1930-32). Husserl-Archief te Leuven (Belgium).
Ms. E I 5 (1933). Husserl-Archief te Leuven (Belgium).

WORKS BY HEIDEGGER

Gesamtausgabe, Vol. 12. *Unterwegs zur Sprache.* Edited by Friedrich-Wilhelm von Herrmann. Frankfurt a. M.: Vittorio Klostermann, 1985.
Gesamtausgabe, Vol. 15. *Seminare.* Edited by Curd Ochwadt. Frankfurt a. M.: Vittorio Klostermann, 1986.
Gesamtausgabe, Vol. 17. *Einführung in die phänomenologische Forschung.* Edited by Friedrich-Wilhelm von Herrmann. Frankfurt a. M.: Vittorio Klostermann, 1994.
Gesamtausgabe, Vol. 18. *Grundbegriffe der aristotelischen Philosophie.* Edited by Mark Michalski. Frankfurt a. M.: Vittorio Klostermann, 2002.
Gesamtausgabe, Vol. 19. *Platon: Sophistes.* Edited by Ingeborg Schüßler. Frankfurt a. M.: Vittorio Klostermann, 1992.
Gesamtausgabe, Vol. 20. *Prolegomena zur Geschichte des Zeitbegriffs.* 3rd edition. Edited by Petra Jaeger. Frankfurt a. M.: Vittorio Klostermann, 1994. *History of the Concept of Time: Prolegomena.* Translated by Theodore Kisiel. Bloomington: Indiana University Press, 1985.
Gesamtausgabe, Vol. 21. *Logik: Die Frage nach der Wahrheit.* 2nd edition. Edited by Walter Biemel. Frankfurt a. M.: Vittorio Klostermann, 1995.
Gesamtausgabe, Vol. 22. *Die Grundbegriffe der antiken Philosophie.* Edited by Franz-Karl Blust. Frankfurt a. M.: Vittorio Klostermann, 1993.
Gesamtausgabe, Vol. 24. *Die Grundprobleme der Phänomenologie.* Third edition. Edited by Friedrich-Wilhelm von Herrmann. Frankfurt a. M.: Vittorio Klostermann, 1997. *The Basic Problems of Phenomenology.* Translated by Albert Hofstadter. Bloomington: Indiana University Press, 1988.
Gesamtausgabe, Vol. 26. *Metaphysische Anfangsgründe der Logik im Ausgang von Leibniz.* 2nd edition. Edited by Klaus Held. Frankfurt a. M.: Vittorio Klostermann, 1990. *The Metaphysical Foundations of Logic.* Translated by Michael Heim. Bloomington: Indiana University Press, 1984.
Gesamtausgabe, Vol. 27. *Einleitung in die Philosophie.* Edited by Otto Saame and Ina Saame-Speidel. Frankfurt a. M.: Vittorio Klostermann, 1996.

Gesamtausgabe, Vol. 29/30. *Die Grundbegriffe der Metaphysik: Welt – Endlichkeit – Einsamkeit.* Edited by Friedrich-Wilhelm von Herrmann. Frankfurt a. M.: Vittorio Klostermann, 1983. *The Fundamental Concepts of Metaphysics: World, Finitude, Solitude.* Translated by William McNeill and Nicholas Walker. Bloomington: Indiana University Press, 1995.

Gesamtausgabe, Vol. 56/57. *Zur Bestimmung der Philosophie: 1. Die Idee der Philosophie und das Weltanschauungsproblem. 2. Phänomenologie und transzendentale Wertphilosophie.* Edited by Bernd Heimbüchel. Frankfurt a. M.: Vittorio Klostermann, 1987.

Gesamtausgabe, Vol. 58. *Grundprobleme der Phänomenologie (1919/20).* Edited by Hans-Helmuth Gander. Frankfurt a. M.: Vittorio Klostermann, 1993.

Gesamtausgabe, Vol. 59. *Phänomenologie der Anschauung und des Ausdrucks: Theorie der philosophischen Begriffsbildung.* Edited by Claudius Strube. Frankfurt a. M.: Vittorio Klostermann, 1993.

Gesamtausgabe, Vol. 60. *Phänomenologie des religiösen Lebens: 1. Einleitung in die Phänomenologie der Religion. 2. Augustinus und der Neuplatonismus. 3. Die philosophischen Grundlagen der Mittelalterlichen Mystik.* Edited by Matthias Jung, Thomas Regehly, and Claudius Strube. Frankfurt a. M.: Vittorio Klostermann, 1995.

Gesamtausgabe, Vol. 61. *Phänomenologische Interpretationen zu Aristoteles: Einführung in die phänomenologische Forschung.* Edited by Walter Bröcker and Käte Bröcker-Oltmanns. Frankfurt a. M.: Vittorio Klostermann, 1985. *Phenomenological Interpretations of Aristotle: Initiation into Phenomenological Research.* Translated by Richard Rojcewicz. Bloomington: Indiana University Press, 2001.

Gesamtausgabe, Vol. 63. *Ontologie (Hermeneutik der Faktizität).* 2nd edition. Edited by Käte Bröcker-Oltmanns. Frankfurt a. M.: Vittorio Klostermann, 1995. *Ontology – The Hermeneutics of Facticity.* Translated by John van Buren. Bloomington: Indiana University Press, 1999.

Kant und das Problem der Metaphysik. 6th edition, identical with Vol. 3 of the *Gesamtausgabe.* Edited by Friedrich-Wilhem von Herrmann. Frankfurt a. M.: Vittorio Klostermann, 1998. *Kant and the Problem of Metaphysics.* Translated by Richard Taft. Bloomington: Indiana University Press, 1973. [Translation of *KPM*, pp. xii-xviii, 1-246, 271-296.]

Wegmarken. 3rd edition, identical with Vol. 9 of the *Gesamtausgabe.* Edited by Friedrich-Wilhelm von Herrmann. Frankfurt a. M.: Vittorio Klostermann, 1996. *Pathmarks.* Edited by William McNeill, translated by William McNeill et al. Cambridge: Cambridge University Press, 1998.

Holzwege. 6th edition. Frankfurt a. M.: Vittorio Klostermann, 1980.

Sein und Zeit. 17th edition. Tübingen: Max Niemeyer Verlag, 1993. *Being and Time.* Translated by John Macquarrie & Edward Robinson. Oxford: Blackwell, 1962.

Der Begriff der Zeit: Vortrag vor der Marburger Theologenschaft Juli 1924. 2nd edition. Edited by Hartmut Tietjen. Tübingen: Max Niemeyer Verlag, 1995. *The Concept of Time.* Translated by William McNeill. Oxford: Blackwell, 1992.

Zur Sache des Denkens. 4th edition. Tübingen: Max Niemeyer Verlag, 2000. *On Time and Being.* Translated by Joan Stambaugh. Chicago: The University of Chicago Press, 2002.

Was heißt Denken? 5th edition. Tübingen: Max Niemeyer Verlag, 1997.

"Phänomenologische Interpretationen zu Aristoteles: Anzeige der hermeneutischen Situation." Edited by Hans-Ulrich Lessing. *Dilthey-Jahrbuch für Philosophie und Geschichte der Geisteswissenschaften* 6 (1989): 237-274. "Phenomenological Interpretations with Respect to Aristotle." Translated by Michael Baur. *Man and World* 25 (1992): 358-393.

"Wilhelm Diltheys Forschungsarbeit und die gegenwärtige Kampf um eine historische Weltanschauung: 10 Vorträge. (Gehalten in Kassel vom 16.IV.-21.IV.1925)." Edited by Frithjof Rodi. *Dilthey-Jahrbuch für Philosophie und Geschichte der Geisteswissenschaften* 8 (1992-93): 143-180.

"Über das Prinzip 'Zu den Sachen selbst'." Edited by Friedrich-Wilhelm von Herrmann. *Heidegger Studies* 11 (1995): 5-8.

"Edmund Husserl zum siebenzigsten Geburtstag." In *Edmund Husserl – Martin Heidegger: Phänomenologie (1927)*, edited by Renato Cristin, 64-66. Berlin: Duncker & Humblot, 1999. *Psychological and Transcendental Phenomenology and the Confrontation with Heidegger.* Translated by Thomas Sheehan and Richard E. Palmer. Dordrecht: Kluwer Academic Publishers, 1997.

"Preface/Vorwort." In William J. Richardson, S. J., *Heidegger: Through Phenomenology to Thought*, viii-xxiii. The Hague: Martinus Nijhoff, 1963.

Husserliana, Vol. IX. *Phänomenologische Psychologie.* [See "Works by Husserl" for full information. This volume, although mainly containing material written by Husserl, contains a draft of the *Encyclopaedia Britannica* article edited by Heidegger, as well as several comments and an important letter written by Heidegger. A translation of this material is found in E. Husserl, *Psychological and Transcendental Phenomenology and the Confrontation with Heidegger.* Translated by Thomas Sheehan and Richard E. Palmer. Dordrecht: Kluwer Academic Publishers, 1997].

WORKS BY OTHER AUTHORS

Adorno, Theodor W. *Zur Metakritik der Erkenntnistheorie: Studien über Husserl und die phänomenologischen Antinomien. – Drei Studien zu Hegel. Gesammelte Schriften*, Vol. 5. Edited by Rolf Tiedemann. Frankfurt a. M.: Suhrkamp Verlag, 1970.

Aguirre, Antonio. *Genetische Phänomenologie und Reduktion: Zur Letztbegründung der Wissenschaft aus der radikalen Skepsis im Denken E. Husserls.* The Hague: Martinus Nijhoff, 1970.

Alweiss, Lilian. *The World Unclaimed: A Challenge to Heidegger's Critique of Husserl.* Athens, Ohio: Ohio University Press, 2003.

Aristotle. *The Complete Works of Aristotle.* Vol. 2. Edited by Jonathan Barnes. Princeton: Princeton University Press, 1984.

Berkeley, George. *Principles of Human Knowledge. – Three Dialogues between Hylas and Philonius*. Edited by Roger Woolhouse. London: Penguin Books, 1988.

Bernet, Rudolf. "Die ungegenwärtige Gegenwart: Anwesenheit und Abwesenheit in Husserls Analyse des Zeitbewußtseins." *Phänomenologische Forschungen* 14 (1983): 16-57.

——. "Die Frage nach dem Ursprung der Zeit bei Husserl und Heidegger." *Heidegger Studies* 3/4 (1987/1988): 89-104.

——."Husserl and Heidegger on Intentionality and Being." *Journal of the British Society for Phenomenology* 21, no. 2 (1990): 136-152.

——."Phenomenological Reduction and the Double Life of the Subject." In *Reading Heidegger from the Start: Essays in His Earliest Thought*, edited by Theodore Kisiel and John van Buren, 245-267. Albany: State University of New York Press, 1994.

Bernet, Rudolf; Kern, Iso; Marbach, Eduard. *Edmund Husserl: Darstellung seines Denkens*. 2nd edition. Hamburg: Felix Meiner Verlag, 1996.

Biemel, Walter. "Husserl Encyclopaedia-Britannica Artikel und Heideggers Anmerkungen dazu." *Tijdschrift voor Philosophie* 12 (1950): 246-280.

——. "Die Entscheidenden Phasen der Entfaltung von Husserls Philosophie." *Zeitschrift für philosophische Forschung* 13 (1959): 187-213.

——. *Martin Heidegger in Selbstzeugnissen und Bilddokumenten*. Reinbek bei Hamburg: Rowohlt, 1973.

Blattner, William D. "Existential Temporality in *Being and Time* (Why Heidegger is not a Pragmatist)." In *Heidegger: A Critical Reader*, edited by Hubert Dreyfus and Harrison Hall, 99-129. Oxford: Basil Blackwell, 1992.

Boehm, Rudolf. "Zijn en tijd in de filosofie van Husserl." *Tijdschrift voor Philosophie* 21 (1959): 243-276.

——. *Vom Gesichtspunkt der Phänomenologie: Husserl-studien*. The Hague: Martinus Nijhoff, 1968.

——. "Zur Phänomenologie der Gemeinschaft." In *Vom Gesichtspunkt der Phänomenologie, Zweiter Band: Sudien zur Phänomenologie der Epoché*, 91-111. The Hague: Martinus Nijhoff, 1981.

Boelen, Bernard. "Martin Heidegger as a Phenomenologist." In *Phenomenological Perspectives: Historical and Systematical Essays in Honor of Herbert Spiegelberg*, edited by P. J. Bossert, 93-114. The Hague: Martinus Nijhoff, 1975.

Bruzina, Ronald Charles. "Gegensätzlicher Einfluß - Integrierter Einfluß: Die Stellung Heideggers in der Entwicklung der Phänomenologie." In *Zur Philosophischen Aktualität Heideggers. Band 2: Im Gespräch der Zeit*, edited by Dietrich Papenfuss and Otto Pöggeler, 142-160. Frankfurt a. M.: Vittorio Klostermann, 1990.

——. "Translator's Introduction." In E. Fink, *Sixth Cartesian Meditation*, translated by R. Bruzina, vii-xcii. Bloomington: Indiana University Press, 1995.

Buckley, R. Philip. *Husserl, Heidegger, and the Crisis of Philosophical Responsibility*. Dordrecht: Kluwer Academic Publishers, 1992.
Cairns, Dorion. *Conversations with Husserl and Fink*. The Hague: Martinus Nijhoff, 1976.
Caputo, John D. "The Question of Being and Transcendental Phenomenology: Reflections on Heidegger's Relationship to Husserl." *Research in Phenomenology* 7 (1977): 84-105.
———. *Heidegger and Aquinas: An Essay on Overcoming Metaphysics*. New York: Fordham University Press, 1982.
———. "Husserl, Heidegger, and the Question of a 'Hermeneutic' Phenomenology." *Husserl Studies* 1 (1984): 157-178.
Carman, Taylor. "On Being Social: A Reply to Olafson." *Inquiry* 37 (1994): 203-223.
Carnap, Rudolf. "Überwindung der Metaphysik durch logische Analyse der Sprache." *Erkenntnis* 2 (1931): 219-241.
Carr, David. *The Paradox of Subjectivity: The Self in the Transcendental Tradition*. New York: Oxford University Press, 1999.
Cerbone, David R. "World, World-entry, and Realism in Early Heidegger." *Inquiry* 38 (1995): 401-421.
———. "Heidegger and Dasein's 'Bodily Nature:' What is the Hidden Problematic?" *International Journal of Philosophical Studies* 8 (2000): 209-230.
Claesges, Ulrich. *Edmund Husserls Theorie der Raumkonstitution*. The Hague: Martinus Nijhoff, 1964.
Courtine, Jean-François. *Heidegger et la phénoménologie*. Paris: J. Vrin, 1990.
Crowell, Steven Galt. *Husserl, Heidegger, and the Space of Meaning: Paths toward Transcendental Phenomenology*. Evanston, Ill.: Northwestern University Press, 2001.
———. "Subjectivity: Locating the First-Person in *Being and Time*." *Inquiry* 44 (2001): 433-454.
———. "Does the Husserl/Heidegger Feud Rest on a Mistake? An Essay on Psychological and Transcendental Phenomenology." *Husserl Studies* 18 (2002): 123-140.
———. "Facticity and Transcendental Philosophy." In *From Kant to Davidson: Philosophy and the Idea of the Transcendental*, edited by Jeff Malpas, 100-121. London: Routledge, 2003.
Dahlstrom, Daniel O. "Heidegger's Method: Philosophical Concepts as Formal Indications." *Review of Metaphysics* 47 (1994): 775-795.
———. "Heidegger's Critique of Husserl." In *Reading Heidegger from the Start: Essays in His Earliest Thought*, edited by Theodore Kisiel and John van Buren, 231-244. Albany: State University of New York Press, 1994.
———. *Heidegger's Concept of Truth*. Cambridge: Cambridge University Press, 2001.

De Boer, Theo. "Heideggers kritiek op Husserl." *Tijdschrift voor Filosofie* 40 (1978): 202-250, 452-501.
Dennett, Daniel C. *Consciousness Explained.* London: Penguin Books, 1993.
Derrida, Jacques. *Speech and Phenomena: And Other Essays on Husserl's Theory of Signs.* Translated by David B. Allison. Evanston, Ill.: Northwestern University Press, 1973.
——. *Of Spirit: Heidegger and the Question.* Translated by Geoffrey Bennington and Rachel Bowlby. Chicago: The University of Chicago Press, 1989.
Descartes, René. *The Philosophical Writings of Descartes,* Vol. II. Translated by John Cottingham, Robert Stoothoff, and Dugald Murdoch. Cambridge: Cambridge University Press, 1984.
Dostal, Robert J. "Time and Phenomenology in Husserl and Heidegger." In *The Cambridge Companion to Heidegger*, edited by Charles B. Guignon, 141-169. Cambridge: Cambridge University Press, 1993.
Dreyfus, Hubert L. "Introduction." In *Husserl, Intentionality, and Cognitive Science*, edited by Hubert Dreyfus, 1-27. Cambridge, Mass.: The MIT Press, 1982.
——. *Being-in-the-World: A Commentary on Heidegger's* Being and Time, *Division I.* Cambridge, Mass.: The MIT Press, 1991.
Drummond, John J. "Husserl on the Ways to the Performance of the Reduction." *Man and World* 8 (1975): 47-69.
——. "On Seeing *a* Material Thing *in* Space: The Role of Kinaesthesis in Visual Perception." *Philosophy and Phenomenological Research* 40 (1979-80): 19-32.
——. *Husserlian Intentionality and Non-Foundational Realism: Noema and Object.* Dordrecht: Kluwer Academic Publishers, 1990.
Elliston, Frederick. "Phenomenology Reinterpreted: From Husserl to Heidegger." *Philosophy Today* 21 (1977): 273-283.
Elveton, R. O. "Husserl and Heidegger: The Structure of the World." *The New Yearbook for Phenomenology and Phenomenological Philosophy* 1 (2001): 203-240.
Fichte, Johann Gottlieb. *Versuch einer neuen Darstellung der Wissenschaftslehre: Vorerinnerung, Erste und Zweite Einleitung, Erstes Kapitel. (1797/98).* Edited by Peter Baumanns. Hamburg: Felix meiner Verlag, 1984.
Figal, Günter. *Martin Heidegger: Phänomenologie der Freiheit.* Frankfurt a. M.: Athenäum, 1988.
——. *Martin Heidegger zur Einführung.* Hamburg: Junius, 1992.
Fink, Eugen. *Studien zur Phänomenologie 1930-1939.* The Hague: Martinus Nijhoff, 1966.
——. *Nähe und Distanz: Phänomenologische Vorträge und Aufsätze.* Edited by Franz-Anton Schwarz. Freiburg/Munich: Verlag Karl Alber, 1976.
——. *VI. Cartesianische Meditation. Teil 1: Die Idee einer transzendentalen Methodenlehre.* Edited by Hans Ebeling, Jann Holl, and Guy van Kerckhoven. Dordrecht: Kluwer Academic Publishers, 1988.

———. *VI. Cartesianische Meditation. Teil 2: Ergänzungsband*. Edited by Guy van Kerckhoven. Dordrecht: Kluwer Academic Publishers, 1988.

Føllesdal, Dagfinn. "Husserl's Notion of Noema." *The Journal of Philosophy* 66 (1969): 680-687.

———. "Husserl and Heidegger on the Role of Actions in the Constitution of the World." In *Essays in Honour of Jaakko Hintikka*, edited by Esa Saarinen, Risto Hilpinen, Ilkka Niiniluoto, and Merrill Provence Hintikka, 365-378. Dordrecht: D. Reidel Publishing Company, 1979.

———. "Absorbed Coping, Husserl, and Heidegger." In *Heidegger, Authenticity, and Modernity: Essays in Honor of Hubert L. Dreyfus*, Vol. 1, edited by Mark Wrathall and Jeff Malpas, 251-257. Cambridge, Mass.: The MIT Press, 2000.

Frege, Gottlob. "Der Gedanke: Eine Logische Untersuchung." In G. Frege, *Logische Untersuchungen*, ed. Günther Patzig, 30-53. Göttingen: Vandenhoeck & Ruprecht, 1993.

———. "Über Sinn und Bedeutung." In G. Frege, *Funktion, Begriff, Bedeutung*, ed. Günther Patzig, 40-65. Göttingen: Vandenhoeck & Ruprecht, 1994.

Gadamer, Hans-Georg. "Die phänomenologische Bewegung." In *Gesammelte Werke*, Vol. 3: *Neuere Philosophie I*, 105-146. Tübingen: J. C. B. Mohr (Paul Siebeck), 1987.

———. "Die Wahrheit des Kunstwerks." In *Gesammelte Werke*, Vol. 3: *Neuere Philosophie I*, 249-261. Tübingen: J. C. B. Mohr (Paul Siebeck), 1987.

———. *Wahrheit und Methode. Gesammelte Werke*, Vol. 1: *Hermeneutik I*. Tübingen: J. C. B. Mohr (Paul Siebeck), 1990.

———. "Erinnerungen an Heideggers Anfänge." In *Gesammelte Werke*, Vol. 10: *Hermeneutik im Rückblick*, 3-13. Tübingen: J. C. B. Mohr (Paul Siebeck), 1995.

Gethmann, Carl Friedrich. *Verstehen und Auslegung: Das Methodenproblem in der Philosophie Martin Heideggers*. Bonn: Bouvier Verlag Herbert Grundmann, 1974.

———. *Dasein: Erkennen und Handeln. Heidegger im phänomenologischen Kontext*. Berlin: Walter de Gruyter, 1993.

Gibson, W. R. Boyce. "From Husserl to Heidegger." Edited by Herbert Spiegelberg. *The Journal of the British Society for Phenomenology* 2 (1971): 58-83.

Gorner, Paul. "Husserl and Heidegger as Phenomenologists." *Journal of the British Society for Phenomenology* 23, no. 2 (1992): 146-155.

———. "Heidegger's Phenomenology as Transcendental Philosophy." *International Journal of Philosophical Studies* 10 (2002): 17-33.

Grondin, Jean. *Sources of Hermeneutics*. Albany: State University of New York Press, 1995.

Gronke, Horst. *Das Denken des Anderen: Führt die Selbstaufhebung von Husserls Phänomenologie der Intersubjektivität zur transzendentalen Sprachpragmatik?* Würzburg: Königshausen & Neumann, 1999.

Haney, Kathleen M. *Intersubjectivity Revisited: Phenomenology and the Other*. Athens: Ohio University Press, 1994.

Hart, James G. *The Person and the Common Life: Studies in a Husserlian Social Ethics*. Dordrecht: Kluwer Academic Publishers, 1992.

———. "Being and Mind." In *The Truthful and the Good: Essays in Honor of Robert Sokolowski*, edited by John J. Drummond and James G. Hart, 1-16. Dordrecht: Kluwer Academic Publishers, 1996.

Haugeland, John. "Heidegger on Being a Person." *Noûs* 16, no. 1 (1982): 15-26.

Held, Klaus. *Lebendige Gegenwart: Die Frage nach der Seinsweise des transzendentalen Ich bei Edmund Husserl, entwickelt am Leitfaden der Zeitproblematik*. The Hague: Martinus Nijhoff, 1966.

———. "Das Problem der Intersubjektivität und die Idee einer phänomenologischen Transzendentalphilosophie." In *Perspektiven transzendentalphänomenologischer Forschung*, edited by Ulrich Claesges and Klaus Held, 3-60. The Hague: Martinus Nijhoff, 1972.

———. "Einleitung." In E. Husserl, *Die phänomenologische Methode: Ausgewählte Texte I*, edited by Klaus Held, 5-51. Stuttgart: Philip Reclam jun., 1985.

———. "Heidegger und das Prinzip der Phänomenologie." In *Heidegger und die praktische Philosophie*, edited by Annemarie Gethmann-Siefert and Otto Pöggeler, 111-139. Frankfurt a. M.: Suhrkamp Verlag, 1988.

Herrmann, Friedrich-Wilhelm von. *Subjekt und Dasein: Interpretationen zu "Sein und Zeit."* 2nd, expanded edition. Frankfurt a. M.: Vittorio Klostermann, 1985.

———. *Hermeneutik und Reflexion: Der Begriff der Phänomenologie bei Heidegger und Husserl*. Frankfurt a. M.: Vittorio Klostermann, 2000.

Holmes, Richard H. "The World According to Husserl and Heidegger." *Man and World* 18 (1985): 373-387.

Hopkins, Burt C. *Intentionality in Husserl and Heidegger: The Problem of the Original Method and Phenomenon of Phenomenology*. Dordrecht: Kluwer Academic Publishers, 1993.

———. "The Husserl-Heidegger Confrontation and the Essential Possibility of Phenomenology: Edmund Husserl, *Psychological and Transcendental Phenomenology and the Confrontation with Heidegger*." *Husserl Studies* 17 (2001): 125-148.

Kant, Immanuel. *Kritik der reinen Vernunft*. Edited by Wilhelm Weischedel. Frankfurt a. M.: Suhrkamp Verlag, 1974. *Critique of Pure Reason*. Translated by J. M. D. Meiklejohn. London: George Bell and Sons, 1890.

Keller, Pierre. *Husserl and Heidegger on Human Experience*. Cambridge: Cambridge University Press, 1999.

Kern, Iso. "Die drei Wege zur transzendental-phänomenologischen Reduktion in der Philosophie Edmund Husserls." *Tijdschrift voor Filosofie* 24, no. 1 (1962): 303-349.

———. *Husserl und Kant: Eine Untersuchung über Husserls Verhältnis zu Kant und zum Neukantianismus*. The Hague: Martinus Nijhoff, 1964.

Kisiel, Theodore. "On the Way to *Being and Time*: Introduction to the Translation of Heidegger's Prolegomena zur Geschichte des Zeitbegriffs." *Research in Phenomenology* 15 (1985): 193-226.

——. *The Genesis of Heidegger's Being and Time*. Berkeley: University of California Press, 1993.

——. "Husserl and Heidegger." In *Encyclopedia of Phenomenology*, edited by Lester Embree, Elizabeth A. Behnke, *et. al.*, 333-339. Dordrecht: Kluwer Academic Publishers, 1997.

Krell, David Farrell. *Intimations of Mortality: Time, Truth, and Finitude in Heidegger's Thinking of Being*. University Park: The Pennsylvania State University Press, 1986.

Lafont, Cristina. *Sprache und Welterschließung: Zur linguistischen Wende der Hermeneutik Heideggers*. Frankfurt a. M.: Suhrkamp Verlag, 1994.

Landgrebe, Ludwig. *Der Weg der Phänomenologie: Das Problem einer ursprünglichen Erfahrung*. Gütersloh: Gütersloher Verlagshaus Gerd Mohn, 1963.

Lee, Nam-In. *Edmund Husserls Phänomenologie der Instinkte*. Dordrecht: Kluwer Academic Publishers, 1993.

——. "Edmund Husserl's Phenomenology of Mood." In *Alterity and Facticity: New Perspectives on Husserl*, edited by Natalie Depraz and Dan Zahavi, 103-120. Dordrecht: Kluwer Academic Publishers, 1998.

Lenkowski, William Jon. "What is Husserl's Epoché? The Problem of the Beginning of Philosophy in a Husserlian Context." *Man and World* 11 (1978): 299-323.

Levin, David Michael. "The Ontological Dimension of Embodiment: Heidegger's Thinking of Being." In *The Body: Classic and Contemporary Readings*, edited by Donn Welton, 122-149. Oxford: Blackwell Publishers, 1999.

Levinas, Emmanuel. *Totality and Infinity: An Essay on Exteriority*. Translated by Alphonso Lingis. Pittsburgh: Duquesne University Press, 1969.

——. *The Theory of Intuition in Husserl's Phenomenology*. 2nd edition. Translated by André Orianne. Evanston, Ill.: Northwestern University Press, 1995.

——. *Discovering existence with Husserl*. Translated and edited by Richard A. Cohen and Michael B. Smith. Evanston, Ill.: Northwestern University Press, 1998.

Luft, Sebastian. "Husserl's Phenomenological Discovery of the Natural Attitude." *Continental Philosophy Review* 31 (1998): 153-170.

Margolis, Joseph. "Phenomenology and Metaphysics: Husserl, Heidegger, and Merleau-Ponty." In *Merleau-Ponty Vivant*, edited by M. C. Dillon, 153-182. Albany: State University of New York Press, 1991.

Marion, Jean-Luc. *Reduction and Givenness: Investigations of Husserl, Heidegger, and Phenomenology*. Translated by Thomas A. Carlson. Evanston, Ill.: Northwestern University Press, 1998.

Melle, Ullrich. *Das Wahrnehmungsproblem und seine Verwandlung in phänomenologischer Einstellung: Untersuchungen zu den phänomenologischen*

Wahrnehmungstheorien von Husserl, Gurwitsch und Merleau-Ponty. The Hague: Martinus Nijhoff, 1983.

Merker, Barbara. *Selbsttäuschung und Selbsterkenntnis: Zu Heideggers Transformation der Phänomenologie Husserls*. Frankfurt a. M.: Suhrkamp Verlag, 1988.

Merleau-Ponty, Maurice. *Phenomenology of Perception*. Translated by Colin Smith. London: Routledge, 1962.

———. *The Primacy of Perception: And Other Essays on Phenomenological Psychology, the Philosophy of Art, History and Politics*. Edited by James M. Edie. Translated by J. M. Edie et al. Evanston, Ill.: Northwestern University Press, 1964.

Misch, Georg. *Lebensphilosophie und Phänomenologie: Eine Auseinandersetzung der Diltheyschen Richtung mit Heidegger und Husserl*. 3rd, expanded edition. Stuttgart: B. G. Teubner, 1967.

Mohanty, J. N. *The Possibility of Transcendental Philosophy*. Dordrecht: Martinus Nijhoff, 1985.

Moran, Dermot. "Heidegger's Critique of Husserl's and Brentano's Accounts of Intentionality." *Inquiry* 43 (2000): 39-65.

———. *Introduction to Phenomenology*. London: Routledge, 2000.

Morrison, James C. "Husserl and Heidegger: The Parting of the Ways." In *Heidegger's Existential Analytic*, edited by Frederick Elliston, 47-59. The Hague: Mouton Publishers, 1978.

Mulhall, Stephen. *On Being in the World: Wittgenstein and Heidegger on Seeing Aspects*. London: Routledge, 1990.

Nagel, Thomas. *The View from Nowhere*. New York: Oxford University Press, 1986.

Natanson, Maurice. *Edmund Husserl: Philosopher of Infinite Tasks*. Evanston, Ill.: Northwestern University Press, 1973.

Øverenget, Einar. *Seeing the Self: Heidegger on Subjectivity*. Dordrecht: Kluwer Academic Publishers, 1998.

Okrent, Mark. *Heidegger's Pragmatism: Understanding, Being, and the Critique of Metaphysics*. Ithaca: Cornell University Press, 1988.

Olafson, Frederick A. "Heidegger *à la* Wittgenstein or 'Coping' with Professor Dreyfus." *Inquiry* 37 (1994): 45-64.

———. "Individualism, Subjectivity, and Presence: A Response to Taylor Carman." *Inquiry* 37 (1994): 331-337.

Orth, Ernst W. *Edmund Husserls "Krisis der europäischen wissenschaften und die transzendentale Phänomenologie"*. Darmstadt: Wissenschaftliche Buchgesellschaft, 1999.

Ott, Hugo. *Martin Heidegger: Unterwegs zu seiner Biographie*. Expanded edition. Frankfurt a. M.: Campus Verlag, 1992.

Oudemans, Th. C. W. "Heideggers 'logische Untersuchungen'." *Heidegger Studies* 6 (1990): 85-105.

Overgaard, Søren. "Epoché and Solipsistic Reduction." *Husserl Studies* 18 (2002): 209-222.
——. "Heidegger's Concept of Truth Revisited." *Sats: Nordic Journal of Philosophy* 3, no. 2 (2002): 73-90.
——. "Heidegger's Early Critique of Husserl." *International Journal of Philosophical Studies* 11 (2003): 157-175.
——. "On Levinas' Critique of Husserl." In *Metaphysics, Facticity, Interpretation: Phenomenology in the Nordic Countries*, edited by Dan Zahavi, Sara Heinämaa, and Hans Ruin, 115-138. Dordrecht: Kluwer Academic Publishers, 2003.
——. "Heidegger on Embodiment." Forthcoming in *Journal of the British Society for Phenomenology*, 2004.
Philipse, Herman. *Heidegger's Philosophy of Being: A Critical Interpretation*. Princeton: Princeton University Press, 1998.
Pietersma, H. "Husserl and Heidegger." *Philosophy and Phenomenological Research* 40 (1979): 194-211.
Plato. *The Collected Dialogues*. Edited by Edith Hamilton and Huntington Cairns. Princeton: Princeton University Press, 1989.
Pöggeler, Otto. "Heideggers logische Untersuchungen." In *Martin Heidegger: Innen- und Außenansichten*, edited by Siegfried Blasche, Wolfgang R. Köhler, et al., 75-100. Frankfurt a. M.: Suhrkamp Verlag, 1989.
——. "Die Krise des phänomenologischen Philosophiebegriffs (1929)." In *Phänomenologie im Widerstreit: Zum 50. Todestag Edmund Husserls*, edited by Christoph Jamme and Otto Pöggeler, 255-276. Frankfurt a. M.: Suhrkamp Verlag, 1989.
——. *Der Denkweg Martin Heideggers*. 4th edition. Stuttgart: Verlag Günther Neske, 1994.
Prufer, Thomas. "Heidegger, Early and Late, and Aquinas." In *Edmund Husserl and the Phenomenological Tradition: Essays in Phenomenology*, edited by Robert Sokolowski, 197-215. Washington, D.C.: The Catholic University of America Press, 1988.
Richardson, John. *Existential Epistemology: A Heideggerian Critique of the Cartesian Project*. Oxford: Clarendon Press, 1986.
Richardson, William J. *Heidegger: Through Phenomenology to Thought*. The Hague: Martinus Nijhoff, 1963.
Ricœur, Paul. *Husserl: An Analysis of His Phenomenology*. Translated by Edward G. Ballard and Lester E. Embree. Evanston, Ill.: Northwestern University Press, 1967.
Rorty, Richard. *Contingency, Irony, and Solidarity*. Cambridge: Cambridge University Press, 1989.
Rosales, Alberto. *Transzendenz und Differenz: Ein Beitrag zum Problem der ontologischen Differenz beim frühen Heidegger*. The Hague: Martinus Nijhoff, 1970.
Ruin, Hans. *Enigmatic Origins: Tracing the Theme of Historicity through Heidegger's Works*. Stockholm: Almqvist & Wiksell International, 1994.

———. "The Passivity of Reason – On Heidegger's Concept of Stimmung." *Sats: Nordic Journal of Philosophy* 1, no. 2 (2000): 143-159.
Ryle, Gilbert. *The Concept of Mind*. London: Penguin Books, 2000.
Sallis, John. *Echoes: After Heidegger*. Bloomington: Indiana University Press, 1990.
———. *Delimitations: Phenomenology and the End of Metaphysics*. 2nd, expanded edition. Bloomington: Indiana University Press, 1995.
Sartre, Jean-Paul. *Being and Nothingness: An Essay on Phenomenological Ontology*. Translated by Hazel E. Barnes. London: Routledge, 1996.
Scanlon, John. "Husserl's *Ideas* and the Natural Concept of the World." In *Edmund Husserl and the Phenomenological Tradition: Essays in Phenomenology*, edited by Robert Sokolowski, 217-233. Washington, D.C.: The Catholic University of America Press, 1988.
Schacht, Richard. "Husserlian and Heideggerian Phenomenology." *Philosophical Studies* 23 (1972): 293-314.
Schmitz, Hermann. *Husserl und Heidegger*. Bonn: Bouvier Verlag, 1996.
Schneider, Robert O. "Husserl and Heidegger: An Essay on the Question of Intentionality." *Philosophy Today* 21 (1977): 368-375.
Schulz, Walter. "Über den philosophiegeschichtlichen Ort Martin Heideggers." In *Heidegger: Perspektiven zur Deutung seines Werks*, edited by Otto Pöggeler, 95-139. Königstein, Ts.: Athenäum, 1984.
Seeburger, Francis F. "Heidegger and the Phenomenological Reduction." *Philosophy and Phenomenological Research* 36 (1975): 212-221.
Sepp, Hans Rainer. "Zeit und Sorge: Eine Anmerkung zu Heideggers Kritik an Husserl." In *Die erscheinende Welt: Festschrift für Klaus Held*, edited by Heinrich Hüni and Peter Trawny, 275-290. Berlin: Duncker & Humblot, 2002.
Sheehan, Thomas. "Husserl and Heidegger: The Making and Unmaking of a Relationship." In E. Husserl, *Psychological and Transcendental Phenomenology and the Confrontation with Heidegger*, edited and translated by Thomas Sheehan and Richard E. Palmer, 1-32. Dordrecht: Kluwer Academic Publishers, 1997.
Sheets-Johnstone, Maxine. *The Primacy of Movement*. Amsterdam: John Benjamins Publishing Company, 1999.
Soffer, Gail. "Phenomenologizing with a Hammer: Theory or Practice." *Continental Philosophy Review* 32 (1999): 379-393.
Sokolowski, Robert. *The Formation of Husserl's Concept of Constitution*. The Hague: Martinus Nijhoff, 1964.
———. "Ontological Possibilities in Phenomenology: The Dyad and the One." *Review of Metaphysics* 29 (1975-76): 691-701.
———. "Intentional Analysis and the Noema." *Dialectica* 38, no. 2-3 (1984): 113-129.
Sommer, Manfred. "Fremderfahrung und Zeitbewußtsein: Zur Phänomenologie der Intersubjektivität." *Zeitschrift für philosophische Forschung* 38 (1984): 3-18.
Spiegelberg, Herbert. "The 'Reality-Phenomenon' and Reality." In *Philosophical Essays in Memory of Edmund Husserl*, edited by Marvin Farber, 84-105. Cambridge, Mass.: Harvard University Press, 1940.

———. *The Phenomenological Movement: A Historical Introduction.* 2nd edition. Vol. 1. The Hague: Martinus Nijhoff, 1965.
Stapleton, Timothy J. *Husserl and Heidegger: The Question of a Phenomenological Beginning.* Albany: State University of New York Press, 1983.
Steinbock, Anthony J. *Home and Beyond: Generative Phenomenology after Husserl.* Evanston, Ill.: Northwestern University Press, 1995.
Streeter, Ryan. "Heidegger's Formal Indication: A Question of Method in *Being and Time.*" *Man and World* 30 (1997): 413-430.
Ströker, Elisabeth. *Husserls transzendentale Phänomenologie.* Frankfurt a. M.: Vittorio Klostermann, 1987.
Taminiaux, Jacques. "Heidegger and Husserl's Logical investigations: In Remembrance of Heidegger's Last Seminar (Zähringen, 1973)." In J. Taminiaux, *Dialectic and Difference: Finitude in Modern Thought*, edited and translated by Robert Crease and James T. Decker, 91-114. Atlantic Highlands, N. J.: Humanities Press, 1985.
———. "From One Idea of Phenomenology to the Other." In J. Taminiaux, *Heidegger and the Project of Fundamental Ontology*, edited and translated by Michael Gendre, 1-54. Albany: State University of New York Press, 1991.
———. "The Husserlian Heritage in Heidegger's Notion of the Self." In *Reading Heidegger from the Start: Essays in His Earliest Thought*, edited by Theodore Kisiel and John van Buren, 269-290. Albany: State University of New York Press, 1994.
Theunissen, Michael. *Der Andere: Studien zur Sozialontologie der Gegenwart.* 2nd, expanded edition. Berlin: Walter de Gruyter, 1977.
Tugendhat, Ernst. *Der Wahrheitsbegriff bei Husserl und Heidegger.* 2nd edition. Berlin: Walter de Gruyter, 1970.
———. "Das Sein und das Nichts." In *Philosophische Aufsätze*, 36-66. Frankfurt a. M.: Suhrkamp Verlag, 1992.
———. "Heideggers Seinsfrage." In *Philosophische Aufsätze*, 108-135. Frankfurt a. M.: Suhrkamp Verlag, 1992.
van Buren, John. *The Young Heidegger: Rumor of the Hidden King.* Bloomington: Indiana University Press, 1994.
Waldenfels, Bernhard. *Das Zwischenreich des Dialogs: Sozialphilosophische Untersuchungen in Anschluss an Edmund Husserl.* The Hague: Martinus Nijhoff, 1971.
Watanabe, Jiro. "Categorial Intuition and the Understanding of Being in Husserl and Heidegger." In *Reading Heidegger: Commemorations*, edited by John Sallis, 109-117. Bloomington: Indiana University Press, 1993.
Welton, Donn. "World." In *Encyclopedia of Phenomenology*, edited by Lester Embree, Elizabeth A. Behnke, *et. al.*, 736-743. Dordrecht: Kluwer Academic Publishers, 1997.

———. "Soft, Smooth Hands: Husserl's Phenomenology of the Lived-Body." In *The Body: Classic and Contemporary Readings*, edited by Donn Welton, 38-56. Oxford: Blackwell Publishers, 1999.

———. *The Other Husserl: The Horizons of Transcendental Philosophy*. Bloomington: Indiana University Press, 2000.

Wentzer, Thomas Schwartz. *Bewahrung der Geschichte: Die hermeneutische Philosophie Walter Benjamins*. Bodenheim: Philo Verlagsgesellschaft, 1998.

Wittgenstein, Ludwig. *Tractatus Logico-Philosophicus*. Translated by D. F. Pears and B. F. McGuinness. London: Routledge and Kegan Paul, 1961.

———. *On Certainty*. Edited by G. E. M. Anscombe and G. H. von Wright. Translated by Denis Paul and G. E. M. Anscombe. Oxford: Basil Blackwell, 1969.

———. *Notebooks 1914-1916*. Edited by G. H. von Wright and G. E. M. Anscombe. Translated by G. E. M. Anscombe. 2nd edition. Oxford: Basil Blackwell, 1979.

Zahavi, Dan. "The Self-Pluralisation of Primal Life. A Problem in Fink's Husserl-Interpretation." *Recherches husserliennes* 2 (1994): 3-18.

———. *Husserl und die transzendentale Intersubjektivität: Eine Antwort auf die sprachpragmatische Kritik*. Dordrecht: Kluwer Academic Publishers, 1996.

———. *Self-Awareness and Alterity: A Phenomenological Investigation*. Evanston, Ill.: Northwestern University Press, 1999.

———. "Beyond Empathy: Phenomenological Approaches to Intersubjectivity." *Journal of Consciousness Studies* 8 (2001): 151-167.

———. *Husserl's Phenomenology*. Stanford: Stanford University Press, 2003.

———. "Husserl's Noema and the Internalism-Externalism Debate." Forthcoming in *Inquiry*, 2004.

INDEX OF NAMES

Adorno, T. W., 51n28
Aguirre, A., 26n29
Alweiss, L., 3n5, 104n3, 108n11, 144n20, 159n38, 197n38
Aristotle, 29n39, 73, 75n10, 102, 159

Berkeley, G., 35n6, 81
Bernet, R., 8n13, 13n9, 27n34, 80n16, 82n20, 98n42, 138, 138n10, 172n8, 174n12, 192n30
Biemel, W., 44n14, 65n49, 74n8, 137n8
Blattner, W. D., 179n21
Boehm, R., 66, 66n54, 67n55, 68n58
Boelen, B., 77n14
Brentano, F., 62, 69
Bruzina, R. C., 67n57, 171n6
Buckley, R. P., 99n44

Cairns, D., 171n6
Caputo, J. D., 36n7, 90n29, 169n4
Carman, T., 18n20
Carnap, R., 28n36
Carr, D., 46n18, 51n27, 186, 186n24, 192n29
Cerbone, D. R., 159n39, 169n4
Claesges, U., 152nn27-28
Courtine, J.-F., 27n34
Crowell, S. G., 3n5, 48n23, 82n21, 86n25, 108n12, 140n14, 196n36, 200n40, 204-205n1

Dahlstrom, D. O., 3n5, 9n1, 83n22, 85n24, 126n35, 159n38, 169n3, 172n8, 179n21, 194nn32-33
De Boer, T., 94n37
Dennett, D. C., 48n22
Derrida, J., 46, 46n19, 174n12, 197n37
Descartes, R., 7, 32-33, 35nn5-6, 42, 93, 104, 104n2, 138n9, 162, 187n26
Dostal, R. J., 174n12
Dreyfus, H. L., 13n8, 14n10, 18n20, 61n45, 65n53, 71nn2-3, 120n30, 137n8, 159n38, 178-179, 178nn18-20, 179n21
Drummond, J. J., 23n26, 34n3, 56n36, 152n27

Elliston, F., 76n12

Fichte, J. G., 138n9
Figal, G., 27n35, 28, 28n37, 104n2, 131n1, 147n21

Fink, E., 7n8, 7n10, 19n21, 26nn29-31, 29, 30n40, 35n5, 36-37, 37n8, 44n15, 55, 55nn33-34, 67, 67nn56-57, 68n58, 140n13, 171n6, 185n23
Føllesdal, D., 56-57, 56n35, 57n37, 175n14, 179n21
Frege, G., 40n11, 205n1

Gadamer, H.-G., 10n2, 34n3, 49n24, 59-60, 59n41, 60n42, 65n48, 104n1, 116n24, 123n32, 124, 125n34, 130n43
Gethmann, C. F., 3n5, 27n34, 65n53, 94n36, 95n39, 111n17, 137n8, 142, 142n16, 162n42, 194n33
Gibson, W. R. B., 49n24
Gorner, P., 90n29, 120n30
Grondin, J., 36n7
Gronke, H., 43n13

Haney, K. M., 16n15
Hart, J. G., 46n20, 133n3, 172n7
Haugeland, J., 118n28
Hegel, G. W. F., 19
Held, K., 44n14, 52n30, 116n25, 131n1, 192n30, 195, 195n35
Herrmann, F.-W. v., 3n5, 49n25, 79n15, 88n26, 104n3, 109n14, 110, 110n16
Holmes, R. H., 126n36
Hopkins, B. C., 3n5, 115n23, 140n14

Jakobsson, J., 175n13

Kant, I., 34n2, 36n7, 46n18, 46n20, 52-53, 64, 90, 94n38, 116n26, 139, 186, 186n25
Keller, P., 3n5, 18n20, 106-108, 106nn4-8, 107nn9-10, 108n11
Kern, I., 8n13, 24n28
Kisiel, T., 1n1, 7n9, 14n10, 15n13, 27n33, 83n22, 84n23, 92n33, 120n29, 125n34, 159n40, 183n22
Krell, D. F., 6n7, 74n8, 125n34

Lafont, C., 194n33
Landgrebe, L., 7n11, 34n3, 109, 109n15, 116n25
Lee, N.-I., 65n48, 130n42
Lenkowski, W. J., 27n32
Levin, D. M., 159n39

Index of Names

Levinas, E., 49n24, 68n58, 80n16, 130n43, 134n4, 137n8, 142n16
Luft, S., 19n22, 27n32

Marbach, E., 8n13
Margolis, J., 169n4
Marion, J.-L., 3n5, 27n34, 61n45, 68n59, 89n27, 98n43, 101n47, 104n3
McDowell, J., 205n1
Melle, U., 40n11
Merker, B., 3n5, 13n6, 173n10
Merleau-Ponty, M., 1n3, 3, 3n6, 16, 17n16, 41, 41n12, 138, 138n11, 158, 158n35, 200n39
Misch, G., 94n37
Mohanty, J. N., 36n7
Moran, D., 75n10, 190n28
Morrison, J. C., 68n59, 102n48
Mulhall, S., 176n16

Nagel, T., 65n47
Natanson, M., 61n44

Øverenget, E., 80n17, 148n24
Okrent, M., 118n28, 168n2, 169n3, 178n17
Olafson, F. A., 18n20
Orth, E. W., 10n2
Ott, H., 1n1
Oudemans, T. C. W., 83n22, 90nn29-30
Overgaard, S., 26n29, 133n3, 134n4, 159n39, 173n9, 194n33

Philipse, H., 74n8
Pietersma, H., 169n4
Plato, 29n39, 73
Pöggeler, O., 7n9, 83n22, 95n39, 123n32, 124-125, 195n34, 200n40
Prufer, T., 45n16, 172n7

Richardson, J., 92n33
Richardson, W. J., 97n42
Ricœur, P., 19n22, 157n33
Rorty, R., 75n11
Rosales, A., 101n47
Ruin, H., 99n45, 125n33
Ryle, G., 141, 141n15, 168

Sallis, J., 36n7, 73nn5-6, 195n34
Sartre, J.-P., 16, 17n16, 28, 28n38, 51n27, 135n6, 137, 137n7, 156n31, 169n5, 188, 188n27, 196
Scanlon, J., 16n14
Schacht, R., 1n2, 61n45
Scheler, M., 142n17
Schmitz, H., 3n5
Schneider, R. O., 43n13

Schulz, W., 92n35
Seeburger, F. F., 94n37
Sepp, H. R., 81n19
Sheehan, T., 1n1
Sheets-Johnstone, M., 158n36
Soffer, G., 14n11, 174n11
Sokolowski, R., 56n36, 65, 65nn51-52, 172n7
Sommer, M., 132n2
Spiegelberg, H., 34n3, 43n13, 77-78, 77nn13-14
Stapleton, T. J., 3n5, 68n58, 104n3, 109n14, 111n17, 116n27, 206n2
Steinbock, A. J., 115n23
Streeter, R., 84n22
Ströker, E., 34n4

Taminiaux, J., 68n59, 80n17, 109n13
Theunissen, M., 134n4
Tugendhat, E., 2n5, 3n5, 28n36, 73n4, 82n21, 120n29, 143n18, 194n33

Van Breda, H. L., 67n57
van Buren, J., 8n12, 83n22, 89n27, 95n39, 125n34

Waldenfels, B., 16n15, 134n4
Watanabe, J., 80n17
Welton, D., 7n11, 111n19, 115n23, 126n36, 128n37, 151n26, 158n34
Wentzer, T. S., 100n46
Wittgenstein, L., 22n24, 23n25, 24n27, 33n1, 50, 50n26, 176n16

Zahavi, D., 17n16, 26n31, 27n34, 46n20, 66n54, 108n11, 132n2, 136n6, 151, 151n26, 154n29, 158n34, 196n36

Phaenomenologica

1. E. Fink: *Sein, Wahrheit, Welt.* Vor-Fragen zum Problem des Phänomen-Begriffs. 1958
   ISBN 90-247-0234-8
2. H.L. van Breda and J. Taminiaux (eds.): *Husserl et la pensée moderne / Husserl und das Denken der Neuzeit.* Actes du deuxième Colloque International de Phénoménologie / Akten des zweiten Internationalen Phänomenologischen Kolloquiums (Krefeld, 1.–3. Nov. 1956). 1959
   ISBN 90-247-0235-6
3. J.-C. Piguet: *De l'esthétique à la métaphysique.* 1960   ISBN 90-247-0236-4
4. *E. Husserl: 1850–1959.* Recueil commémoratif publié à l'occasion du centenaire de la naissance du philosophe. 1959   ISBN 90-247-0237-2
5/6. H. Spiegelberg: *The Phenomenological Movement.* A Historical Introduction. 3rd revised ed. with the collaboration of Karl Schuhmann. 1982   ISBN Hb: 90-247-2577-1; Pb: 90-247-2535-6
7. A. Roth: *Edmund Husserls ethische Untersuchungen.* Dargestellt anhand seiner Vorlesungsmanuskripte. 1960   ISBN 90-247-0241-0
8. E. Levinas: *Totalité et infini.* Essai sur l'extériorité. 4th ed., 4th printing 1984
   ISBN Hb: 90-247-5105-5; Pb: 90-247-2971-8
9. A. de Waelhens: *La philosophie et les expériences naturelles.* 1961   ISBN 90-247-0243-7
10. L. Eley: *Die Krise des Apriori in der transzendentalen Phänomenologie Edmund Husserls.* 1962
    ISBN 90-247-0244-5
11. A. Schutz: *Collected Papers, I.* The Problem of Social Reality. Edited and introduced by M. Natanson. 1962; 5th printing: 1982   ISBN Hb: 90-247-5089-X; Pb: 90-247-3046-5
    Collected Papers, II *see* below under Volume 15
    Collected Papers, III *see* below under Volume 22
    Collected Papers, IV *see* below under Volume 136
12. J.M. Broekman: *Phänomenologie und Egologie.* Faktisches und transzendentales Ego bei Edmund Husserl. 1963   ISBN 90-247-0245-3
13. W.J. Richardson: *Heidegger. Through Phenomenology to Thought.* Preface by Martin Heidegger. 1963; 3rd printing: 1974   ISBN 90-247-02461-1
14. J.N. Mohanty: *Edmund Husserl's Theory of Meaning.* 1964; reprint: 1969   ISBN 90-247-0247-X
15. A. Schutz: *Collected Papers, II.* Studies in Social Theory. Edited and introduced by A. Brodersen. 1964; reprint: 1977   ISBN 90-247-0248-8
16. I. Kern: *Husserl und Kant.* Eine Untersuchung über Husserls Verhältnis zu Kant und zum Neukantianismus. 1964; reprint: 1984   ISBN 90-247-0249-6
17. R.M. Zaner: *The Problem of Embodiment.* Some Contributions to a Phenomenology of the Body. 1964; reprint: 1971   ISBN 90-247-5093-8
18. R. Sokolowski: *The Formation of Husserl's Concept of Constitution.* 1964; reprint: 1970
    ISBN 90-247-5086-5
19. U. Claesges: *Edmund Husserls Theorie der Raumkonstitution.* 1964   ISBN 90-247-0251-8
20. M. Dufrenne: *Jalons.* 1966   ISBN 90-247-0252-6
21. E. Fink: *Studien zur Phänomenologie, 1930–1939.* 1966   ISBN 90-247-0253-4
22. A. Schutz: *Collected Papers, III.* Studies in Phenomenological Philosophy. Edited by I. Schutz. With an introduction by Aron Gurwitsch. 1966; reprint: 1975   ISBN 90-247-5090-3
23. K. Held: *Lebendige Gegenwart.* Die Frage nach der Seinsweise des transzendentalen Ich bei Edmund Husserl, entwickelt am Leitfaden der Zeitproblematik. 1966   ISBN 90-247-0254-2
24. O. Laffoucrière: *Le destin de la pensée et 'La Mort de Dieu' selon Heidegger.* 1968
    ISBN 90-247-0255-0
25. E. Husserl: *Briefe an Roman Ingarden.* Mit Erläuterungen und Erinnerungen an Husserl. Hrsg. von R. Ingarden. 1968   ISBN Hb: 90-247-0257-7; Pb: 90-247-0256-9
26. R. Boehm: *Vom Gesichtspunkt der Phänomenologie* (I). Husserl-Studien. 1968
    ISBN Hb: 90-247-0259-3; Pb: 90-247-0258-5
    For *Band II* see below under Volume 83

Phaenomenologica

27. T. Conrad: *Zur Wesenslehre des psychischen Lebens und Erlebens.* Mit einem Geleitwort von H.L. van Breda. 1968 ISBN 90-247-0260-7
28. W. Biemel: *Philosophische Analysen zur Kunst der Gegenwart.* 1969
ISBN Hb: 90-247-0263-1; Pb: 90-247-0262-3
29. G. Thinès: *La problématique de la psychologie.* 1968
ISBN Hb: 90-247-0265-8; Pb: 90-247-0264-X
30. D. Sinha: *Studies in Phenomenology.* 1969 ISBN Hb: 90-247-0267-4; Pb: 90-247-0266-6
31. L. Eley: *Metakritik der formalen Logik.* Sinnliche Gewissheit als Horizont der Aussagenlogik und elementaren Prädikatenlogik. 1969 ISBN Hb: 90-247-0269-0; Pb: 90-247-0268-2
32. M.S. Frings: *Person und Dasein.* Zur Frage der Ontologie des Wertseins. 1969
ISBN Hb: 90-247-0271-2; Pb: 90-247-0270-4
33. A. Rosales: *Transzendenz und Differenz.* Ein Beitrag zum Problem der ontologischen Differenz beim frühen Heidegger. 1970 ISBN 90-247-0272-0
34. M.M. Saraiva: *L'imagination selon Husserl.* 1970 ISBN 90-247-0273-9
35. P. Janssen: *Geschichte und Lebenswelt.* Ein Beitrag zur Diskussion von Husserls Spätwerk. 1970
ISBN 90-247-0274-7
36. W. Marx: *Vernunft und Welt.* Zwischen Tradition und anderem Anfang. 1970
ISBN 90-247-5042-3
37. J.N. Mohanty: *Phenomenology and Ontology.* 1970 ISBN 90-247-5053-9
38. A. Aguirre: *Genetische Phänomenologie und Reduktion.* Zur Letztbegründung der Wissenschaft aus der radikalen Skepsis im Denken E. Husserls. 1970 ISBN 90-247-5025-3
39. T.F. Geraets: *Vers une nouvelle philosophie transcendentale.* La genèse de la philosophie de Maurice Merleau-Ponty jusqu'à la 'Phénoménologie de la perception.' Préface par E. Levinas. 1971 ISBN 90-247-5024-5
40. H. Declève: *Heidegger et Kant.* 1970 ISBN 90-247-5016-4
41. B. Waldenfels: *Das Zwischenreich des Dialogs.* Sozialphilosophische Untersuchungen in Anschluss an Edmund Husserl. 1971 ISBN 90-247-5072-5
42. K. Schuhmann: *Die Fundamentalbetrachtung der Phänomenologie.* Zum Weltproblem in der Philosophie Edmund Husserls. 1971 ISBN 90-247-5121-7
43. K. Goldstein: *Selected Papers/Ausgewählte Schriften.* Edited by A. Gurwitsch, E.M. Goldstein Haudek and W.E. Haudek. Introduction by A. Gurwitsch. 1971 ISBN 90-247-5047-4
44. E. Holenstein: *Phänomenologie der Assoziation.* Zu Struktur und Funktion eines Grundprinzips der passiven Genesis bei E. Husserl. 1972 ISBN 90-247-1175-4
45. F. Hammer: *Theonome Anthropologie?* Max Schelers Menschenbild und seine Grenzen. 1972
ISBN 90-247-1186-X
46. A. Pažanin: *Wissenschaft und Geschichte in der Phänomenologie Edmund Husserls.* 1972
ISBN 90-247-1194-0
47. G.A. de Almeida: *Sinn und Inhalt in der genetischen Phänomenologie E. Husserls.* 1972
ISBN 90-247-1318-8
48. J. Rolland de Renéville: *Aventure de l'absolu.* 1972 ISBN 90-247-1319-6
49. U. Claesges und K. Held (eds.): *Perspektiven transzendental-phänomenologischer Forschung.* Für Ludwig Landgrebe zum 70. Geburtstag von seiner Kölner Schülern. 1972 ISBN 90-247-1313-7
50. F. Kersten and R. Zaner (eds.): *Phenomenology: Continuation and Criticism.* Essays in Memory of Dorion Cairns. 1973 ISBN 90-247-1302-1
51. W. Biemel (ed.): *Phänomenologie Heute.* Festschrift für Ludwig Landgrebe. 1972
ISBN 90-247-1336-6
52. D. Souche-Dagues: *Le développement de l'intentionalité dans la phénoménologie husserlienne.* 1972 ISBN 90-247-1354-4
53. B. Rang: *Kausalität und Motivation.* Untersuchungen zum Verhältnis von Perspektivität und Objektivität in der Phänomenologie Edmund Husserls. 1973 ISBN 90-247-1353-6
54. E. Levinas: *Autrement qu'être ou au-delà de l'essence.* 2nd. ed.: 1978 ISBN 90-247-2030-3
55. D. Cairns: *Guide for Translating Husserl.* 1973 ISBN Pb: 90-247-1452-4

Phaenomenologica

56. K. Schuhmann: *Die Dialektik der Phänomenologie, I.* Husserl über Pfänder. 1973
ISBN 90-247-1316-1
57. K. Schuhmann: *Die Dialektik der Phänomenologie, II.* Reine Phänomenologie und phänomenologische Philosophie. Historisch-analytische Monographie über Husserls 'Ideen I'. 1973
ISBN 90-247-1307-2
58. R. Williame: *Les fondements phénoménologiques de la sociologie compréhensive: Alfred Schutz et Max Weber.* 1973 ISBN 90-247-1531-8
59. E. Marbach: *Das Problem des Ich in der Phänomenologie Husserls.* 1974 ISBN 90-247-1587-3
60. R. Stevens: *James and Husserl: The Foundations of Meaning.* 1974 ISBN 90-247-1631-4
61. H.L. van Breda (ed.): *Vérité et Vérification / Wahrheit und Verifikation.* Actes du quatrième Colloque International de Phénoménologie / Akten des vierten Internationalen Kolloquiums für Phänomenologie (Schwäbisch Hall, Baden-Württemberg, 8.–11. September 1969). 1974
ISBN 90-247-1702-7
62. Ph.J. Bossert (ed.): *Phenomenological Perspectives.* Historical and Systematic Essays in Honor of Herbert Spiegelberg. 1975. ISBN 90-247-1701-9
63. H. Spiegelberg: *Doing Phenomenology.* Essays on and in Phenomenology. 1975
ISBN 90-247-1725-6
64. R. Ingarden: *On the Motives which Led Husserl to Transcendental Idealism.* 1975
ISBN 90-247-1751-5
65. H. Kuhn, E. Avé-Lallemant and R. Gladiator (eds.): *Die Münchener Phänomenologie.* Vorträge des Internationalen Kongresses in München (13.–18. April 1971). 1975 ISBN 90-247-1740-X
66. D. Cairns: *Conversations with Husserl and Fink.* Edited by the Husserl-Archives in Louvain. With a foreword by R.M. Zaner. 1975 ISBN 90-247-1793-0
67. G. Hoyos Vásquez: *Intentionalität als Verantwortung.* Geschichtsteleologie und Teleologie der Intentionalität bei Husserl. 1976 ISBN 90-247-1794-9
68. J. Patočka: *Le monde naturel comme problème philosophique.* 1976 ISBN 90-247-1795-7
69. W.W. Fuchs: *Phenomenology and the Metaphysics of Presence.* An Essay in the Philosophy of Edmund Husserl. 1976 ISBN 90-247-1822-8
70. S. Cunningham: *Language and the Phenomenological Reductions of Edmund Husserl.* 1976
ISBN 90-247-1823-6
71. G.C. Moneta: *On Identity.* A Study in Genetic Phenomenology. 1976 ISBN 90-247-1860-0
72. W. Biemel und das Husserl-Archiv zu Löwen (eds.): *Die Welt des Menschen – Die Welt der Philosophie.* Festschrift für Jan Patočka. 1976 ISBN 90-247-1899-6
73. M. Richir: *Au-delà du renversement copernicien.* La question de la phénoménologie et son fondement. 1976 ISBN 90-247-1903-8
74. H. Mongis: *Heidegger et la critique de la notion de valeur.* La destruction de la fondation métaphysique. Lettre-préface de Martin Heidegger. 1976 ISBN 90-247-1904-6
75. J. Taminiaux: *Le regard et l'excédent.* 1977 ISBN 90-247-2028-1
76. Th. de Boer: *The Development of Husserl's Thought.* 1978
ISBN Hb: 90-247-2039-7; Pb: 90-247-2124-5
77. R.R. Cox: *Schutz's Theory of Relevance.* A Phenomenological Critique. 1978
ISBN 90-247-2041-9
78. S. Strasser: *Jenseits von Sein und Zeit.* Eine Einführung in Emmanuel Levinas' Philosophie. 1978
ISBN 90-247-2068-0
79. R.T. Murphy: *Hume and Husserl.* Towards Radical Subjectivism. 1980 ISBN 90-247-2172-5
80. H. Spiegelberg: *The Context of the Phenomenological Movement.* 1981 ISBN 90-247-2392-2
81. J.R. Mensch: *The Question of Being in Husserl's Logical Investigations.* 1981
ISBN 90-247-2413-9
82. J. Loscerbo: *Being and Technology.* A Study in the Philosophy of Martin Heidegger. 1981
ISBN 90-247-2411-2
83. R. Boehm: *Vom Gesichtspunkt der Phänomenologie II.* Studien zur Phänomenologie der Epoché. 1981 ISBN 90-247-2415-5

Phaenomenologica

84. H. Spiegelberg and E. Avé-Lallemant (eds.): *Pfänder-Studien.* 1982   ISBN 90-247-2490-2
85. S. Valdinoci: *Les fondements de la phénoménologie husserlienne.* 1982   ISBN 90-247-2504-6
86. I. Yamaguchi: *Passive Synthesis und Intersubjektivität bei Edmund Husserl.* 1982
      ISBN 90-247-2505-4
87. J. Libertson: *Proximity. Levinas, Blanchot, Bataille and Communication.* 1982
      ISBN 90-247-2506-2
88. D. Welton: *The Origins of Meaning.* A Critical Study of the Thresholds of Husserlian Phenomenology. 1983   ISBN 90-247-2618-2
89. W.R. McKenna: *Husserl's 'Introductions to Phenomenology'.* Interpretation and Critique. 1982
      ISBN 90-247-2665-4
90. J.P. Miller: *Numbers in Presence and Absence.* A Study of Husserl's Philosophy of Mathematics. 1982   ISBN 90-247-2709-X
91. U. Melle: *Das Wahrnehmungsproblem und seine Verwandlung in phänomenologischer Einstellung.* Untersuchungen zu den phänomenologischen Wahrnehmungstheorien von Husserl, Gurwitsch und Merleau-Ponty. 1983   ISBN 90-247-2761-8
92. W.S. Hamrick (ed.): *Phenomenology in Practice and Theory.* Essays for Herbert Spiegelberg. 1984
      Hb: ISBN 90-247-2926-2; Pb: 90-247-3197-6
93. H. Reiner: *Duty and Inclination.* The Fundamentals of Morality Discussed and Redefined with Special Regard to Kant and Schiller. 1983   ISBN 90-247-2818-5
94. M.J. Harney: *Intentionality, Sense and the Mind.* 1984   ISBN 90-247-2891-6
95. Kah Kyung Cho (ed.): *Philosophy and Science in Phenomenological Perspective.* 1984
      ISBN 90-247-2922-X
96. A. Lingis: *Phenomenological Explanations.* 1986   ISBN Hb: 90-247-3332-4; Pb: 90-247-3333-2
97. N. Rotenstreich†: *Reflection and Action.* 1985   ISBN Hb: 90-247-2969-6; Pb: 90-247-3128-3
98. J.N. Mohanty: *The Possibility of Transcendental Philosophy.* 1985
      ISBN Hb: 90-247-2991-2; Pb: 90-247-3146-1
99. J.J. Kockelmans: *Heidegger on Art and Art Works.* 1985
      ISBN Hb: 90-247-3102-X; Pb ISBN 90-247-3144-5
100. E. Lévinas: *Collected Philosophical Papers.* 1987
      ISBN Hb: 90-247-3272-7; Pb: 90-247-3395-2
101. R. Regvald: *Heidegger et le problème du néant.* 1986   ISBN 90-247-3388-X
102. J.A. Barash: *Martin Heidegger and the Problem of Historical Meaning.* 1987
      ISBN 90-247-3493-2
103. J.J. Kockelmans (ed.): *Phenomenological Psychology.* The Dutch School. 1987
      ISBN 90-247-3501-7
104. W.S. Hamrick: *An Existential Phenomenology of Law: Maurice Merleau-Ponty.* 1987
      ISBN 90-247-3520-3
105. J.C. Sallis, G. Moneta and J. Taminiaux (eds.): *The Collegium Phaenomenologicum. The First Ten Years.* 1988   ISBN 90-247-3709-5
106. D. Carr: *Interpreting Husserl.* Critical and Comparative Studies. 1987.   ISBN 90-247-3505-X
107. G. Heffernan: *Isagoge in die phänomenologische Apophantik.* Eine Einführung in die phänomenologische Urteilslogik durch die Auslegung des Textes der *Formalen und transzendentalen Logik* von Edmund Husserl. 1989   ISBN 90-247-3710-9
108. F. Volpi, J.-F. Mattéi, Th. Sheenan, J.-F. Courtine, J. Taminiaux, J. Sallis, D. Janicaud, A.L. Kelkel, R. Bernet, R. Brisart, K. Held, M. Haar et S. IJsseling: *Heidegger et l'idée de la phénoménologie.* 1988   ISBN 90-247-3586-6
109. C. Singevin: *Dramaturgie de l'esprit.* 1988   ISBN 90-247-3557-2
110. J. Patočka: *Le monde naturel et le mouvement de l'existence humaine.* 1988 ISBN 90-247-3577-7
111. K.-H. Lembeck: *Gegenstand Geschichte.* Geschichtswissenschaft in Husserls Phänomenologie. 1988   ISBN 90-247-3635-8
112. J.K. Cooper-Wiele: *The Totalizing Act.* Key to Husserl's Early Philosophy. 1989
      ISBN 0-7923-0077-7

Phaenomenologica

113. S. Valdinoci: *Le principe d'existence*. Un devenir psychiatrique de la phénoménologie. 1989
    ISBN 0-7923-0125-0
114. D. Lohmar: *Phänomenologie der Mathematik*. 1989   ISBN 0-7923-0187-0
115. S. IJsseling (Hrsgb.): *Husserl-Ausgabe und Husserl-Forschung*. 1990   ISBN 0-7923-0372-5
116. R. Cobb-Stevens: *Husserl and Analytic Philosophy*. 1990   ISBN 0-7923-0467-5
117. R. Klockenbusch: *Husserl und Cohn*. Widerspruch, Reflexion und Telos in Phänomenologie und Dialektik. 1989   ISBN 0-7923-0515-9
118. S. Vaitkus: *How is Society Possible?* Intersubjectivity and the Fiduciary Attitude as Problems of the Social Group in Mead, Gurwitsch, and Schutz. 1991   ISBN 0-7923-0820-4
119. C. Macann: *Presence and Coincidence*. The Transformation of Transcendental into Ontological Phenomenology. 1991   ISBN 0-7923-0923-5
120. G. Shpet: *Appearance and Sense*. Phenomenology as the Fundamental Science and Its Problems. Translated from Russian by Th. Nemeth. 1991   ISBN 0-7923-1098-5
121. B. Stevens: *L'apprentissage des signes*. Lecture de Paul Ricœur. 1991   ISBN 0-7923-1244-9
122. G. Soffer: *Husserl and the Question of Relativism*. 1991   ISBN 0-7923-1291-0
123. G. Römpp: *Husserls Phänomenologie der Intersubjektivität*. Und Ihre Bedeutung für eine Theorie intersubjektiver Objektivität und die Konzeption einer phänomenologischen Philosophie. 1991
    ISBN 0-7923-1361-5
124. S. Strasser: *Welt im Widerspruch*. Gedanken zu einer Phänomenologie als ethischer Fundamentalphilosophie. 1991   ISBN Hb: 0-7923-1404-2; Pb: 0-7923-1551-0
125. R.P. Buckley: *Husserl, Heidegger and the Crisis of Philosophical Responsibility*. 1992
    ISBN 0-7923-1633-9
126. J.G. Hart: *The Person and the Common Life*. Studies in a Husserlian Social Ethics. 1992
    ISBN 0-7923-1724-6
127. P. van Tongeren, P. Sars, C. Bremmers and K. Boey (eds.): *Eros and Eris*. Contributions to a Hermeneutical Phenomenology. Liber Amicorum for Adriaan Peperzak. 1992
    ISBN 0-7923-1917-6
128. Nam-In Lee: *Edmund Husserls Phänomenologie der Instinkte*. 1993   ISBN 0-7923-2041-7
129. P. Burke and J. Van der Veken (eds.): *Merleau-Ponty in Contemporary Perspective*. 1993
    ISBN 0-7923-2142-1
130. G. Haefliger: *Über Existenz: Die Ontologie Roman Ingardens*. 1994   ISBN 0-7923-2227-4
131. J. Lampert: *Synthesis and Backward Reference in Husserl's* Logical Investigations. 1995
    ISBN 0-7923-3105-2
132. J.M. DuBois: *Judgment and Sachverhalt*. An Introduction to Adolf Reinach's Phenomenological Realism. 1995   ISBN 0-7923-3519-8
133. B.E. Babich (ed.): *From Phenomenology to Thought, Errancy, and Desire*. Essays in Honor of William J. Richardson, S.J. 1995   ISBN 0-7923-3567-8
134. M. Dupuis: *Pronoms et visages*. Lecture d'Emmanuel Levinas. 1996
    ISBN Hb: 0-7923-3655-0; Pb 0-7923-3994-0
135. D. Zahavi: *Husserl und die transzendentale Intersubjektivität*. Eine Antwort auf die sprachpragmatische Kritik. 1996   ISBN 0-7923-3713-1
136. A. Schutz: *Collected Papers, IV*. Edited with preface and notes by H. Wagner and G. Psathas, in collaboration with F. Kersten. 1996   ISBN 0-7923-3760-3
137. P. Kontos: *D'une phénoménologie de la perception chez Heidegger*. 1996   ISBN 0-7923-3776-X
138. F. Kuster: *Wege der Verantwortung*. Husserls Phänomenologie als Gang durch die Faktizität. 1996
    ISBN 0-7923-3916-9
139. C. Beyer: *Von Bolzano zu Husserl*. Eine Untersuchung über den Ursprung der phänomenologischen Bedeutungslehre. 1996   ISBN 0-7923-4050-7
140. J. Dodd: *Idealism and Corporeity*. An Essay on the Problem of the Body in Husserl's Phenomenology. 1997   ISBN 0-7923-4400-6
141. E. Kelly: *Structure and Diversity*. Studies in the Phenomenological Philosophy of Max Scheler. 1997   ISBN 0-7923-4492-8

Phaenomenologica

142. J. Cavallin: *Content and Object.* Husserl, Twardowski and Psychologism. 1997
ISBN 0-7923-4734-X
143. H.P. Steeves: *Founding Community.* A Phenomenological-Ethical Inquiry. 1997
ISBN 0-7923-4798-6
144. M. Sawicki: *Body, Text, and Science.* The Literacy of Investigative Practices and the Phenomenology of Edith Stein. 1997   ISBN 0-7923-4759-5; Pb: 1-4020-0262-9
145. O.K. Wiegand: *Interpretationen der Modallogik.* Ein Beitrag zur phänomenologischen Wissenschaftstheorie. 1998   ISBN 0-7923-4809-5
146. P. Marrati-Guénoun: *La genèse et la trace.* Derrida lecteur de Husserl et Heidegger. 1998
ISBN 0-7923-4969-5
147. D. Lohmar: *Erfahrung und kategoriales Denken.* Hume, Kant und Husserl über vorprädikative Erfahrung und prädikative Erkenntnis. 1998   ISBN 0-7923-5117-7
148. N. Depraz and D. Zahavi (eds.): *Alterity and Facticity.* New Perspectives on Husserl. 1998
ISBN 0-7923-5187-8
149. E. Øverenget: *Seeing the Self.* Heidegger on Subjectivity. 1998
ISBN Hb: 0-7923-5219-X; Pb: 1-4020-0259-9
150. R.D. Rollinger: *Husserls Position in the School of Brentano.* 1999   ISBN 0-7923-5684-5
151. A. Chrudzimski: *Die Erkenntnistheorie von Roman Ingarden.* 1999   ISBN 0-7923-5688-8
152. B. Bergo: *Levinas Between Ethics and Politics.* For the Beauty that Adorns the Earth. 1999
ISBN 0-7923-5694-2
153. L. Ni: *Seinsglaube in der Phänomenologie Edmund Husserls.* 1999   ISBN 0-7923-5779-5
154. E. Feron: *Phénoménologie de la mort.* Sur les traces de Levinas. 1999   ISBN 0-7923-5935-6
155. R. Visker: *Truth and Singularity.* Taking Foucault into Phenomenology. 1999
ISBN Hb: 0-7923-5985-2; Pb: 0-7923-6397-3
156. E.E. Kleist: *Judging Appearances.* A Phenomenological Study of the Kantian *sensus communis.* 2000   ISBN Hb: 0-7923-6310-8; Pb: 1-4020-0258-0
157. D. Pradelle: *L'archéologie du monde.* Constitution de l'espace, idéalisme et intuitionnisme chez Husserl. 2000   ISBN 0-7923-6313-2
158. H.B. Schmid: *Subjekt, System, Diskurs.* Edmund Husserls Begriff transzendentaler Subjektivität in sozialtheoretischen Bezügen. 2000   ISBN 0-7923-6424-4
159. A. Chrudzimski: *Intentionalitätstheorie beim frühen Brentano.* 2001   ISBN 0-7923-6860-6
160. N. Depraz: *Lucidité du corps.* De l'empirisme transcendantal en phénoménologie. 2001
ISBN 0-7923-6977-7
161. T. Kortooms: *Phenomenology of Time.* Edmund Husserl's Analysis of Time-Consciousness. 2001
ISBN 1-4020-0121-5
162. R. Boehm: *Topik.* 2002   ISBN 1-4020-0629-2
163. A. Chernyakov: *The Ontology of Time.* Being and Time in the Philosophies of Aristotle, Husserl and Heidegger. 2002   ISBN 1-4020-0682-9
164. D. Zahavi and F. Stjernfelt (eds.): *One Hundred Years of Phenomenology.* Husserl's *Logical Investigations* Revisited. 2002   ISBN 1-4020-0700-0
165. B. Ferreira: *Stimmung bei Heidegger.* Das Phänomen der Stimmung im Kontext von Heideggers Existenzialanalyse des Daseins. 2002   ISBN 1-4020-0701-9
166. S. Luft: *"Phänomenologie der Phänomenologie".* Systematik und Methodologie der Phänomenologie in der Auseinandersetzung zwischen Husserl und Fink. 2002   ISBN 1-4020-0901-1
167. M. Roesner: *Metaphysica ludens.* Das Spiel als phänomenologische Grundfigur im Denken Martin Heideggers. 2003   ISBN 1-4020-1234-9
168. B. Bouckaert: *L'idée de l'autre.* La question de l'idéalité et de l'altérité chez Husserl des *Logische Untersuchungen* aux *Ideen I.* 2003   ISBN 1-4020-1262-4
169. M.S. Frings: *LifeTime. Max Scheler's Philosophy of Time.* A First Inquiry and Presentation. 2003
ISBN 1-4020-1333-7

Phaenomenologica

170. T. Stähler: *Die Unruhe des Anfangs.* Hegel und Husserl über den Weg in die Phänomenologie. 2003 ISBN 1-4020-1547-X
171. P. Quesne: *Les* Recherches philosophiques *du jeune Heidegger.* 2003 ISBN 1-4020-1671-9
172. A. Chrudzimski: *Die Ontologie Franz Brentanos.* 2004 ISBN 1-4020-1859-2
173. S. Overgaard: *Husserl and Heidegger on Being in the World.* 2004 ISBN 1-4020-2043-0

Previous volumes are still available

Further information about *Phenomenology* publications is available on request

Kluwer Academic Publishers – Dordrecht / Boston / London